PENGUIN BOOKS

A LIFE IN DIPLOMACY

MAHARAJAKRISHNA RASGOTRA joined the Indian Foreign Service in 1949, and in a long and distinguished career, held several important posts in Indian diplomatic missions abroad and in the ministry of external affairs.

He was deputy chief of mission in Washington DC, ambassador of India in Morocco, Tunisia, Nepal, Holland and France, and twice India's high commissioner in London.

He was foreign secretary of India from 1982 to 1985 under prime ministers Indira Gandhi and Rajiv Gandhi, conducting important negotiations with Islamabad, Washington DC, Moscow and Beijing. SAARC was founded in his time as foreign secretary. After his retirement, he has written extensively on international relations in Indian journals and has lectured on the subject in India and abroad. He was a visiting professor at New Delhi's Jawaharlal Nehru University, president of the Delhi College of Arts and Commerce and regents professor at the University of California at Los Angeles.

Rasgotra was member of the National Security Advisory Board from 1999 to 2001 and chairman of the Board from 2005 to 2007.

A LIFE
in
DIPLOMACY

MAHARAJAKRISHNA RASGOTRA

PENGUIN BOOKS

An imprint of Penguin Random House

PENGUIN BOOKS

USA | Canada | UK | Ireland | Australia
New Zealand | India | South Africa | China | Singapore

Penguin Books is part of the Penguin Random House group of companies
whose addresses can be found at global.penguinrandomhouse.com

Published by Penguin Random House India Pvt. Ltd
4th Floor, Capital Tower 1, MG Road,
Gurugram 122 002, Haryana, India

Penguin
Random House
India

First published in Viking by Penguin Books India 2016
Published in Penguin Books by Penguin Random House India 2019

ISBN 9780143447276

Typeset in Bembo Std by Manipal Digital Systems, Manipal
Printed at Manipal Technologies Limited, India

www.penguin.co.in

MIX
Paper | Supporting
responsible forestry
FSC® C043100

This is a legitimate digitally printed version of the book and therefore might not
have certain extra finishing on the cover.

To Kadambari, my life's companion, counsellor
and co-sharer of the burdens of my tasks

Now the last day of many days
All beautiful and bright as thou,
The loveliest and the last, is dead:
Rise, Memory, and write its praise!
Up—to thy wonted work! come, trace
The epitaph of glory fled,
For now the Earth has changed its face
A frown is on the Heaven's brow.

—P.B. Shelley, *The Recollection*

CONTENTS

~

ACKNOWLEDGEMENTS

~

I am indebted to four very close personal friends—veteran journalist and editor, H.K. Dua; former ambassador and Member of Parliament, Vice Admiral (retd.) K.K. Nayyar, a rare intellectual at home equally in security strategies and foreign affairs; and two former colleagues, Ambassador Ashok Sajjanhar and Harish Shukla—for their support and encouragement without which this book might not have seen the light of day. I cannot thank them enough for the time and effort they spent on reading the manuscript, and for the suggestions they made to improve its contents and format.

The keen interest my son, Dilip Krishna, a busy financial executive in London, took in the book gave me much gratification. He read the entire manuscript with the utmost care as the writing progressed and made several useful suggestions.

Last but not the least, I am deeply obliged to Ranjana Sengupta, my editor, for the care, time and attention she devoted to this book. Chapter 4 (About Myself) was written by me at her insistence. She made several other valuable suggestions for the book's improvement. Her enthusiasm about the book, her painstaking and sympathetic reading of it made it a pleasure for me to work with her.

PREFACE

~

When I finished with government service in March 1990, I took a firm decision not to write a book. I was simply too tired to write any more: In a career of nearly forty years in the Indian Foreign Service, I must have filled several reams of paper with my writings—office memoranda, reports of various kinds, policy notes, special dispatches on my talks with foreign heads of state/government. I recall all this not to claim credit for having contributed anything of great value to the archives of the ministry of external affairs, but simply to confess to a state of overpowering writing fatigue. Great was my relief when fairly early in my term as foreign secretary, Prime Minister Indira Gandhi told me not to send her any files, but personally discuss problems, issues and required policy initiatives with her, and implement the decisions reached in such discussions.

I held to that resolve for twenty-four years, till one day towards the end of 2013, the director general of the Indian Council of World Affairs (ICWA), Ambassador Rajiv Bhatia, asked me to give a talk at the council about what I had seen of India and the world in my time, the origins and development of India's Foreign Office, the Indian Foreign Service and how we dealt with important global issues and problems of international relations of direct interest to India etc. In the weeks and months following my extempore talk at the ICWA, I was overwhelmed with approaches from young scholars, university teachers, some of my former colleagues in the Indian Foreign Service and others interested in international relations—all urging me to write a book on what I had spoken about at the ICWA. It was all new to them, they said, as there was little by way of comprehensive eyewitness accounts of important developments in international relations and the successes and failures of India's foreign policy in the first half century of India's life as an independent nation. Weakness possessed me, and I promised to give thought to their suggestions.

A Life in Diplomacy was written mostly from memory in ten months, from December 2014 to September 2015. I had not kept any official papers with me; nor did I keep a diary. So I had to depend on my memory which is still good. As foreign secretary, I had to sit in on Prime Minister Indira Gandhi's important meetings with foreign VIPs. I never took notes on such occasions but later that day, or even a few days later, I would dictate from memory a near-verbatim record of the meeting, whatever its length, and send the same to the prime minister. On the second such occasion, she asked me whether I had used a small recorder in those meetings which, of course, was not the case. A bright young IFS officer, Arif Khan, who headed my office for two years when I was foreign secretary, used to say that a guardian angel had implanted a mini recorder and a tiny camera in my head to bless me with an audio-visual memory.

The book is not my autobiography, though I have included in it a chapter about my early life, which shows that there was nothing in my upbringing to qualify me for the diplomatic profession and that there are opportunities galore for young men and women of humble origins to rise through hard work and serve the country in positions of responsibility in a growing number of unfamiliar fields of work.

My personal participation in the events of the period figures in the book here and there, but it is more a story of India in that period, of the trials and tribulations it faced, of the men and women who defined its policies and shaped its destiny and its role and influence in the world. It was an interesting but not an easy time of mutual adjustment between the world and India, a big new entrant in it with its own interests and its humanist goals and ideals influenced by its millennial tradition. Thus, the book is also the story of the world of those times to the extent circumstances enabled me to observe it first-hand.

The world in which India awoke to freedom was not an entirely friendly one. In particular, the first two-and-a-half decades of Independence were a period of constant struggle to overcome the hostility of one or another great power. We have come a long way since then. Today there is hardly an area of activity in which the world can do without India: Indeed, today, the world wants India to succeed and wants to be a partner in its success.

I hope this book will fill at least some of the gaps in the knowledge of that period. It is also my hope that it does not disappoint those whose insistence drove me to this endeavour.

New Delhi
1 December 2015

chapter one

FOREIGN POLICY IN
INDEPENDENT INDIA

~

At the beginning of the era of Independence, by way of a foreign policy establishment, India only had Jawaharlal Nehru. Nehru was the foreign minister without a Foreign Office and without a Foreign Service to represent India abroad. But he had a foreign policy which he spelt out in a steady stream of hitherto unheard of ideas, about the nature of external relations and a series of actions, which he launched in the pursuit of that policy and its goals. And though he was without a Foreign Office and without a corps of trained diplomats to elaborate and project his ideas abroad, the world listened to him with attention when he spoke because his voice was the voice of an India which the modern world had not heard for two hundred years.

In fact, Nehru had enunciated his foreign policy for India even before the country became independent. On 7 September 1946, five days after joining the Governor General's Executive Council as vice chairman and member in charge of external affairs, Nehru proclaimed that policy and its immediate goals in the following words:

> We propose, as far as possible, to keep away from the power politics of groups, aligned against one another, which have led in the past to two world wars and which may again lead to disasters on an even vaster scale . . .

1

We believe that peace and freedom are indivisible and the denial of freedom anywhere must endanger freedom elsewhere and lead to conflict and war. We are particularly interested in the emancipation of colonial and dependent countries and peoples, and in the recognition in theory and practice of equal opportunities for all races . . .

The world, in spite of its rivalries and hatreds and inner conflicts, moves inevitably towards closer cooperation and the building up of a world commonwealth. It is for this One World that free India will work, a world in which there is the free cooperation of free peoples, and no class or group exploits another.

In South Africa racialism is the State doctrine and our people are putting up a heroic struggle against the tyranny of a racial minority. If this racial doctrine is going to be tolerated it must inevitably lead to vast conflicts and world disaster . . .[1]

Elaborations would follow, but in these 170 words Nehru had described the foreign policy of newly independent India, given it a name—Non-alignment—which meant, as he had outlined in the radio address, 'keeping away from power groups aligned against one another' and defining its practical agenda for the immediate future. To its threefold programme of Liberation of Colonies, One World United for Peace and Cooperation, and Opposition to Racism, would soon be added a fourth: General and Complete Disarmament, a Ban on Nuclear Tests and the Elimination of Nuclear Weapons, which was an extension of India's commitment to non-violence.

That Nehru's concept of Non-alignment did not envisage an inflexible posture of equidistance between the two power blocks, led by the USA and the USSR, is implied in the phrase 'as far as possible' in the very first line of this first authoritative statement of his foreign policy. What Non-alignment essentially meant was independence of judgement of events and issues and of doing the right thing, not only for India, but also for world peace. The limited concept of keeping 'away from the power politics of groups, aligned against one another' arose directly from the Cold War division of the world into two hostile blocks at the time of India's Independence. The rest—the unchanging emphasis on peace, the belief in the relevance of a non-violent approach in international relations, cooperation for peace and progress and tolerance and coexistence—are all reflexes of India's age-old cultural tradition going back to Vedic revelations and Vedanta philosophy, which informed the politics and governance in the great ages of Indian history—the centuries of the rule of the Mauryas, the Guptas and the Mughals (especially the period of Emperor Akbar's rule).

This cultural tradition is the inheritance not only of the intellectual ruling elites; it is embedded also in the consciousness of our common people. A hymn in the Rig Veda (8.58.2) draws the reader's attention to 'unity in diversity'. Upanishads in hyperbole speak of freedom as the 'creator and sustainer of the universe'. 'The world is a family' (*vasudhaivakudumbakam*) is another basic concept of Vedanta thought. The Mahabharata, the great Indian epic which has many lessons on the science of polity, puts the same thought into more majestic words with scientific undertones: 'The whole world of mortals is an inter-dependent organism'. Peace (*Shantih* in Sanskrit) is frequently invoked in an Indian's daily life). A Hindu's prayers for various occasions are not for his own happiness but for the well-being of all humanity; the prayer most commonly cited on auspicious occasions simply says: 'May all the people be well, comfortable and happy.'[2]

A prayer from the Kath Upanishad, which Indira Gandhi often invoked at the end of her speeches to foreign audiences, runs as follows:

May He protect us both together;
May He nourish us all together;
May we both acquire power (of knowledge) together;
Let our study be brilliant;
May we not cavil at each other.
Om Shantih, Shantih, Shantih.[3]

The Upanishadic prayer which I like the most is the following:

Om, may all become happy,
May all be free from illness.

May all see what is auspicious,
May no one suffer.
Om, peace, peace, peace.[4]

Nehru, the scholar and historian, had a sound knowledge of Vedanta thought. In a discussion of current and ancient philosophies he writes: 'Marxist philosophy did not satisfy me completely, nor did it answer all the questions in my mind; and, almost unawares, a vague idealist approach would creep into my mind, something rather akin to the Vedanta approach.'[5]

The awareness of India's socio-cultural tradition informed Nehru's thinking on international relations and was evident in his formulation of India's foreign policy. He referred to this 'conditioning' of the foreign policy he had enunciated in the debate on foreign policy in the Lok Sabha on 9 December 1958:

It is incorrect to call our policy 'Nehru' policy. It is incorrect because all that I have done is to give voice to that policy. I have not originated it. It is a policy inherent in the circumstances of India, inherent in the whole mental outlook of India, inherent in the conditioning of the Indian mind during our struggle for freedom and inherent in the circumstance of the world today.

The most powerful element in our struggle for freedom was non-violence, as interpreted and practised by Mahatma Gandhi. And this too was a part of the Indian tradition since the Buddha. It was his teachings that the emperor Ashoka had applied in the governance of a vast empire covering the entire subcontinent and stretching from Burma in the east to central Asia in the west. Nehru was trying, I have often thought, to formulate and practice a non-violent foreign policy, Ashoka style. The attempt failed because of the circumstances surrounding India's birth—for example a hostile Pakistan and uncertainties attendant on the rise of a powerful and revolutionary communist China. An independent policy of peace works best when it is backed by a deterring military force held in reserve. Emperor Ashoka's non-violent policy succeeded because he maintained a huge army—perhaps the largest in the world of his time.'

Nehru was familiar with the teachings of Kautilya and Shukracharya on the fundamental importance of safeguarding the security of the state. In *Discovery of India*, there are long sections on Kautilya's Arthashastra (fourth century BC) and on Shukracharya's Nitisar (tenth century), which show that Nehru had studied these works on the science of polity with great care. They both emphasize the importance of security in the formulation of policy. A weak state, Kautilya says, invites attack.

The only explanation for Nehru's comparative neglect of India's military security, especially on the northern border with China, is that he did not expect an attack from China. Also, because of his overriding concern about the crushing poverty that blighted the lives of the great masses of Indian people, he did not want too much of the meagre resources available for development diverted to military purposes.

In the declaration of September 1946, Nehru had indicated his intention to work for a 'close association of free countries' of Asia; for, as he put it, 'we are of Asia and the peoples of Asia are nearer and closer to us than others'. And in his Asian policy he accorded particular importance to China, 'that mighty country with a mighty past, our neighbour . . . throughout the ages'. Nehru believed that friendship with China 'will endure and grow'. This belief apparently arose from his inadequate knowledge of imperial China's history and of revolutionary China's ambitions and policies about which he was not well-served by his ambassadors to China. Ambassador K.M. Panikkar, for example, described China's revolutionary leaders as harmless agrarian reformers of friendly disposition towards India.

Nehru's long search for a united Asian identity and his emphasis on cooperation among Asian nations found early expression in the Asian Relations Conference in New Delhi in March–April 1947, and in the conference he convened in New Delhi in January 1949 to condemn the Dutch military attack to recapture recently liberated Indonesia. Eighteen independent countries of South Asia, west Asia and the Far East (including Australia) attended the latter conference, a historic first gathering of Asian and Arab powers. The only invited country which failed to send a representative was Turkey. Africa, whose liberation was still ten to fifteen years in the future, was represented by Ethiopia. Such as it was, this was the first manifestation of the so-called Third World.

Six years later, at the Bandung Conference in Indonesia in April 1955, Afro-Asian solidarity was reasserted, and Non-alignment and Panchsheel, or the Five Principles of Co-existence, were given a global profile. But some Asian countries had already joined—and more would soon join—one or the other military alliances of the Cold War period. Rifts among Asian countries had surfaced during the Bandung Conference, which also saw the coming together of China and Pakistan in an informal pact against India.

The Panchsheel, or the Five Principles of Peaceful Co-Existence,[6] had been formulated in the Agreement between India and China on Trade and Intercourse between the Tibet Region of China and India, signed in Peking on 29 April 1954. Nehru apparently had a hand in defining the Five Principles which rule out the use of force. It is noteworthy, though, that seven years after Nehru's death, Zhou En-Lai, in his talks with Henry Kissinger, claimed that the principles were formulated by China. Beijing's massive, carefully planned invasion of India in 1962 casts serious doubt on China's sincerity in agreeing to them in the first place. China had no use for the Five Principles after it had consolidated its hold on Tibet.

Nehru's concern for Tibet was long-standing. He had invited a separate delegation from Tibet to the Asian Relations Conference in March–April 1947, and took care of their board and lodging and other expenses to establish the delegation's separate, autonomous identity in an international gathering. The Chinese delegation at the conference made several attempts to take the Tibetan delegation under its wing but with Nehru's support the latter successfully resisted their blandishments.

In another informal and personal initiative on Tibet, soon after India's Independence Nehru sent a confidant of his—a Bengali gentleman—to the Tibetan capital to explain to members of the

Kashag, the Dalai Lama's cabinet, the importance of the recently established United Nations, and how countries were seeking to become members. The emissary was to ask whether Lhasa wanted to apply for membership. But though he stayed in Lhasa for several days, the Tibetans showed little interest. A year later, Nehru sent another emissary to Lhasa with the same message; but he, too, failed to elicit any response from the Tibetan government. Implicit in these gestures was the suggestion that if the Tibetans themselves sought UN membership, friendly countries could perhaps render some help in obtaining it. These moves were not without some historical justification. For, after the Manchu dynasty's demise in 1911, Tibet was effectively an independent country; it had stopped sending the annual tribute-bearing mission to Peking.

At the time of the two visits of Nehru's emissaries to Tibet, the post of India's representative in Lhasa was still held by an Englishman because a suitable Indian was not available. There is no evidence that Nehru took him or the Indian Foreign Office or any of his cabinet colleagues into his confidence about the matter. The Tibetans woke up to the significance of Nehru's initiatives too late, after the Chinese army marched into their country in January 1950. Lhasa then requested Nehru to sponsor Tibet's case for membership of the UN. But it was too late, and Nehru refused to take any action on their appeals.

Against Nehru's advice, an attempt was made to raise the issue at the Dalai Lama's initiative, by the delegation of El Salvador in the UN General Assembly. The question was discussed in the assembly's political committee and the matter was allowed to die without further action. In 1960, Ireland's highly respected permanent representative to the UN, Ambassador Boland, tried, without success, to mobilize some support for the issue. I was at the UN then and I remember Ambassador Boland trying to convince me of the importance of safeguarding Tibet's autonomy and its distinct religion and culture. But Tibet had missed its chance. Already in 1950 the realist in Nehru had recognized the reality of China's effective reoccupation of Tibet, and his further efforts were focused on negotiating a dignified withdrawal from Tibet of India's extraterritorial privileges—a representative at

Lhasa with a small military escort and Indian trading posts at Yatung and Gyantse inherited from the British. The new situation was finally formalized in the 1954 India–China Agreement on Tibet.

If all of Nehru's initiatives were known to Secretary General Sir Girija Shankar Bajpai[7] or to Sardar Vallabhbhai Patel, perhaps the latter's famous letter of 7 November 1950[8] (see appendix pp. 397–403) to Nehru about the new threat on India's northern horizon because of China's reoccupation of Tibet might never have been written. Nehru wrote back to Patel saying that he would discuss the matter with him after the latter's return from an internal tour, on which he was to proceed the following day. The meeting could not take place as Patel never returned to Delhi from his tour and died within a few days of the exchange of letters between him and Prime Minister Nehru.

There has been some speculation about the authorship of or the inspiration behind the letter. I personally am convinced that the letter was drafted by Bajpai. The mastery of the detail of China's policy, the comments on Nepal, Bhutan and Sikkim and the suggestion about entering into a defence pact with Burma—which the Burmese leader U. Aung San had proposed, and India's representative in Burma Gundevia[9] had strongly supported, but Nehru had rejected—all point to the drafting of the letter by an expert of the highest calibre. Moreover, the letter's phrasing and diction have a close resemblance to Bajpai's writing style.

In the top echelons of the MEA bureaucracy there was a feeling that Ambassador K.M. Panikkar was too ready to take China's professions of friendship for India at face value, and was misleading Nehru in his China policy. There was a good deal of antipathy between Secretary General Bajpai and Ambassador Panikkar, not only because of their differing assessments of Chinese policies and diplomacy, but also because of the gap between Bajpai's wider experience of world affairs and his habitual dislike of communism and Panikkar's somewhat narrower focus on the importance of India–China relations. There is little doubt in my mind that the letter was actually drafted by Bajpai in the hope that Patel's intervention might help introduce a measure of circumspection in India's China policy. Bajpai was liked and respected by senior members of Nehru's cabinet and had easy access, notably, to Rajagopalachari and Vallabhbhai Patel. Panikkar, meanwhile, was acting in accord with Nehru's instructions and had his full support in cultivating China's revolutionary leaders. The task was not easy and he went about it energetically, in full awareness of the notorious egocentrism of the Chinese leaders.

Understandably, in those early years Nehru depended a great deal on these two intellectual giants among his collaborators in the foreign policy arena, but there was no love lost between them. In 1955, Panikkar was Ambassador Bhagwan Sahay's guest in Kathmandu for several days and I (second secretary in the embassy then) spent a lot of time with him escorting him to meetings and on sightseeing trips. In private conversations he would often deride Bajpai as 'that little man with little understanding of China'.

Bajpai's assessments of China's policies and objectives and his warnings of future portents were borne by later events. Though Nehru often disagreed with Bajpai and sometimes overruled him, Bajpai had his full confidence and he (Nehru) appreciated Sir Girija's candour, his unmatched ability to analyse critical issues with cool objectivity and his boundless capacity for hard work despite his indifferent health. On ten or eleven occasions, when Bajpai wanted to quit the Foreign Office because of differences with Nehru on issues of importance, the prime minister would go out of his way to persuade him to stay on the job. Bajpai alone, among the MEA's senior officials, could stand up to Nehru, and occasionally even made the prime minister change a decision made on impulse.

I should like to begin with the early days of the creation of the requisite wherewithal of independent India's foreign policy—an adequately manned Foreign Office and a corps of trained diplomats to man India's diplomatic missions abroad. For decades, imperial New Delhi had both a Foreign Office and a Foreign and Political Service, but in both cases Indians mostly had access to them only at the clerical levels. All senior officers of the service were British.

The origins of an Indian Foreign Office of sorts go far back to 1784; the British government of India had set up a Secret and Political Department to deal with independent power centres, which had, thus far, escaped the grasp of Calcutta's expanding empire, and to manage the affairs of tribal populations in northeast and northwest India. This nucleus of a Foreign Office went through several changes of nomenclature and in the nature and scope of its responsibilities. In 1842, the department was renamed the Foreign Department without any significant change in its functioning. In 1914, in response to the growing need to deal systematically with subjugated Indian princes, a 'political' wing was added and the merged entity was designated the Foreign and Political Department. The foreign wing continued to be responsible for the affairs of India's tribal areas, Sikkim, Bhutan, the Indian possessions of France and Portugal, the neighbouring countries of Afghanistan, Nepal and Tibet, as well as the territories under British rule or influence in the Gulf region.

Even as the range of its activities expanded, the senior ranks of the foreign wing of the department continued to be manned exclusively by British personnel. Its policies and actions continued to be dictated from Whitehall in London and implemented under the governor general's direction without consultation with, or knowledge of, any Indian member of his executive council. All this would change with Nehru joining the Governor General's Executive Council as vice chairman and member in charge of external affairs in 1946.

A further change in the department's nomenclature occurred with the adoption, by the British Parliament, of the Government of India Act, 1935. In order to keep the affairs of the princely states out of the purview of Indian members of the Governor General's Executive Council, the political wing was separated from the department and placed directly under the viceroy as the crown representative. The Indian government, also headed by the governor general, had no authority to pry into the relations between the imperial power and its Indian satrapies. In August 1947 this political wing became the 'States Department' under the first home minister of independent India, Sardar Vallabhbhai Patel.

In a parallel development in 1941, a Department of Indians Overseas was set up to deal with the work which, till then, was handled within the Indian government's Department of Education, Lands and Development. In 1946, when Nehru took charge of it along with the External Affairs Department, he gave it a new name—the Department of Commonwealth Relations.

As Independence approached, British officers who occupied all senior positions in the External Affairs Department were preparing to return to Britain or to go over to Pakistan.[10] Nehru's first foreign secretary, an English gentleman named Creighton, who was a member of the old Foreign and Political Service, had also indicated his desire to return to Britain, and he actually left for home in August 1947. Clearly, a thorough overhaul of the outdated External Affairs Department was needed. As a first step Nehru merged the two departments of Commonwealth Relations and External Affairs into the new ministry of external affairs, and entrusted the tasks of its reorganization to Sir Girija Shankar Bajpai, whom he had summoned from Washington to head the new ministry as secretary general.

chapter two

CREATION OF THE INDIAN FOREIGN SERVICE

~

It fell to Sir Girija Shankar Bajpai to begin the process of creating an Indian Foreign Service from scratch and to man the Foreign Office with competent personnel. His experience as India's agent general in Washington DC would have been useful even though it was not a diplomatic post in the conventional sense. The main purpose for its creation was to have a senior and respected Indian member of the ICS in the American capital to aid the British government's war propaganda, disparage the Indian Independence movement and its leaders, and justify or explain away the brutal repression unleashed by the government on the Indian National Congress and its supporters after Mahatma Gandhi launched the Quit India Movement on 15 August 1942; in short, to tell a lot of lies about India to unsuspecting Americans on behalf of his wily British masters.

It is hard to say that Bajpai's heart and soul were in his unsavoury anti-national mandate. In any case, his success in the particular task of maligning the Independence movement and leaders of the Indian National Congress did not seem to have made a dent in the reputation Gandhi and Nehru enjoyed in the United States, or in the admiration mixed with curiosity with which Americans viewed the non-violent character of the movement for Independence led by Gandhi.

Nehru's sister, Vijaya Lakshmi Pandit made countrywide lecture tours of the United States to tell the truth about India, while Bajpai was still in occupation of the post of agent general, and this had a far greater effect in generating sympathy and support for India's Independence in America's official and non-official circles. As war approached India from the East and American soldiers and other Americans started arriving in India in large numbers, criticism grew in America of London's folly in alienating the most popular political force in India—the Indian National Congress.

Did Bajpai know that Pandit was evacuated from India without a passport in an American military plane with President Roosevelt's approval, and that she had several meetings with senior State Department officials in Washington during her long lecture tour? In any case, there was nothing he could do except take Pandit's campaign in his stride. For him those five years were also an opportunity to observe from his high perch in the US capital—which would soon overtake London, Paris, Bonn and Moscow in importance, the changing facets of national and international policies of great powers at a critical time in world affairs. Quite unintentionally, the British had opened the portals of the world's best school for observing and absorbing the intricacies of international relations and diplomacy to a man who was going to be Nehru's most valued and unerring adviser on foreign policy during the first five years of Independence.

If Nehru had any misgivings about Bajpai's loyalty, he never showed it. That Nehru recognized the worth of Bajpai's experience, his knowledge of world affairs and of the routine and detail of day-to-day diplomatic functioning, and his qualities as an upright and reliable civil servant, is obvious. Whether there was some special or secret reason which made Nehru repose total confidence and trust in Bajpai to reshape or create the two institutions, which he was to use directly for the execution of his foreign policy, remains in the realm of speculation. The two tasks Bajpai took in hand were rebuilding the Indian Foreign Office and creating the Indian Foreign Service in July 1947.

Bajpai was a thoroughly disciplined and organized person with a polished and formal deportment. His speech and writing were characterized by directness and clarity, precision and economy in the use of words. The buildings and furnishings he acquired for our embassies in Washington DC and Paris are evidence of his highly refined taste in matters of architecture and the arts. I was fortunate to sit in, as a note taker, on a couple of Bajpai's meetings with Dr Frank Graham, the UN Good Office's man on the Kashmir issue. Graham was a bit long-winded about the virtues of peace and the importance of settling the problem with Pakistan for the overall good, progress and prosperity of both countries. Graham was soon reduced to taking notes of the points Bajpai made. The secretary general concluded the tutorial on Kashmir by saying that 'without uttering a threat', he wanted to advise Graham to warn the authorities in Pakistan that there are limits to India's patience and they should facilitate a peaceful settlement by being reasonable.

The relationship that developed between Nehru and Bajpai in the next five years is unique in the annals of relations between a top civil servant and his minister (who in this case also happened to be a powerful prime minister). Nehru and Bajpai differed often on issues big and small, such as Nehru's China policy, Krishna Menon's insulting behaviour towards senior MEA officials or Radhakrishnan's lofty but unauthorized initiatives for world peace in Moscow, or on routine administrative matters like the training of Foreign Service officers etc. Sometimes disagreements came to such a pass that Bajpai felt compelled to send his letter of resignation to Nehru, giving reasons for his actions. In five years as secretary general, Bajpai tendered his resignation on ten or eleven occasions. But Nehru would not let him go. More often than not Nehru went along with Bajpai's view, but even when he stuck to his own position, he would go out of his way to persuade Bajpai to stay on the job.

One such occasion arose in the early weeks of their association. On Bajpai's suggestion, Nehru agreed that thirty Indian officers of the ICS, with some experience of overseas service, should constitute the nucleus of the new Indian Foreign Service; but in agreeing to this, and also to the recruitment of another eighty to hundred overage professionals through interviews by the Union Public Service Commission, Nehru had also told Bajpai that entrants to the service should be informed beforehand that ambassadorial posts would be beyond their reach, as all such posts would be filled by eminent persons chosen by the government from public life. Bajpai protested against that stipulation. He recognized, he said, the foreign minister's prerogative to select some heads of mission from public life, but a general embargo denying top posts to career officers, as a rule, would dissuade persons with ability from joining the new service. He told the prime minister that he would not accept responsibility for implementing his decision and the task should be entrusted to someone else—a politely worded threat of resignation. Nehru saw the point and did not press his idea further.[1]

A more serious disagreement arose in 1950 on Krishna Menon's alleged ill treatment of MEA officials and on some other issues on which Nehru had simply ignored Bajpai's advice. Bajpai felt he had outlived his use in the ministry and wrote a long letter of resignation explaining his reasons for the action. Nehru reassured Bajpai of his deep appreciation of the great value of his work and persuaded him to withdraw his resignation. This, and other such incidents say a lot about Bajpai's administrative foresight and his firmness when convinced that a point of principle that he had raised was sound . . . They also do credit to Nehru's generosity of spirit and his readiness to acknowledge an error of judgement. Their close working relationship was based on mutual regard and respect, which, however, did not prevent serious disagreements and occasional confrontations on issues about which either felt strongly.

On China policy, for example, where Nehru had overruled Bajpai and persisted in a course recommended, allegedly, by Ambassador K.M. Panikkar and which Bajpai considered flawed, he did not push matters to breaking point. For in such matters Bajpai ungrudgingly acknowledged the prime minister's prerogative as the final authority in making policy. Nehru, on his part, saw no reason why the secretary general should agree to any basic policy to which he was opposed. When the time came finally for Bajpai to retire for reasons of health in 1952, Nehru, in consideration of his services and healthcare needs, rewarded him with the coveted governorship of undivided Bombay.

Soon after taking over as secretary general, Bajpai recalled Subimal Dutt from Bengal where he was secretary, Agricultural Department, to take over as commonwealth relations secretary in the department. Dutt had earlier worked under Bajpai in a Central government department and had also served as agent of the Government of India in Malaya. K.P.S. Menon, who was India's agent general at Chungking, was brought back to take over as foreign secretary. This core team then assembled another twenty-seven ICS officers to fill posts at headquarters and abroad. Eight of this constellation of stars—R.K. Nehru, S. Dutt, M.J. Desai, Y.D. Gundevia, C.S. Jha, Rajeshwar Dayal, T.N. Kaul and Kewal Singh, became foreign secretaries one after another. Their reign in the MEA ended when Jagat Mehta—a war service recruit from the Royal Indian Navy, took over as foreign secretary on Kewal Singh's retirement in 1976. Mehta was followed in that post three years later by R.D. Sathe, who had been transferred from the Indian army to the External Affairs Department in 1945, and posted in the agent general's office in Chunking as second secretary.

Bajpai and K.P.S. Menon did not join the new service, but the other twenty-seven were seconded into different grades of it, in accordance with their seniority in their old cadre. Even among those who did not reach the top posts of foreign secretary and secretary general, there were men of great ability, like Azim Hussain for example, who missed becoming foreign secretary because the considerations of seniority worked against him. All of them were men of good calibre, with extensive knowledge of Indian conditions. They combined some experience of overseas service, a high degree of self-assurance and a suave demeanour. At headquarters or abroad, they went about their tasks with a spring and swagger in their gait and dealt with complex, unanticipated problems with ease and impressive efficiency. The only problem with the induction of such a large number of comparatively young ICS officers was that they blocked the promotion prospects of the next lot of eighty overaged members of the IFS for many years, causing much frustration down the ranks.

In addition, another ten or twelve ICS officers, who did not join the IFS, were also given senior assignments at headquarters and in missions abroad. Notable among them were N.R. Pillai, who followed Bajpai as secretary general, H.S. Malik (ambassador in Paris), C.C. Desai (high commissioner in Colombo), C.S. Venkatachari (high commissioner in Canada), B.R. Sen (CDA/ambassador in Washington DC, from where he went to the FAO as its head for many years), L.K. Jha (ambassador in Washington), B.K. Nehru (minister economic) and later ambassador in Washington and high commissioner in London). B.K. Gokhale and Bhagwan Sahay distinguished themselves as ambassadors in Kathmandu, in some respects the most important and prestigious but trying post for an Indian ambassador. B.K. Nehru's long and most successful tenures in the US and Britain put him in a special category of his own.

In my early years of service I was privileged to work under Nehru, Sen, Gokhale and Sahay and learnt much from them about the form and substance of diplomacy. They were men of great wisdom and outstanding God-given diplomatic skills. They met and dealt with presidents and prime ministers, kings and queens on equal footing and won their respect. It was my great good luck to enjoy their affection, paternal guidance, trust and confidence. What I learnt working under their watchful and sympathetic gaze in those formative early years stood me in good stead later in my career. The best part of a young IFS officer's training lies in his assignments in the first four or five years under caring, interested and sympathetic ambassadors in active missions abroad.

Clearly, there was immediate need for at least eighty to hundred or more persons with good educational backgrounds and professional competence in suitable vocations to fill posts at home and abroad. For this purpose the Union Public Service Commission of India prescribed educational and other qualifications, including experience of work in existing central and provincial services, the academia and other fields, and invited applications. On the basis of the results of interviews, the commission recommended three or four hundred candidates for entry into the Foreign Service, but the secretary general was not satisfied with the commission's selections, out of which he accepted only sixty or sixty-five for the new Indian Foreign Service.

Bajpai then set up a small committee of secretaries headed by himself, to select a score or more candidates through interviews, without advertising the posts or the qualifications required for them. To give the committee a public face, a well-known industrialist, Lala Shri Ram, was included in it as a member. There was criticism of this irregular procedure in Parliament and the press, and complaints also reached the prime minister. Clearly some favouritism and wrongdoing was involved. Some of those candidates selected by the Bajpai Committee were as young, some even younger than, the candidates who joined the service through the Commission's competitive examination for All India Services in 1948–49: they should have taken the exams route.

The prime minister did not take too serious a note of the complaints and only asked Bajpai to include in the committee's selections a few persons from the minority community and some officers of the disbanded Indian National Army whose personnel, even educated and qualified ones, were finding it difficult to get suitable employment. The Bajpai Committee complied with this request of the prime minister, but grudgingly. It selected only five former INA officers for the service: C.J. Stracey, Abid Hasan Safrani, K.M. Kannam Pillay, M.M. Khurana and Mahboob Ahmad. The seniority allotted to these patriotic gentlemen was not commensurate either with their age or the national service they had rendered, and this worked against their rise to the high positions they merited in their careers. For us, junior members who entered the service through competitive examinations, they were heroes.

Of this entire lot of entrants into the IFS, eighteen came from the armed forces, four from the former Indian National Army, six from the old Indian Foreign and Political Service and other central and provincial services, half a dozen were princes from the former ruling houses, a handful came from the media and the remaining from academic and legal professions. There was no time to impart any kind of training to this heterogeneous group with wide differences in age, educational background and professional experience. They were straightaway deployed in a wide variety of tasks at headquarters and in missions abroad, with which they had no prior acquaintance.

Among them there were some very able men, for example, R.G. Rajwade, I.J. Bahadur Singh, K.V. Padmanabhan, J.C. Kakar, B. Rajan (a former Cambridge don who left the service after a few years) and Rikhi Jaipal—but ambassadorial posts were long in coming to them. In particular, important embassies remained beyond their reach because ICS incumbents outstayed them in the service and in the posts of that category.

An exception was K.R. Narayanan, who not only rose to be India's ambassador in China and the United States but, post-retirement, successfully fought an election, won a seat in the Lok Sabha and, in course of time, became India's vice president, and later, President. Another exception was P.N. Haksar, an intellectual giant who replaced a non-IFS officer of the ICS, L.K. Jha as Prime Minister Indira Gandhi's principal secretary and filled that post with distinction during the critical years of the Bangladesh War and the Emergency. Later, he was deputy chairman of the Planning Commission, a post carrying cabinet rank. However, overall they were all highly competent men, and unfamiliar as they were with the manner and substance of diplomatic functioning, they brought much credit to Indian diplomacy in a tension-filled and Cold War-stricken world. What is more, they, rather than the elite ICS group, gave the nascent service its esprit de corps.

chapter three

NEHRU'S AMBASSADORS OF TRUTH AND GOODWILL: THEIR ACHIEVEMENTS AND FAILURES

~

Many foreign countries had expressed the desire to open their embassies in Delhi, and Nehru himself had also decided to send resident ambassadors to forty countries. With the limited induction of about 100 persons in the Foreign Service, independent India's Foreign Office had become a functional entity and Nehru proceeded to select ambassadors who would head the new embassies and high commissions. The target of forty Indian diplomatic missions abroad was reached in 1950.

Because of the paucity of career officers of sufficient seniority at least in the first round of appointments to ambassadorial posts, the prime minister had no choice except to select eminent persons from public life. He sent Vijaya Lakshmi Pandit to Moscow followed by Dr S. Radhakrishnan; Asaf Ali to Washington; Krishna Menon to London; K.M. Panikkar to Peking followed by N. Raghavan of the INA;[1] Sri Prakasa to Karachi; B.N. Rao as permanent representative to the UN; Abdur Rauf to Rangoon; C.P.N. Singh to Kathmandu; Diwan Chaman Lall to Ankara; Minoo Masani to Brazil; Ali Zaheer to Tehran; Apa Pant to Kenya; Ali Yawar Jung to Argentina; Niranjan Singh Gill, an INA hero, successively to Ethiopia, Thailand and Mexico. Kesava Menon, an activist in the Independence movement and the founder and chief editor of *Mathrubhumi*, was sent to Colombo where he was succeeded by V.V. Giri as high commissioner in Colombo in 1951–52. Dr Tara Chand, a historian, was sent to Tehran, following Ali Zaheer's retirement. A few more important public figures were given ambassadorial appointments especially in London and Washington, as and when these posts fell vacant: Benegal Rama Rau, G.L. Mehta and M.C. Chagla went to Washington; B.G. Kher and Dr J.N. Mehta became high commissioners in London after Krishna Menon.

Vijaya Lakshmi Pandit and all the others were members of the Indian National Congress or supporters and sympathizers of its non-violent struggle for freedom. They were not given any training in diplomatic functioning or formal instruction except, as I learnt later from some of them, that in informal conversations Nehru told them that he was not sending them abroad to lie for their country; that the world knew little about India and its problems and there was curiosity about it and its policies. 'So, explain our problems and policies truthfully and offer India's friendship to the countries to which you are accredited, and win their goodwill and friendship.'

Two of those eminent public figures, V.V. Giri and S. Radhakrishnan, later filled the highest position as India's presidents. Krishna Menon joined the cabinet as defence minister and was also the designated permanent leader of Indian delegations to the UN. M.C. Chagla rose to be India's foreign minister. Of the rest, only Vijaya Lakshmi Pandit, K.M. Panikkar, C.P.N. Singh, Apa Pant and Ali Yavar Jung were honoured with repeat appointments as heads of mission.

G.L. Mehta, who followed Vijaya Lakshmi Pandit as ambassador in Washington and held that post for a period of six years (1952–58), deserves a special mention for keeping India–US relations on an even keel at a time of many differences and difficulties between the two countries.

C.P.N. Singh will be long remembered for his bold and imaginative decision to give asylum to King Tribhuvan and his family when they drove into his residence in Kathmandu. He later helped to fly them out to India, defying threats of the Rana prime minister—the de facto ruler of Nepal. This put an end to a 104-year long rule of the Ranas and changed Nepal's history. Apa Pant and Ali Yawar Jung were known in India and foreign diplomatic circles for their youthful enthusiasm, sophistication, personal elegance and the ability to make friends.

Another notable, though a later appointee from public life, was Gopalaswami Parthasarathy, who distinguished himself as India's ambassador in a number of difficult assignments, notably in China from 1958 to 1961, when India–China relations were on a downward slide, and in Pakistan from 1962 onwards, a tough period for Indian diplomacy between the Sino-Indian war of 1962 and the Pakistan–India war of 1965. He also filled with distinction the post of India's permanent representative to the UN. With his imperturbable temperament, Parthasarathy combined extraordinary negotiating skills, tact and patience which he used to help resolve international problems as well as long-pending contentious domestic issues. For many years he was a close and trusted adviser of prime ministers Nehru and Indira Gandhi.

All these were persons of eminence in India's public life as politicians, freedom fighters, lawyers, writers and thinkers, who had made a mark in their respective fields of activity. Four of them, Vijaya Lakshmi Pandit, Sarvepalli Radhakrishnan, V.K. Krishna Menon and K.M. Panikkar were already internationally known figures. Much has been written about them, in praise and in criticism of their achievements and failures—and they had some failures too—as India's representatives abroad. I was fortunate to know them fairly well, had opportunities to work under them or observe them in action in the world's most important capitals. Their pioneering work in the unfamiliar domain of diplomacy was truly remarkable and it influenced my own life in diplomacy a good deal.

I have very fond memories of my association with them and if I recall some of them here I do so not in judgement, but as tributes of a disciple to his gurus:

MRS VIJAYA LAKSHMI PANDIT

The embassy in Moscow was India's first diplomatic mission to be opened, and Mrs Pandit's appointment as ambassador to the USSR, just a few days before Independence, showed the importance Nehru attached to developing relations with that country. However, during her tenure in Moscow from August 1947 to March 1949, Stalin showed little appreciation of Nehru's gesture and never received Mrs Pandit, because it was said that he was seriously ill throughout her stay in Moscow. But that was a pretext. The fact is that Stalin was in doubt about India's Independence, as Mountbatten was still in Delhi as governor general and British officers remained in command of the Indian army and the Indian navy. Be that as it may, Nehru had other uses for this highly talented diplomatist with a magnetic personality, who was already a prominent world figure. If Stalin chose not to meet her, so much the worse for the old man: the loss was his! Prime Minister Nehru sent her to Washington as India's ambassador in advance of his own first visit to the United States in 1949.

While Mrs Pandit was personally popular in America's social, cultural and political circles, she could not do much to improve US–India relations because of irreconcilable differences between the two governments on the Japanese peace treaty, the Korean War and Cold War-related issues. Though Nehru was received with much respect and cordiality in the US in 1949, the American establishment's aversion to his policy of Non-alignment came in the way of better understanding between the two countries. Even in London, where she was a popular and much respected high commissioner for India for seven years, she could not achieve any change in the anti-India British policy on Kashmir. She did, however, succeed in raising Indo-British relations to a high level of cordiality and left a huge lot of goodwill in political and social circles of Britain, including the royalty.

Earlier, in 1946, Mrs Pandit had made a tremendous impact on the UN General Assembly (UNGA) at Lake Success and established her reputation as a forceful, yet conciliatory, stateswoman when pressing India's complaint against racial discrimination in South Africa. It was Mahatma Gandhi's decision that she should lead the delegation to the UNGA's first session. In a personal talk with her, the Mahatma had said that Field Marshall Jan Smuts was his friend and, even though he himself had opposed his politics, he knew Smuts to be a man of God whose friendship and respect he would not like to lose for the sake of a majority vote. She did not disappoint him. Her restrained advocacy of India's case won a two-thirds majority for the Indian resolution in the UNGA. Throughout the debate she extended all respect and courtesy to Smuts and even seemed to have won the saddened elderly statesman's esteem and affection. But as a result of South Africa's defeat in the UN, Smuts lost the next election, discriminatory practices worsened under his successor and decades went by before racial discrimination against people of Indian origin ended and the apartheid regime was dismantled. Nevertheless, seven years of her leadership of Indian delegations to the UNGA had so enhanced her prestige, authority and popularity in international circles that in 1953 she was unanimously elected president of the UN General Assembly. She was the first woman to receive that honour.

The arrival of a woman ambassador in the cloistered domain of diplomacy, with its strict adherence to protocol, practice and precedence, was a bundle of embarrassments. For how should she be seated at a dinner table? As a spouse, or a woman invitee or an ambassador? Or, where would she retire when men and women separated after dinner in two different rooms—the former for cigars and cognac and the latter for gossip? Surely she should join the ladies? But Mrs Pandit would have none of it. 'I am an ambassador,' she would say to the dean of Moscow's diplomatic corps,' and I assert my right to be treated as such. I do not smoke or drink cognac but I shall join the men for political talk.' And that is what she did.

In Washington Mrs Pandit's wish to be treated as ambassador—as a man that is—met with even stronger objection from Dean Acheson, secretary of state. He could not reconcile himself to the idea of a woman representing her country as ambassador! 'I cannot accept you as India's official representative,' he told her. 'Why do pretty women want to be like men?' 'They don't,' replied Pandit, 'they only want equal rights and privileges, and I insist on having mine.'[2]

She says: It was 'an uphill struggle during the first few weeks to insist on this recognition, but I succeeded in obtaining it . . . A few ambassadors felt uncomfortable in the beginning but they soon got used to my presence, and, I might say, liked it!'

How the women took it is not known, but Mrs Pandit enjoyed the experience, even the initial discomfiture of her male colleagues.

After Mrs Pandit's election as President of the UN General Assembly, Prime Minister Winston Churchill invited her to visit the United Kingdom. When she arrived in London, Churchill was recuperating from a stroke in his country home, Chartwell. His illness had been kept from the public and though not fully recovered, he wanted to meet her and invited her to Chartwell. The old India-hater had already acquired some respect and affection for his former enemies, Nehru and his sister. But he told her he did not care for women in politics: 'I have accepted you, but don't start trying to incite everyone here.' Mrs Pandit said to him there were many women already in England more qualified than her to hold positions of high responsibility and asked how long he was going to keep them out. 'As long as I can,' said the prime minister of the world's oldest democracy! At the end of a long, warm and friendly meeting he paid Mrs Pandit the same tribute which he had paid to Jawaharlal Nehru: 'You have conquered two of man's greatest enemies—hate and fear.'

On another occasion Churchill remorsefully said to her: 'We killed your husband, didn't we?' Her response could only have come from a deeply spiritual person: 'Every man lives his allotted span of life.' Churchill was moved and described her words as 'nobly spoken'. It was this calm acceptance of life's trials and suffering, as well as its responsibilities, that made Mrs Pandit such a popular figure not only in India but wherever her responsibilities took her.

Mrs Pandit was the first woman ever to appear at the Court of St James as a foreign ambassador and, even though London was accustomed to the rule of queens, on her arrival in London as India's high commissioner, there was some discussion about protocol in those circles as to how she should be addressed—as His Excellency, or Her Excellency—as there was no precedent. The tortuous processes through which British protocol reconciled itself to respecting the femininity of a woman ambassador is not known.

Departure from tradition and habit does not come easy to the British. In British towns where the mayor's elective post is held by a woman, she is, when spoken to by male or female interlocutors, addressed as Mr Mayor, not Madam Mayor.

I came up against this conundrum at a side meeting of the Conservative Party's Annual Conference in Blackpool in October 1989, when I was posted in London as India's high commissioner. These are meetings organized by local or regional leaders which foreign ambassadors are sometimes invited to address; the German ambassador and I were special guests at this large gathering, and I was invited to be one of the speakers, the last one, to conclude the discussion on a political theme. The meeting was chaired by a good-looking lady, thirty-five or forty years of age. Every speaker, including a woman speaker and the ambassador of Germany addressed her as Mr Mayor, and neither the lady mayor nor anyone else seemed to mind that. Incidentally, this was the time when a great Englishwoman, Margaret Thatcher was in her eighth or ninth year of Britain's prime ministership!

When my turn came to speak, I bowed to the chair and said, 'Many English men and women were in my country for nearly 200 years; we tried to understand them, their ways of doing things and the secret of their power that had made them rulers of half the world. When we said goodbye to them in 1947, we thought we had got the hang of it all. But here today I have discovered yet one more of the Englishman's mysterious powers. You gentlemen take a perfectly good lady, very obviously a woman of beauty and charm, and by some alchemy almost like the power of a god, you make a man out of her to give her an office—even the office of a modest elevation such as that of mayor!' The mixed gathering of 300, seemingly apprehensive that the Indian high commissioner was about to berate them for Britain's misdeeds in India, broke out into loud cheers and laughter.

'It cannot be I am sure,' I said, 'pure and simple male chauvinism. But with little personal knowledge of such things I cannot definitely assert also that it might even be something worse.' More laughter and clapping followed, and someone shouted: 'Go on high commissioner, we want more . . .'

I then turned to the chair and said, 'I seek your permission, mayor, to address you as Madam Mayor!' Bravos, clapping and laughter followed.

The lady nodded, and I resumed:

Madam Mayor, when they were out there in India we learnt some things from them, Englishmen; and we also tried to teach them something of our millennial lore, one part of which says that, in or out of office, a woman remains a woman, that she should be respected and admired as such and that there are many ways of showing her your adoration and love without imagining her as a man, or worse, making a man out of her!

Amid much merriment a connoisseur from the back rows shouted: 'Kama Sutra!'

Finally, I said, 'Madam Mayor, I hope and pray that the effects of the transmogrification practised on you are not irreversible.'

The laughter seemed unending and I could not even touch on the afternoon's political theme—something about the relevance or importance of democracy. Madam Mayor herself was in splits. She got up, gave me a hug and led me, hand in hand, to the tea table. During the next day or two of the conference, the good lady was my friendly guide to the intricacies of the Conservative Party politics, and through her I met a large number of constituency party leaders.

The English love a joke: more so a joke on themselves. Had we known this, we might have laughed them out of India long before 1947! Or, maybe not; for in India they ceased to be British or English. They were imperialists—the rulers of a conquered race without even the right colour of skin!

Mrs Pandit had great capacity to laugh and make others laugh. I had first met her at Prime Minister Nehru's residence in 1951 at a family gathering through the courtesy of her son-in-law, Gautam Sehgal, a good friend of mine. The room resounded with laughter as she regaled us with the foibles, eccentricities and vanities of the high and mighty she had met at the UN and elsewhere. I was privileged to meet her often during the following years in Delhi and abroad. In 1954, I accompanied her on her week-long official visit to Sri Lanka as UNGA president, and observed her dealing with men and matters at several public gatherings and in a few tête-à-têtes. She was quick to discern a hidden contretemps or some lurking contrariness in an opponent's argument and conjure up an anecdote with an infectious touch of humour to diffuse the awkwardness of the moment.

Her ability to deal with complex and difficult problems and situations with natural ease and sympathetic understanding always left a favourable impact on situations and people she dealt with.

Mrs Pandit was a natural master of the art of diplomacy. Though she failed to achieve much in Moscow or Washington, she was a great success at the UN and during her seven-year tenure as high commissioner in London.

DR SARVEPALLI RADHAKRISHNAN

Mrs Pandit's successor as India's ambassador in Moscow, the eminent scholar and philosopher, Dr Sarvepalli Radhakrishnan was Nehru's most imaginative choice for the post at that particular time. Stalin had to be convinced of the genuineness of India's Independence, of the depth of India's concern over Cold War tensions and its desire for peace and for Russia's friendship and cooperation. The usual diplomatic approach would be of no avail, and Radhakrishnan was just the man for the complex task. On the eve of his departure for Moscow, Nehru had said in a speech in Delhi on 24 August 1949 that Radhakrishnan would go to Russia as the symbol of India, that he had the capacity to understand the Soviet Union and world developments and also to make the world understand what India stood for.[3]

A contemporary of Bertrand Russell's, Radhakrishnan was already a towering figure in the world's philosophical circles. A humanist thinker and an eloquent public speaker, he was known internationally for his forceful advocacy of human brotherhood and a world of harmony, peace and cooperation. In 1936, he became the Spalding professor of Eastern Religions and a fellow of All Souls College at Oxford. He wrote several books on Hindu religion and Vedanta philosophy and was regarded as their most authoritative interpreter. His knowledge of other religions—Judaism,

Christianity, Buddhism and Islam—and their scriptures, was equally impressive. His lean, tall figure and austere appearance made him look like a modern messiah. When he spoke, his audiences were mesmerized. In private conversation he was an absolute charmer and could make even the stolid Russian Foreign Minister Andrei Gromyko laugh.

He took to diplomacy with effortless ease because he chose to remain what he was, and introduced in diplomacy's stilted narrative a touch of informality, candour and humour, mixed with moral fervour. Stalin was intrigued by this uncommon ambassador's reputation as a philosopher of the urgings of the soul of man, and by the reports he had received of his austere appearance and ascetic way of life.

Before Radhakrishnan arrived in Moscow, the Russians had conducted a nuclear test challenging the United States' nuclear monopoly. It was a time of growing tensions and the lengthening shadow of conflict between the two power blocks. There were also new uncertainties in Asia caused by the victory of communists led by Mao in China, and the conflicts in the Korean peninsula and Vietnam. In those circumstances Radhakrishnan felt impelled to enlarge his own role way beyond the normal remit of an ambassador, to nudge the US and the USSR towards better understanding of each other and a possible detente.

According to Dr S. Gopal,[4] Radhakrishnan's son and biographer, the ambassador believed that accommodation between the Soviet and Western ways of life was not impossible; nor was the blame for tensions wholly on one side, and that intolerance was not peculiar to Russian communism. He felt it was wrong on the part of Western powers to summarily reject Stalin's repeated statements about the possibility of peaceful coexistence. He then went on, without Nehru's approval or instructions, to emphasize the urgency and importance of a meeting of six heads of government—two from Asia (including India) and two from Europe, to join those of the United States and the Soviet Union—'to dissipate the blinding mist of misunderstanding and break through the mounting wall of prejudice'. He declared his support also for the idea of a four-power summit, which had been floated by Moscow earlier.

All this was embarrassing for the government, and it did not cut ice with the Western powers. Neither the US, nor the European powers were in favour of such a meeting. Its public support by the Indian ambassador in Moscow only caused annoyance in Washington. But Moscow was delighted with Radhakrishnan's enthusiastic support and the fact that he was disseminating Stalin's ideas and proposals not only in Russia but also globally from the platform of the UNESCO General Conference. Again, without authorization or instruction from Delhi, the ambassador had engaged in negotiations with the American ambassador in Moscow concerning the proposed summit meeting. Also he had meetings with British Prime Minister Attlee to convince the latter of Stalin's sincerity.

Stalin was curious and asked him over to the Kremlin for a meeting at 9:30 p.m. on 15 January 1950. Radhakrishnan opened the conversation by saying that India's independent foreign policy of Non-alignment sought peace and friendship with all nations, and that India attached special importance to the Soviet Union's understanding and friendship. Stalin asked whether the Indian army was still commanded by British officers and whether India had a navy. Two more intriguing questions followed: Why was Ceylon not a part of India? And did Maldives belong to India? To all these queries, the ambassador gave appropriate answers. Finally, after deploring the Cold War, the ambassador suggested that the Soviet Union should take the initiative to end it. When Stalin said that there was also another side responsible for it and it takes two to clap, the ambassador's solution to the problem left him without an answer: 'As a peace-loving country the Soviet Union should withdraw its own hand as it takes two hands to clap.'[5]

The two austere men, both direct and blunt in speech, had apparently hit it off. Stalin's satisfaction with the meeting was made known to the Indian embassy, and new warmth began to characterize the Indian embassy's dealings with the Russian Foreign Office. These were the first results of the impact of Radhakrishnan's personality, his sincerity and candour, his transparent goodwill, his humanist thinking and love of peace.

Radhakrishnan's informality and directness, accompanied by unpredictable touches of teasing humour, served him well in the months that followed. In a meeting with Foreign Minister Andrey Yanuarevich Vyshinsky, the ambassador suddenly asked him why Russia was not supporting India on the Kashmir issue in the Security Council. Taken by surprise by this unanticipated query on an important foreign policy issue, Vyshinsky mumbled something about India never having asked for Soviet help in the matter. 'But that's what I am doing now, am I not?'

It was that simple; but the results were far-reaching. In the next meeting of the Security Council in 1951 in Paris, the Soviet Union's representative blasted the UK and the USA for meddling in Kashmir's internal affairs. The inevitable next step followed in due course: From then on all Western resolutions in the Security Council, not acceptable to India, were vetoed by the Russian representative. All this took place on the ambassador's own initiative, without consultation with anyone in India. Even Nehru was surprised how it had happened. He was apprehensive that the Soviet Union's support would make Kashmir a Cold War issue. But that fear was misplaced as Britain and America had already made Kashmir a Cold War issue by committing their support to Pakistan in utter disregard of the facts of the case.

When Radhakrishnan was to return to Delhi to take up the post of vice president, Stalin received him for the second time. At this meeting Radhakrishnan, while referring to some common ideals shared by India and the Soviet Union, emphasized India's commitment to democracy.

This was in response to Stalin's remarks about India's soft treatment of the princes and landlords. Stalin was sceptical of any peaceful advance to socialism in such easy ways: 'When a Russian peasant sees a wolf, he knows how to deal with it. Liquidate, Mr Ambassador.' Radhakrishnan asserted that India's peaceful methods to get rid of exploiters would show a new way for other nations. The discussion concluded with an unexpected assurance from Stalin: 'Both you and Nehru are persons we do not consider as our enemies. This will continue to be our policy and you can count on our help.'[6]

Radhakrishnan had not only achieved a breakthrough in India–USSR relations, he had pioneered a new course in Indian diplomacy.

On the other hand, the ambassador's unauthorized public drumming up of Stalin's sincerity, and the genuineness of his desire for peace from Moscow and from UNESCO's platform, was raising new doubts about India's Non-alignment. Radhakrishnan personally was losing credibility in the West where people were asking whether he was India's ambassador to Russia or Stalin's ambassador to the world. His unauthorized initiatives to enter into negotiations with the American ambassador in Moscow and the British prime minister produced no result. An excess of zeal never does any good in diplomacy.

The philosopher-ambassador got so carried away by his own success in Moscow that he proposed to Nehru that India and the USSR should enter into a Treaty of Peace and Friendship. Nehru promptly and categorically rejected the idea to stop the ambassador from further floating ideas, which at that time were not in accord with his policy of Non-alignment.

V.K. KRISHNA MENON

Krishna Menon, high commissioner for India in London from 1947 to 1952, and the leader of Indian delegations to the UN General Assembly and Security Council till 1962, though controversial in both roles, was a notable actor on the world stage in his time. He was a versatile man of great intellectual powers, but his creative energy and other abilities were not attuned to tasks of political management or high administrative responsibilities like those of a defence minister.

Menon's political career began when as a student in the Law College Madras he got actively involved in the Home Rule Movement, where he got to know Annie Besant,[7] His ability and capacity for hard work had impressed her and she arranged a scholarship for him to go to England in 1924 for higher theosophical studies. Menon availed of the scholarship, but in London his interest shifted to scholarly pursuits of a worldly kind. He joined University College, London, to study for a master's degree in psychology. He then joined the London School of Economics (LSE) for an MSc in economics. There, Menon came under the influence of Harold Laski, whose patronage helped him to embark on a political career as a young member of the British Labour Party. In 1929, he founded the India League, and as its secretary till 1947, used it to lobby for Indian Independence in Britain's parliamentary and public circles. It was during this long and tireless campaign that he won the admiration, comradeship and affection of Jawaharlal Nehru, India's future prime minister.

Menon's hunger for knowledge was insatiable. He was a voracious reader on a variety of subjects, such as law, politics and governance, economics, history and world affairs, war, arms and disarmament, psychological and crime thrillers and classics. So even while he was immersed in political activity, a part of his great talent blossomed in another direction for which book lovers the world over owe him a debt of gratitude. With his colleague, Sir Allen Lane, he co-founded and edited Penguin and Pelican Books.

As a campaigner for Indian Independence in Britain, Menon had lived a stoic's life in one small room in circumstances of unrelieved impecuniousness. He was so accustomed to that lifestyle that even later, as the head of one of the most prestigious Indian diplomatic missions, he did not feel inclined to move out of it. He shunned the space, comfort and elegance of 9 Kensington Palace Gardens, the Indian high commissioner's government-owned residence, and made himself comfortable in a small room behind the high commissioner's office in India House, and stuck to that skeletal arrangement for the next five years. He dressed well, but never seemed to have the appetite for a proper meal. His diet consisted of countless cups of light milk tea and the occasional toast or one medium-sized baked tomato. But he was a good host and derived vicarious enjoyment from feeding close friends and young protégés. Amid friends and people he trusted he was an engaging and amusing conversationalist. Only a few knew this side of his personality. He had a sense of humour, which often had a sharp Swiftian sting to it. At the conference table he commanded attention and respect, and in an argument the last word was always his.

As a man in politics his worst flaw was his 'notorious incapacity to suffer fools gladly'. Nor was he good at hiding his dislike of his equals. When Nehru offered him membership of India's delegation to the UN, he accepted it on the condition that he would not have to work under Mrs Pandit, who was leader of the delegation. Since Nehru wanted to move Menon out of London, he gave him independent charge of the Korean issue at the UN. Eventually he became leader of the Indian delegation to the UNGA and the Security Council. There Menon was in his element, enjoyed himself hugely, and soon acquired the reputation of a chastiser of sanctimonious imperialists who dominated the UN Security Council.

In the early years of his high commissionership for India in London, he enjoyed high prestige and was personally popular with the Indian community in whose welfare he took keen interest. Indian students, whose numbers in Britain at that time were quite sizeable, were his special favourites. In addition to his diplomatic work, he was running hostels for them. At their functions, he mixed freely with them and they responded enthusiastically to his interest in their welfare and activities.

But there was a noticeable decline in his relationship with Attlee's Labour government, and all his efforts failed to make the slightest dent in Britain's adversarial position on the Kashmir issue. Worse, ignoring his protests and pleas, the Attlee government imposed restrictions on the supply of arms to India at a time when Britain was its traditional and exclusive supplier.

Menon had been feeling frustrated and unhappy. In 1952 he addressed a personal letter to Attlee saying his presence in London had hardly helped to advance Indo-British relations and he was therefore thinking of quitting his post. It is not known whether Attlee wrote back, and if so what his response was. In late 1951 or early 1952, Prime Minister Attlee had confidentially conveyed to Nehru that he would like to deal with him on important matters through the British high commissioner in Delhi and not through Menon, because the latter had employed several undesirable persons— known British communists—in the High Commission, posing risk to the confidentiality of communications between them. This was tantamount to declaring Menon persona non grata, which obliged Nehru to withdraw him from London despite the latter's reluctance to leave Britain.

In 1955, while Menon was dealing with the Korean problem at the UN, there was an American attempt to use him to convey a message to Peking that until China released all Americans captured by its forces in the Korean War, there would be no negotiations on other outstanding issues. In this connection Menon had two meetings with President Eisenhower in March and May of that year. Eisenhower noted that while discussing Indian philosophy Menon 'made one or two disparaging, and therefore astonishing, remarks about communists'. In Washington there was a widespread belief that Menon was a communist. In all probability this might have been an attempt on Menon's part to convince Eisenhower of his objectivity and impartiality as a negotiator on Korea. Eisenhower was not impressed by Menon's criticism of communism and communists. In a note on his meetings with Menon he commented:

> Krishna Menon is a menace and a bore. He is a bore because he conceives himself to be intellectually superior and rather coyly pretends to cover this under a cloak of excessive humility and modesty. He is a menace because he is a master at twisting words and meanings of others and governed by an ambition to prove himself the master international manipulator and politician of the age.[8]

Menon, of course, had something of an actor in him. But his mastery of the English language was well known, and he had the uncommon ability to draw out and convincingly put across the implied or hidden meanings of words. In fact, these attributes had made him such a successful negotiator of seemingly insoluble problems, like the ones faced by the Geneva Conference on Vietnam.

I saw a totally different side of Menon's persona in a meeting with another noted political personage of the time, Lord Beaverbrook, who was a conservative politician and a close friend of Winston Churchill's. In March or April 1962, Beaverbrook had invited Menon to Canada to deliver a lecture in Montreal, to be followed by a private meeting and tea at his residence. I was commanded by Menon to accompany him to Montreal and also be with him for tea with Beaverbrook. The lecture, which took place in a huge hall, packed to capacity, was a great success. During tea, Beaverbrook heaped much praise on Menon for saving the Commonwealth and the good work he was doing in New York as leader of India's delegation. Among other things, he said Americans were fools: Top officials in Washington, instead of listening to Menon's advice, were jealous of him etc. Menon, whom Eisenhower considered a menace, was like a docile and devoted disciple in Beaverbrook's presence, listening and reverentially asking questions. With tea, a domestic brought a plateful of small cupcakes, and Beaverbrook told him he had the cakes especially baked for him. Wonder of wonders, the abstemious Menon ate four without a fuss!

K.M. PANIKKAR

K.M. Panikkar was a scholar and poet, a historian and university teacher. He had translated several Greek plays into Malayalam verse. In the mid-1920s, he joined service in Indian princely states, some of which pretentiously maintained foreign offices for their dealings, presumably, with other native states and the viceroy's representatives—called residents—positioned in their capital cities to watch over the conduct of the ruling princes. Panikkar had served as foreign minister of two large Indian states—Patiala and Bikaner— when he was appointed secretary to the chancellor of the Chamber of Princes. Nehru had appreciated Panikkar's work in the Indian princely states, his moderating influence on the princes and his quiet sympathy with the activities of the States' Peoples' Congress, led by Nehru, to introduce democratic reforms in those remnants of feudal India.

The publication, in 1945, of his book *India and the Indian Ocean* had established Panikkar's reputation as a strategic thinker. It is a seminal work which highlights the critical importance of the Indian Ocean to India's security and to its relations with South East Asian neighbours and other littoral regions. The book gave rise to more studies of the subject after Independence. His *Survey of Indian History*, published in August 1947, captures in a short volume of some 300 pages the millennial panorama of the romance and tragedy of India, the rise and fall of its dynasties and its revival and resurgence as a civilization and a state. *Asia and Western Dominance*, published in 1953, is a unique volume, written from an Asian perspective, on European relations with Asia.

China was in turmoil, and with the prospect of an uncertain and difficult transition from the collapsing Kuomintang regime to communist rule and to forge India's relations with the new government, Nehru saw in this versatile scholar-statesman just the man for the ambassador's post in revolutionary China. The ambassador's task in China was bound to be of more than usual complexity because the leadership of China's communist revolution were an unknown quantity, and cultivating Mao and his senior colleagues was going to require uncommon political savvy and an abundance of virtues, which according to nineteenth century American political theorist Benjamin Franklin, are indispensable in diplomacy—'sleepless tact, immovable calmness and a patience that no folly, no provocations, no blunders can shake'. Panikkar had all that and more.

After China's invasion of Tibet in 1950, Panikkar was wrongly accused in India of having misled Nehru about China's communist rulers, or that he failed to understand the motives underlying China's policy towards India. In fact, the ambassador had foreseen China's action in Tibet and had been advising Chinese leaders to avoid use of force and resolve the problem peacefully through negotiations with the Dalai Lama. Delhi was fully in the picture about the developing situation, but was in no position to effectively intervene to prevent China's reoccupation of Tibet. Those who criticize Nehru and Panikkar for India's China policy had exaggerated notions of India's economic and military strength to confront and make revolutionary China reverse its Tibet policy.

Revolutionary China, even in victory, was an angry country. Its leaders were scornful of India's non-violent revolution and spoke contemptuously of Indian leaders, including Nehru, as 'running dogs of imperialism'. In New Delhi, Nehru, foreseeing future difficulties over Tibet in particular, had rightly decided to persevere in a conciliatory approach towards China. His advice to Panikkar was to do his best to cultivate the friendship of China's new leaders, and Panikkar worked with exemplary patience and diligence to eliminate misunderstandings, suspicions and rivalry, and succeeded in bringing about a change in the attitude of China's leaders towards India. He had no illusions about the nature of his task in Peking. He knew there were serious issues on which disagreements were bound to arise between India and China and as he himself notes, 'with a communist China cordial and intimate relations were out of the question, but I was fairly optimistic about working out an area of cooperation by eliminating causes of misunderstandings, rivalry etc. The only area where our interests overlapped was in Tibet.'[9]

In regards to Tibet, his knowledge of China and Chinese history had convinced him that the British policy of maintaining with force India's special political interests could not be sustained. Nehru was in general agreement with that view. It would have been a foolhardy act for India to seek to continue with outdated British policy in Tibet. Tibet had come up in one of the ambassador's meetings with Zhou En-Lai, and he had expressed the hope that China would sort out differences with the Tibetans through peaceful negotiations. Zhou En-Lai's response was that while they themselves preferred negotiations to military action, 'to liberate Tibet was China's sacred duty'. In the circumstances, as a realist and far-sighted diplomatist, all Panikkar could do was to prepare the ground for peaceful removal, through patient negotiations, of the meaningless relics left behind by a retreating imperial power. That goal was achieved by the 1954 India–China agreement on Tibet.

The border problem had not acquired prominence during Panikkar's assignment in Peking, which ended in 1952. For various reasons border negotiations had not even begun then. The souring of India–China relations occurred in the late 1950s primarily for two reasons: grant of asylum to the Dalai Lama in 1959, and the opposition in Parliament, egged on by the empty theatrics of inflexible leaders like Acharya Kripalani, to Nehru taking any pragmatic initiative to find a mutually accommodative solution to the complex border issue through friendly negotiations with Zhou En-Lai. Panikkar had no role in those events.

So, by and large, in the course of the early years of Independence these great ambassadors had not only established friendly relations with important countries, they had also elaborated and explained India's distinctive foreign policy of Non-alignment, and defined the areas of practical action at the global level to achieve its goals of liberation of colonial peoples, cooperation for world peace, disarmament and development, poverty alleviation and halting the nuclear arms race. These humanitarian concerns of India soon became the most pressing agenda of the United Nations and its specialized agencies. The quality of the performance of these representatives of a newly independent country, and the scale of their achievements in the unfamiliar area of international relations and diplomacy, were truly praiseworthy—a few setbacks and false steps due to an excess of zeal notwithstanding.

To the younger IFS officers in the MEA and in missions abroad, this star-quartet—Mrs Pandit, S. Radhakrishnan, Krishna Menon and K.M. Panikkar—of Nehru's ambassadors from public life, were larger-than-life heroes without any blemish or error. Those of us who were lucky to have the opportunity to work under one or more of them found them all most kind and considerate towards us. They were good teachers, and we learnt much from them and from the way they dealt with people, problems and issues of policy.

However, the top bureaucracy in the MEA from Secretary General Bajpai down was openly critical, and often scornful of at least three of them. They criticized Panikkar for his zealous approbation of Mao and his communist cohorts; Krishna Menon for his abrasiveness and radical leftism; and Radhakrishnan for his 'flights of fancy',' woolliness and naivety'! Towards Mrs Pandit they were understandably deferential, not only because she was the prime minister's sister, but because of her undoubted diplomatic skills— even the stern Sir Girija was appreciative of her sterling performance at the UN. The real reason for the top bureaucracy's resentment was that for instructions and advice, these four ambassadors dealt directly with Nehru who was appreciative of their pioneering work in high-level diplomacy and the fact that despite many difficulties inherent in their tasks they had helped raise India's image in the world. That riled the ICS bureaucrats in New Delhi all the more. But the ambassadors did not care, and Nehru was deaf to the grumbling and whining of their critics.

It wasn't that Nehru was unaware of the flaws in their diplomatic functioning. He had noted, for example, Panikkar's 'habit of seeing further than perhaps facts warrant'. There was a large element of deception in China's India policy which Panikkar had failed to detect. He thought Zhou En-Lai's cordiality and friendship and his silence on the border issue meant his acceptance of India's position. Occasionally he even overstepped his role as a transmitter of messages to second-guess China's policy or motives. In 1950, Panikkar was instructed by Nehru to convey a message from the United States to China saying that US forces would not cross the 38th parallel without specific authorization from the UN, and therefore China should not react sharply to the success of the ongoing American military campaign in South Korea. Instead of conveying the message to the Chinese he sent back to Nehru his own view that there was no possibility of China entering the war unless Russia did so and a world war resulted! Clearly he had not fully grasped the significance of the American message.

Both Radhakrishnan and Panikkar were unduly alarmed over the likelihood of the Korean War or the Cold War tensions deteriorating into a world war. Bluster apart, neither China nor Soviet Russia was really prepared for a big war; nor were the American people, their hatred of communism notwithstanding. President Truman wanted to bring the Korean War to an end, but he had a problem with General MacArthur and it took him some time to get rid of him. The scare spread by Radhakrishnan, Panikkar, and Nehru himself about an impending world war because of the intensity of the Cold War and the nuclear arms race had no real basis, and even for peace in northeast Asia we need not have indulged China to use us. There were no worthwhile rewards for India's peace zealotry. Moscow did not like our meddling in the Korean issue which was of much closer and deeper concern to them, and it did no good to the already difficult India–US relationship.

However, those were early days in the making and implementing of the foreign policy of a huge new and complex country on the world stage, and Nehru was not very particular about disciplining his senior ambassadors. His bemused tolerance of their unauthorized, out-of-line initiatives or faux pas is best summed up in Gopal's biography of Nehru:[10]

> The war hysteria and the drift to a world conflict gathered pace, and at this moment Nehru found his cluster of powerful ambassadors almost an embarrassment, for they began to display the disadvantages of their eminence. Each pursued an almost independent foreign policy. Vijaya Lakshmi [Pandit] was eager to talk to President Truman, Krishna Menon met Attlee repeatedly, Panikkar saw himself as China's line of communication to the world, Radhakrishnan, with his formidable personal prestige, conducted his own private negotiations for peace with the Soviet Foreign Office and the American ambassador in Moscow.

Overall, Nehru was not satisfied with the performance of most of his non-career ambassadors. S. Dutt, Nehru's trusted foreign secretary—who was with him at the Foreign Office for twelve years—records Nehru's disappointment with his non-career ambassadors in the following words:

> I recall having suggested to Nehru a number of times in 1958 and 1959 that he might consider selecting some public men for three or four of the more important embassies, since there was a dearth of sufficiently senior officers in the permanent cadres. Every time I referred to the suggestion he kept quiet. That was his characteristic way of expressing dissent. Had he learnt by experience?[11]

Of course he had; but regardless of Nehru's experience, his successors in the following decades continued to make political appointments in important diplomatic posts. And, their experience of non-career ambassadors' work was no different from Nehru's.

chapter four

ABOUT MYSELF

~

I was born on 11 September 1924 in a Dogra-Brahmin family in a
village called Shakargarh, located on the banks of a perennial stream,
Baiyn-nadi, which originated in the hills of the nearby Jammu
province of the Indian State of Jammu and Kashmir (J & K). My
father was headmaster of a middle school in a village named Khanna,
seven or eight kilometres away from Shakargarh, on the other side of
the Baiyn. Every morning and evening, six days a week, he used to
ride his mare to and fro from the school. He was a self-taught, self-
made man who had overcome—by sheer will and perseverance—
circumstances of extreme difficulty, which I shall explain shortly.

In the rainy season the Baiyn became a river, almost a kilometre or
more wide of muddy water, but in the winter months the width of the
continuous flow of water would be reduced to eight or ten metres,
with a depth of no more than two feet of cool, crystal clear water.
Shakargarh is located a few kilometres south of the foothills of the
Himalayas, in a fertile region (now in Pakistan) with an abundance of
mango groves and agricultural fields, green round the year with one or
another crop. My father's younger sister (my bua) owned a couple of
large groves of good quality mangos; so we had plenty of that luscious
fruit in its season. From the banks of the Baiyn, on clear mornings we
had a clear view of the snow-clad Himalayan mountain range.

My bua's husband, a tall, handsome philanderer, had abandoned
her for a merry time with girls in Rajasthan. Later in life when he

wanted to rejoin his wedded wife, he was not allowed to re-enter his own home in the village named Chujwana. So he went back to his women in Rajasthan. He had no care for the substantial landed property and the mango groves, which he had left behind for delights of the flesh away from home. My bua was in full possession of those properties and was managing them well with the help of a number of hired hands whose families were also beneficiaries of her generosity and care.

I was nine or ten years old when I got to know that branch of the family well, especially my bua and her daughter Vidya, her only child, about six years my senior in age. Vidya, a beautiful, affectionate, kind, caring and gentle girl, became my icon of feminine loveliness and virtue. There was an ethereal quality to her presence, her voice and her touch, and I imagined myself deeply in love with her in a devotional and reverential sort of way. In return she showered much tender care and affection on me. When I got to know her she had been suffering from tuberculosis, which was in the incurable terminal phase. Nevertheless, there was never a hint of sadness or fear of death in her; in fact, when we were together she was always full of good cheer with the radiance of inner happiness on her face.

I was spending a weekend in Vidya's home, when one late evening she suddenly breathed her last, with her mother and myself at her bedside. That moment haunted me for years; it broke something inside me and I didn't quite know how to contain or express the emptiness that I felt within and around me. That night, I cycled back to my home five or six kilometres from Vidya's village to inform my parents about the death of their niece. For countless days that followed I attended school, did home work as an automaton and during those countless nights I sobbed and wept silently till sleep numbed my senses. Even in my early years of youth, Vidya remained the icon by which to judge beauty, tenderness, poise and goodness in a woman. When I started composing poems at the age of fourteen, I wrote several short compositions to describe the gossamer delicacy of her beauty, but they left me cold. In my only book of Hindi poems I later published—*Do Parten*—there are two short compositions that reflect something of that paragon of the mystic allure and God-given adornments of a simple village girl.

The origins of all branches of my Dogra-Brahmin family go back to Jammu. We were preceptors for religious rites and ceremonies of the state's Dogra rulers. What has come to us as family history by hearsay is that one of my paternal ancestors, four or five generations ago, had fallen for a Kashmirī girl and married her in preference over a Dogra-Brahmin damsel. And perhaps because of the displeasure he had thus earned of the extended family, he left the state with his young Kashmiri bride to settle down just outside the state's northwestern border, in a village named Aimalpur on the west bank of the Jhelum River. There he acquired lands which were cultivated by hired farming hands. It was a happy marriage and soon my Kashmiri great-great-grandmother presented her doting husband with a son, who was named Devi Das (popularly called Deva Shah), in gratitude to the famous shrine of Vaishno Devi in Jammu. Since then, two blood streams of Kashmiri Pandits and Jammu's Dogra-Brahmins have coursed in the veins and arteries of Deva Shah's descendants.

In course of time, his son, my grandfather, Pandit Lalo Ram, moved to Shakargarh for unknown reasons, perhaps to be closer to the province of the family's origin, Jammu. Lalo Ram was an extravagant spendthrift, fond of horses, and was known to give his favourite mare a drink or two of country liquor every day. His elder son, Kishen Chand died early followed, before long, by Lalo Ram himself and his wife, leaving my father, Harcharan Dass, an orphan at a very young age, without money or property to make both ends meet. A once well-off family of Samskrita scholars had fallen on bad times.

My father educated himself in the three Rs, Urdu and Persian, and got a job as school teacher in a government school. Within a few years he rose to be headmaster of a middle school with Urdu as the medium of instruction. He married the daughter of a modest Dogra-Brahmin family, who bore him three sons including myself, and two daughters. Teachers were not paid well in those days, but at great personal sacrifice he educated his three sons up to the matriculation level in English-medium high schools, within a distance of ten to twelve kilometres from Shakargarh, and the two girls in the only local Hindi-medium school for girls up to the eighth class. For higher education, he sent my elder brother Prem Nath to DAV College, Lahore, and six years later I joined the Hindu College, Amritsar, because Prem was already in a job in that city and I would not have to live in a hostel.

For obvious reasons my early education was in village schools where my father taught or which were close by. Totally unacquainted with Samskrita himself, my father saw to it that I studied that language and its literature from my fifth year in school till my BA degree. For two years of my high school education, I cycled twelve kilometres to and fro every morning and evening to Ghulam Din Islamia High School, owned and managed by a Sunni-Muslim family, in a village called Maingri, which, incidentally, had a good Samskrita teacher, who also gave the school's Hindu students daily instruction in the basic tenets of Hinduism.

Thus, during the first fourteen years of my life, Shakargarh was my base. As I grew in years, the village grew in size and population; a fair mix of Hindus and Muslims who lived and worked together in friendship and cooperation. The essentials of daily consumption like wheat and rice, lentils, vegetables, milk and ghee, poultry and mutton—all produced locally—were unbelievably cheap, and one rupee went a very long way. A year's requirement of wheat for a family of five, for example, cost no more than four or five rupees! Good, clean and tasty water for household use was drawn from wells at the end of each street. On my mother's insistence my father had a bore well sunk in our courtyard with a surface handpump to draw perfectly delicious and health-giving water from the earth's depths without much physical exertion. My mother generously allowed women of the neighbouring homes to draw water from our pump, but only when my father was not around.

The village had quite a few interesting characters—a separate book will be needed to narrate their traits and tales. I shall recall just one here which I cannot push out of my mind. A former sepoy in the Indian army, Ghulam Din, a tall, well-built, middle-aged man lived a few doors away from us on the same street. He had seen active fighting in the First World War in Italy and France. He was happily married to a woman even though the couple had remained childless. He could not afford a buffalo or a cow on his small pension and the few extra rupees he earned from casual labour, but he kept a goat and drank goat's milk for daily nourishment.

We, children of eight to fifteen years, used to gather round Ghulam Din now and then, to urge him to tell us of his heroics in the battles he had fought in faraway Europe. He would conclude those impromptu sessions with a tale or two of his non-martial exploits, the flings he had with English, French and Italian girls. These tales always concluded with the same exhortation every time: 'Boys, when you grow up, go to Italy. Forget Bartania (Britain), France and all other countries. Forget Amrika (America). Go to Italy, I say'—and here he would name some towns—'the girls there are more beautiful than the Taj Mahal!' And if someone asked whether he had seen that famous monument he would retort: 'What if I have not seen the Taj Mahal? I have seen those girls, hey! I tell you they are whiter than the marble of Taj Mahal! Go to Italy, boys, just to look at those houris. Their soft white skins, so translucent that when they drink water, you can see it going down their throats!'

He would not guide us further down along the flow of that blessed little stream of fluid to its terminal point.

In the schools I had attended, turban was de rigueur: Sitting in the classroom bare-headed was considered an insult to the teacher. So when I landed up at the Hindu College in Amritsar, with my turban firmly on my head day after day, week after week, I became a figure of fun in my class till one day, after being the object of ridicule for several months by city boys, on the advice of a sympathetic boy, Shyam Sundar Nayar I gave up the turban. Shyam chided, rebuked and quarrelled with boys who used to make fun of me. He became my most cherished, lifelong friend.

Meanwhile, after the third or fourth month of classes, there was a test in essay writing in English on a subject given by the teacher. Thanks to my English teachers in those village schools, my essay was judged the best. And when in response to Professor Manek Chand

Kapoor's call for the writer to stand up and show himself—it was a large class of forty-five or fifty boys seated on wooden benches—I stood up with my turban and all, there was stunned silence in the classroom, till Shyam Sundar clapped, then the professor clapped and the whole class joined in. Professor Kapoor then read out my piece to the class as a model of essay writing. In the next year, another teacher, Professor Raghuvansh Kishore Kapur (R.K.), an Oxford graduate who headed the department of English at the college, helped me improve my accent and pronunciation and made me editor of the college magazine—*Shivalay*. Thanks to his encouragement and instruction, within a year or so I became a confident and reasonably good public speaker in English. During my last two years at the Hindu College, I was twice elected President of the College Union.

When the government brutally suppressed the Congress in 1942, the All India Hindu Student's Federation (AIHSF), an affiliate of the Hindu Maha Sabha, became active, especially as the All India Hindu Maha Sabha's annual session was to take place in Amritsar in December 1943. The most prominent non-Muslim Indian leader out of jail at the time, Shyama Prasad Mookerjee, had been invited to preside over the session. The AIHSF, which would have a role in the event, elected me as its general secretary. A couple of days before the big event, the deputy commissioner of Amritsar imposed a ban on processions and on gatherings of more than five persons in the city. On Mookerjee's advice it was decided to apply for permission for a procession in the evening preceding the event and for public meetings on the two following days, in a large open area with three or four entrance and exit gates in the low walls surrounding it. Seating arrangements had been made there for a crowd of 100,000 people.

The following morning, the ground was filled to capacity with people, and Mookerjee, in his presidential address, fired up the audience with strong condemnation of the Firangi sircar for its crime in creating artificial famine conditions to kill millions of Bengalis. The Muslim League's demand for Pakistan was on the agenda and Mookerjee asked me to speak on the subject in the main session. In about twenty minutes I made three or four points: the absurdity of a population of converts claiming to be a separate nation, the financial unsustainability of the areas that might comprise two separated lands, Mr Jinnah would never get a Pakistan comprising all the areas he was claiming and, finally, Pakistan was a scheme of the wily English to leave behind a weak India and an even weaker Pakistan, forever dependent on its benefactor Britain and other powers for security. When I finished speaking Mookerjee got up and gave me a big pat on the back, then started clapping and the crowd also broke into loud cheers.

Mookerjee had wanted me to stay in politics, but my teachers were getting annoyed that I was ignoring my studies. I too realized that I owed it to my family to complete my education satisfactorily and find a good job. So, in the remaining one year at the Hindu College and the next two in Government College, Lahore, I devoted all my time and energies to my studies. The Hindu Maha Sabha politics, in their nationalist phase under Shyama Prasad Mookerjee's leadership in 1942–43, were my first and last brush with Indian politics.

At the end of it all, I was still the same old, small-time, diffident village boy from Shakargarh. Therefore when the first All India Services Competitive Examination was announced early in 1948, I saw the notification in the newspapers and ignored it. After taking the master's degree in English literature in early 1946, I had been teaching the subject to undergraduates for almost two years. I was happy doing it and thought I had found my métier for the rest of my life. A bureaucrat's life held no interest for me.

My first appointment as a college lecturer in English was in the Sanatan Dharma College for Girls in Sialkot. It was a degree college and though it carried a Hindu denomination, there were several Muslim girl students also in my classes. The allure of teaching Keats and Shelley to young and beautiful Punjabi damsels with romance in their hearts and dreams in their big eyes is not without risks for a twenty-two-year-old innocent. Occasionally the atmosphere in the classroom became a bit difficult. Grown-up girls—there were a few aged about nineteen or twenty in my senior class—in an all-girls college can be very naughty, especially when the teacher is a young, vulnerable male. The bolder ones would wink, stare, make faces, do anything to get attention. Coming from a conservative background, for a few days I found this sort of thing embarrassing. But after a few weeks I learnt to deal with the mischief by responding with a harmless joke or introducing a diversionary note to provoke a discussion on the subject of the lecture, or sometimes just by snubbing the offender. Sialkot was a small, conservative town in those days but, as they say, girls will be girls.

Soon there was talk about arguments among the girls, as to who among them was the teacher's favourite. All this despite the fact that I always left the doors and windows of the classroom open and assiduously avoided meeting any of the students alone in college or outside. Talk travels and word about it reached the ears of the college principal.

So, one late afternoon in September or October 1946, the principal, a kind, elderly gentleman whom we addressed as Panditji, called me to his office and spoke to me, in strict man-to-man privacy and confidence, about the guile and wiles of women. He knew, he said, I was without blame, but these girls—ah! Be very careful, Rasgotraji. He added by way of a suggestion that I try and introduce some teaching of good moral behaviour, and even some religion in my lectures! You are a good teacher, Panditji went on, there is a long career ahead of you and I do not want to see a blemish fall on you because of these girls! They have got hold of some of your Hindi poems and there is speculation whether you are still composing poems and if so who among them will be the inspiration behind your new poems!

The poems Panditji was referring to were written and published when I was studying for my BA degree at the Hindu College, Amritsar. I explained that I had neither written nor published anything recently because I was concentrating on my work for the master's degree. Since my arrival in Sialkot I hadn't breathed a word about my being a poet of sorts, but a couple of my poems had been published in a Hindi journal recently of which copies might have found their way to Sialkot. Panditji said he was not blaming me for anything, only cautioning me since I was new to teaching young girls!

The principal was a conservative gentleman, but a well-meaning and sympathetic person. I also knew he liked me: He had welcomed me with great warmth as a new entrant into the time-honoured teaching profession. But I knew no way of mixing Vedantic axioms and verses from the Bhagavad Gita with English poetry in my lectures. T.S. Eliot's 'Waste Land' had not yet found a place in Indian textbooks. But I seriously thought over Panditji's fatherly advice, and decided to lookout for an opening in a safer haven for my future career as a college teacher.

Fortunately, two or three weeks later an advertisement of a vacancy in Arya College, Ludhiana, came to my notice for the post of head of the Department of English, which would mean promotion of rank from a simple lecturer and possibly also higher emoluments. I took four-day leave and went to Ludhiana to present myself for the interview. To my great relief, after a not very exacting interview, the college principal, Mr Kalia, offered the post to me and asked me to join duty within a week to ten days.

Panditji was shocked when I placed my resignation letter in his hands, along with the offer to surrender a month's salary in lieu of notice as stipulated in the contract. He said he did not want me to leave, that I had misunderstood his advice etc. He seemed genuinely reluctant to let me go, but I insisted and told him that the new job was that of head of department in a bigger men's college and with higher pay. He agreed finally and we parted as friends.

Sialkot was basically a quiet military cantonment town, with a small supporting civilian population and India's best-known sports goods industry. Ludhiana, in contrast, was a bustling commercial city known for its large hosiery industry and several other industrial clusters. The city also had several good schools and at least three colleges, including one exclusively for women. The largest and most prestigious of these educational institutions was the Government College, with its sprawling campus in a quiet area at the town's edge. Close by was the modest building of the Arya Degree College with a large open compound around it.

The college had a good but small faculty and a very large body of students, with forty or more students to a class. Some distance away from these two male bastions was a small, high-walled redoubt which housed an all-girls college with an all-female faculty, headed by a charming spinster, whose only known name was Miss Sen. Her faculty included a few more confirmed spinsters and an equal number of still marriageable young women with little actual prospect of marriage, because in those days in that Jat-dominated region highly educated women were considered 'too forward' and not good candidates for marriage! Except in very big cities like Lahore and Amritsar romance and even harmless friendly contacts between men and women were taboo. My generation's youthful years were wasted in very arid times.

Panditji's gentle words of caution leading to my quick exit from Sialkot turned out to be a stroke of great good luck for me and my family. Soon the country was partitioned, leaving my entire family stranded in Pakistan. For weeks I could not contact them or get news of their safety. My aged parents, my unmarried younger sister and younger brother and two little daughters of my elder brother were in our home town, Shakargarh, which we had expected would remain in India but was given to Pakistan by the Boundary Commission headed by Sir Cyril Radcliffe. My elder brother Prem Nath, who was heading a dyes and chemicals firm in Multan, was stranded there with his wife and two other little daughters. Both areas were badly affected by violence and other atrocities. I cannot find words to describe my agony and anguish mixed with a debilitating sense of shame at my not being with them in their ordeal.

After a couple of weeks of futile efforts to get some news of their safety, in utter despair I addressed a letter marked personal to Prime Minister Nehru pleading for his help. Within days I received a simple acknowledgement of my letter and a few days later I was informed that my parents' party had moved out of Shakargarh with a group of other Hindus from the area who had been forced out of their homes. They had been found walking towards the Jammu border escorted by a jeep-load of Gurkha soldiers led by a British officer. The group would be provided a resting place for a few days inside J & K, and then my family members would be transported to Ludhiana as soon as possible.

The safety of my elder brother and his family was still uncertain, and we heaved a sigh of relief when they were evacuated to Amritsar by air in November 1947. Both parties had lost everything that goes under the description of property, possessions and wealth. When they reached Ludhiana, all they had was the clothes they were wearing. But they were now all safe and we were all together in my semi-detached, five-room bungalow on Dr Hira Singh Road, which I had hired at a rental of fifteen or twenty rupees a month; my emoluments as a college lecturer at that time were around Rs 150 per month.

The shock of Partition, the loss of comforts of a settled home and assured means of livelihood were lightened somewhat by the fact that I had a job, however inadequate financially for the sustenance of a large family. All of us being together under one roof at a time of unimaginable trauma was a source of solace and strength. Prem soon moved to Amritsar to re-establish himself in his old business of dyes and chemicals, but did not succeed too well and shifted to Delhi where he found more satisfying employment in the growing agro-industries sector. Inder Krishna, my younger brother resumed his disrupted studies in Ludhiana, graduated from Government College, and later received his master's degree in English from St Stephen's College in Delhi. He entered the Railway Accounts Service through the annual competitive examination for All India Services.

My tenure at Arya College was not long. The Partition had resulted in the temporary location of East Punjab's Education Department at Ludhiana—its main offices were later shifted to Shimla. Among the high officials of the department was one of Punjab's highly-respected educationists, Rai Bahadur Harish Chandra Kathpalia who was the United Punjab's inspector of schools. During his inspection tours before the Partition, he had met my father, then headmaster of a school in a village close to the Jammu border in West Punjab. In the new Education Department at Ludhiana, Mr Kathpalia was the inspector of Training Institutions in the truncated East Punjab—a very senior position. When I was introduced to him at a function in Ludhiana, he asked whether I was related to a Pandit Rasgotra—a teacher, headmaster of a school somewhere in the Sialkot district. Yes, sir, I answered; Pandit Harcharan Dass Rasgotra is my father. After a few more inquiries about my family and my educational career, Mr Kathpalia said something to the effect that Arya College was hardly the place for an MA degree holder from Government

College, Lahore. I didn't get the sense of what he had said, and mumbled something in praise of Arya College.

Thereafter I was invited to the Kathpalia's home every now and then. Soon Mr Kathpalia's intercession would lead to my induction in the Punjab Education Service (Class II) and my posting as a lecturer in English in Government Degree College at Dharamshala.

In those days Dharamshala was a small, idyllic town, unspoilt by tourism, in the lap of a Himalayan middle range called Dhaulidhar. The college premises were a lovely little campus, with windows of classrooms opening on verdant valleys on one side and snow-clad mountain peaks on the other. I loved my treks with my students on the snowy heights of Dhaulidhar and my daily walks between the college and 'Mount Pleasant', the bungalow nestled high up on a hillside, which I shared with a colleague. But Mr Kathpalia had other plans for me. My stay in Dharamshala was also very short.

East Punjab's director of Public Instruction, G.C. Chatterjee, came to Dharamshala to inspect our college. In the absence of suitable accommodation for him in the town, he was put up in a spare room in 'Mount Pleasant'. In the course of a chat with me one evening, he mentioned that a vacancy was likely to arise in the English department in Government College, Ludhiana, and I might be asked to go there; if that was okay with me, he advised that I remain ready to move to Ludhiana at short notice when the transfer order came. He added that he had mentioned it to Principal Gomti Prasad and he would not stand in the way of my move!

This was indeed a great favour to a young man who had entered government service just a few months earlier. I was back in Ludhiana, in April or May 1948 as a lecturer in the English department in East Punjab's premier institution of higher education. This, I discovered later, was no happenstance. Mr Kathpalia had taken over as principal of the Government College in February that year and had asked for me to be transferred to his college. Out of sheer goodness of heart Rai Bahadur Sahib had taken firm charge of my career. He would soon steer my course into the Indian Foreign Service.

My admiration for, and love of the teaching profession, was due to the fact that both in school and college I had excellent teachers who seemed happy and contented with their lives. Their lessons fired my imagination and opened before me new vistas of thought and inquiry, and it became my sole ambition to follow them into the noble teaching profession. But Mr Kathpalia thought I was being foolish; he chided me for having missed the first All India Services Competitive Examination in early 1948.

Refugees from Pakistan were coming to Ludhiana in large numbers; the district administration's resources were stretched. On Deputy Commissioner Narottam Sehgal's request, Government College agreed to manage a tented camp of some 30,000 refugees. I was involved in this work and spent a lot of time helping, or often simply talking with those traumatized people whose losses and suffering were much greater than what my own family had gone through. Some of them had seen their homes looted and burnt, and their kith and kin forcibly taken away, abused and murdered in cold blood. They were all in a terrible state of deprivation, loss and grief. Our management tasks included meeting their immediate needs of shelter, food and clothing, medical attention and providing such comfort and solace as was possible pending their permanent resettlement.

There is enough suffering and sorrow in the life of an individual human being, but to see such misery in the mass as I saw in the Jawahar Refugee Camp in Ludhiana, is a truly shattering experience. The Buddha had said about life: 'All is misery, utter misery; all is momentary, nothing but momentary.'[1] Lord Krishna, in the Bhagavad Gita, agrees that life is misery, but offers no cure for it, only the palliative of unswerving devotion to him. He says: 'Having come into this impermanent and unhappy world, remember me, worship me.'[2] There is a promise of redemption, of release from the cycle of birth and death in all this, but no present alleviation of, or escape from suffering and travails of life. Only death brings the end of present misery and perhaps also impermanence. A seer who had guided me at different stages of my life once said to me in a truly revelatory moment: 'It is all here; there is nothing beyond death.' Nevertheless, God or Nature has granted man the gifts of resilience, determination and the will to fight and overcome adversity. In that vast sea of loss, grief and misery, which the Jawahar Camp was, I also saw signs of hope and determination to rebuild broken lives. And that filled me with a rare level of contentment, which has remained a long remembered experience of my later years.

Even as the shock and trauma of the Partition receded, one incident during my student days in Lahore has remained fresh in my mind. In the winter of 1945–46, some students of the Punjab University had picked a quarrel with the university authorities on some insignificant matter, which I cannot now recall. Perhaps it was related to some aspect of the examination system or the students' demand for a change in the schedule of examinations. A few students had gone on hunger strike and a small representative group of five student leaders from different colleges, including myself, had been formed to mobilize moral support for the hunger strikers, and to launch protests with the university authorities, and also to contact ministers of the Punjab government in the hope that they might influence the university administration in favour of the students' demands. In this latter undertaking we had no success at all with any member of Sir Khizar Hyat Tiwana's cabinet: We could not get a meeting with any of them.

While this agitation was going on, Mr Mohamad Ali Jinnah happened to visit Lahore for two or three days. He was staying at the residence of an important Muslim League leader, Raja Gazanfar Ali Khan. We requested a meeting with him and were told that he had a very heavy schedule of meetings, but would meet with us for a few minutes in the evening on a given date before leaving the residence for dinner with another Muslim League leader. We reached Raja Sahib's bungalow at the appointed time, around 7:00 or 7:30 p.m. Mr Jinnah's car was already stationed in the porch and we did not have to wait long. Mr Jinnah came out, greeted our group of five and asked what the problem was. We had chosen a leader to narrate our grievances and he did a good job of it in a well-rehearsed oration of three or four minutes. Jinnah asked a couple of short questions to which others responded briefly in turns. He was patient and attentive and expressed his sympathy. He advised us that the hunger strike should end; young lives should not be wasted in that way. To our pleas that he should tell Premier Khizar Hyat and his ministers to address the students' grievances, his response was that he would do whatever was possible and added: 'What am I to say to these idiots? Hard to expect them to do anything sensible.'

He shook hands with each one of us, me being the last. The others had moved a few steps away, and in a completely spontaneous move, as I held his soft delicate hand, I asked: 'Sir, the country is drifting towards a division, isn't it still possible for us to remain together as one nation?' Jinnah gently laid his hand on my shoulder and said: 'It is too late *now* young man.'

That *now* in Mr Jinnah's response bothered me for quite some time. Was Partition avoidable? Did Jinnah really want India to remain united? His secret correspondence with Churchill, with whom he was in regular touch since 1940, led one to a different conclusion. Churchill was encouraging him to persevere in his struggle against the 'Caste Hindus'. Jinnah himself also was adamant on his demand for a sovereign, independent Pakistan.

It is true that Mr Jinnah had accepted the Cabinet Mission Plan, which contemplated a federal structure of three semi-independent units because it offered, after a specified period, the right to secede to the Muslim-dominated western and eastern units—the former including the whole of Punjab and the latter comprising a huge region of the whole of Bengal, Assam and all the other territories in India's northeast. Secession, virtually unavoidable in the circumstances of those times, would give Mr Jinnah a much larger Pakistan than what he actually got in the end. Nehru had foreseen this mischief in the Cabinet Mission Plan and was right in rejecting it. I myself have never regretted the Partition. We rebuilt our lives as best we could, and neither I, nor any other member of my family has felt the least bitterness towards Pakistan.

I have gone into this part of the story of my life at some length because it explains my total lack of interest in any new prospect of a more prestigious and remunerative engagement with life. I had no intention of appearing in any examination for All India Services. I was happy teaching, being with young people and seeing them grow in understanding, wisdom and responsibility. I would argue this with Principal Kathpalia from time to time; he would listen with sympathy and patience but insist that independent India needed young people like me in its service at higher levels of responsibility. One day, in the privacy of his office I received a proper comeuppance: I was being foolish, Mr Kathpalia said; I needed to have my head examined, I must think the matter over etc.

Even while I was at Arya College, and more so now that I was under his direct charge in Government College, I was a guest at Principal Kathpalila's dinner table often, especially on occasions when a senior official of the department, or a VIP from Delhi, was being entertained. He would present me to them as an exemplary product of the good quality of education in schools in our villages, then teasingly speak of my being too much in love with teaching and, finally, point to the country's need for well-educated, dedicated, young men in the new All India Services being constituted in place of the old ICS. On one such occasion at his residence, I was introduced to one Mr R.N. Banerjee ICS, who, I later learnt, was chairman of the Union Public Service Commission (UPSC). A month or two later when the time came to sign up for the second competitive examination to be held in December 1948–January 1949—the last I could have taken because of the prescribed age limit—Mr Kathpalia summoned me to his office and made me fill the forms and complete other formalities necessary for one to sit for the examination.

In the end, I took the examination after such little preparation, as was possible in the short time available. The results came out on 13 June 1949, and to my surprise, I qualified in the written test. In July 1949, the call came for me to go to Delhi for an interview (it used to be called the viva voce) at the UPSC. I was the last candidate to be interviewed on a hot summer afternoon by a high-powered board of six or seven members seated behind a table on a raised platform with the interviewee's chair facing them at a slightly lower level—a pretty intimidating set-up! At the head of the board was Mr R.N. Banerjee himself, chairman of the UPSC. I must admit I failed to recognize him: There was not too much light in the room as the windows were shuttered or covered with fragrant *khastattis* to shut out the summer heat. If Mr Banerjee recognized me, he did not show it. The interview lasted for about forty minutes.

The range of questions put to me was wide, but the questions were not too difficult to deal with. A few related to the internal situation in India; the Partition (whether it could have been avoided: in this context I told them of my meeting with Mr Jinnah) Indian princely states, priorities in economic development, my hobbies etc. The concluding part, which I can still recall clearly, went as follows:

Q. What is your ambition for India?
A. A powerful and prosperous country.

Q. The worst problem facing India?
A. Poverty.

Q. Noting that the IFS was my first option, a member asked me to describe India's foreign policy.
A. Non-alignment; I said and cited a sentence or two from Nehru's first radio broadcast on the subject in 1946.

Q. How is foreign policy made? What goes into its making?
A. Considerations of national security, and national interest are the most important factors. The country's history, geography, cultural tradition and the prevailing world situation are influencing elements. Sometimes events intervene to shape or reshape policy.

Q. Do we have the institutional framework for such a complex process?
A. For the present, Sir, India's foreign policy is made by Pandit Jawaharlal Nehru. Institutional framework will be developed in due course. The MEA and the IFS are part of that.

Q. What is India's most pressing national interest today?
A. Peace at home and in the world.

There was a short pause and a booming voice came out with the shocker of my viva voce:

Q. Mr Rasgotra, you offered one or two papers in history. Have you heard of, or come across a person called Thailand? (Siam had recently adopted that name).

A. A person called Thailand? No Sir, I have not heard of a person of that name. But, Sir, there is a country of that name. But, perhaps, Sir, there might be a person named Thailand also! It is a big world, Sir.

A ripple of laughter swept the table; the chairman's booming voice a notable part of it. The interview ended after one or two more questions of a routine nature, and the chair dismissed me with a not unpleasant 'Thank you Mr Rasgotra'.

As I came out of the interview, I felt a bit nervous, wondering whether I had been rude in responding to the chairman's question. I was lingering, wending my way out in a long corridor, when I felt a friendly pat on my back and a gentleman, who was part of the board, said: 'Well done, Mr Rasgotra. Well done. I am Ray.' I said: 'Sir, I was afraid I might have offended the board by the manner of my response to the chairman's question. I should have been polite and respectful.' 'Oh, no,' said Mr Ray. 'They all enjoyed that response. Did you not notice, it was the chairman, who laughed the loudest? You are in, Mr Rasgotra. It will be the IFS; you will hear from the government before long.'

Principal Kathpalia was delighted when I recounted all this to him. Mr Ray, he told me, was secretary of the UPSC. 'If he said you are in, you are in, my boy!' In the first week of September, I received a telegram from the ministry of external affairs saying I had been selected for the IFS, that I should report for duty to the under secretary, Mr M.K. Narayanan, in the MEA on 20 or 22 September 1949, and come prepared to leave for England for training a few days later.

My discharge from the Punjab Education Service (Class II) was sorted out within days with Principal Kathpalia's help. When the time came to part with my benefactor, it was with a very heavy heart that I took leave of that kindest, most generous and affectionate of men I was to know in my life.

There is much misinformation about the Indian Foreign Service in India still, after the experience of sixty-five years. People nostalgically speak of the popularity the IFS enjoyed in early years, when only the top four or five candidates were considered worthy of the elite service. The truth is very different. In the final list of successful candidates in 1949, I had figured somewhere in the high twenties or the low thirties! I managed that rank because of my very high marks in the viva voce test. Only a very small number—perhaps no more than six—had opted for the IFS, of which four were finally accepted on combined grounds of merit and suitability. Few Doon School-wallahs were interested in the services; most competitors came from humbler backgrounds like mine. Obviously there was talent in the countryside too, but successful candidates from such circumstances had family responsibilities which could be better attended to through employment in one of the home-based services. As I discovered later, the IFS boys were looked upon with favour only in one very small constituency of highly educated, sophisticated and ambitious girls of marriageable age and their even more pretentious socialite mothers!

We have been very conservative in our recruitment policy and the country is now suffering from shortage of senior personnel in the IFS. The selectors should go as far down the list of successful candidates as necessary to select thirty or more candidates every year of the right aptitude, with willingness to spend two-thirds or more of a career of thirty-five or forty years in service abroad. Impeccable social manners and a degree of sophistication are useful in diplomatic life and these can be acquired by intelligent young men and women in the course of their training years, given good academic qualifications. I am not sure it is still fully recognized that what makes a good diplomat is the quality of training he receives in the first two or three years, and how he is treated and what he is taught by his superiors, especially the heads of mission in his first couple of postings abroad, or by his seniors at the headquarters.

chapter five

TRAINING FOR DIPLOMACY

~

In my first-ever journey by air, as a Sabena Airliner carried me to London, a medley of thoughts and feelings assailed my mind and body: The plane's noisy rise into the sky was an exhilarating experience of liberation, of overcoming the downward pull of gravity even though the wings on which I rose heavenward were not integral to my body. The thought of going out into the big world beyond India filled my mind with excitement, mixed with wonder and awe. Awe, because despite my MA degree and two years of teaching I had remained my villagey self, a simpleton in fear of being lost in the big world. It was a dark night and though lights inside the plane were also switched off, I did not get a wink of sleep. The day dawned as we approached Rome, and then opened up the grand panorama of the Alps and the immense spread of the green land mass of Europe as the aircraft flew over it to Brussels, and then to London.

London, somehow, seemed familiar, perhaps because of my acquaintance with parts of it through my studies of English history and literature and also because of what I had heard about the great metropolis from my teachers in college, both Indian and British, who had studied in London, Cambridge or Oxford. Four years after the end of the Second World War, the debris of the destruction caused by it still pockmarked the great city. About this also I had read a good deal in newspapers. A pleasant surprise was the large number of women, young and not so young, at worksites, on shop floors and in offices. The war had taken a heavy toll on the young generation of British males.

The main purpose of sending IFS probationers to England was to expose them to life and learning in leading Western universities and to the sophistication and complexity of the wider world. So, after a few days in London and a couple of pep talks by High Commissioner Krishna Menon, I made my way to Oxford and to a room in one of Oxford's older and smaller colleges, Wadham, which was founded in 1610 AD. High Commissioner Menon had written to the warden of Wadham, Sir Maurice Bowra, about the purpose of my being sent to Oxford and my educational qualifications etc. As a result, throughout my stay at Oxford I had the benefit of Sir Maurice's kind personal care and guidance.

Life in victorious Britain in 1950 was austere. Throughout my three terms at Wadham College in Oxford, I remember eating a fish called kipper, more bones than flesh, for breakfast day after day. Eggs were in short supply and chocolates were a luxury. Cigarettes and liquor were forbiddingly expensive because of extremely high taxes. Britain was deep in debt, economic recovery was slow, and with India already out of it, the British Empire was unravelling fast. A comment often heard in London and Oxford was: Does Britain matter in the world any more?

Indeed, Britain was passing through a most difficult period of adjustment from a central power in the world to a diminished, small island power, dwarfed in comparison with the new leading world powers, the United States of America and Soviet Russia. In a few years, as its economy strengthened and the new enlarged commonwealth gained in international stature, Britain would regain some of its standing and influence in world affairs, but for the present the grandiloquent pronouncements of Foreign Minister Ernest Bevin on world affairs reflected London's difficulty in getting reconciled to the present-day reality. A far more interesting figure in British politics at that time was a young Labour leader, Aneurin Bevan, who was health minister in Attlee's government.

Bevan's initiative to create the National Health Service (NHS), which would provide free medical services such as free consultation and prescription by physicians, free medicines and hospitalization, had given rise to much public controversy and polarization in politics. The measure was popular with the common people but was bitterly opposed by the Tories whom Bevan had described as 'vermin', which had been eating away the nation's wealth. The doctors feared the measure would reduce their incomes and were opposed to it.

John Maynard Keynes and his revolutionary theory of modern macroeconomics, which marked a break with Adam Smith's laissez-faire economics, was another buzzword in London and in the academic circles of Britain. Keynes had died in 1946, but his theories were being validated by their adoption in government policies in the 1950s. The core of his teaching recommended state intervention, through monetary and fiscal measures to mitigate the harmful effects of the recurring cycle of economic recessions and depressions. Keynes' ideas influenced postwar economic arrangements in all major countries, including the United States of America.

My room in Wadham had a comfortable bed, a desk and a chair and a small almirah for clothes, a rack for books and a deluxe item—a wash basin with running hot and cold water! This last-named facility was available only in a small number of rooms in the college and was offered to privileged scholars. A part-time helper called Scout was allotted to me to keep the room clean, to take care of changing the bed and bath linen with unfailing regularity twice a week and to provide any other help I might need. Cyril, my scout, was a most helpful and pleasant young man, who never had to be told what to do. He was always there when I needed some help or information. During a brief illness I had, he was a most accomplished and thoughtful nurse; in short, he did everything possible to make me feel at home.

A large, wall-sized window of my room opened on the New Bodleian Library across the road and the spires of a couple of colleges beyond. Also across the street below the New Bodleian Library was Oxford's largest bookshop, Blackwell's, where one could browse new titles for hours without the obligation to purchase a book. Delighted with the prospect of life as a student once again, I could not have asked for more.

The town of Oxford and the beautiful countryside surrounding it had not suffered any noticeable damage in the war. The university was humming with activity—lectures and tutorials by learned dons, pretentious and noisy undergraduate politics, debates in the University Union in which political personages from London participated at the Union president's invitation, and were often brought down a peg or two by the audience of irreverent young undergraduates. I took part in one debate on the issue of racial discrimination and didn't think the standard of discussion very high. Wit and humour and turn of phrase, more than the intellectual content of discussion, carried the day. Among the 'darkies' speaking for elimination of racism and racist regimes were myself, my probationer colleague, Ajai Mitra and three or four other students. Anti-racism was popular with Oxford's undergraduate population and our side won the debate with a very large voice vote. The general environment of Oxford University was truly international, with students from all parts of the world contributing to the unique intellectual fervour of the place.

High Commissioner Krishna Menon had advised me to concentrate on economics and world history, including European diplomatic history, during the ensuing academic year at Wadham. I read a lot on international relations and attended lectures on those subjects. Fortunately for me, in the two subjects mentioned by the high commissioner, Wadham had two well-known Oxford dons. My economics tutor, Professor Donald Macdougal, was a respected authority on the subject. He later visited India at Prime Minister Nehru's invitation to advise the government on economic planning. He rose to the high positions of chief economic adviser to the British Treasury and head of the government's economic service. Professor Arthur Thompson was my history tutor. His narration of historical figures and the events of a long, dead past would vibrate with life and fun in his tutorials. The weekly tutorials were not big gatherings: Just my tutor and me in a quiet room of the college for an hour or more of discussion of a short paper I had written or of a subject in which the tutor chose to instruct me. I was free to attend lectures on these subjects delivered by other dons in other colleges also or spend hours in Oxford's magnificent libraries of which the high-domed old Bodleian, with its unrivalled collection, was my favourite haunt.

In pursuance of High Commissioner Krishna Menon's advice that I should also take part in students' political activities, I had joined the university's Labour Club. Out of curiosity, I also attended a couple of meetings of an extreme Left group. At one of these the chairman asked me why the Indian government had sent its Gurkha soldiers to help British imperialists suppress and kill freedom fighters in Malaya? Bewildered silence followed when I informed the meeting that the British army had several battalions of Gurkhas directly recruited from Nepal and some of those units—not any Indian troops—were engaged in the fighting in Malaya's jungles. The chairman insisted that the Gurkhas were Indians. I firmly told him that he was ill informed; that India had its own Gurkhas and also recruited some from Nepal under an agreed arrangement, but the British army's Gurkha units were recruited directly and entirely from Nepal, and those were the troops fighting in Malaya. Overall my impression was that student politics in Oxford was not very well informed about the ground realities in the world beyond Europe.

In applying for membership of the Oxford Labour Club, I must have written a letter or filled a form giving my full name—Maharajakrishna Rasgotra—and the name of my college etc. This caused me no end of embarrassment during my stay at Oxford. Some bright spark spread the word that an Indian ruling prince, 'the maharaja of Krishna Rasgotra' was a resident scholar at Wadham! Curious young undergraduates started visiting my college for meetings with 'His Highness'. One or two I actually met wanted to know the size of my kingdom and the strength of my army!

My protests about being an Indian citizen of very modest origin only led to flattering accusations of undue modesty and humility on my part! This farce went on for weeks, and when I reported this to Professor T.C. Keeley, who was a sort of guardian to me at Wadham, he was amused by my predicament and advised me to let things be and enjoy myself. But he must have done something to save me further embarrassment, for soon the number of curious visitors to Wadham declined and no one was allowed to knock at my door.

Britain's fascination with Indian princes had a very long life. Thirty-eight years later, when I was India's high commissioner in London, my wife and I were guests of a member of the British royalty at a Royal Ascot racing event. A well-known society magazine, *Tatler,* publicized the presence at the event of an Indian princely couple, the 'maharaja and maharani of Rasgotra'!

During one of the college breaks, High Commissioner Krishna Menon had arranged for us a week or ten days' training in the British Foreign Office where we got acquainted with the British diplomatic tradition of formal speech lightened by an occasional touch of typical British humour. We were received with great courtesy by a number of senior officials who talked to us about British foreign policy and the state of the world in general. There must have been more to that short spell of training, but at this long distance in time, I have distinct memory of only two things that I had observed then: A big globe adorned the office of every senior official, and some officers still wore striped trousers. We Indian trainees were a group of four—Ms Muthamma, B. Deva Rao, Ajai Mitra and myself. At the same time a larger group of Pakistani Foreign Service officers was also there and the two groups were moving in opposite directions doing the same round of meetings. Our paths did cross now and then in the corridors of the Foreign Office, but without any possibility of interaction or comparing of notes between the two groups.

It was now time for intensive language training in the countries of the languages allotted to us. Ajai Mitra went to Madrid to polish his Spanish, Deva Rao to Moscow where that brilliant officer—a strict vegetarian—contracted TB, which caused a serious setback to his health and to his career prospects. Muthamma and I were sent to Tours in the Loire Valley—the region of the best spoken French and also known for two good white wines—Vouvray and Sancerre. The magnificent cathedral of Chartres is one of France's great attractions for tourists from all over the world. While at Oxford I had studied the basics of the French language with a tutor—an English lady with a rather heavy accent to her French. In Tours I stayed with a French family—M and Mme Pinson and their children, none of whom were allowed to converse with me in English.

My limited French was the cause of quite a few gaffes on my part and much hilarity at the family dining table. But hearing good conversational French and the compulsion to speak to family members in that language gave me a measure of proficiency in it. A short course at the Sorbonne University in French language and culture, along with some routine activity at the Indian embassy, completed my training abroad as an IFS probationer. In early 1951, I returned to India and a much busier and better organized but still small MEA, to be yoked into active duty as an assistant to India's first and much celebrated chief of protocol, Inder Sen Chopra, who became my guide and mentor for the next eighteen months.

Protocol duties were considered of special importance largely because New Delhi was now host to a growing number of foreign embassies, and helping them with their problems of housing and other needs was a priority with the MEA. Having recently become a capital city of international importance, New Delhi was conscious of the necessity of doing everything involving foreign embassies and diplomats properly and in strict accordance with the fixed rules of protocol. Official New Delhi was still a very formal capital. Even at cocktail receptions, which usually began at 6 or 6:30 p.m., for foreign diplomats and Indian bureaucrats black tie was de rigeur. Politicians, including ministers and MPs, disregarded the dress code completely, and even on formal occasions at Rashtrapati Bhavan turned up in their habitual apparel. The example of meticulously dressed Nehru and the advisory notes circulated by the chief of protocol had not the slightest effect in achieving uniformity in the matter of dress. Eventually, after much unavailing effort over the years in this regard, even protocol had to acquiesce in a typically Indian solution: Dress as you like, but be properly covered! For Indian diplomats though, a prescribed dress code remains in force for formal occasions only; these days even in the Indian prime minister's office senior officials go about in safari suits or multicoloured shirts and trousers!

The city of Delhi was undergoing important changes in other ways as well. The population of Delhi had increased substantially because of the influx of refugees from Pakistan, who were being resettled in new colonies around Lutyens' Delhi—Paharganj, west Patel Nagar and Karol Bagh. A city of no more than 4,00,000 inhabitants in 1946 was now host to 2,000,000 people. New markets were coming up and business activity was on the increase. However, in South Delhi, Teen Murti House still marked the city's outer limit, and in the east there was no habitation beyond the Ambassador Hotel. For the comparatively better off emigrants from Pakistan, preferred housing sites were Model Town beyond the Delhi University in the north, and Hauz Khas, a kilometre or so south of the Safdarjung airport.

Motorized traffic was on the increase because of vehicles owned by foreign diplomatic missions. The tonga, a two-wheeled passenger vehicle drawn by one horse, was still much in use. In 1946, I had hired a tonga in Connaught Place to take me to Daryaganj. The driver spoke to his horse in polished Urdu to encourage the beast to speed up. I asked him his name and where he lived in Delhi. Mohammed Sarwar Mughal said he had a two-room house in one of the back lanes in the walled city. 'Mughal' intrigued me and I quizzed him a little more about his ancestry. He was a descendent, he said, of the great Mughal dynasty and was the recipient of a pension of two or three rupees a month originally sanctioned by the Angrez sircar!.

Plots were being marked out in what is now Sunder Nagar, where land was available at a few rupees per square yard, but there were few buyers because the area—still jungle with a good deal of wildlife in it—was considered too far from the main markets of Connaught Place and Gole Market. A friend of mine advised me to invest Rs 20,000 or Rs 30,000 in a decent sized plot for a house to be built later at my convenience, but I rejected the idea!

Changes in the capital's cultural environment were even more noticeable in two or three other aspects. A city dominated by Tamils or others from the deep south before Independence was fast acquiring a Punjabi bearing in tone of voice, food and dress. Soft Tamil and Malayali cadences were being lost in the colloquial din and vigour of the Punjabi language. An Urdu poet dejectedly summed up this change in a single line of a couplet: 'Dilli kabhi aap thee, ab tusi hai.'[1]

The south Indian clerical inhabitants of New Delhi for decades were happy riding to and from work in the city's bus service, no matter how long the wait for the next arrival of the bus. The impatient Punjabi babu—his numbers in the secretariat had grown rapidly since Independence—wanted his own wheels under him. One evening, at office closing time, I was escorting Prime Minister Nehru in his car from the Parliament building for a meeting at his residence, when we found our way blocked by hundreds of bicycle riders gliding into the vast Vijay Chowk on their way home. The prime minister ordered his car stopped for the bicycle traffic to ease. A little bemused, he watched that mobile mass for a moment or two, and then said to himself: India is now in the bicycle age!

To meet the acute shortage of housing for diplomats and accommodation suitable for embassy offices, plans were afoot for clearing the uninhabited scrubland which is now the prized Chanakyapuri. Clearing of the area was hastened as a huge pandal and tented sleeping accommodation had to be erected for the annual session of the Indian National Congress. Since Nehru, the foreign minister was also president of the ruling Congress party, the entire protocol division of the ministry got involved in the arrangements for security, proper reception and seating etc. of members of the diplomatic corps, who would be invited to observe the proceedings. After the event, a meeting of concerned officials, and others including engineers, architects, town planners, was convened by the chief of protocol to discuss the layout of the area and decide issues like whether the entire area should be an exclusive diplomatic reserve, or whether parts of it should accommodate civil society housing and markets. Another question to be decided urgently for some reason was that of the name to be given to the area. Diplomatic Enclave, suggested by someone, was quickly rejected by the chief. After some further unrewarding discussion, he turned to me and said: 'You Samskrita scholar, Rasgotra! Have you any ideas?' I said the place should be named after an Indian authority on diplomacy and foreign policy like Kautilya; Kautilya Nagari for example. Mr Chopra thought about it for a while, muttered Kautilya Nagari two or three times and said it sounded a bit 'heavy', a bit pedestrian also!

I then recalled Kautilya's other name—Chanakya—and suggested Chanakyapuri. 'That's it; Chanakyapuri sounds much better,' said Mr Chopra. He carried the suggestion to the foreign secretary and Prime Minister Nehru; they both liked the name and the matter was settled.

Protocol duty for a young officer carries risks as well as advantages. A faux pas can cause the government embarrassment and land you in trouble. But a job well done brings you to the attention of senior officials, cabinet ministers, the prime minister and, on some special occasions, even the President. I was lucky to have as my boss so sympathetic and encouraging a person as Mr Chopra, who would readily cover any flaws in my performance and correct my shortcomings in private—never chastise me in the presence of others.

On Mr Chopra's recommendations I was given a number of important protocol duties. In another chapter, I have mentioned my attachment to Dr Graham, who came to India as the UN Security Council's Good Office's man on Kashmir. For a few weeks I was placed on duty with the two queens of Nepal's King Tribhuvan—according to established custom the king had married two sisters: the practice was discarded by the heir apparent, Crown Prince Mahendra. The queens were in India for several weeks for medical treatment and were the government's honoured guests. On another occasion I acted as a French interpreter at Prime Minister Nehru's meetings with a large Turkish delegation. I did liaison duty with British Prime Minister Harold Macmillan during his visit of four or five days. Prime Minister Nehru had put up Macmillan, his wife Lady Dorothy and their two assistants in Teen Murti House, and he had personally instructed me to accompany Macmillan to all his meetings and brief him (Nehru) personally in the evening about the day's happenings.

Another important assignment given to me was to escort a Canadian minister, Clarence Decatur Howe and his wife, Lucy Worcester and their party to Agra to see the Taj Mahal. On that occasion Prime Minister Nehru himself instructed me to take them to the Taj and the Fort of course, but also to show them I'timād-ud-Daulah's tomb across the river, an exquisite jewel of a mausoleum not many people knew about. The minister and his party were wonderstruck by the beauty and splendour of the Mughal monuments, but the minister's wife was so enchanted with the Taj Mahal that when they sat down on a marble bench for the customary photograph, she said to her husband: 'Darling if you promise to build something like this for me, I shall die right now.' To which the honourable minister promptly responded: 'But I do not want you to die ever, my love!' On our return from Agra, Prime Minister Nehru had a hearty laugh when I narrated the little romantic exchange between the minister and his wife.

The prime minster apparently entertained very special regard for the couple. The next evening he accompanied them to a classical vocal recital by Pandit Omkarnath Thakur in the AIR building's small auditorium. The prime minster and his two guests sat in the front row with myself behind them in the second row of chairs. From time to time, Nehru would whisper something to one or the other of his guests who obviously were not familiar with the intricacies of Indian classical ragas. This seemed to disturb Omkarnath, who a little higher up on the stage, close to the first row, was warming up to raise the tempo of the raga after a short 'alap'. Apparently Nehru's whispers broke Omkarnath's concentration and he suddenly stopped singing. The accompanying tabla, sarangi and the tanpura naturally also came to a dead stop. Nehru asked Omkarnath what had happened, why he had suddenly stopped singing. The master vocalist responded: 'Sir, you finish your talks first, I shall then resume.' It was an embarrassing moment saved by Nehru's gracious apology: 'I am sorry Panditji,' he said, 'I was trying to explain to our foreign guests aspects of classical Indian music; do please resume.'

Omkarnath complied and we had a wonderful, highly animated rendering of an evening raga by the master vocalist. At the end Nehru warmly thanked Omkarnath and introduced the visiting minister and his wife to him. The incident says a great deal about the prevailing democratic spirit of those days: A great artiste thought nothing of publicly upbraiding India's powerful prime minister, who, in turn, acted with great humility and decency in promptly apologizing for his mistake.

My most important assignment as a protocol officer came towards the end of 1951. The Mao government's first-ever Chinese cultural delegation to be sent abroad came to India in November for an extensive tour of our country. It had twenty or so members from different walks of life and was headed by China's vice minister of culture, Ting Si Lin—a thoughtful, soft-spoken and highly cultivated gentleman. Because of the importance Nehru attached to India–China relations, the delegation was put up at Rashtrapati Bhavan and great care was devoted to preparing the programme of their visit to ensure that they saw not only India's historical sites or places of touristic and cultural interest like Ajanta and Ellora, but also something of India's development since Independence—new educational and scientific institutions, laboratories, factories and industrial estates, community development centres, big dams and massive irrigation projects. Ms Leelamani Naidu, deputy secretary in the MEA, was appointed the chief liaison officer with me as her deputy, to accompany the delegation throughout their tour of the country and ensure that arrangements made by the concerned state governments were satisfactory in every respect.

Travel in those days was mostly by road, and our cavalcade of ten or twelve cars was heading towards Bhopal in Madhya Pradesh when we came upon an unexpected scene. There we saw Nehru addressing a small wayside gathering of a few hundred unlettered villagers and their children. The first parliamentary elections were to take place in early 1952 and the Congress president was on his electioneering tour. He was telling his enraptured audience to send their children to schools and colleges to learn science, maths and other subjects. His government was opening new schools closer to remote villages and establishing new colleges and universities to make educational facilities more easily accessible. India needed doctors, engineers and scientists in very large numbers, he was telling them, to become a strong and prosperous nation. 'In the modern world,' he emphasized, 'science is very important, a nation can become strong and make progress only if it is good in science and maths and engineering.' He talked to them about big dams and canals, small irrigation projects, agricultural universities and new fertilizer factories—the scientific infrastructure of a green revolution his government was laying which would, in the course of a decade, greatly increase productivity in India's farms and factories.

In 1951–52, despite a paucity of resources and other problems confronting India, the country's mood was one of self-discovery, enthusiasm and hope. The Chinese visitors were quick to notice this and were impressed with what they saw in different regions of India. They evinced special interest in the size and the low estimated cost of the Bhakra-Nangal project. The Nilokheri community development project near Delhi seemed to rouse their curiosity, and they were impressed by India's new educational institutions and industrial undertakings as well. They had found it particularly intriguing to see Nehru speaking about the importance of scientific and technical education to villagers in a remote area. They wondered how the prime minister of the country could be away from the seat of power for long spells for no better purpose than electioneering.

In the following days, in their conversations with Leelamani Naidu and myself, members of the delegation kept recalling the encounter with Nehru on his election campaign. How had Nehru's audience been gathered there? Were there highly educated people in the audience to whom his remarks about science and engineering and college education etc. were addressed? The leader of the delegation was much taken, in particular, with Nehru's emphasis on science and technology as the tools for India's reconstruction and advancement. The Chinese delegation's grand tour of India was a great success. In Calcutta, where the visit ended, Ting Si Lin openly spoke about India's impressive progress in scientific education and industrialization and of the importance of friendship and cooperation between Asia's two largest countries. He hoped that an Indian cultural delegation would visit China as soon as possible.

On our return to Delhi, both Leelamani and I met Prime Minister Nehru and mentioned to him what we thought were the delegation's impressions of India. He asked: Any mishaps? Any embarrassments? Any inadequacy in arrangements anywhere? He was pleased when we told him all had gone smoothly and well. He thanked us graciously and we took leave.

I was about to step out of the room when he called me back to say he had seen a paper about my being posted to the embassy in Washington DC on my first regular assignment in a diplomatic mission. 'There is much to learn from that country,' he said, 'but do not stay there too long—two years, no more. You are not married?' 'No, Sir,' I answered, 'and no plans for at least the next five years. ''Good,' he said and patted me on the shoulder. What a blessing for the start in my career in diplomacy! A month or so later I set off to Washington DC by sea via England and joined the embassy as third secretary/vice consul in April 1952.

chapter six

WASHINGTON DC: EARLY WARNINGS OF AN INDO-US RIFT

~

In my first encounter with them, the United States of America seemed quite different from the rest of the world and the American people a race apart. The unique character of the city of New York, where I disembarked one early morning in late April 1952 after a week's voyage from Southampton in Britain, also accentuated the country's uniqueness. The bustle and energy of that city was an unforgettable experience. Throughout the day, and during the better part of the night, I spent in New York before boarding a train for Washington the following morning—the city hummed with activity. A break for rest or sleep seemed alien to New Yorkers.

The brash informality of the New York cabbie I had hired for the day for sightseeing was another new experience. While remaining glued to his seat, he stretched an arm to unlock the door to the taxi's passenger seats and beckoned me to get in and shut the door. The London cabbie, even on a cold winter morning, would get out of the cab, open the door for you, spread a blanket on your knees and talk, if at all, about the weather. But my New York cabbie was more engaging, wanted to know who I was, what my business was in the US etc. When I told him I was an Indian diplomat on my way to the Indian embassy in Washington, he exclaimed: 'Oh, one of those cookie-pushers! That's what diplomats do here, push cookies

75

around at cocktail parties. I guess they do the same down there in Washington.' We had a little laugh over that remark, and then, he had more to say: 'You Indians are religious people, the hindoos, you know; everybody says India is a democracy and Nehru is a good man. Then, why do you fellahs love the Russians so much, those godless communists? They are bad people; no freedom in that country. We are the good guys, you know. Why don't you love us?'

Dave, the cabbie, was a good-natured fellow and in what he had said there was no anger or unfriendliness, only disappointment tinged with indignation about India's lack of love for liberty-loving America and Americans. So, I felt obliged to respond to his comments. 'Our religion and philosophy teach us,' I said, 'to regard all humanity as one family and be tolerant of diversity. As for politics, India, like America, is a democracy and that is a strong bond between our two countries, and we have learnt much from American history and its Constitution. India has many problems: poverty and unemployment, poor agriculture and lack of industry and the crippling inadequacy of educational and healthcare facilities for our large population. India needs peace to devote all its resources, energy and attention to those great tasks facing it. Therefore it must avoid getting dragged into the fights of the Big Boys. That's what you Americans did in the early years of Independence,' I added. 'It was good policy; it gave young America time to develop and become a rich and powerful country.' 'I guess you are right, friend,' said Dave. There was no more political talk during the remainder of the day while he was taking me around all the various sights of his city. Dave turned out to be a pleasant tourist guide.

During a sandwich lunch in a small restaurant, where he was my guest, he filled me in with lot of information about New York, about life and politics in America and his own family. At the day's end we were almost chums. As I settled the fare and we shook hands, he asked whether I would let him take me to the railway station the following morning, to which I readily agreed. He turned up at the hotel on time and drove me to the railway station. He would not accept payment for the trip or a tip. As we got out of the taxi and

I took out a cigarette, he lit it for me, advised me to smoke cigars instead, and gave me one for my rail journey to Washington.

That was America, its foreign policy and diplomacy for me on my first day in the New World!

In 1952, in contrast with New York, Washington was a placid little town totally without the ceaseless activity and hubbub of New York. There wasn't much vehicular traffic in the streets—old-fashioned trams still ran in the middle of Columbia Street and one or two other main arteries of the town. It was a good, clean and green city for walking, and many office-goers preferred to walk to work. The city is located in a depression on the banks of the Potomac River. The State Department had recently moved into its new premises close to the river and the wags had appropriately nicknamed it Foggy Bottom. There were no skyscrapers, no great shopping malls, only a few hotels and restaurants and little else by way of places of evening entertainment. The high-domed congressional complex on the 'hill', housing the Senate and the House of Representatives, the Congressional library and the numerous supporting offices and lobbies, was the only truly imposing edifice of architectural interest. The White House, or what of that famed residence of the American President is above ground, had the appearance of a fair-sized colonial bungalow.

The city's two monuments commemorating presidents Thomas Jefferson and Abraham Lincoln are among its major attractions. The austere beauty of the huge statues of the two former presidents and the simplicity and elegance of the buildings in which they are placed are enhanced by the large open spaces and water bodies nearby. The Basin at one end of which stands the Jefferson Memorial is bordered with cherry trees, gifted to the US by Japan before World War I. In early spring, when for a couple of weeks the trees are covered with blossoms of shaded hues of pink, tourists flock to Washington to catch a glimpse of that evanescent vision of beauty from some other world. The trees decked out in their floral glory and the blossom-petals gently floating down to unite with their reflections in the water below are an enchanting sight.

The seemingly easy pace at which life moved in that calm, idyllic environment was deceptive. In the two years I spent in the American capital, the Cold War tensions were high and the city was adjusting itself to its new role as the capital of the leading world power. The conduct of government officials displayed awareness of their nation's economic and military might. To an independent and not unfriendly observer, the government's contemporary policies seemed to move in contrary directions abroad and at home. Washington was generously helping to revive and rebuild Europe from the ashes of the world's most destructive war, but in Asia it appeared determined to blunder into new armed conflicts. It preached the virtues of democracy to the world but supported military dictators and autocratic rulers in Asia. Despite its love of liberty and human freedoms, the nation passively watched the worst ever witch-hunt of decent citizens of liberal orientation launched by Senator Joseph McCarthy and his bunch of political bigots.

My post in the embassy carried the designation of third secretary/ vice consul and my responsibilities included attending to all kinds of work relating to passports and visas, canvassing for increase in the annual immigration quota of 100 for Indians, looking after the welfare of Indian citizens of whom there were no more than 2000 or 3000 at that time in the entire country, taking visiting Indian VIPs on sightseeing tours and to meetings etc. And, more interestingly, preparing the first draft of the embassy's monthly report and giving talks in faraway towns, schools and colleges to inquisitive audiences about Indian politics, economy, religions and culture. In addition, any cases from the Indian consulate general in New York and San Francisco requiring to be taken up with the State Department or immigration authorities would be handled by me. The workload was heavy but to dispose of it I had enough staff support and a good measure of autonomy.

My consular work put me in touch with a wide variety of American officials, journalists, businessmen and writers intending to visit India. India was still popular in the country at large, but in the sophisticated, elitist circles of Washington, it was common to hear Indians being denounced as 'communist-loving neutrals', 'mugwump's'(roughly, one who didn't want to conform), 'fence-sitting bastards', or worse. But among the common citizens of the country there was a great deal of inquisitiveness and hunger for information about India. There was also a disarming childlike simplicity, freshness and candour in their desire for being liked, even loved, which many voiced freely. All this made it easy to like them and be friends with them.

The embassy used to receive a lot of requests for speakers from a variety of groups from different parts of the country, and often the ambassador would ask me to go there and do the talking. On one such occasion I was the guest speaker at the annual evening function of an all-white women's group. The audience consisted of about 200 or so elegantly turned out, good looking women of different ages. It was an attentive and disciplined audience and everything was prim and proper and well perfumed in the small hall of a school. After I had spoken for about thirty or thirty-five minutes about India's political system, economic situation, present plans and aspirations for the future, there followed an hour or so of questions (and answers) in which I was grilled about Indian spirituality, Hinduism, Yoga, Hindu gods and goddesses, the caste system, Gandhi and how he managed to throw the British out of India without war and violence. I dealt with all that suitably and the meeting ended with warm words of thanks from the presiding lady and much clapping from the audience.

We were about to move into another room for refreshments, when a well-groomed, elderly lady approached me, held my hands in both of hers, and said: 'Young man I wish you were a Christian!' There wasn't the least hint of intolerance or bigotry in her remark; those words were spoken gently and with a smile. She meant no offence. Perhaps, this was her way of complimenting me on the way I had spoken and the content of my talk.

So, I said to her: 'Ma'am I have studied the gospels and I have profound respect for your religion; all religions are paths to the same one God. What matters is that a Christian should be a good Christian and a Hindu a good Hindu.' I do not know whether this satisfied her, but there was no more talk of religion while we sat together at the same table for refreshments.

American society in those days was deeply religious with profound attachment to family ethics and moral values. Marriage was regarded a sacrosanct bond, and one rarely heard or read in the papers of breakups. Family bonds were strong and teenagers—boys and girls—behaved responsibly and there was seldom a case of rape or teenage pregnancy. There was an appealing simplicity and innocence, warmth and instinctive generosity of spirit in the common American citizen. The sex revolution and the cult of free love, which erupted in full fury in the wake of the Kinsey Report on female sexuality, the pill, drug use, the Beatles' New York visit followed by the explosion of new music and the Woodstock Youth Festival were still a decade or two in the future.

The ruling elite of Washington were a sophisticated lot determined to retain world dominance through the use of the country's military and economic might. They fully expected the world to fall in line with their goals and their ways to achieve them. And yet, among the two score or more foreign offices in the world I must have personally interacted with in my long career in the Indian Foreign Service, I found the State Department the easiest to deal with regardless of serious differences of policy and objectives between the governments of India and the US. As a rule, the department officials were informal, personally friendly, forthright, and even bluntly frank without being offensive in expressing their personal viewpoints or in communicating their government's policies or decisions on specific issues.

During my very first call on the State Department's India-desk team, we got on to first-name terms—their preferred style. Williams L.S. Williams, the India-desk team leader, took the initiative to set the tone: addressing me as Mr Maharajakrishna Rasgotra, he said, 'I am Bill, your name is too long; I am told you are known as Krishna to your friends. Even that is a bit long; we are going to call you Krish. Is that okay?' So from then on it was Bill and Krish. Williams and his beautiful Argentinian wife, Arlita, became good friends and through them I soon met several others, in the State Department and in other wings of government, whom I needed to contact from time to time for consular matters.

In one of my meetings with him a few weeks later, Williams said to me, 'Krish, strictly between you and me, New Delhi's preaching peace to us is pushing my seniors closer to Pakistan.' I said there was no preaching; New Delhi's concern and worry should be appreciated.

China, and conflicts and tensions in Korea and Vietnam, are not far from the subcontinent. He acknowledged all that and added that he thought, nevertheless, that as a friend he should share with me the thinking of American policymakers on a personal basis. My seniors in the embassy rejected this early warning as 'typical bragging by a junior State Department official'! Bill wasn't all that junior either; he was the senior-most official on the India desk.

At the personal level it was all courtesy and bonhomie between us in the embassy and the American officials, but US–India relations were moving from differences and disagreements to serious trouble. Prime Minister Nehru had paid his first visit to the US on President Truman's invitation in 1949, and though he had been received with great cordiality and warmth in Washington and in every other place he visited in the country, his substantive talks with the President, and especially with Secretary of State Dean Acheson had not gone well.

Nehru's advocacy of early recognition of Mao's government and its admission into the UN, and his frequent assertion that communism as a doctrine was alien to the Chinese mind had caused much dismay and irritation to Dean Acheson. Nor did Nehru's forthright condemnation of Dutch and French actions to suppress freedom movements in Indonesia and Indo-china go down well with the Europe-oriented secretary of state. Acheson thought Nehru's stance on Kashmir unreasonably rigid and uncompromising. Nehru, on the other hand, felt that Washington and London had deliberately diverted the UN Security Council's attention away from the basic issue of Pakistan's aggression to appease Pakistan, a country they looked to as the most important future link in the Islamic security crescent they were priming up against the USSR in the north and against China in the east.

While Acheson's knowledge of Asia and Asian problems was rather limited, Nehru's narrative was suffused with expressions of the Asian continent's suspicions, grievances and aspirations. So, there was no meeting of minds and little effort to find some common ground and explore areas of joint action on big issues of the day—the lessening of Cold War tensions, possible American cooperation in

India's agricultural and industrial development or even a common approach to resolving the Kashmir problem bilaterally on the basis of the actual situation on the ground.

It is not that Acheson was not keen to befriend Nehru; only the chemistry between the two strong personalities was all wrong. After a formal dinner Acheson had hosted for him, he took Nehru to his residence for a private talk in the hope of establishing a rapport with him. Acheson sums up the results of that meeting as follows:

> I had hoped that, uninhibited by a cloud of witnesses, we might establish a personal relationship. But he would not relax. He talked to me, as Queen Victoria said of Mr Gladstone, as though I were a public meeting.[1]

On Kashmir, in particular, Acheson failed to appreciate Nehru's strong feelings on complete withdrawal, from the state, of Pakistan's regular and irregular forces before any consideration of the modalities of a plebiscite in the state. That is, in fact, a clearly stipulated precondition to plebiscite arrangements in the UNCIP's resolution of 13 August 1949. Britain and the US had deliberately shifted the focus away from that resolution, which alone furnished the basis for a UN supervised plebiscite. They had also pushed the Security Council into naming an American, Admiral Nimitz, as the plebiscite administrator. Nehru was willing for a plebiscite in accordance with the UNCIP resolution under an impartial administrator from a small, neutral country, but he was not willing to accept or acquiesce in these partisan manoeuvres.

However, regardless of the important differences that had surfaced in Nehru's talks in Washington, Acheson was not lacking in appreciation of the importance of India or of Nehru in world affairs. He concludes his comments on Nehru's talks with him as follows:

> Having talked from 10:30 (p.m.) till past one 'o clock in the morning after a strenuous day, my guest had clearly earned a rest. For my part, I was becoming a bit confused. We therefore adjourned this interesting talk. It made a deep impression on me. I was convinced that Nehru and I were not destined to

have a pleasant personal relationship. He was so important to India and India's survival so important to all of us, that if he did not exist—as Voltaire said of God—he would have to be invented. Nevertheless, he was one of the most difficult men with whom I have ever had to deal.[2]

The official part of Nehru's visit was clearly not a success in initiating a positive trend in relations between the two great democracies, but on the American public Nehru had left a positive impact. The public acclaim for him was reflected in the large crowds that gathered to see and hear him wherever he went, and in the numerous personal tributes paid to him as an outstanding democratic leader and a towering world figure. The *Christian Science Monitor* described him as a 'World Titan'. At the public meeting in Chicago on 26 October 1949 to welcome Nehru, Adlai Stevenson described him 'as one of those tiny handful of men who have influenced the impeccable forces of our time . . . He belongs to the even smaller company of figures who wore a halo in their own lifetimes'. But all the public adoration showered on Nehru by Americans was of little help in arresting the drift in official relations between Washington and New Delhi.

Deep differences had arisen between the two countries on the Japanese peace treaty, and on China, Korea and Vietnam. With the passage of time other issues would arise to deepen the divide between them: Nuclear Non-proliferation Treaty (NPT) for example. The relations between the two countries worsened after John Foster Dulles succeeded Acheson as secretary of state. The Middle Eastern Defense Organization (MEDO), the Baghdad Pact, and South East Asia Treaty Organization (SEATO) were all created by Dulles, with Pakistan at the centre of all those military pacts. To enable the Pakistan army to play its new role, the US undertook to increase its strength and equip it with modern American weapons. The irony of ironies: Dulles, who had condemned Non-alignment as evil, on a visit to New Delhi in 1956 had the temerity to tell Nehru to join SEATO and change it from within!

The changeover from Acheson to Dulles had occurred while I was still in Washington. The new secretary of state was intolerant of dissent and utterly ignorant about Asian sensitivities. Nor was he strong on his facts. He was driven by the zeal to destroy communism. When Walter Lippmann[3] asked him why he was boosting Pakistan so much, Dulles answered he was doing that because Pakistan had the best fighters in the world—the Gurkhas! Such was his knowledge of South Asia.

Dean Acheson was far more sophisticated and cultivated, with a kinder, gentler side to his personality. In the first few weeks of my stay in Washington, I was without a car and I used to walk from a hotel on 16th Street to the Indian Chancery at 2107 Massachusetts Avenue. One morning, to my surprise, I saw Dean Acheson walking to his office from the opposite direction. As we drew nearer, I wished him good morning and he graciously wished me back. On the second or third such chance encounter when I wished him 'good morning', he stopped for a moment and asked who I was and whether I knew him. I said: 'Sir, the whole world knows the secretary of state. I am an Indian diplomat; third secretary in the Indian embassy.' He said he was glad to meet me. We shook hands and moved on.

On 4 July 1952, the US's National Day, every single diplomatic officer, right down to third secretary in all of the fifty or so embassies, was invited to the midday reception at the White House, where President Truman and Mrs Truman stood at the receiving line to personally greet the guests. While standing in the queue awaiting my turn to greet the President, I saw Dean Acheson talking to some guests nearby. I was quite sure the great man had not noticed me. But a few minutes later, as my turn came to approach the President, Acheson appeared on the spot, caught me by the hand and presented me to him saying: 'Mr President, this young friend of mine is a secretary in the Indian embassy.' The President greeted me with a smile and a warm handshake. The reception room was crowded and I did not think anyone could have noticed this act of extraordinary kindness on Acheson's part, but one of my senior colleagues in the embassy and someone from the India desk had observed the event.

There was quite a buzz about it in the embassy for weeks, and it made my dealings with the India desk in the State Department even easier and more pleasant.

But the relations between India and the United States continued to decline, not only because of Dulles' condemnation of India's Non-alignment policy as evil, but because he considered Indian policies concerning China and other Asian issues—the Korean truce negotiations, the Japanese peace treaty etc.—as anti-American, pro-communist and pro-Soviet Russia. Vice President Richard Nixon, who entertained similar views had visited India (and Pakistan) in late 1952. He was lionized in Pakistan but in India he was given VIP treatment appropriate, protocol wise, to his status. On return he complained that his meetings with Nehru were a long lecture by the prime minister on world affairs, as if he (Nixon) was an ignorant novice. Consequently he nursed a lifelong grudge against India, Nehru, and his daughter Indira. He did his worst to spread prejudice against India in Washington's political circles.

However, all the blame for the downward drift in relations does not lie with the American side. Some of our own policies and actions of that early period were questionable. Why did India have to pitch in so firmly against the US, at considerable risk to US–India relations, on issues like the Japanese peace treaty's failure to include the return of Formosa to China and of South Sakhalin and the Kurile islands to Russia? India also objected to the continuing presence of American troops in Japan and American trusteeship over the small Japanese islands of Ryukyu and Bonin. Those were issues to be resolved between the US, China, Russia and Japan. No vital Indian national interest was involved in any of those issues, and we should not have allowed differences over them to become a fundamental problem between India and the United States.

America is an inheritor of the European political and diplomatic tradition. Dean Acheson and other power-wielders in Washington were statesmen in the European mould. Newly independent India had awoken to its own inheritance of a millennial tradition, which regarded the world as one family and valued human dignity, tolerance, peace and cooperation above all else. China was the inheritor of its own tradition, very different from India's, and at least in its reliance on power as the arbiter in international policies, it was closer to the Euro-US tradition. In the circumstances, while Non-alignment was the right policy, Nehru's championship of Asia and Asian causes was premature. He rightly regarded Asian cooperation and solidarity in India's national interest, but these were not existing realities, but distant goals to be worked for not only by India but China and others as well. Was the policy of Non-alignment intended to have relevance only to the US–USSR power struggle? It might have served Indian interests better if Nehru had decided to remain non-aligned in the ensuing contest between the USA and communist China also.

THE US DECISION TO GIFT MODERN ARMS TO PAKISTAN

Pakistan was firmly on America's political and foreign policies agenda. On a hot summer day in June or July 1953, on a hint from Bill Williams, I invited him to lunch in a quiet restaurant not far from our chancery, which I often used for a quick hot meal instead of a sandwich and coffee in the chancery canteen. Williams had said he wanted to talk to me about a very important matter but not in the State Department or anywhere in its vicinity. He was a very pleasant person, always with a smile on his face and an impish sense of humour, but on this occasion his demeanour was serious. So, as we sat down, he said as a friend he wanted to share with me some highly confidential information, provided I promised to protect him as its source. I assured him suitably and he told me of the decision his government had reached to give arms aid of the book value of $20–25 million to Pakistan. The decision had been taken, he said, after months of consideration of pros and cons and it seemed irreversible, meaning it had received presidential approval.

In answer to my queries he confirmed that arms would be a gift and book value meant concessional evaluation; therefore the market value of the arms aid might be of the order of $35–40 million. He agreed with me that this would seriously tilt the existing military balance between India and Pakistan in the latter's favour, enhance tensions between them and also affect US–India relations.

On returning to my office, I recorded a brief note on the disturbing information Williams had given me and took the paper to First

Secretary J.C. Kakkar, who at once grasped its significance, and together we went to Minister S.N. Haksar's room where the counsellor, I.J. Bahadur Singh, was already present. They both showed surprise, for neither had received the slightest hint of any such development in their frequent contacts with senior US officials. The discussion that followed was about Williams, and how responsible an officer was he? Was he doing some kite flying on his own? Could he be taken seriously? Regardless, Kakkar suggested that he might forward my note with a Demi Official (D.O.) letter to the concerned joint secretary in the MEA, but the idea was shot down on the grounds that drawing such pointed attention to a bit of information, unconfirmed or unverified at senior levels, might create unnecessary panic in Delhi. Finally, it was decided that a few lines about it be included in the mission's monthly report, which was due to go to the MEA within a couple of days.

In the MEA, a bright under secretary read and reread those few lines, highlighted them and sent the report up to the joint secretary T.N. Kaul for special attention. Kaul, recognizing the importance of the information, took the report to Foreign Secretary K.P.S. Menon, who mentioned its contents to the prime minister. Nehru was quick to see the serious nature and dangerous implications of what Williams had conveyed to me. He immediately ordered quiet, further investigations by the concerned authorities in Delhi. Meanwhile, after some weeks of cogitation, the British government decided to mention the US government's decision to Nehru and they asked their high commissioner in Delhi to seek a personal meeting with the prime minister for the purpose. The high commissioner was also instructed to tell the prime minister that Washington had taken the decision to arm Pakistan, against Britain's advice. Nehru, apprehensive of the pact bringing the Cold War tensions to India's frontiers, launched a fierce campaign against it. It was only in November 1953 that Assistant Secretary of State Henry Byroade told our deputy chief of mission, S.N. Haksar that the US defence department was 'now focused on Pakistan's military'! The pact was formally signed in February 1954.

A lesson I learnt from this episode was never to reject out-of-hand information brought by a junior officer or spurn its source.

America, I would learn again and again, used this mode of conveying significant information, either to trigger negotiations or simply to forewarn the target of unpleasant future events. For example, later when I was in the MEA in March or April 1965, Douglas Heck, counsellor in the US embassy in Delhi, came to my office at very short notice to say: 'Krish, your army seems to be readying for big battles in the Rann of Kutch. Kutch is a ruse, a diversion. Look north: they [Pakistan army] have been putting war paint on their tanks.' I passed this on to Foreign Secretary C.S. Jha, who took appropriate action and the Indian army was ready to blunt Pakistan's attack in Kashmir and carry the war into the aggressor's territory.

PAKISTAN REJECTS A GENUINE OFFER OF A KASHMIR SETTLEMENT

The planning of arms aid by the US to Pakistan under the Mutual Security Act was taking place at a time when India and Pakistan were close to resolving the Kashmir problem bilaterally, through a plebiscite with voting in the whole state of J & K, followed by the state's partition on the basis of the results. Nehru had made this offer to Pakistan's Prime Minister Mohammad Ali Bogra during the latter's state visit to Delhi in August 1953. It actually amounted to what Pakistan had been asking for. Apparently, Nehru had thought through all its implications and 'if this meant the loss of the Valley, he was prepared for it'.[4] In Delhi, Bogra had agreed to the appointment, before May 1954, of a plebiscite administrator from a small neutral country in place of the American Admiral Nimitz, but on return to Karachi he went back on that understanding under American pressure. Not for the first time, nor the last, Washington had intervened to sabotage a real possibility of a peaceful, bilateral settlement of the Kashmir problem.

Washington's policy of creating a balance of arms[5] between India and Pakistan, favourable to the latter, was to have many dangerous consequences for the South Asian region. But, perhaps, its most disastrous long-term effect fell on Pakistan itself. It led to the militarization of that country's thinking and its foreign policy. The rapid expansion and arming of Pakistan's Armed Forces encouraged the generals to stage a coup every now and again, seize power from legitimate, elected regimes and embark on a course of confrontation and armed conflict with India. One delayed, but most serious and permanent consequence of this policy was the 1971 India–Pakistan war and, as its result, the emergence of the independent state of Bangladesh.

By the time I was to leave Washington in early 1954, the drift in US–India relations had steadily gathered pace, deepening the estrangement between the world's two largest democracies. As soon as the arms pact with Pakistan was signed, President Eisenhower, in his letter of 24 February 1954 to Nehru, offered a similar arrangement for arms supply to India, which Nehru politely refused on the ground, as he put it, 'If we object to military aid being given to Pakistan, we would be hypocrites and unprincipled opportunists to accept such aid ourselves.' New problems, such as the nuclear test ban, the non-proliferation issues and sanctions on technology trade with India, kept arising to widen the gulf between the two countries.

One part of my work in Washington, namely VIP duty with important Indian visitors, was time-consuming, but it provided opportunities to meet important politicians, ministers and senior officials of central and state governments, scientists and scholars, business leaders, social figures, film stars and other bigwigs from India's film world. I learnt much from these contacts of human behaviour, of negotiating tactics and diplomacy in action. I was assigned for a few days to Mrs Vijaya Lakshmi Pandit, president of the UN General Assembly, when she was on a visit to Washington, to accompany her on her calls on American authorities and meetings with other important figures in Washington. Through her I got to know many high personages, notably Paul Robeson, the legendary African American singer and actor. A victim of many racist slights, criticized and condemned for his leftist political views, Robeson was a noble figure with the voice of a god.

An even more interesting experience was the meeting with Albert Einstein, when Mrs Pandit visited with him at his residence in the Institute for Advanced Study in Princeton. He talked with great feeling about Mahatma Gandhi, Jawaharlal Nehru and his policies, and about the dangers the world faced from the nuclear arms race between the US and the Soviet Union. Western policies, he remarked, were power driven and divorced from moral, even human considerations. It was the same with the Soviet Union. The talk turned to spirituality and I asked him whether science had a rational basis for denying the existence of a supreme power called God. No, he said, science had not reached a level of understanding of even the visible natural phenomena, where it could deny or confirm the existence of God.

Einstein died a year and a half later, and we were lucky to spend a couple of hours with him while he was still in good health. He looked like an ascetic Indian sage. Just to be in his presence was an elevating experience.

A funny little episode keeps bubbling up in my memory. A small delegation from Bollywood, consisting of Sunil Dutt, Nargis whom he married later and a couple of minor actors led by the Indian film world's big man, Chandulal Shah—I think that was his name—was in Washington for a week. Throughout their stay they kept me busy, organizing their meetings, getting their visas extended and accompanying them on sightseeing trips etc. In between appointments they would drop in for a cup of tea in my office and a little chit-chat on sundry matters. They were a friendly lot, full of good humour and were very good company. On the last day of their stay, Chandulal Shah said to me, 'My friend, you are wasting your time in government service. Come to Bombay; I promise you a big career in the films. Dutt agrees with me.' Nargis chipped in with 'Rasgotraji Bombay aa jaiyae' (Rasgotraji, do come to Bombay). 'That is a good joke Mr Shah,' I said, 'but, no thanks. I hope my services here as a government official have not disappointed you.' He insisted he was serious, gave me his card and asked me to think it over and call or write to him and he would 'fix everything else'. I saw them off at the airport and never gave the matter another thought. Thirty-eight years later, Dutt came to London and I, as high commissioner of India, chaired a couple of public meetings for him to raise funds for treatment of cancer, the disease that had taken Nargis's life. He recalled that occasion in my office in 1953 and we had a good laugh. But Chandulal, a talent hunter, was serious, Dutt said; he had fully expected a positive response from me and was disappointed at my silence.

RACISM IN THE UNITED STATES

Sometime in late 1953, in response to a call for the embassy's help in resolving a consular problem, I travelled by air to a town in Texas, the southern state in which racial discrimination and segregation was the way of life and African Americans had no civil or political rights. I came out of the airport, hailed a cab and one pulled up with a black cabbie driving it. As I had only hand luggage with me, I opened the door and settled down in the rear seat of the taxi. I politely asked the driver to take me to a certain hotel where a room had been reserved for me for the night. He looked back at me for a moment or two and said he could not take me any place at all. Why? Because I was a white man! His cab was only for black people! 'I am not a white man,' I protested. 'I am an Indian from India.' 'No, Sir, for me here you are a white man. You even talk like a white man!' When I insisted, he pleaded, 'Sir, you are new here. You don't understand, if I drive you to the hotel, I will be beaten up, even killed by white people.' This shocked me. I got out of the taxi, gave the cabbie a dollar tip for his time, hailed another cab with a white driver who took me to the hotel which was situated in an all-white zone of the town. This disturbing incident remained the worst memory of my two-year stay in the US for a long time. Because of their race and colour a whole section of the population was living in segregation and in fear in a country which, except for this evil of racism, was way ahead of the rest of the world in its openness, love of liberty and in its liberality of spirit and generosity in helping others.

Much earlier, during one of my visits to New York, I had spent several hours one day talking to the people in Harlem in their shops, restaurants and places of entertainment. Harlem was also a shock, but not as intense as the deeply disturbing experience in Texas; for in Harlem, African Americans had created a self-contained world of their own with its distinctive traits of cultural and social activity, its music, dance and entertainment. Not even a casual visitor could miss the dynamism and vibrancy of that little world, nor could one fail to see the cauldron of seething anger and resentment just below the surface calm.

The two streams of life—white and black—could not exist in one country for long in their separate habitats without a future disaster. Meanwhile, racist exclusion and neglect of the African American citizen would disfigure the national character and identity of the United States. Nor would it now be possible for the white American to do to his black compatriots what he did with the indigenous American inhabitants—Red Indians, so-called—namely their elimination. On the other hand, the inevitable blending of the two life streams would right a historic wrong and result in the rise of a new, more wholesome, diverse and united American humanity. America struck me as a civilization in the making.

The real question was how long it would take the country to reach that inevitable result. Thirty-six years later, in 1988, a black taxi driver in New York told me that if the whites continued to deny them their rights 'we will destroy this country'. However, even in the late 1950s there were positive factors in the situation, such as the growing humanism within America's white society, recognition of the sacrifices of black soldiers in the war and the inspiring effect of the arrival of black leaders of newly independent African nations at the United Nations in New York. America's own growing engagement with people of brown, yellow and black races in the Asian and African continents was helping to mellow American attitude towards issues of race and colour. There was also the growing popularity of Mahatma Gandhi, and finally, the rise and martyrdom of an American Gandhi—Martin Luther King Jr.

In retrospect, America has not done badly in removing racial discrimination. Continuing progress in that area over five or six decades resulted recently in the election of an African American citizen of great distinction and ability as the country's President. Even in the mid-twentieth century, African American arts were enriching America's cultural life by injecting in it their distinctive originality, youthful vigour and enthusiasm. In music, for example,

Duke Ellington had elevated jazz to a classical art form. In vocal music I had personally witnessed Nat King Cole, Harry Belafonte, Ella Fitzgerald and Eartha Kitt hold all-white American audiences in spell for hours of an evening. Blues music, which I heard for the first time in Harlem, left a very deep impression on me.

In March 1954, the ministry ordered me to proceed to Kathmandu where I would have a promotion of rank as second secretary in the embassy. I have mentioned elsewhere my earlier contacts with the Nepalese royalty. Nepal, with its long snow-capped Himalayan ranges, its torrential rivers and its lush-green valleys is one of the most scenic lands on earth. I loved the country and was looking forward to my new assignment. I was told I was needed in Kathmandu urgently; therefore no leisurely sea voyage of three or four weeks. I was flown out to reach Delhi in a matter of twenty-four hours, only to be diverted to another short-term assignment with Mrs Vijaya Lakshmi Pandit before joining my new post a month or so later.

chapter seven

NEIGHBOURHOOD DIPLOMACY: NEPAL

~

By giving asylum to King Tribhuvan and his family in the Indian embassy in November 1950, and by arranging for them to fly out to India in defiance of Rana Prime Minister Mohan Shamsher's protests and threats, Indian ambassador to Nepal, C.P.N. Singh had changed Nepal's history. On his triumphant return to Kathmandu in February 1951, the king, for a while, needed and relied on C.P.N. Singh's advice and support in several critical decisions he had to make on issues of political importance, such as cabinet formation and the creation of a new administrative framework for the country. The remnants of the Rana regime and their henchmen, and even some disgruntled elements in the democratic political parties, resented it and kicked up a shindy about India's interference in Nepal's domestic affairs. C.P.N. Singh had served Nepal and India well, and at the end of his normal tenure as ambassador, Nehru summoned him to a series of equally important other assignments. His successor, B.K. Gokhale, a highly respected member of the former ICS, was ambassador in Kathmandu when I reported for duty as second secretary in April 1954.

Nepal was passing through a difficult transition from autocratic rule to democratic governance and it needed all kinds of help from India. Managing that change in the nature and scope of India–Nepal relations was not going to be easy. For while Nepal was in dire need of reviving and reorganizing its military, economy and administration, which were destroyed by the widespread armed insurrection triggered by King Tribhuvan's voluntary exile, India ran the risk of getting too deeply involved in the process and attracting criticism and accusations of interfering in Nepal.

What India had not anticipated or suspected was that anti-India criticism would be inspired and encouraged by a weak Nepal government to divert the blame for its failures to alleged Indian interference and intervention. That made the Indian embassy's task of forging a new relationship between Nepal and India even more complicated. Ambassador Gokhale had all the wisdom, tact, patience and tolerance for dealing with the situation, but he needed additional experienced personnel to spread the word among the Nepalese people that India's sole interest in Nepal was its stability, the steady progress of its democratic process and its rapid economic development. For that role, the embassy was grossly understaffed. Against the ambassador's demand for three or four Foreign Service officers, the MEA sanctioned just one post of second secretary, to fill which I was transferred from Washington. The MEA just did not have more officers to spare for Nepal.

On arrival in Kathmandu, I was lodged in the Nepal government's small guest house at the end of the city's short, metalled road, running from the Indian embassy to the end of Tundikhel—a huge open ground in the heart of the city. The following morning I was getting ready to leave for the embassy when I saw a gentleman alight from a small hill pony and walk up to greet me. He introduced himself. 'I am Prakat Man Singh, chief of protocol,' he said after we had exchanged our 'namastes'. We sat down for a cup of tea in the guest house, where I was actually the Nepal government's guest. I said to Mr Singh that it was really for me to call on him and whether I could, at least, return the call. That would not be right, he said, and that was that. Sardar Prakat Man Singh's courtesy call on me—a humble second secretary in the Indian embassy—was indicative of India's political prestige in Nepal. It was symbolic also of the old-world courtesy and cultural values that the Nepalese cherished.

In a detailed, personal briefing to me a day or two later, Ambassador Gokhale said that the embassy had no information at all about what was happening in the country beyond the valley of Kathmandu, and because of acute shortage of personnel we knew little even about the goings-on in the valley's political circles, whose numbers and activities had multiplied manifold after the end of Rana rule. Access to those circles would pose no problems but it required a degree of finesse and sophistication in enhancing routine contacts into friendship for India. In particular, we needed to develop contacts with outstation members of the newly created Advisory Assembly, which would be convened shortly. The valley's cultural, academic and social circles also needed to be cultivated on a sustained basis. Clearly, it was going to be a new learning experience for me in neighbourhood diplomacy.

The ambassador wanted the intelligence wing also strengthened and on his urgings, the government had posted an experienced officer from Uttar Pradesh, R.N. Shukul to join the embassy as additional first secretary. Shukul's predecessor, a middle-level police officer from Bihar—he will remain nameless—was a good soul, with informal, homely ways and disarming simplicity of manners, bearing and behaviour. He went about his tasks with an unusual degree of naivety. As my contacts in Kathmandu's political circles expanded, my frequent, open meetings with leaders and workers of different political parties to discuss politics and aid projects seemed to cause him some discomfiture, and he innocently asked some of his earlier collocutors: 'Why do you talk to Rasgotra so much? I am the guy from the police, you know!' When the gaffe reached the embassy, there was much merriment, but all of us took it in our stride. And the ambassador, in his good-natured way, explained to him the difference between his functions and mine. His normal term of duty ended a few months later, and his post was upgraded to accommodate Shukul.

I had mentioned to Ambassador Gokhale that I had liaised with King Tribhuvan's entourage during His Majesty's stay at the Hyderabad House in New Delhi, and after the king's triumphant return to Kathmandu in 1951 I was attached to the two queens, as their protocol assistant, during their six-week stay in India, and that I also had got to know the Crown Prince Mahendra and his two brothers, Himalaya and Basundhara, during their stay in Delhi.

So, would it be in order for me to renew contacts with them? He advised that in such matters it were best to leave the initiative to the royalty; that in a few days my presence in Kathmandu would become known, and I might await developments. Sure enough, I received an invitation to a restricted social occasion organized by one of the princes, where I met the other two as well. And soon enough an opportunity arose for me to make a quiet visit to the royal palace to pay my respects to Their Majesties, the two queens!

One of the highlights of my early months in Kathmandu was the tiger shoots in the Terai forests, to which the crown prince, Mahendra Bir Bikram Shah, had invited me to accompany him. His Royal Highness was a good poet in the Gurkhali language, and after the days' shoot, we would all sit together in the common room of the hunting lodge or under a tent and he would recite his poems, someone would sing, while another member of the party would play the tabla or the harmonium; all good, clean fun and much needed relaxation for the next day's shoot.

In the course of Ambassador Gokhale's instructions to me mentioned earlier, I had asked whether he would permit me to travel to other parts of the country. He welcomed the idea; for, he said, the embassy did not know whether Indian aid was needed in the countryside. Thus far all our aid activity was confined to the Kathmandu valley. But he cautioned, 'There are no roads, nor any regular means of transport. And what about your security and your meals in those remote places?' I assured him trekking was my hobby and I would take with me a couple of Nepalese porters, who would carry the necessary supplies for a week or two of the trip. He asked me to plan out something and we would discuss the matter further. I did not have to wait long.

In June and July 1954, there were heavy rains and floods in several districts of Nepal Terai, followed by the occurrence of malaria, cholera and other infectious diseases in several districts and there was the added threat of epidemics spreading to neighbouring hill areas. At the Nepal government's request, India had decided to send several medical teams to treat the affected population and immunize others who might be at risk. But the administration in

Kathmandu could not tell us where to deploy the medical teams to provide the much-needed medical help. Ambassador Gokhale asked whether I would like to go down to the Terai and pinpoint areas and population centres that needed urgent medical attention. So, I went down to the Terai, and in about two weeks walked the entire length of the densely forested region except for some short stretches where a pony, bullock cart, or elephant became available to provide relief for my legs. Leaders of medical teams accompanied me on some of my travels in the Terai and the areas for their work were defined in consultation with local authorities and political party workers. One team was to cover the Nepalganj area in western Nepal, two would cover central Terai (Birgunj and neighbouring districts) and the remaining two teams would spread out in eastern Terai, from Janakpur to Nepal's eastern border with India.

The teams had worked well, with much public appreciation and support, for some weeks, when we started receiving complaints from them that district authorities were not cooperating and they were not getting the necessary support that Kathmandu had promised by way of transport, needed for their movement from place to place. The teams deployed in the Birgunj area were the worst sufferers in this regard.

I had joined the two teams in Biratnagar in the eastern Nepal Terai in mid-October and travelled with them in badly affected districts east and west of the Kosi River, and then turned westwards, after crossing the Bagmati River, to Birgunj. Villagers in both areas were very friendly and supportive. They wanted the medical teams to provide medical relief in their villages and would go out of their way to help them. Often they walked miles with me from one village to the next. After mobilizing the people's support and district officials' cooperation with the teams in both areas, I flew to Pokhara in central Nepal and trekked down to Bhairahawa and Nepalganj to join the team at work in the western Terai. I was able to contact members of the Advisory Assembly and some political party workers of the area and obtain their cooperation. They walked with me to a few affected villages, and having seen the team's good work they chastised the officials and urged them to extend all possible cooperation and help to the teams.

Most bada hakims (district governors) were happy to have the teams and wanted to help them, but did not have the funds to incur expenditure on hiring porters, or elephants for movement in flood-affected areas. The cost of hiring such help was a pittance and I gave some money to the teams, and advised them to pay liberally for the services received by them. In some districts, the bada hakims or rich landlords were pleased to lend their own jeeps and elephants free of charge, which went a long way in facilitating the teams' and my movement in affected areas. As information spread about the good work our medical teams were doing, requests were received from district governors, zamindars and delegations of common people from areas, which were not on the original schedules for the teams' visits, for medical help in their respective regions. I criss-crossed virtually the entire Terai three times in 1954 and 1955. The east-west highway and some roads were built years later, more or less along the dense jungle tracks I had walked on in those two years.

But there was mischief afoot, especially in areas where members of Prime Minister Matrika Prasad Koirala's party, the Rashtriya Praja Parishad, had preponderance in numbers and influence. In the Biratnagar-Janakpur area, for example, friendly people said they had been told that the two medical teams had been sent to Nepal by the Americans, and medical supplies had also been given by the US government. Or, that the teams had only a few useless medicines and poorly trained doctors to dispense them!

A more serious allegation in circulation in Biratnagar was that the Indian government had sent the teams to alienate the Terai from Nepal. I was told that the false information was being spread by workers of Prime Minister Koirala's party 'under instructions from above'. Simple, credulous village folk, who had nothing but goodwill for India, were being misled by a government that Nehru had gone out of his way to help.

The false propaganda ceased after my visit; our medical teams completed their allotted tasks and went back to India. A spreading epidemic had been controlled and eliminated, and the Terai remained as firmly a part of Nepal as ever.

The Terai was governed then, as it is now, by the ruling elite of Kathmandu as a colony. Throughout my travels I never met a Teraian high administrative or police officer or even a petty official—they all came from Kathmandu. In due course the development of roads facilitated other economic development activity and the spread of education and awareness among the Teraians of their citizenship rights. The present struggle in the Terai is the result of the denial of those rights to the inhabitants who account for nearly half the country's population. Now that democracy is deepening its roots in the country, the Terai population is not likely to tolerate its subservient second-class citizenship status. The attempt in the new Constitution, to gerrymander the Terai's parliamentary constituencies to keep the Terai's representatives in a minority in the national Parliament, has given rise to a widespread rights movement in the entire Terai region, with secessionist undertones in some sections of the population. It is to be hoped that Kathmandu's ruling elite will resolve this problem with wisdom and expedition.

LESSONS IN DIPLOMACY WITH SMALL NEIGHBOURS

For me it was a vitally important experience in neighbourhood diplomacy, and I drew some conclusions for future guidance. One, that a smaller neighbour fears even the good that a big neighbour can do for the smaller country's populace; two, that our embassies in such circumstances must develop direct contacts with the people to ascertain their real needs for development; three, too close an embrace and an excess of generosity on the part of the bigger neighbour does not always generate goodwill and may, in fact, rouse suspicions; four, that the bigger country must not grudge its small neighbour the benefits it expects or can obtain from other donors; and finally, a country like Nepal which views itself as a 'yam between two stones' will not be able to resist the temptation of playing one 'stone' against the other to avoid being crushed between them.

My education in Nepal's 'public' diplomacy had begun within a few weeks of my arrival in Kathmandu. In the middle of May 1954 the Indian Parliament went into recess and a group of MPs, led by Radha Raman, an influential political figure in the Congress party of Delhi, decided to pay a goodwill visit to the next-door democratic neighbour 'at their own expense', except for whatever limited hospitality the Nepal government might voluntarily offer them.

It was a difficult time in Kathmandu in the matter of availability of accommodation. Preparations were also afoot for convening the newly created Advisory Assembly, even as the Koirala government was faced with internal difficulties and attacks from some ambitious, veteran dissenters like Tanka Prasad Acharya. It is not normal for parliamentary delegations to impose themselves on a target of their love and goodwill; but neither the MEA, nor the prime minister's office in Delhi, nor Ambassador Gokhale chose to firmly dissuade Raman from embarking on his goodwill expedition at that particular time. The Nepal government then decided to deal with the situation in its own way, not directly but through proxies, who were always at hand for a bit of fun and other rewards to boot. On deplaning at Gauchar airfield, Raman's delegation was given a reception memorable enough in a way: They faced a huge and abusive demonstration and a few poorly aimed stones thrown with the clear intention to avoid causing bodily harm to the honoured visitors. I for one could not help but admire the fine art the Nepalese had made of deterring encroachments on their sovereign independence. If I am not mistaken, for several years after this incident no Indian parliamentary delegation saw much merit in paying a goodwill visit to Kathmandu.

There were apologies galore and repeated expressions of unhappiness, even sorrow at such an ugly incident from high quarters in Kathmandu, which Ambassador Gokhale accepted with grace and a grimace. But in Delhi, Prime Minister Nehru was furious. In a letter dated 4 June 1954 to Koirala he wrote:

> The recent incident (hostile demonstration against our MPs) has produced strong reactions in India. I must say that I have been powerfully affected by it too. I have a feeling that

India is not getting a fair deal in Nepal. We go all out to help the Nepal government, financially and otherwise, and yet our people are subjected to insults there and intrigues against India continue . . . I am disturbed and distressed by all this and therefore I am writing to you quite frankly on this subject.

But what could all this avail? For in the same letter Nehru also, quite unnecessarily, went on to write:

I know that your government is not responsible for this and has expressed its regret. I know that it is the Nepali Congress and the Gurka Parishad, may be helped by foreign money.

That virtually absolved Koirala and his government of all guilt for unfriendly behaviour. Apparently this implausible tale of involvement of the Nepali Congress, Gurkha Parishad and foreign money had been sold by M.P. Koirala directly to Nehru in Delhi. In his reply, on 24 June 1954, to Nehru's letter, Koirala spun the same yarn again in different words:

You know Kathmandu has been the seat of the Ranas for the last century and their money and their hangers-on do try to exploit the situation. This has been manifest on many previous occasions . . . The recent demonstration against the visiting parliamentarians was also one of them. We had thought primarily to put a ban on processions and meetings before the arrival of these visitors, but in our later consideration we thought that would have produced even worse propaganda and reaction. Hence we had to defer that.

All this was duplicitous hogwash of course. A couple of weeks later a reliable source, a member of Prime Minister Koirala's party told me that the whole thing was organized by Koirala's henchmen with his approval: There was no Rana or Rana money involved in the unsavoury business!

This kind of behaviour on the part of a so-called democratic leader of Nepal was an upsetting and saddening experience for a decent, upright and unsuspecting gentleman like Ambassador Gokhale. And there were good reasons for his disappointment. For Radha Raman MP, who took the initiative for the visit, had discussed the same with a visiting Nepalese minister in Delhi in late April or early May, and the minister, Bhadra Kali Mishra, had seen no difficulty in the way of the visit taking place. A week before the visit, on 16 May, Ambassador Gokhale had written to Prime Minister Koirala to alert him about the visit, and they discussed this matter in a pre-scheduled meeting the same evening and Koirala raised no problem or difficulty concerning it. If he had the slightest reservation about the timing or any other aspect of the visit he needed only to mention it to the ambassador, who would have advised Radha Raman to postpone or simply drop the idea. I do not know what Koirala gained by insulting Indian parliamentarians, but he lost Ambassador Gokhale's trust completely and he caused offence to Nehru, whose support he badly needed.

Actually Nehru's disenchantment with Matrika Prasad Koirala's functioning had begun within months of his taking over as prime minister in November 1951. He would seek Nehru's advice on sundry matters, and then, the advice eagerly sought and enthusiastically accepted would be ignored, allegedly because of a campaign against 'Indian interference', inspired by him and organized by his henchmen. Koirala had asked for a huge number of Indian personnel to help organize his administration and train Nepalese police, and additional clerical Indian staff for the cabinet and virtually every department of government. Nehru went out of his way to send all requested personnel to Nepal on deputation, despite a great need for them at home, but after their arrival in Nepal their services and expertise remained unutilized and, instead, a fresh campaign was launched against Indian interference.

Nehru reacted to all this in a letter to Koirala on 21 June 1952. Concerning allegations of interference and unwanted advice, he wrote:

We have tried deliberately not to interfere in Nepal's internal matters. It was only when our advice was sought or our help asked for in any particular matter that we gave that advice or help. In spite of this, however, the Government of India are continually blamed for all the troubles of Nepal. We are supposed to interfere and intervene. You have asked us for all kinds of help from time to time and we have been reluctant to give it because of our desire not to intervene . . . As a matter of fact, looking back at the last few months, I find that our advice has seldom been followed, although it has often been accepted when given.

On the non-utilization of Indian deputationists, Nehru said bluntly that he had no desire to send Indian officers to Nepal when they had no opportunity of doing good work and had to function in an atmosphere which was hostile to them and to India. He added that he had a feeling the Nepal government was not playing fair with him, that he was not used to that kind of politics in a government and if the Nepalese government did not 'wish to act up to its previous undertakings to India, then the sooner those were revised the better'.

Here was an opportunity for Koirala to ask for an amendment to or abrogation of existing arrangements, and assert the right to borrow or recruit needed personnel from some other country. But he had neither the intention, nor the courage to do that. Instead, he asked Nehru for more: A military mission to reorganize and train Nepal's army! Nehru of course, sent a small military mission and, of course, it became the target of criticism almost from the day of its arrival in Kathmandu.

Nehru had a very soft corner in his heart for Nepal, especially because of his respect and affection for King Tribhuvan, who was responsible for introducing democracy in Nepal under a constitutional monarchy. The king was in poor health and Nehru did not want to trouble him with the growing problems in Nepal–India relations. But he was losing patience with Koirala's machinations and he ended his letter of 21 June 1952 with the accusation that Koirala was responsible for the anti-India campaigns, and he challenged him to come up with suggestions for a changed relationship with India:

My interest in Nepal is to see progress and stability there. It is not my concern what kind of government the Nepalese people would like to have themselves. But if something happens in Nepal which endangers our own security, then of course this is a matter of great consequence to us. Also, if a continuous campaign, supported in high quarters, of vilification of India continues, that is also a matter of concern to us. History and geography have thrown India and Nepal together. We cannot forget that history or change geography. Those governing factors continue and will inevitably influence action both in India and Nepal. But within those limits there can be much variation and it is for your Government and for us to consider what exactly our relations should be. I hope I have made my meaning clear.'

As a result of Nehru's admonition, the mischief stopped for a year or so, but, as I have narrated, it was the same old story in 1954.

A LITTLE PAKISTAN IN NEPAL

During my tour of the Biratnagar area, I heard reports about a new settlement of Muslims and the continuing flow of Pakistani nationals into an isolated pocket about six to eight square miles in area, which used to be a grazing field before 1947. The nucleus of this enclave was the village of Bhutaha, with ancillary villages on all four sides giving the exclusive Muslim settlement the shape of what armies call the 'box formation'. People living in villages around the 'box' told me that the settlement enjoyed the Nepal government's secret support.

When I entered the rectangular box from its northern end, I found my passage through it lined by hundreds of its inhabitants not to welcome but simply gaze in annoyance at the unwelcome intruder. The un-walled fortress seemed to have a system of informing the whole colony of any unwelcome intrusion. I later learnt that a substantial number of the inhabitants of Bhutaha were professional dacoits who lived on the earnings of their nightly labours in India as well as Nepal; some others had purchased land with the booty thus acquired and settled down as farmers. Smuggling of arms was a regular activity of some others. The nearest police station was fifteen miles away in Biratnagar, but the police did not dare mess with this protected community of lawbreakers.

What I found of particular interest was the attitude of the Nepalese political parties towards this Muslim settlement. While the Jan Congress led by Bhadrakali Mishra, and the Terai Congress led by Vedanand Jha, were openly apprehensive about this 'little Pakistan'—that was its locally given name—and its potential for serious mischief in the future, members of the Rashtriya Praja Parishad, Prime Minister Koirala's party, were favourably disposed to it. From my talks with workers of different political parties I gathered that M.P. Koirala and his lieutenants regarded this Muslim pocket as their trump card against India's growing prestige and popularity in the Terai population. A steady trickle of Muslims was continuing from East Pakistan into that pocket. Whether that 'little Pakistan' was the result of some dark design of those not too well disposed towards India, I could not say then. But perhaps some policy of the kind has been in place these several decades. For today Nepal Terai's Indian border is a 'Maginot Line' of mosques and Islamist madrasas from east to west.

During my tour of the Terai, my visit to the town of Janakpur in the Mahottari district of Nepal had evoked a long-dormant emotional feeling. On entering the town I involuntarily touched the hallowed ground in reverence, took a pinchful of it and rubbed it on my forehead. The district was once the garden country of Mithila, the glory of which is so well described in the Ramayana of Tulsidas. Here the Sage King Janak's daughter, Sita, had married Rama after the young prince, at her swayamwara, had lifted and mounted the irate Parashurama's great 'bow', which no other prince, not even Ravana of Lanka, was able to move even slightly from where it lay as a challenge to their might.

Though Janakpur possessed little of the glamour and glory that characterized the former capital of Mithila, it was still, with its mango groves, gardens, innumerable sacred tanks and streams and green surroundings, one of the most attractive towns of Nepal. The country around Janakpur bore resemblance to the one described by Tulsidas in his Ramacharitmanas. But no excavations had been carried out to prove its historical identity or to find relics of archeological and historical interest that might be lying underneath the ground.

The spacious and impressive temple of Sita attracted many local worshippers and a large number of pilgrims from India every year. The existing temple was constructed by an Indian prince some thirty years earlier on the site of the old temple which had crumbled and fallen. The temple of Rama was humbler in outlay and architectural grandeur, but it had a far larger income—Rs 60,000 per year, a very substantial sum in those days—all of which went to the mahant. Everyone I talked to said that legend had it that the temple was situated on the exact spot where Rama had mounted Parashurama's huge bow. Regrettably neither Nepal nor India have done much for decades to develop Janakpur, and Lumbini, as major centres of pilgrimage for Hindus and Buddhists of India and the world.

After leaving the teams to their good work in the Terai districts, which needed their services, I took the same route back to Raxaul and I could now see that the epidemic had been checked. The people were full of praise for our doctors and their work, and were thankful for the advice they had given them and medicines they had left with them for use in emergencies to prevent any recurrence of disease.

After a night's halt in our embassy's dak bungalow at Raxaul I took the Nepal government's narrow-gauge train to Amlekgunj, the terminal station at the foot of the hills. It was a hilarious experience. This narrow-gauge railway, introduced during the Rana period in the 1920s, moved at about four miles an hour. The carriages had slatted wooden benches which gave little comfort to a weary traveller's behind, and I would get down, now and then, walk alongside the moving train, and duly refreshed after a mile or so, hop back into my carriage.

Near Amlekgunj, in a camp of the Indian army engineers, I met the tall, dark, handsome Colonel Ratnaswamy—the hero of Han Suyin's book *The Mountain is Young*. He told me that the jeep track (the initial phase of Tribhuvan Rajpath) had been completed and though the gravelling of some small sections was yet to be done, it would be possible for me to drive my American Ford Sedan, which had arrived from Washington, to Kathmandu. I started off the following morning, with Ratnaswamy in the lead in his own jeep part of the way, to inspect ungravelled sections of the jeep track. It was very slow going not more than ten miles an hour because of the small width of the jeepable track. He had arranged for my night-halt midway in the engineers' camp, from where one of his men accompanied me to Kathmandu. For me it was an enjoyable pioneering experience to drive my own car on that road. On the second day of my journey I made it to Kathmandu in the afternoon without a mishap. And there, a memorable surprise awaited me.

Until that day, cars used to be transported from Bhimphedi over the steep mountain range, tied up atop a huge wooden platform which was carried by several scores of sturdy Nepalese men! Mine was the first car to reach Kathmandu on its own power and I was the first man to do the feat. Someone doing the journey to Kathmandu on foot the previous day must have seen my car moving on the freshly cut road to the valley and spread word in Kathmandu of the wonder event. A cheering, clapping crowd of men, women and children greeted my car just outside the city of Kathmandu. I stopped the car and came out to stretch my legs. Half a dozen people came forward with garlands, not to garland me, but to pay homage to my path-breaking Ford Sedan!

MY TOUR OF WESTERN NEPAL HILLS

As the word spread about my explorations of the country, several of my young friends, members of the Advisory Assembly (AA), began pressing me to visit their constituencies with the object of having some Indian aid diverted to their regions. In consultation with two friends—Kashi Raj and Jai Prasad Sharma—I planned a trek in the hill districts of western Nepal from where large numbers of Nepalese young men had been joining the Gurkha regiment of the Indian army since British times. When I told Ambassador Gokhale that two AA members, Kashi Raj and Jaya Prasad Sharma would be with me in the more difficult sectors of my travels, his fears about my safety were allayed somewhat and he agreed to my taking a seven- or eight-day tour of the hill districts in the Pokhara-Bhairahawa sector.

I reached Pokhara by air from Kathmandu in the morning one day in late October. The scenic Pokhara valley running east–west below the snow-clad Annapurna range, had seven lakes and numerous streams and rivulets, and yet the valley was drought prone and very poor in agriculture. Its tourist attractions were obvious, but there was no board and lodging facilities for tourists. Harnessing of the valley's perennial streams for minor irrigation and power-generation projects would greatly improve its agriculture and make it a hub of power-driven small and medium industrial enterprises. But the Kathmandu government had not paid attention to the valley's development possibilities.

The only government hospital had been without a doctor for two years; its four rooms for indoor treatment were without hospital beds and other necessary equipment. It had very few medicines which the compounder in charge, I was told, sold to patients after diluting them. All this while medical equipment, including a number of beds for indoor treatment of patients, and medicines supplied by India for hospitals in Nepal, had been lying unused for months in a government store in Kathmandu.

Some distance away from the town, a hospital run by half a dozen British missionary women belonging to the All Nepal Evangelical Mission Society was the only good medical facility in Nepal's second largest valley. I visited the premises late in the evening of the day of my arrival in Pokhara. The lady in charge of the hospital, a kind and elderly person, showed me round the premises and introduced me to her staff of six other missionary women workers. The hospital had provision for six indoor patients and was well stocked with medicines. Those brave women were carrying on their humanitarian work in the face of persistent and vociferous opposition from the Brahmin community of the area. A few conversions to Christianity had roused their ire and they had threatened the missionary women with murder. The good ladies were nevertheless continuing their work with zeal, though proselytization had been given up. The hospital was quite popular as I could see from the steady trickle of visitors pouring into the premises from nearby villages even during late hours of the evening. In token return of the chief lady doctor's kindness in showing me round the establishment, I presented to her a copy of Gandhiji's *My Experiments with Truth*, which she gratefully accepted.

Educational facilities were grossly short of actual requirement. The valley's only high school, run by pro-India workers of the Nepali Congress, was in dire financial straits. No fee was charged but the students had to pay for the benefit of education by arranging strikes and taking out processions when told to do so. The assistant headmaster invited me to tea along with a large number of students who good-humouredly complained about the political conditioning they were subjected to at the school. The assistant headmaster confided in me that the boys actually liked the fun of taking part in strikes and processions. The boys said they wanted more books in the library. I noted their needs and on my return to Kathmandu, books and some money were sent to the school for its library.

Nepalese officials in Kathmandu were full of praise for the village extension work being done by the United States Operations Mission (USOM) in the Pokhara valley. Two villages were mentioned in this connection—Gerjati and Serenghot. I made a quick visit to both villages and talked with several local inhabitants. But neither in those two villages, nor anywhere else, was there a sign of any extension work being done by USOM or its local employees.

As in Biratnagar and Birgunj, USOM had rented an impressive-looking building which was being used as office-cum-residence for its eight Nepalese employees. They had been given two new jeeps in which they did their running about in the valley, and also lent them out freely to those willing to return the favour by spreading propaganda for USOM and American aid. I met a couple of USOM's Nepalese employees in their office, and they told me that the American village extension programme was still at the stage of preliminary reconnaissance and planning. It had rested there for nearly two years! USOM's much tom-tommed humanitarian activities comprised little more than selling D.D.T. at the reduced rate of Rs 2.5 per lb.

The town of Pokhara was a three-kilometre long straggling bazaar running from north to south, with dirty narrow streets meandering out of it in all directions. The town had no simple, clean accommodation with toilet and bath facilities for a visitor.

Thanks to the Nepal army chief's courtesy, I was made comfortable for the night in a room in the army barracks. The merchandise in the bazaar consisted largely of coarse printed cloth and a few other goods from India, such as glass bangles and beads of which women wore a bending load, and rough grey Nepalese woollen shawls and blankets. There was an abundance of filthy little restaurants and shops selling rakshi—a home-distilled rice liquor—all decorated exclusively with coloured prints of plumpish beauties from the world of Indian films. Nowhere else have I seen so many pictures of Indian film stars in one place. There were literally thousands of them, pinned up row upon row of buxom glamour, on the walls of every restaurant and shop of that long bazaar.

In my young days it was a common belief in our womenfolk that buxomness was an enhancer of their other God-given allures; for if a man saw beauty on a female human frame, he would want more of it in throbbing flesh and blood to have and to hold. Men agreed: There were few takers among them, then, for the latter-day idea of skeletal loveliness popularized by unsmiling, desiccated models.

Before leaving for the hills my two Gurkha porter-comrades and I stopped at a shop to pick up a bottle or two of rakshi to sustain and energize us during the tough mountaineering ahead, and I noticed my two companions looking longingly at the pictures of full-bodied dazzlers pinned up on the shop's long wall. I told them to choose one each, and gave the same to them. Later during the journey, I asked what they would do with the prints on their return to their villages. The elder, Ram Bahadur, said he would give the print to a young, unmarried friend in the village; he would visit the friend now and then to look at the 'girl'. 'Can't keep it at home, Sir. Wife is young and very strong!' The younger one, Bal Bahadur, said he would pin it up on the wall: 'Wife will then stop looking at other men!' Gurkhas certainly have a sense of humour.

The strategic, political and economic importance of the Pokhara valley lies in its geographic location at the crossroads of Tibet and Mustang to the north and India to the south. On that ancient trade route Bhutia nomads still carried wool and other quaint merchandise on their ponies to India via Nuwakot, Palpa and Bhairahawa. Pokhara town was, in those days, and perhaps still is, the trading post for the outlying hill districts of western Nepal.

I was late in starting off on my trek of twenty or so miles in the forenoon of the following day, 28 October 1953. My destination was nowhere in sight at sunset when darkness suddenly enveloped the hills. It had been a tough day going up and down two steep and difficult ascents and descents. With no place for shelter in sight, my Gurkha companions braced themselves for walking the last stretch of whatever distance lay between us and a welcoming shelter with the light of two big torches. I took out my own torch meant for such emergencies. Ram and Bal unsheathed their khukries—a curved dagger with a razor-sharp cutting edge and killer point—to deal with any threat. And they started singing—perhaps to allay unacknowledged fear, or, as they said, to ward off a lurking wild animal in the vicinity.

After about two hours of walking single file in this surreal situation, cautious slow step followed by cautious slow step, Ram Bahadur saw one glimmer of light some distance ahead and shouted in its direction the arrival of three weary travellers in need of a resting place for the night. The raised mud platform, open on one long side and covered by a roof of straw, was unoccupied and we were told it was ours for the night. I opened my bedroll and told the two Bahadurs to take out of the food box whatever they liked. But the lady of the house came over and said, 'The guests God has sent to my humble hut will not go to sleep hungry.' Soon, three thalis filled with rice and curry of dried buffalo meat, laced with home-made rakshi, were placed before us. The meat was unchewable but I swallowed as much of it as I could. No meal had ever tasted as good. I slept like a log that night and swore to never again walk in the hills after sundown.

The following morning I offered a fair sum of money to our hostess but she would not touch it. She said it was her good luck that God had sent three good people to find rest and sleep under her roof. Finally after much pleading by my Gurkha companions, she accepted one of the two bottles of rakshi and a packet of biscuits which were now surplus to our need. In the morning we realized our destination for the previous day's trek was still an hour's walk from where we had spent the night. From there our path to Nuwakot and Syangja lay along the Krishna Gandaki part of the way. This was the most gruelling march of twenty miles across one of the worst terrains I would ever walk on in Nepal. But happily for me, at Syangja, my friends, Jai Prasad Sharma and Kashi Raj would be waiting for me. They had been instrumental in organizing the Indo–Nepal Friendship Society three months earlier, and were keen for me to visit some districts in their region. From Syangja onwards they would be travelling with me to Bhairahawa and back, by air, to Kathmandu.

My reception in Syangja was one of the unique experiences of my life. It was embarrassing, even a bit unnerving, but also hilarious and deeply moving at the same time. This was the one occasion of which I have kept a short pen-picture to entertain my friends and to rejoice in my remembrance of it. I reproduce below the little piece I had written on it sixty years ago:

Two miles outside of Syangja, I was met by two armed sentries who asked to know whether I was 'Rasgotra Sahib Bahadur'. As soon as I confirmed my identity, they stood to attention, saluted me, raised their 303 rifles and fired two shots in the air. The gun salute, they said, would also inform the townspeople of the approach of their august guest.

Then, one sentry fell in line ahead of me, and the other behind me to cover the rear in our march to the town. A mile or so down the path, two flute players sprang up in front of us and led the procession while playing folk tunes to soothe my fatigued senses. After another mile or so, my hosts, the assistant bada hakim and gentry of the town, along with my two friends, met me in the dry bed of the Andhi stream. Then, as we approached the main street, I saw about a thousand men, women and children lined up in their colourful costumes on both sides of the street, whispering to one another in hushed excitement.

How did I feel? Elated, moved, thankful for the affection and respect of those simple people. How did I look? Flushed with embarrassment at the quaintness of my apparel and the

utter inadequacy of my appearance for this grand welcome—
the brim of my jungle cloth-hat drooping right over my ears
and eyes, shirt sleeves and the bottoms of my trousers rolled
up in cavalier fashion, walking stick in hand, and a bit out
of breath not so much from fatigue of the journey but the
excitement of the occasion. Our pace was dictated by the
slow steps of the flautists, and as the procession moved up the
street women sprinkled rice grains and flower petals on me,
men garlanded me, a lovely little girl did aarti while others
sang sweet songs of love and blessings for their guest. The
sentiment behind and significance of such a welcome to a
visitor can be understood and appreciated only in Hindu
society. Syangja had adopted me as its son!

The children of the Syangja school staged a thoroughly enjoyable
song and dance show for me. My hosts had also summoned a couple
of bards of the area to entertain me. Their ballads were about the
lives of Nepal's heroes—Prithvi Narayan Shah who had founded
modern Nepal and the Shah dynasty, one or two of the Rana prime
ministers, and their living hero, Dr K.I. Singh. Equally entertaining
were their snippety biting compositions on present-day social and
political issues. One of these ditties ran as follows:

O God, what a government have you given us!
Of all these gentlemen, K.I. Singh was a good man,
But he has fled to Tibet!
The rains and the floods come year after year,
And the bridges go down;
But these are not repaired, nor new ones erected
Look southward beyond the hills,
They are bridging the Ganga!
O God, give us a leader like Gandhi
And a raja like Nehru.

Dr K.I. Singh was a popular revolutionary leader of this region and a
good deal of folklore had grown around his name. He had fallen out

with Matrika Prasad Koirala, the Nepali Congress president during the uprising against the Ranas. He staged a coup against the Koirala government which failed and he fled to Tibet. He was a stubborn and wayward man and, on occasion, indecisive. But he was a man of courage and determination, honest, incorruptible and straightforward to the point of folly. Undoubtedly, he was the single-most popular man in Nepal at the time. In western Nepal, especially, his was a name to conjure with.

Rumour in Nepal had it that during his exile in Tibet, K.I. Singh had turned bitterly anti-India. He suddenly turned up in Kathmandu one day in the early summer of 1955 to a hugely enthusiastic reception by the people of the valley. India baiters were disappointed when he rang up the embassy two or three days later to ask for an appointment to pay his respects to the ambassador of India. Ambassador Bhagwan Sahay invited him to lunch at the residence the following day, at which First Secretary N.B. Menon and I were also present. He said his very first visit outside his home to pay his respects to the ambassador would show to everybody that he was pro, not anti-India. He spent three hours in the embassy, discussing politics, his exile and narrated some hilarious tales about the Chinese trying to indoctrinate him against India.

To return to my trek in the hills of western Nepal; after a couple of happy and restful days in Syangja, followed by a half day's brisk walking over hill and dale, I crossed the Krishna (or Kali) Gandaki at midday in Ramdighat, a place of pilgrimage for the Hindus of both India and Nepal. We bathed in the sacred river before proceeding to Palpa. This whole region is the habitat of the gallant warrior tribes— Gurungs, Magars and Thakalis—whose sons form the backbone of Gurkha units of the Indian army. Fine particles of gold could be seen in the sands of the river almost all along its banks, but gold-sifting was being done only at three or four places; the process was difficult and slow and the yield was small. But apparently worthwhile quantities of gold were being retrieved from the river's sands; for I saw women everywhere wearing large nose rings, earrings, pendants and a round, sunflower-shaped flat ornament called a phool. The phool is worn only by married women on their foreheads. The custom of the land,

I was told, was that the father of the girl would hand her over to the bridegroom only after she had been presented with the auspicious phool by her chosen one.

Nepal's hill regions are a land of captivating natural beauty and guileless human simplicity and romance. On several occasions I saw separate groups of young men and young women, while at work on opposite hillsides singing away to each other in competition and courtship. Nepal awaits a Wordsworth to celebrate the ethereal beauty of the hill and dale of western Nepal and the good, simple and honest men and women that blend so artlessly with their environment. The lyrics of Madhav Prasad Ghimire, Nepal's poet laureate, and one of my dearest friends in Nepal, captures some of the fabulous beauty and grandeur of western Nepal's mountains rivers and valleys.

PILGRIMAGE TO LUMBINI

This tour was of about 120 miles in six days excluding the two days of rest in Syangja, and at the end, tired though I was, the promise of Lumbini, the birthplace of Lord Buddha, so near at hand, drew me away from the rest and comfort at the palatial residence of the friendly governor of Bhairawaha. On the afternoon of 3 or 4 November, I hired a pony and proceeded to Lumbini, thirteen miles west of Bhairawaha. My progress on this path even on pony-back was extremely slow. It took me four or five hours to reach my destination. There are three rivers on the way and a multitude of shallow seasonal streams. The culverts and bridges were all broken and one had to wade through the rivers which in places were waist-deep. The owner of the pony helped the little beast negotiate these successfully, with me perched precariously on its back. It would soon take revenge for my uncivil behaviour. The Lumbini compound was surrounded by a moat filled with water, which to my untrained eye looked shallow. So, without waiting for its master, who had fallen some distance behind us, I goaded my mount into the murky water. Midway in the moat, the four-foot dwarf started swimming, obliging me to dismount and wade my way through waist-deep water to the other end.

The local zamindar, chairman of the Lumbini Managing Committee, gave me a room in the Nepal government's guest house in the compound. Perhaps because of the stagnant water in the moat surrounding the sacred site or the marshy areas nearby, the place had become the breeding ground of South Asia's finest mosquitoes. The battle began as soon as I snuffed the two candles that lit my room. Those night fighters of Lumbini came in swarms, and they drew blood. The sting of Lumbini's mosquitoes was as sharp as the prick of a khukri's sharp point. It was an unequal fight, and that night was one long spell of misery for me, relieved to a point by my efforts to meditate on the Lord and his teachings. In 1951, I had encountered a near similar breed of mosquitoes of more or less the same sting-power in Bodh Gaya. Between the two, though, the night fighters of Nepal had an edge over their Indian incarnates. No wonder then, that at the end of it all, Lord Buddha, born in Lumbini and enlightened in Gaya, found life to be all 'Dukkha'—endless suffering.

Be that as it may, Lumbini, such as it was, had something in its air, its earth and water that awakened a long-dormant layer in my inner self, and I became a devout follower, albeit an unconventional one, of the Lord.

Of what was once the beautiful Lumbini gardens, and of the dense sal forest surrounding the area, there was no trace left. The Ashoka Pillar still stood outside the entrance to the temple of Maya Devi, with its capital of three lion heads laid low at its base, reminding the visitor of Emperor Ashoka's pilgrimage to his spiritual master's birthplace.

A lot of history lies buried in that holy ground, which was now a forlorn ruin. Some excavations haphazardly carried out in the time of Prime Minister Juddha Shumsher Jang Bahadur Rana had yielded a few exquisite stone carvings and coins belonging possibly to the Gupta period of Indian history. I was also shown a wealth of beads, signet rings and statuettes and a large number of terracotta heads with Greek faces and hairstyles. Some of the finer, small pieces were kept in biscuit tins. Repeated requests from the managing committee to the Government of Nepal, for a lockable showcase in which these treasures could be displayed safely, had been met with no response! A dozen or more terracotta figures lay in a heap in a dingy old room near the cookhouse, where some damage had occurred owing to leakages in the roof in rainy seasons and careless handling by the keepers.

Visitors from China, Taiwan, Japan, Burma, Ceylon and India had recorded, year after year, their dismay at the sad state of Lumbini and urged the Nepal government to restore the dignity and sanctity of the sacred site. Buddhist societies of Burma and Ceylon had offered to restore and maintain the place, but their generous offers were not accepted by Kathmandu. Indian visitors were content with criticizing the Nepal government for not doing this, that or the other, without ever making any positive offer or taking some concrete action themselves.

Lumbini, when I saw it, was a disgrace to both Nepal and India, and nothing much seems to have been done since to improve the site and its surroundings. The Nepal government could not be blamed; it had inherited an empty treasury from the Rana regime, and understandably, it had other, far more pressing priorities for the meagre financial and other resources at its disposal. But what explains the apathy of the Government of India towards the sacred site of the birth of the most illustrious son of India and Nepal? What keeps it from offering all necessary financial and technical assistance to develop Lumbini into a most attractive place of pilgrimage in South Asia?

The offer by a Chinese organization recently to restore, develop and maintain Lumbini at a cost of several million US dollars caused some panic in India for no good reason. There are many devout followers of Lord Buddha in China, though it is no longer the Buddhist country it once was. Other countries, including India, are also interested in seeing Lumbini developed as one of the Indian subcontinent's most important and attractive centres of international pilgrimage. Perhaps the best way to recreate a Lumbini worthy of the memory of the founder of one of the world's great religions might be for Nepal to constitute an international consortium for the purpose.

My exploration of the country had to be suspended for some time because the new ambassador, Bhagwan Sahay wanted me to be with him on his calls on ministers, and other meetings with eminent political, social and cultural figures of the country. Really only one region remained to be surveyed—hill districts of northwestern

Nepal. My senior colleague, First Secretary N.B. Menon, covered that region in his long trek of ten days to Muktinath and Mustang. He brought the same kind of reports from this region as I had from others, of poverty and poor governance, absence of development activity, and the common people's respect, friendship and goodwill for India, despite the absence of any Indian presence there.

THE BEGINNINGS OF A NEW ERA IN NEPAL

1955 was an eventful year in Nepal. King Tribhuvan, who had been ailing for some time, passed away while under treatment in Europe. Tribhuvan, a benign monarch who had rid the country of autocratic Rana rule and introduced democracy under a constitutional monarchy was hugely popular in Nepal. The country went into a long period of mourning followed by the coronation of his son, Mahendra Bir Bikram Shah Dev; the first such occasion since the Ranas usurped the monarch's powers 104 years ago. India sent a high-powered delegation, led by Vice President Radhakrishnan, to witness the ceremonies and felicitate the young king.

A few months later at President Rajendra Prasad's invitation, King Mahendra paid his first state visit to India lasting nearly two weeks, including four days in Delhi. The king and queen were received with great warmth by the President and the prime minister on their arrival at Safdarjung airport. I accompanied the royal party throughout their Indian visit as liaison officer. Our media gave warm and extensive coverage to the royal couple. The king enjoyed his stay in Delhi, of which the special features were the banquet at the Rashtrapati Bhavan and a friendly lunch hosted by Prime Minister Nehru at his residence. The king was happy with his private talks with the prime minister and with some senior Indian ministers who called on him at the Rashtrapati Bhavan. In the rest of the country the king liked what he saw—our development projects such as the Bhakra Dam, the Sindri Fertilizer Factory, industrial estates, community development projects, new educational and scientific institutions, cultural sites like Ajanta and Ellora, and the dance and music recitals arranged in his honour in various places. They were particularly intrigued by the dancing style and the quaint make-up and elaborate costumes of Kathakali dancers in Travancore and Cochin.

Two of our chief ministers had impressed the king in particular. In Mumbai, Chief Minister Morarji Desai's sumptuous vegetarian lunch was a treat to remember. It was served in large, sparking silver 'thalis' laden with silver katoris filled with a variety of delicious vegetarian dishes—I counted ten in my thali and another two or three were placed around it after we had started eating. During the lunch, the chief minister regaled us with stories about his experiences of life in British jails during the struggle for Independence. He also explained to the royal couple some aspects of Gandhiji's teachings on truth and non-violence. Chief Minister Kengal Hanumanthaiah of Karnataka and his government gave a huge public reception followed by a dinner in honour of the royal couple. What the king liked in particular was Hanumanthaiah's simplicity and openness. He enjoyed his talks with the chief minister who explained to the guest, with much amusement, the intricacies of Indian politics. The king described him as 'Thulo Mancha'—Nepali for a 'great man and a wise one'.

In a lighter moment during the tour, the king had threatened that he and the queen would turn up at my residence in Kathmandu to find out how I managed to run the 'Kamal Pokhari Bangalow'— my residence—without a woman. So, on my return to Kathmandu I invited Their Majesties to dinner. They graciously accepted, and I asked whether they would like anyone else to be invited to the dinner. 'Only Ambassador Bhagwan Sahay and Mrs Sahay,' said the king. The matter was settled. Four weeks later, the dinner at my residence in Kathmandu was a long, informal and happy evening. Francis, my Goan cook, excelled himself in preparing a meal for the royal couple. One dish I had cooked myself for my royal guests— butter chicken—also received their fulsome approval.

THE EMBASSY'S CHANGING ROLE

Though we had a strong Indian presence in Kathmandu—the embassy, the Aid Mission, the Indian Military Training Mission, and several

Indian deputationists loaned by India on the Nepal government's request—it was there that we first felt the need for a special kind of public relations effort to reach out to different sections of the general public. To fill this need, a library-cum-cultural centre was established in the busiest section of the city. Its inauguration by Ambassador Bhagwan Sahay was followed by a recital of classical Indian music by the celebrated vocalist, Pandit Omkarnath Thakur. Three or four concerts following the centre's inauguration proved hugely popular events, and the demand grew for more recitals of classical Indian music and dance. The embassy therefore made it a practice in later years to bring leading Indian classical musicians and dancers to Kathmandu, at least twice a year, on India's Independence Day and Republic Day. This helped meet a genuine hunger for high-quality entertainment among the public, and also promote contacts between the cultural communities of the two neighbouring countries. The centre's library, with its big reading room and large collection of Hindi, Nepali and English books, became popular with the student community, and therefore, also a solid target, when the need arose, for the officially sponsored stoning of it. Overall the experiment was a notable success.

THE BACHCHANS IN NEPAL

I had known modern Hindi's best lyrical poet of all time, Dr Harivansh Rai Bachchan since my college days at Hindu College in Amritsar in the early 1940s. He was a popular lecturer in English at Allahabad University, but the cause of his great fame was the publication of his two early books of Hindi poetry, *Madhushala* (the House of Wine) and *Madhubala* (the Cup-bearer Damsel). In a short time, *Madhushala* went through several editions and was also translated into English verse by Marjorie Boulton—an English poet from Oxford. No other volume of modern Hindi poetry has achieved such magnitude of circulation and recognition.

Though Bachchan's best poetry was yet to come, these two books brought him a flood tide of acclaim and appreciation, and there were demands not only for the books but also for personal, hours-long recitals by the poet of his *Madhushala* and *Madhubala*. There was such magic in Bachchan's well-modulated voice that when he recited, every listener's heart throbbed with the beat of his own. Before Bachchan's arrival on the scene, modern Hindi love poetry was mostly mystical expression of a vague longing of the poet's soul for another beauteous but elusive, unbodied spirit. Bachchan gave full and free expression in these, and in his later poems, to human emotions of love, loss and grief, renewal of hope, the excitement and troubling uncertainty of courtship and the ecstasy and calm of love's fulfillment. Bachchan had made modern Hindi poetry a powerful medium for the portrayal of secular, human emotions.

When Allahabad University closed for the summer recess, I invited the Bachchans to spend the vacation as my guests in Kathmandu. The poet, his wife Teji, and their two little boys, Amitabh and Ajitabh, arrived in Kathmandu in late June or early July 1955. During the next six weeks, Amit and Ajit filled my house with their laughter, fun and frolic and playful pranks. Amitabh recently recalled those happy times in a blog post he wrote after meeting me at a dinner at the house of one of our common friends, Suhel Seth, an internationally reputed public relations guru.

As the news spread of Bachchan's presence in the city, requests poured in for meetings with the poet. Kathmandu had quite a few poets, playwrights and other writers in the Nepali language. To begin with, we planned three or four evenings at my residence of recitations and readings by poets, playwrights and others from their works, and an evening of discussion on global and subcontinental trends in modern writing. These first gatherings of creative writers to meet with Bachchan led to requests from others to attend or take part in such meetings as well. As a result, for the next three or four weeks of the Bachchans' stay in Kathmandu, my house, Ambassador Bhagwan Sahay's residence and, on occasion, the Indian embassy's open compound, became the venues of Bachchan's recitals of his poems, and a veritable India–Nepal literature festival. Those evenings, beginning at 8 or 8:30 p.m. after dinner, ended, generally, an hour or two after midnight with light refreshments.

One memorable and deeply moving experience was the night-long recital by Bachchan at my residence of his 'Nisha Nimantran' (Call of the Night), beginning at 9 p.m. and ending at the break of dawn. Bachchan wrote this long poem in 100 short lyrical parts, when he was sunk in gloom following his first wife's death. Each lyric, of twelve lines, suffused with the poet's feelings of the moment, is a reflection of the night's mood at that particular moment. It is a sad but gripping poem, its gloom occasionally relieved by nature's hope-giving phenomena—the light of a shooting star, the rumble of the clouds followed by gentle rain, or the early morning chirping of a bird. The audience consisted of some committed Nepalese devotees of the Muse. For us, his listeners, and in some sense for Bachchan himself, this was a night of catharsis of our own private losses and sorrows.

Throughout the Bachchans' stay I kept an open house and the poet's very own private muse, Teji Bachchan, looked after the preparation of meals and light refreshments for those present. Under her overall direction and encouragement, Francis, my Goan cook, and his two Nepalese assistants stood up well to the demands of those special occasions. Teji was a lovely woman, always full of energy and good humour. She had a most attractive singing voice which melded well with Bachchan's, when the two sang his love lyrics together.

One result of all this activity and the response to it of Nepal's cultural elite was the addition of the post of a cultural attaché in the embassy, to be filled by a leading literary figure of India with a modicum of PR talent. Its first occupant, Shivmangal Singh Suman, a well-known Hindi poet, held the post with distinction. He was followed by other luminaries from the world of Hindi writers on short visits or to fill posts in the embassy.

But perhaps the most important effect of all these small, unusual things we did, including our countrywide contacts with the common people was to generate a fund of goodwill, fellowship and friendship for India. These new contacts gave us the benefit of information and advice on Nepalese affairs to which hitherto we had no access. Quite unconsciously we had pioneered a new dimension in the embassy's functioning. We did not even think of a name for what the MEA has recently christened Public Diplomacy.

chapter eight

TEETHING PROBLEMS OF
A NEW FOREIGN SERVICE

~

A few days after Mahendra's coronation on 2 May 1956, I was transferred to the ministry of external affairs as under secretary in charge of Foreign Service personnel—US (FSP). The post dealt with a variety of work pertaining to branch A of the Indian Foreign Service, such as recruitment, training, postings, promotions of officers, financial sanctions and administrative work to facilitate the smooth functioning of our missions abroad. The incumbent under secretary functioned as a junior manager of the service who was expected to propose or initiate action on these and other related matters for consideration by the senior joint secretary in charge of administration—JS (ADI) or the additional or special secretary (administration). The final arbiter of problems concerning IFS personnel was of course the foreign secretary (FS). The implementation of the decisions made by them or collectively by the Foreign Service Board comprising the MEA's three secretaries and the secretary, ministry of commerce, was one of US (FSP)'s important responsibilities.

Till May 1956, this post had been held by a succession of Central Secretariat Service (CSS) officials who had never served abroad. Understandably, they were sticklers for the rules. The trouble was with the rules. In the ninth year of Independence, India's diplomatic service was being managed under outdated CSS Rules of Service, which bore no relevance to the functioning of India's diplomatic personnel and diplomatic missions abroad. Some work had been initiated to frame the IFS Rules of Service and I was told to finalize them and pursue action for their promulgation after obtaining the approval of all concerned.

In the early weeks of my handling the post's administrative work I came up against the iron control exercised by the finance ministry's officers on virtually every item of expenditure to be incurred by the Foreign Office and the financial controller's belief in the immutability and universal applicability of CSS rules. The MEA had posted an officer of first secretary/counsellor rank in one of India's diplomatic missions in Europe—I do not now remember for sure but, perhaps, it was our embassy in Brussels—and the embassy had hired an unfurnished house or apartment for the officer and requested the ministry's sanction of a certain amount of money for local purchase of furnishings to make the bare premises habitable. It was a fairly modest demand, but our financial advisers would have none of it. The deputy financial adviser (DFA) cited rules and asserted that officers serving abroad were entitled to the same furnishings as were admissible to an officer of equal seniority working in India, namely a few wooden chairs and tables, cotton dhurries in lieu of carpets, a number of string charpais etc.

Notably, the list included a contraption called the commode—a wooden box with an open top giving the user access to a removable toilet bowl underneath. In common parlance the contraption was called 'thunderbox'. It was an import from Britain introduced in India in the days of Company sircar.

The DFA was impatient with my arguments about the way of life in the West, namely representational—the need to entertain appropriately—obligations of our diplomatic officers, unsuitability in European climatic conditions of the Indian furnishings proposed for a diplomat in Brussels, or the local unavailability of such items in foreign countries. He was adamant the rules must apply equally to officers working in India and abroad; there must be no discrimination, and India, a poor country, could not afford Western luxuries for its officers.

All that we could agree on was that since these items were not available locally in Europe, all of them, with adequate spares would have to be sent from India; future replacements would also have to be sent from India, and a competent Indian carpenter might have to be added to the embassy's staff to carry out emergency repairs.

I gave the DFA's list of Indian furnishings, admissible to the first secretary in Brussels, to Cox & Kings and requested them to prepare an estimate of expenditure on: i) purchasing the listed items in Delhi; ii) costs of packing, insurance and shipment to Brussels; iii) replacement from India of damaged items due to normal wear and tear (around 20 per cent of the original lot after every two or three years). The gentleman from Cox & Kings was nonplussed and wondered what was up. I simply told him to give me just the fair costs without padding. The estimate he brought a week later was considerably higher than the amount requested by the embassy for local purchase of furnishings. I added to it the cost of stationing an Indian carpenter at Brussels and sent the file to the financial advisor saying we were ready to comply with his advice, and requested his early concurrence.

Days went by without a response from him. Finally with a sheepish grin, he sanctioned the amount requested by the embassy. And our future dealings with our financial advisers on administrative matters became cooperative and smooth. The finance ministry's control eased further when the IFS Rules of Service were promulgated a few months later.

In 1956, the MEA had a total of only about 130 officers in branch A of the IFS to deploy at headquarters, and in forty diplomatic missions and a few consular posts abroad. It was a very unsatisfactory situation. The number of independent states' members of the UN had grown from fifty-seven in 1947 to eighty in 1956, and there was a procession of African colonial territories lined up for independence and UN membership. Also there were requests from a few countries for resident Indian diplomatic missions in their capitals. We just did not have the personnel to meet those friendly requests.

We were still recruiting four or five officers per year through the competitive examination. In our internal discussions I argued for recruitment of fifteen officers every year, but the high authorities in the MEA were fixated on the idea that only the brightest and the top five or six deserved to join the elite Foreign Service of India. Very reluctantly though, they agreed to set the recruitment target from 1956 onwards at ten per year, subject to availability of top-drawer talent. However, despite these teething problems, our missions were functioning well, and there were heartening signs of the development of a strong esprit de corps.

Our planning and replanning of the IFS cadre was never really adequate for the expanding requirement of senior diplomatic personnel. The number of India's missions and posts abroad, today, is close to 200. The officer strength of the ministry and its posts abroad needs immediate expansion of the order of 50 per cent at the very least. With its 900 IFS (A) officers, the ministry simply does not have the manpower to meet the international responsibilities of a country of India's size and importance.

We do not have to follow the wasteful personnel policies of the US, Britain or China, but we need a minimum IFS (A) strength of around 2000, compared with the present 900. Even with the present recruitment of thirty to forty officers a year, that required strength may be reached only in thirty or more years! Meanwhile critical shortages can be met by inducting officers from other wings of government for a couple of assignments, each of three years in our missions abroad.

But this is only part of the story and there is no justification for criticism by American commentators about India's alleged incapability to become a world power because of a comparatively small senior branch of the IFS. There is its branch B, whose members competently fill numerous diplomatic posts abroad. Besides, we should continue the practice of filling financial, commercial and other technical posts in the embassies with officials of the concerned ministries of the Government of India. This practice has served India well, and it has the merit of keeping the IFS integrated in the overall functioning of the Central government.

OBSOLETE MARRIAGE RULES

The MEA's early decisions concerning recruitment of women in the Indian Foreign Service were very conservative. Prejudice against women's recruitment in the diplomatic service prevailed even in the democratic societies of the United States, Britain and other European countries. Despite Prime Minister Nehru's liberal views in the matter of women's rights and capabilities, some of the prevailing prejudices had crept into the thinking of our senior civil servants responsible for framing the rules of recruitment. A woman member of the IFS was required to resign from the service on getting married. Ms C.B. Muthamma, an outstanding officer, who was the first young woman to join the Foreign Service through the competitive examination, chose to remain single. Savitri Kunnadi, a talented officer of great personal charm, who joined the service much later, followed Muthamma's example, and had a distinguished career. During my two years as US (FSP), some very bright young women had qualified for the IFS, wanted to join it but opted in favour of Home Services because of their families' fears of imagined hardship and hazards of serving abroad.

A bright young woman, Manorama Kochchar and nine young men had qualified for the IFS in the competitive examination in 1958. They came to my office on 10 April to sign up, and I noticed that Manorama was accompanied by her mother who, according to Manorama, was anxious to talk to me. Mrs Kochchar, Manorama and I talked together for about an hour or more about the work environment in our embassies and the nature of diplomatic work. She wanted to be assured that no harm would come to her daughter, especially while serving abroad and I tried to allay her fears. Finally, I said to Mrs Kochchar that Manorama seemed to have the aptitude for the Foreign Service. Therefore she had made a wise choice and I was certain that she would distinguish herself in the career, bring honour to the country, and make her family proud of her achievements. Mrs Kochchar was also worried about the marriage prohibition rule. That, and related matters, I told her, were under review and I had no doubt that soon the prohibition would go. There were several other questions and nagging doubts in her mind which I tried to dispel as best I could.

Manorama and her batchmate, Hardev Bhalla fell in love while they were under training in Delhi. They were both aware that if they were to marry, Manorama would have to submit her resignation, which course she did not want to adopt and Hardev agreed with her decision. While doing language training in different countries far apart from one another, (Manorama in Germany and Hardev in Japan), they stoically bore the pangs of separation, hoping for divine intervention to reward their penance with the myriad delights of daily intimacies of married life. The divine intervention did occur in the form of a visit in 1961 of Lakshmi Menon, minister of state in the MEA, to Prague where Hardev had been posted a month or two earlier. He pleaded their case with the minister and she told Hardev to advise Manorama to write a letter to the foreign minister, Jawaharlal Nehru, to request his permission for her to marry Hardev Bhalla. After a couple of weeks she received a letter from Nehru giving her permission to marry Hardev. They got married on 14 April 1962 in the house of Ambassador P.A. Menon in Germany. It was a happy marriage. They did well in their careers and were a popular couple in the service. Manorama was not even asked to send her resignation with the letter she wrote to Foreign Minister Nehru, nor was she required to comply with any other condition.

The satisfactory conclusion of this case became a guide for the future. To ensure the couple's happiness and well-being in the early years, the MEA posted them together on four or five occasions in our larger missions, and when they reached ambassadorial seniority an effort was made to post them in two neighbouring countries so that they could spend time together in one or the other capital during holidays.

Because of the ban on IFS members marrying foreigners, we lost a brilliant young woman officer, Surjit Man Singh who married an American national and had to leave the service. Her book, *India's Search for Power* published in 1984, is about the best account I have seen of Indira Gandhi's foreign policy. Though here too, Prime Minister Nehru took a liberal view of the matter and instructed the ministry to consider sympathetically the application of an officer to marry a national of a close and friendly neighboring country like Bhutan, Burma, Nepal or Sri Lanka. K.R. Narayanan's marriage to Usha, a Burmese national, was the most important such case. It was moved away to meet other guests. By the end of the evening all that had passed between us was a handshake and, by way of conversation, 'I hope to see you again' from me, and from her a brief, 'I hope so too.'

But that short meeting, with the lovely girl with big eyes arched over by eye-catching eyebrows and a bashful smile, was enough to make my heart strings break out in a song of love. So, as I drove back to my little apartment behind the old Cottage Industries Emporium on Janpath, four lines from a poem by Robert Burns kept leaping up in my head word by word:

To see her is to love her,
And love but her forever,
For Nature made her what she is,
And never made sic another.

A restless day or two later, I asked my friend to tell me something more about Kadambari. 'Why don't you call her and find out more yourself?' he said; 'You are not a child. She is twenty-one years old, she may also be wanting to know you better.' 'Oh, no! Twenty-one years! So young! I am thirty-two, too old for a lovely young thing like that.' He gave me the Viswanathans' telephone number and ordered: 'Call her, take her out for coffee, lunch or dinner. And tell her you are thirty-two! Not a bad opening from an IFS officer. No?'

Thus it was that Kadambari and I met in August 1956. Intimacy between us grew fast and most of our evenings were spent together walking on Shanti Path in Chanakyapuri, or relaxing and chatting in my apartment, or watching a film followed by dinner and dancing in a restaurant in Connaught Place or in the ballroom of the Imperial Hotel on Janpath. On 24 October 1956—United Nations' day—Kadambari and I were united in marriage in a simple, south Indian wedding ceremony at the Viswanathan's residence on Teen Murti Lane. A week's honeymoon in Srinagar, and I plunged into my work again, while Kadambari took charge of my life and all that goes in the name of the household. Barely a year later we were the blessed parents of a lovely little boy, who brought joy and a new light in our lives. With motherhood Kadambari not only grew in maturity, her personality gained a fresh glow and grace.

No marriage is free from occasional differences, even serious misunderstandings and other difficulties. In the Foreign Service in particular, moving house from one new place to another in foreign countries every two or three years takes a heavy toll on the lives of the wives of IFS officers. Domestic help is always inadequate because of insufficient provision for it in an officer's foreign allowance. Kadambari complained about these matters but managed them. Her support to me, especially in the years of my assignments as head of mission from 1967 to 1990, was as invaluable as it was indispensable. That at the time of writing we are just a year away from the diamond jubilee of our wedding, says something about our marriage.

KING MAHENDRA AND INDIA–NEPAL RELATIONS

In late 1957, the king and queen of Nepal paid their second state visit to India and I was, again, appointed liaison officer to accompany the royal party throughout their visit of about two weeks, which began with a pilgrimage to Amarnath in Kashmir and took us to the states and sites of special developmental and cultural interest Their Majesties had not visited in 1955.

As usual, in the kings's Delhi programme we had kept one evening free for relaxation and a quiet dinner. I asked the king whether he had anything in mind for the free evening. 'Yes,' he said, 'the queen and I would like to spend the evening with you and Mrs Rasgotra. Can we have drinks at your place and then go to Moti Mahal for dinner?' He added that I could invite any number of our friends for drinks, but at dinner there should be just the four of us, any other members of my family, and three or four of his entourage! He had already done me a lot of favours, including two big-game shoots in the Terai jungles; by this latest gesture he had put the seal on our friendship.

But for taking the royal couple to Moti Mahal, a restaurant known for its tandoori specialities, in Daryaganj, I needed approval of higher authorities. When I mentioned to Foreign Secretary Subimal

Dutt what the king had proposed for a quiet private evening, he was dumbstruck for a long minute or two. Finally he asked: 'You know him so well?' I told him that the king and queen had been my guests at dinner at my residence in Kathmandu when I was a mere second secretary in our embassy in their country. 'He sees no barriers to friendship, that is the kind of man he is.' 'Well, if this is what the king wants, what can I say?' said Dutt and added, 'But do mention this to Panditji' (Prime Minister Nehru).

When I got a chance to have a word with the prime minister that evening, he had already heard it from Dutt and I did not have to say much. He approved. 'Well, why not? Do what the young couple want. Bhagwan Sahay (our ambassador in Kathmandu) had told me that the king is a good friend of yours. But ensure security.'

Several senior MEA officers with their wives, Kadambari's parents—Mr and Mrs Viswanathan—a dozen or so of our non-official young friends, and virtually everyone dealing with Nepal in the Government of India were present in my ground floor, DI apartment on Vinay Marg when the royal couple arrived. The king greeted and spoke with each one of our guests and Kadambari, my wife, conducted herself as the hostess with admirable dignity and aplomb as if she were used to entertaining royalty all her life. She took every lady guest to the queen during those two hours from 7 p.m. to 9 p.m. without ignoring any of the other guests. She had personally supervised the preparation, presentation and serving of snacks and drinks to the guests. It was a happy evening with Their Majesties completely at ease, exchanging small talk and pleasantries with the guests. They enjoyed the bonhomie and informality of the evening.

At Moti Mahal, the manager, Kundal Lal, had arranged a small private room for us on the first floor overlooking Daryaganj. We were ten at the table, including Mr and Mrs Viswanathan. From around 9:30 till 11:00 p.m., Kundan Lal and his men—all impressively turned out in pink turbans and white Pathani shalwar kameez suits, served our group one delicacy after another. The food was a treat with every item cooked and flavoured to perfection. The queen was amused at her husband asking for a little more dal makhani with every new dish that was placed before him. The conversation at the table was lively, with Mr Viswanathan regaling Their Majesties with tales from the annals of various dynasties that had ruled India from Delhi. Talk then turned to shikar—big-game shooting in Nepal, the duck shoots in Bharatpur on the maharaja's invitation; I had accompanied Mr Viswanathan on some of those duck shoots in Bharatpur. Kadambari, who was sitting next to the king was with child at the time. He looked at her, then turned to me and said, 'During her present condition you must not kill any animal or bird.' Then he turned to Kadambari and said, 'Don't let him go on shoots while you are in this condition.'

The evening went off well, giving a good start to Their Majesties' two-week tour of the country. As in the earlier visit, the king noted the dynamism and energy of the country and signs of progress in every state he visited. He was happy with his talks with Prime Minister Nehru. In our private conversations, he often mentioned the prime minister's role in the monarchy's restoration in Nepal and his deep interest in Nepal's progress and prosperity. He was equally touched by President Rajendra Prasad's personal simplicity and his goodwill and friendship for Nepal. Before leaving Delhi he extended an invitation to President Rajendra Prasad and Mrs Prasad to visit Nepal. Their visit the following year was a grand success.

Despite occasional pinpricks by disgruntled politicians, even the covert antagonism of unelected prime ministers like M.P. Koirala and Tanka Prasad Acharya, India–Nepal relations were at their peak and a perfect model for good neighbourly relations. The architects of this model relationship were Mahendra's father, King Tribhuvan, and Jawaharlal Nehru—not the leaders of democratic parties of Nepal. It was expected that a benign monarch would guide the democratic process to maturity and gradually train democratic parties in the disciplines and responsibilities of democracy. But Mahendra was disenchanted with the ambitions of popular leaders. In fact even as crown prince he had not quite liked his father's idea of reconstituting Nepal into an elective democracy under a constitutional monarchy. In 1960 he suddenly dismissed the government headed by popularly elected Prime Minister B.P. Koirala, and instituted a system called

Panchayati Raj, which made him the absolute ruler of his country. That action resulted in a serious deterioration in India–Nepal relations.

HAROLD MACMILLAN VISITS INDIA

In March or April 1958, British Prime Minister Harold Macmillan accompanied by his wife, Lady Dorothy, paid an official visit to India. Prime Minister Nehru put them up along with Macmillan's two assistants at Teen Murti House as his personal guests. The two prime ministers had several sessions of private talks on the world situation, the Cold War, the nuclear arms race and the prevailing crisis over Berlin, Kashmir, Pakistan and China. Though the visit of four or five days was rather long for a British prime minister, Macmillan did not want to move out of Delhi, but wanted to see as much as possible of development activity in areas around Delhi. I was attached to him as his liaison officer and Prime Minister Nehru had instructed me to accompany Macmillan everywhere, ensure that no mishap occurred, and in the evening report to him (Nehru) on how the day's events had gone for his guest.

At a public meeting in a village near Gurgaon, a provincial minister tried to introduce Macmillan to a large gathering of village folk and students and teachers from schools in the area: 'Our distinguished visitor is the prime minister of Britain.' That evoked no response from the audience till someone shouted in Hindi: 'Woh to Nehruji hain.' (But Nehruji is the prime minister of Britain.) After laughter subsided, the minister tried another tack: 'You all know the name Macmillan & Co. which is printed on your school books, don't you?' There was a big roar, 'Yes, we do.'

'The company that prepares those books belongs to our honoured guest!' That remark was followed by much clapping and shouts of joy. Clearly the honorable minister had made his point. Macmillan took it all in good spirit and with much amusement.

Every evening, by way of my report of the day, I narrated such happenings which amused Panditji a good deal. On the last day of Macmillan's stay in Delhi he said to me in Hindi: 'Itney jalse huay, gaon ke logon mein se kisi ne Macmillan ke paon nahin chhuey? Kisi ne Macmillan ko hazoor mai-bap nahin kaha?' (In so many meetings with village folk, nobody touched his feet? Or said to him: Sir you are my father and mother?) While people everywhere, men and women alike were eager to shake Macmillan's hand, no one had said 'hazoor mai-bap' to him or showed the least inclination to touch his knees or feet.

Macmillan's last appointment in Delhi was with Vice President Radhakrishnan at the latter's residence in the evening at around 7 p.m. He was looking forward, he had told me, to his meeting with the 'wonderful philosopher who is your vice president'. East–West tensions had been rising over Berlin because of Khrushchev's ultimatum for the withdrawal of NATO troops from West Berlin and recognition, by Western powers, of East Germany as a sovereign state. Macmillan wanted the vice president's advice as to whether Khrushchev and Bulganin would respond to his initiative to reduce tensions in the right spirit and whether he should go ahead with his planned visit to Moscow in early 1959.

Macmillan heaped much praise on the vice president for the way he had dealt with Stalin. The vice president told him that the Western powers missed a chance to make peace with Stalin, sort out the German problem, end the Cold War and halt the wasteful and dangerous nuclear arms race. In his judgement, Stalin was genuinely desirous of peace. He encouraged Macmillan to visit Moscow because he had found Khrushchev and other Russian leaders open-minded and willing listeners. He said there was a positive change in Moscow of which advantage should be taken. He believed Khrushchev would respond positively to a conciliatory approach from Western leaders: 'The initiative you have in mind is a good one. The leaders in Moscow are people you can talk with,' said the vice president.

Macmillan did visit Moscow in February 1959, and in response to his conciliatory approach Khrushchev indicated his willingness even to discuss proposals for a confederation of East and West Germany, provided the social system of the confederation was left to the German people to decide.[1] However, while these talks were going on, John Foster Dulles from Washington threatened the use of force to defend the West's interests in Berlin. The initial

1941: At the University Officers' Training Corps while a student in Hindu College, Amritsar.

1948: Trekking in the snow in the Dhauladhar range overlooking Dharamshala.

1955: PM Nehru hosted a dinner at his residence for King Mahendra and Queen Ratna (seated with him on the sofa).

1956: Our simple, south Indian wedding ceremony
on 24 October.

1960: Kadambari with PM Nehru and Indira Gandhi at a
reception in New York.

1960: Introducing PM Nehru to African delegates at the UN.

1962: Assisting Krishna Menon at a meeting of the UN first committee.

1971: Kadambari with President Nixon at the banquet
for PM Indira Gandhi at the White House.

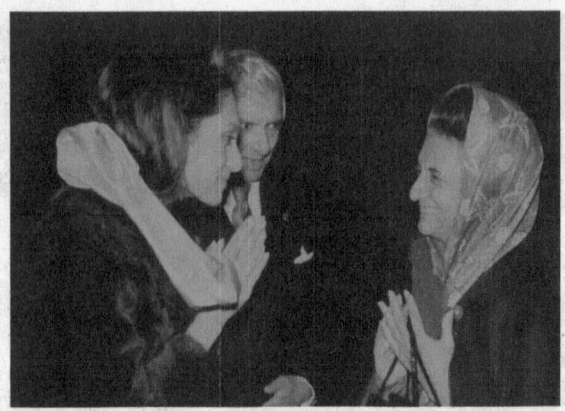

1971: Kadambari at the ambassador's reception in Washington DC.

1972, London: Kadambari, and myself as acting high commissioner, with Labour leader Michael Foot and Mrs Jill Foot.

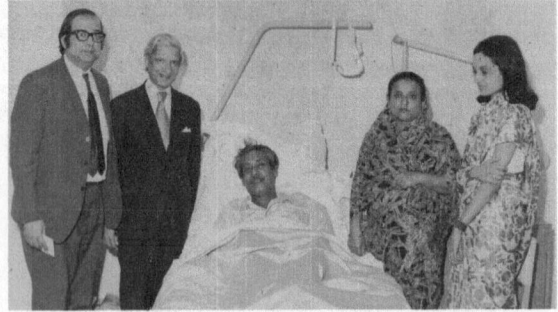

1972, London: Kadambari and I called on Bangabandhu Sheikh Mujibur Rahman, who was recuperating in a hospital in London.

1973, London: Lord Mountbatten with Kadambari
and myself at a reception at India House.

1973: Kadambari welcoming Field Marshal Sam
Manekshaw at our dinner for him.

1973: Presenting a portrait of PM Nehru to Lord Butler,
master of Trinity College, Cambridge. Lord Butler is showing
the portrait to Nehru's former landlady, who had come for the occasion.

1973: In discussion with PM Indira Gandhi on her arrival at Heathrow Airport.

1973: Margaret Thatcher, Britain's education minister, at our residence for dinner after her first visit to India.

November 1973: In conversation with King Birendra of Nepal,
after presenting credentials.

1978, The Netherlands: Amitabh Bachchan with Sujit Kumar and Prem Chopra
(third and fourth respectively from left) at the ambassador's residence for dinner.

February 1979: With President Giscard d'Estaing
at the Élysée Palace, after presenting credentials.

October 1981: PM Indira Gandhi's state visit to
Paris. Kadambari escorting Indira Gandhi to the ornate salon
on the first floor of our residence.

friendly atmosphere of the talks was further vitiated by the British Foreign Secretary Selwyn Lloyd's warnings in Moscow of the grave consequences of a conflict over Berlin because of Khrushchev's ultimatum for the withdrawal of Western troops from the city. Then, not to be left behind, Macmillan added a warning of his own about a very dangerous situation arising if Khrushchev refused to negotiate! Khrushchev resented and rejected the threats, and the talks ended in failure and much personal bitterness between Macmillan and Khrushchev, which led to an ugly scene in the UN General Assembly session in 1960 (see next chapter). The failure of the Moscow talks also put paid to Macmillan's ambition of leadership of the West in negotiations with Soviet Russia. He soon discovered that despite Dulles' threat over Berlin, Washington and Moscow were engaged in bilateral negotiations behind his back.

THE INDIAN FOREIGN OFFICE

The MEA was still a small and intimate place, and its harmonious working environment reflected the warmth of Nehru's personality. Nehru's own quick decision-making also set an example for expeditious disposal of work at all levels in the Foreign Office. Senior officers were easily accessible; and so was the foreign minister.

A few months after my return from Nepal, Foreign Secretary Subimal Dutt handed me a book on Nepal written by a general in the British army who had served in northeastern India. He wanted me to read the book carefully and prepare a two to three-page note objectively summarizing its contents for the prime minister. The intended publisher had sent the manuscript to the Prime Minister Nehru with a letter saying that it was replete with all manner of personal allegations against him and his interventionist policy, which had undermined Nepal's sovereignty, peace and stability etc. The letter also said that they were hesitant to accept the manuscript for publication without bringing it to the prime minister's attention for any comment or advice.

The book was a tissue of lies, misstatements, distortions of facts and false allegations against the prime minister. It was a propagandist piece of writing against Nehru 'the imperialist', the interventionist', 'warmonger' etc. According to the author, the Ranas were good rulers and were popular in Nepal. There was no uprising against the Ranas; it was all Nehru's war on Nepal. Every page of the book reeked with the writer's hatred of India and his vengefulness against Nehru. Dutt read the note in my presence, thanked me for it, and sent it to the prime minister.

The following morning I received a brief note from the prime minister saying he had drafted a reply to the publishers' letter which I could issue! There are not many examples of a prime minister drafting a letter for one of his junior-most officers to sign and send to its destination. I duly issued the letter over my signature. The draft was a perfect precis of the more important points to which I had drawn attention. At the end it thanked the publishing house for the courtesy of bringing this erroneous and prejudiced work to our attention. It added that the facts stated in our letter for their information were easily verifiable; as for publication of the volume, the decision rested entirely with them.

The head of the publishing house wrote back to me the following day thanking me for my letter and saying that they had decided not to accept the book for publication.

For years before joining the Foreign Service I had been writing poems in Hindi, which were published in Hindi journals from time to time. When he was editor of *Illustrated Weekly*, Sardar Khushwant Singh had honoured me by occasionally giving space in that prestigious journal for my own English renderings of some of my poems. In 1957, Harivansh Rai Bachchan,[2] the famous Hindi poet, urged me to publish a selection of my poems because he was confident that some of the experiments I had attempted deserved the attention of Hindi poetry circles. After much hesitation I did bring out, for circulation among friends, a collection of twenty-five poems to which Bachchan contributed an appreciative introduction. I sent a copy of the book to Prime Minister Nehru as an offering from an humble poet to a great writer whose prose touched poetic heights.

I was not expecting anything more than an acknowledgement—if that—from one of the prime minister's personal assistants. What

I received from the great man was a personal letter saying that the previous night he had read all my poems and had liked them!

The MEA was looking around for a Hindi officer of deputy secretary or director's rank, but had not succeeded in finding a suitable person. Panditji asked me whether I knew someone suitable and I mentioned Bachchan, who had a PhD in English literature, was a lecturer in English at Allahabad University, and a prolific poet and prose writer in Hindi. With his mastery of the two languages, I said, Bachchan would be the best man for the job. Panditji said I should give the details to K.P.S. Menon, the foreign secretary, and that he would also speak to him. The foreign secretary spoke to me the following day, and the process of selection was set in motion. Once the necessary formalities were completed, two or three weeks later Bachchan joined the post.

ON SERVING LIQUOR TO GUESTS

All manner of issues pertaining to the IFS's functioning had been under discussion at the highest level on and off during the first decade of Independence. Nehru himself took keen interest in these matters. Now and then, a paper would float down to the ground floor office of the humble US (FSP) revealing the thinking of stalwarts like Secretary General Girija Shankar Bajpai or Foreign Secretary K.P.S. Menon. At a meeting with the prime minister, Foreign Secretary Menon brought up the ticklish issue of the ban on alcoholic drinks being served by our diplomats at dinners and receptions. The idea had been rejected by the prime minister earlier, but Menon persevered and he decided to make another attempt with an argument which he thought would allay the prime minister's hostility. 'A little drink,' said Menon, 'helps loosen the tongue of the guest.'

To which the prime minister rejoined with a clincher: 'Yes, indeed; and what about your own tongues?'

The matter rested there for some years till Menon, now India's ambassador in Moscow, reverted to it on the eve of the prime minister's visit to Moscow in April 1955. He requested the prime minister's permission to serve alcoholic drinks at three functions to be hosted by him during the visit. Menon's main argument was that senior leaders of the Russian government would feel unhappy if vodka and wines were not served at small dinners or other functions for them. While rebutting Menon's argument, the prime minster relented somewhat in the note he recorded on 15 April 1955 for communication to Ambassador Menon:

> At the small dinner to government members the Russians may be served some sherry or light wine or vodka. No champagne to anybody. No Indian present will be served or should accept any alcoholic drink . . . At the reception (one of the three functions Menon had planned) no alcoholic drinks of any kind.[3]

At receptions and dinners hosted by Indian heads of missions, this became the practice for some time. At the next stage, the question of serving alcoholic drinks at receptions hosted by Indian missions in honour of local dignitaries on special occasions was left to the discretion of heads of mission in the light of local protocol and practice. The ban on serving alcoholic drinks at receptions on Independence Day and Republic Day continues to be meticulously observed.

These had been two very busy but rewarding years of my life in many ways. My tenure as US (FSP) began with my promotion to the senior scale in the IFS. It gave me the opportunity to witness the growth and stabilization of the Indian Foreign Service as a confident actor within the Government of India and on the world stage. A very special privilege it was to be noticed and called upon for some small acts of service by one of the tallest world figures of the twentieth century, foreign minister and prime minister of India, Jawaharlal Nehru. All these rewards were capped by a gift of divine grace in the shape of a life companion and co-sharer of the burdens of my official life, Kadambari, the daughter of a celebrated civil servant—Mr V. Viswanathan ICS.

In June 1958 I received orders to proceed to New York to join the permanent mission of India to the UN as first secretary. Khub Chand, the senior joint secretary in charge of administration said to me that the UN posting would give me, at one place, an overview of the world, its problems and the diverse interests and forces in play in international relations, and prepare me for a later appointment as India's permanent representative (PR) to the UN! I did not quite know how to thank him for that flattering advance planning of my career.

chapter nine

CAMPAIGN FOR AFRICA'S
FREEDOM IN THE UN

~

In 1958, the United Nations was still predominantly a club of white nations of Europe and the Americas, and at a pinch they could conjure up enough support to defeat any proposal which affected their interests. Apart from a few Asian members, the organization's strength of sixty or so members included only four African states—Ethiopia, Ghana, Liberia and Sudan. Guinea, whose representatives had been kept waiting at the UN gates, was admitted to membership at the end of 1958. Numerous African countries were still ruled by small European countries like Belgium and Portugal. The UN was not yet fully representative of the world as a whole. The Fourth Committee's work would, therefore, acquire special importance.

On my joining duty in the permanent mission of India to the UN, all work relating to the General Assembly's Fourth Committee—which dealt with decolonization of colonies in Africa and elsewhere ruled by alien powers, and to oversee the work of the Trusteeship Council—was allotted to me. The Trusteeship Council's task was to scrutinize the policies of the colonial powers in their respective territories with the object of hastening the territories' advance towards independence. The examination of the council's reports to the General Assembly formed an important item on the Fourth Committee's agenda.

The council's membership, though equally divided between the countries ruling the Trust Territories and the non-administering members, was somewhat weighted in favour of the former. But it was an open forum with impressive public attendance in the galleries and we, delegates of countries opposed to colonial rule, had ample opportunities of shaming and encouraging colonial powers to do a better job of their responsibilities towards the people they ruled as a sacred trust. The latter's annual reports on their respective Trust Territories were often self-congratulatory and evasive on unpleasant ground realities. The two devices of petitions and the periodic UN visiting missions gave council members a closer view of the actual conditions prevailing in the territories and were helpful in our calling their governments to account. Among the petitioners were some very eminent people, future rulers of their countries—the most impressive and statesmanlike figure among them was Julius Nyerere from Tanganyika.

A large number of islands in the Pacific Ocean captured by American forces from the Japanese in the Second World War had been constituted into a Strategic Trust Territory under the United States' administration. I visited that territory as a member of the UN's visiting mission in 1960. The islands were well governed, the people were prosperous and happy and enjoyed a fair measure of freedom and self-rule. American officials and other US citizens seemed popular and mixed freely with the local inhabitants. American rule of the islands was benign, educational facilities were good and in several places young, local inhabitants formed part of the island's official hierarchy. The general expectation was that in due course these islands would opt for some form of a closer relationship with the United States. Nevertheless, we spoke to them of independence as a goal for a Trust Territory. In the event, the Marshall Islands, Palau and the Federated States of Micronesia all chose independence and were admitted to UN membership in the 1990s. The Trusteeship Council was working with fair speed towards its own demise.

In several islands of Micronesia, when I was introduced to groups of inhabitants as the Indian member of the mission, they wanted me to tell them stories from the Indian epic Ramayana, which I did, at times to the impatience and annoyance of the two British and Belgium members of the visiting mission. The inhabitants I talked with seemed familiar with the names of the epic's heroes and episodes, but the mention of the Mahabharata or of the heroes in that epic evoked no response. I wondered whether their ancestors had ventured into those islands in a post-Ramayana and pre-Mahabharata period. They themselves could not say when, why, how or from where their remote ancestors came to the islands; perhaps they came directly from India or from Bali, Java or some other Indonesian islands where even today stories from the Ramayana are part of the folklore.

In May 1958, when I took over from my predecessor, Rikhi Jaipal, the Trusteeship Council was already discussing modalities for Somalia's independence, and in the next four years another eight or nine Trust Territories would attain independence and become members of the World Organization. Therefore, it was now time for the Fourth Committee to focus on the liberation of the other dependent territories. The information that the colonial powers sent to the UN secretary general on those territories was scant. The secretary general did not do anything with it, nor did the Committee on Information from Non-Self-Governing Territories (NSGTs) do more than take note of it.

Was a UN committee needed just to note that information? Thus far the Fourth Committee had not raised that question, nor invested adequate and sustained effort in delving into the full meaning of the charter provisions on the status and likely future of these colonies. Therefore, the Fourth Committee would have to probe deeply into that information, ask for more and push for the territories' early independence. In my understanding certain words and phrases in Chapter XI of the UN Charter, such as 'sacred trust', 'self-government', 'political aspiration of the peoples', and 'progressive development of their free political institutions' meant that the goal for these territories was the same as for the Trust Territories, namely independence. And clearly, 'sacred trust' implied answerability of the trustees to the UN.

I sought permission from Krishna Menon and our permanent representative to the UN, Ambassador Arthur Lall to begin a vigorous campaign in the Fourth Committee for the independence of African colonies. They both thought it was a good idea. Menon advised me to put together a group of like-minded delegates to join me in the campaign, which I had already taken care of by consulting a few of my colleagues in the Fourth Committee. The initial group, comprising Adnan Pachachi of Iraq, Angie Brooks of Liberia, Yao Turkson of Ghana, Imam Abhikushnu of Indonesia, Najmuddin Al-Rifai of UAR, Rehnama of Iran, Neville Kanakaratne of Sri Lanka, U Tin Maung of Burma, Sidi Baba of Morocco and myself, was joined by another eight or ten young delegates in the Fourth Committee as our campaign began to get noticed. Soon, we were dubbed the Fourth Committee's warriors for Africa's liberation.

The UN's procedure for granting admission to new members is quite simple. The proposal or application for membership has to be considered and approved first by the Security Council. The council's recommendation then goes to the UN General Assembly where a simple majority is sufficient for grant of membership. Guinea had declared its independence from France in early 1958 and applied for UN membership. Fairly early in the UNGA's 13th session, the Security Council had recommended Guinea's admission but the General Committee, which arranges the General Assembly's agenda, had put it down as the last item on the General Assembly's agenda for the session. This meant that Guinea's representatives would not be able to take part in the ongoing session and give the Fourth Committee first-hand information on the situation prevailing in the colonies in Africa. For the UN to disallow Guinea from participating in its ongoing session was incomprehensible to us in the Fourth Committee: We wanted a Guinean delegation to expose the brutal reality of colonial oppression and exploitation in Africa. Therefore we decided to make an issue of the delay, which seemed calculated to accommodate France.

I discussed the matter with my friend Yao Turkson, Ghana's young delegate on the Fourth Committee, and it was decided that at the committee's next meeting he would spring a surprise by proposing, orally or in writing, immediate action by the General Assembly to approve Guinea's UN membership to enable its delegation to take part in the Fourth Committee's ongoing discussion of conditions in African colonies. This was unusual action for a committee, but no rules barred it. I told Yao that if his move led to a procedural wrangle, as indeed it did, I would take over from that point and mobilize the necessary voting support for any procedural move required for the achievement of our objective. The manoeuvre succeeded and the Fourth Committee's assertion in support of a newly independent African country, followed by the appearance of Guinea's representatives in the Fourth Committee on 11 December 1958, created quite a stir in African circles and, of course, also in the UN.

A new era had begun in the Fourth Committee's drive for the elimination of colonial empires in Africa. In welcoming Guinean diplomat Diallo Telli (he went on to become one of the founders of the Organization of African Unity) to the Fourth Committee, many delegations joined me in asserting that the differentiation the founders of the UN had made between the two groups of colonial possessions—the Trust Territories and the Non-Self-Governing Territories—was not justified, that all colonial dependencies were latently sovereign and equally deserving of independence and UN membership. Soon decisions were made by the committee to invite petitioners from and send visiting missions to the NSGTs.

This unavoidably put us at odds with the colonial powers who claimed that they alone were competent to say whether an NSGT should or should not be considered fit for independence. In other words, colonial powers were free to integrate their colonial possessions in their metropolitan territories. In the second half of the twentieth century such views could only be described as stale emanations of a frozen nineteenth-century mindset. Portugal was the most inexorable proponent of this obscurantist idea. But Australia and, occasionally, even France seemed to subscribe to this kind of thinking.

Efforts never ceased on the part of the colonial powers to propose or initiate steps to retain some kind of control on, or preferential links with, their colonies. The Fourth Committee was watchful and prevented or fought off all such moves. Belgium and France, for example, proposed to associate their colonies with the European Economic Community. The measure would bring the territories' trade policies under the overall direction of the community and the latter's tariff barriers would deny the territories the right to decide on their own trade links with other countries. Their resources would also remain under the exclusive control of their erstwhile masters. The move was rejected by the Fourth Committee and by the concerned territories. France's attempt to rope its dependencies into a union with it was frustrated by Guinea's unilateral declaration of independence from France. Senegal, Mali and other territories followed Guinea's example a year later.

All over Africa, change was swift and its sweep wide and throughout the UN's 13th session, the Fourth Committee remained intensely occupied with devising ways to hasten independence of colonies to avoid the spread of incipient violence. Congo, ruled by Belgium, had already exploded in violence, which could spread to other areas of the continent, posing serious threat of a general upheaval and further polarization of international politics. When Belgium could no longer maintain its control on Congo, its retreat from that huge colony precipitated the independence of the neighbouring Trust Territory of Ruanda–Urundi, also ruled by Belgium. On the eve of Congo's independence, Brussels proposed the Trust Territory's merger in Congo's troubled, pro-Belgium province of Katanga, which had declared its independence from Congo! The move was promptly rejected by the Fourth Committee. Ruanda and Urundi were admitted to UN membership as two separate, independent states in 1962. Belgium had done little to prepare its colonies for self-government by educating the people, creating civil service cadres and legislative bodies etc. The independence of the three countries was followed by varying periods of violence and instability.

The question of the mandated territory of South West Africa, administered by the Union of South Africa, was an important item on the Fourth Committee's agenda. A Good Offices Committee (GOC), established by the Fourth Committee to engage in talks with the South African government had, quite unwisely, been drawn into consideration of a proposal floated by the Union government to partition the mandated territory. The Good Offices Committee had clearly exceeded its terms of reference as partition was against the terms of the mandate. To deter the South African government and the Good Offices Committee from any further consideration of the idea, warning notes were sounded in the Fourth Committee about the matter being taken to the International Court of Justice to enforce the terms of the mandate, or to convert South West Africa into a Trust Territory under direct UN administration. Clearly, the struggle for South West Africa's independence was going to be a long and trying one. The territory achieved independence and Namibia became a member of the UN in 1990.

An even worse case was that of Southern Rhodesia, a British colony. Its colonial government had proposed to relocate several black reserves from the richer, southern part of the territory in the northern part to make the former a white majority area, which would be absorbed in the Union of South Africa or become another racist white country in Africa. The poor northern part with its African majority could then decide its own separate future after ascertaining the wishes of its inhabitants in a referendum or by some other mode of consultation. Regrettably, the British government had lent support to the plan, which was rejected by the Fourth Committee.

It is not that there was a clear-cut division in the Fourth Committee between the colonial powers and their supporters on one side of the aisle and the supporters of decolonization on the other. The US and Canada and several European and Latin American delegations voted with those advocating rapid decolonization. My colleagues and I were continually in touch with the other side in a determined search for consensus and compromise on resolutions of fundamental importance. As a result, towards the end of the 13th session, we noticed a change in the attitudes of the colonial powers' delegations from unbending self-righteousness to thoughtful tolerance of constructive criticism and even a willingness to cooperate in the search for consensus.

For us who had spearheaded the Fourth Committee's thrust for independence of all colonies, the most important issue now was the future of the remaining colonies in the continent of Africa which were thirsting for liberty and seething with unrest. In consultation with my Asian and African colleagues I drafted and co-sponsored with them several resolutions, the effect of which was to put pressure on colonial rulers for better performance and to spread the message in Africa of the UN's keen and active interest in their early independence and in the well-being of their people. The most important of those resolutions was on the Attainment of Independence by NSGTs. While the draft resolution emphasized that there would be no compromise on the independence of colonies, its tone and wording were moderate. The resolution was adopted by the Fourth Committee and later by the assembly plenary unanimously.

That landmark achievement of the Fourth Committee triggered an even more important event, namely, the issue, on 14 December 1960, of the *UN Declaration on the Granting of Independence to Colonial Countries and Peoples*, sponsored by the delegation of the Soviet Union. It was followed by the creation of the Decolonization Committee of seventeen members, under Indian chairmanship, to monitor implementation of the declaration on the colonies. An immediate and most gratifying result of these moves was the independence of sixteen African countries and their admission to UN membership during the 15th GA session in 1960.

The Fourth Committee's role in unleashing these developments is best described by one of the UN's most experienced and respected statesmen, Ambassador Frederick H. Boland, permanent representative of Ireland to the UN, who was chairman of the Fourth Committee throughout the 13th session in 1958. At the end of the committee's last meeting in December 1958, Ambassador Boland delivered a most moving closing address, which is summarized in the Fourth Committee's summary records as follows:

He [Ambassador Boland] was immensely proud to have served as chairman of what could justly claim to have been the hardest-working committee in the history of the United Nations. The Fourth Committee had met not only more than 30 per cent more frequently than any other committee of the present session; it had met more frequently than any committee of the United Nations ever before, the present meeting being the 103rd of the session.

Great issues of policy were precisely what had been engaging the committee during the past three months. The problem of South West Africa, the future of Togoland, the destiny of the two Trust Territories of the Cameroons, the independence and future welfare of the Trust Territory of Somaliland, the determination of the frontier between Somaliland and Ethiopia—those were not issues of secondary importance or of merely abstract or academic interest. They were practical problems of great difficulty, of immediate concern and of immense consequence, involving not only the well-being and happiness of millions of human beings but the whole future pattern of political relationships in Africa and between the countries of Africa and the rest of the world.

He [Ambassador Boland] was not trying to pose as an authority on the questions with which the committee dealt. Many members of the committee had far longer and deeper acquaintance with those problems than he. But it was impossible to sit in the chair, as he had done throughout the past three months, without learning at least something. One of the things which had been borne in upon him during his occupancy of the chair had been a sense of the enormous significance of the work being done in the Fourth Committee, not only from the point of view of future world relations but from the point of view of the future of the United Nations itself.

An English statesman had once spoken of calling a new world into existence to redress the balance of the old. Aided by the Fourth Committee, and indeed owing in no small measure to its tireless exertions, a new world was emerging among the dependent territories throughout the world which would not only leave the balance of the United Nations very different from what it had been but would confront the world community as it was today with new challenges, new demands on its sense of responsibility and on its capacity for constructive statesmanship.

chapter ten

THE CONGO TRAGEDY AND
A FAILED WORLD LEADERS' SUMMIT

~

The year 1960 was truly Africa's year in the UN and as such, it is deserving of a special chapter in the world organization's history. However, two other events of the UNGA's 15th session are equally noteworthy—the tragedy of the Congo, and the failed summit of world leaders at the UN.

Belgium had ruled Congo with the help of Belgian civil servants and an army of Congolese troops commanded by Belgian officers. Belgian officials and commercial establishments had methodically robbed the country of its abundant wealth of diamonds, precious gems and other rare metals and minerals. When violence erupted in several provinces of Congo, which Brussels could not control, it entered into negotiations with Joseph Kasavubu and Patrice Lumumba who had led the political agitation for independence. Brussels agreed to grant Congo what in fact turned out to be no more than a form of independence. For, even as under the Loi Fondamentale (Constitution), a parliamentary government comprising an assembly, the Senate, an elected constitutional President (Joseph Kasavubu) and an elected prime minister (Patrice Lumumba) was installed, Belgian civil and military officers retained control of the administration and the Congolese National Army and the country's immense resources.

Since independence brought no improvement in the pay scales and service conditions of the common soldier, mutiny broke out in the army against its Belgian officers, resulting in the breakdown of law and order in the country. Shocked by this unexpected threat to its interests, Brussels dispatched Belgian troops to reoccupy its former colony. Fearing loss of the country's independence, President Kasavubu and Prime Minister Lumumba jointly appealed to the UN for military and economic assistance to safeguard Congo's sovereignty and to stabilize its economy. The Security Council called upon Belgian troops to leave the country immediately; it also agreed to provide military help and economic and technical assistance to restore normality in the country.

The UN Secretary General Dag Hammarskjöld then rapidly put together a 20,000-strong multinational force from twenty different countries, including a brigade from Pakistan. In addition, some 1100 international personnel were sent to Congo to implement the civil assistance programme. Meanwhile, taking advantage of the prevailing confusion, Moise Tshombe, with Belgian support, declared independence of his province, Katanga, which contained 70 or 80 per cent of Congo's diamond and mineral wealth.

In order to prevent Katanga's secession and establish UN presence in that province, Hammarskjöld himself flew into the province on 12 August 1960 with four planeloads of Swedish troops under the UN flag to be stationed in Elizabethville, capital of the Katanga province. This should have led to the withdrawal of Belgian military units from Katanga, but it did not. Besides, the secretary general's action angered Prime Minister Lumumba who felt that he had been bypassed. And it incensed Britain and the United States, who had openly supported Tshombe and his action to declare his province's independence to protect their own commercial interests in Katanga. The Soviet Union, on the other hand, was in favour of firm action against Katanga's secession. So, the already complex problem of Congo got dragged into the vortex of the Cold War.

While Moscow favoured Lumumba, who enjoyed countrywide popularity, Britain and the US backed President Kasavubu with whatever support he needed, widening the breach between him and Lumumba. The American intelligence agency, the CIA, had already, quite unjustly, condemned Patrice Lumumba 'a dangerous communist', for whose elimination plans were hatched.

With Belgian, British and American political and military support, Kasavubu divested Lumumba of prime ministership. He also demanded the withdrawal of all foreign forces under UN command, and Indonesia, Morocco and the UAR promptly agreed to recall their contingents.

Joseph Iléo, whom Kasavubu appointed prime minister in Lumumba's place, was so ineffective that he could not even put together his cabinet. Colonel Joseph Désiré Mobutu, a former petty clerk, whom Lumumba had appointed commander of the Leopold Garrison, staged a coup and in connivance with President Kasavubu ousted the dummy Prime Minister Iléo. Mobutu's forces captured Lumumba and transferred him to Katanga, where Moise Tshombe had that charismatic African nationalist leader brutally murdered in February 1961, leading to further deterioration of the law and order situation in the country. The Indian combatant brigade that Nehru reluctantly sent to Congo on Hammarskjöld's pressing appeals succeeded in restoring law and order, and Tshombe moved over to the neighbouring, white-ruled Southern Rhodesia from where he continued his war against the UN with Western support.

Britain and the USA had suffered a setback and they started putting pressure on Hammarskjöld to resolve the Katanga problem not by force but politically through talks with Moise Tshombe. Under British pressure, Hammarskjöld, who had arrived in Leopoldville in September 1961, decided to go to Southern Rhodesia to meet with Tshombe but his plane crashed en route, ending the life of a strong and dedicated international civil servant who had wanted to save Congo from an impending civil war, and keep the newly independent country out of the Cold War.

WORLD LEADERS' SUMMIT

The idea of a four-power summit meeting of the US, Russia, Britain and France was mooted by Nikita Khrushchev in January 1958 to resolve differences that had arisen over his demand for the withdrawal of Western forces from Berlin and his threat to handover control of the city to the East German government. The US–Russia contacts in 1959 and a meeting of the foreign ministers of the four countries in Geneva had helped reduce tensions. Vice President Nixon's visit to Russia in July was followed by Khrushchev's own visit to the United States in September 1959, which had, from all accounts, gone well.

Moscow's unilateral announcement on 14 February 1960 to reduce Russia's Armed Forces by one-third was indicative of Khrushchev's sincere desire to reach an understanding with the Western powers on disarmament and other issues. A month later, in March 1960 the Soviet Union and the three Western powers discussed Berlin and their respective disarmament plans at the Disarmament Conference in Geneva in a cooperative and friendly manner. These exchanges seemed to have cleared the way for a meeting of Khrushchev, de Gaulle, Macmillan and Eisenhower in May 1960 in Paris. But all of a sudden all hopes for progress were shattered by the U-2 incident.

On May 1, Russia shot down an American U-2 spy plane, which had taken off from an American base in Peshawar in Pakistan, during its flight over Russian territory. The pilot, Gary Powers, captured alive by Russia, was living evidence of the spying nature of the mission. Americans did not know that he had been captured and kept issuing statements about 'a lost plane of NASA on a civilian mission', or 'an unauthorized flight lost over Russian territory'. Khrushchev exposed these lies by revealing that Gary Powers was alive and had confessed to his mission of espionage. The Russian leader felt betrayed and angry and roundly condemned the United States for violation of Russia's borders and international law.

An expression of regret at an appropriate level, and the assurance Khrushchev wanted that the US would stop violating the USSR's borders in the future might have restored calm and saved the four-power summit meeting scheduled for mid-May in Paris. But instead of any such conciliatory move, in a press conference on 11 May 1960, President Eisenhower accepted responsibility for the U-2 flight as part of the various programmes undertaken by his government to secure military intelligence. Understandably, that was viewed by Khrushchev as another affront and the lack of desire to settle differences through friendly negotiations. Regardless, Eisenhower, Khrushchev, Macmillan and de Gaulle met in Paris on 16 May but, alas, only to exchange accusations and harsh words and to announce the summit's failure. Khrushchev, unwisely, cancelled his invitation to Eisenhower to visit Moscow, which the latter had planned for in July.

Khrushchev then sent personal letters to several heads of government, including Prime Minister Nehru, requesting them to join him at the UN in New York in September–October 1960, for a collective high-level review of the world situation. Prime Minister Nehru was sceptical about such a large gathering of world leaders achieving anything, but, nevertheless, arrived in New York on 24 September and attended the UN General Assembly meeting the following day. Eisenhower and Khrushchev had already addressed the General Assembly without holding out any hope of a meeting between them. When Prime Minister Nehru called on Eisenhower, the US President told him that he wanted to talk to Khrushchev, but he did not know how to deal with him because Khrushchev kept hurling abuse and accusations at him. Nehru's advice was that in the interest of world peace a meeting between him and Khrushchev was necessary, but perhaps a little time should be allowed for tempers to cool and then the President might himself make a direct or indirect conciliatory gesture. Prime Minister Nehru had emphasized that in his judgement only a meeting between them would help reduce tensions which were causing great concern and anxiety in the world.

In his speech to the General Assembly, President Eisenhower had emphasized the necessity of espionage by suitable means of the ongoing military activity in the USSR and commended his 'open skies' proposal, which would exclude the possibility of a surprise attack like the one on Hawaii by Japan. Khrushchev's speech was a sweeping condemnation of American hypocrisy and the lack of sincerity in Washington's professions of peace. He also criticized Anglo-American machinations in Congo and alleged that Secretary General Hammarskjöld was in league with the West, was inimical to Soviet Russia's interests in Congo and Africa generally, and that the

UN operation in the conflict-ridden Congo was being directed by the United States and Britain.

Khrushchev proposed Hammarskjöld's replacement by a Troika of three secretaries general, one each from the East and the West and the third from a non-aligned country. Prime Minister Nehru was opposed to the idea of Troika not only because he had full confidence in Hammarskjöld, whom he regarded as an able, effective and impartial UN secretary general but also because he felt Khrushchev's idea was impracticable. A Troika, he felt, would split the UN secretariat three ways and render it ineffective. Khrushchev stuck to his idea, but it gathered no support among the heads of government present in New York, except those from the eastern block.

MACMILLAN'S THEATRICS AND KHRUSHCHEV'S SHOE THUMPING

During Prime Minster Nehru's month-long stay in New York, I was on duty with him for nearly three weeks to keep his papers in good order, keep track of his appointments and be with him in all his movements in the town. One late afternoon while he was talking to a couple of African delegates in the big UN lounge, I noticed lights in the plenary hall even though there was no programme scheduled in the chamber at that time. I discreetly opened one of the glass doors and from behind a pillar saw a strange scene. Five or six officers of the British mission were sitting in different sections of the hall and Prime Minister Macmillan on the speaker's podium was declaiming, making gestures with his arms and hands, pausing as if waiting for clapping to end, roaming his gaze over an invisible audience, bowing slightly as if to acknowledge applause and then resuming the drill. The microphones were not on and I could not hear what he was mumbling, but clearly the prime minister of Britain was rehearsing his next day's address to the UN General Assembly!

Quietly, I made my exit from the plenary hall. Prime Minister Nehru was taking leave of his interlocutors when I joined him. As we went past the plenary hall's main glass doors on our way to the escalator leading to the ground floor and the way out, I said: 'Sir, tomorrow we are going to see some theatre at the plenary meeting.' 'Why? What kind of theatre?' he asked. I told him that Mr Macmillan was rehearsing his speech from the podium, making all kinds of theatrical gestures with his arms and hands. Mr Nehru could not believe it. 'Are you sure?' he asked. I said I had just witnessed the drama; Macmillan was still on the podium and he even had an audience, a few officials of the British mission sitting in different sections of the hall to give him an audience's reactions, so to speak. 'Strange; very strange,' said the prime minister, and we continued down the escalator to the ground floor and on our way to the Carlyle Hotel.

The following day Macmillan was even more theatrical than in the rehearsal the previous day. Physical gestures apart, he would speak a few sentences, then point tauntingly in the direction of Khrushchev, accusing him of creating tensions by demanding withdrawal of Western troops from West Berlin. He rejected Khrushchev's threat to hand over control of the city of Berlin to the Government of East Germany. He justified the necessity of espionage because of lack of openness on the Soviet Union's part. He did not mention the U-2 incident even once; instead he praised Eisenhower's 'open skies' proposal. The plenary hall was filled to capacity and Macmillan's theatrics drew frequent applause. But it was not a speech for peace and reconciliation; it was a performance to tease and taunt, to challenge and humiliate Khrushchev.

At one point Khrushchev shouted at one of Macmillan's provocative remarks: 'That is a lie.' But Macmillan went on in the same vein, provocative gestures and finger-pointing accompanying his words. In uncontrollable anger Khrushchev took off one of his shoes and thumped his desk with it three or four times. A moment's silence followed and Macmillan, pretending to be a bit puzzled asked: 'Will someone translate that for me?' After waiting for a ripple of subdued laughter to subside, he proceeded with the rest of his speech, which was heard in silence. Suddenly the audience seemed to become aware of the seriousness of the situation and Macmillan's peroration fell rather flat.

Krishna Menon did not think it was the right kind of speech for the occasion. Prime Minister Nehru turned to look at me—I was sitting right behind him—and said: 'You saw all that yesterday!' Foreign Secretary Subimal Dutt in the Indian delegation, alone, was impressed with Macmillan's performance. In his book, *With Nehru in the Foreign Office*,[1] he describes Macmillan as 'in his best parliamentary form'! But the UNGA plenary is not the House of Commons where, in the cut and thrust of debate, aggressive posturing is in order and even subjecting your peers on the opposition benches to ridicule is considered fair game. This was a very special gathering of a large number of heads of government who had come to the UN to calm international tensions and engage in a joint search for solutions to issues of war and peace. Macmillan's speech had only added to existing tension and mistrust.

As delegates were rising to leave the hall, an officer of the Russian mission came running to me to say that Khrushchev wanted to have a word with the prime minister and was coming to where we were waiting for the crowd to thin before leaving. I alerted the prime minister and as he rose from his seat to greet the Russian leader he was just three or four steps away. Khrushchev said to the prime minister: 'If you are not doing something terribly important just now, please come to my place for a drink.' The prime minister asked me about his next engagement and I said he had a couple of hours free before dinner, and so he told Khrushchev he would join him at his place.

A DRINK OF VODKA WITH KHRUSHCHEV AND NEHRU

When we reached the Russian Consulate General building, where Khrushchev was staying, its front door opened without my even knocking. Khrushchev was already there to greet the prime minister. Before stepping in, the prime minister told me in Hindi to follow him. I lingered and mumbled something about Khrushchev might be wanting to talk to him alone. 'Arre nahin, aa jao, lekin notes nahin lena,' said Mr Nehru in Hindi. (No, no; come along but don't take notes.) After a warm handshake with Khrushchev, the prime minister introduced me to him saying, 'This young man keeps track of my engagements. He is our expert on decolonization.' Khrushchev gave me a warm handshake and, beckoning me to follow them, led the prime minister hand in hand, to a medium-sized room on the ground floor with two tables, a long one laden with a great variety of cuts of meats and vegetables and an assortment of cheeses, nuts, biscuits and breads, and a smaller table on which were arrayed half a dozen choicest brands of vodka, two or three bottles of Russian wines, two jars filled with orange and tomato juice and a number of small vodka glasses and tumblers. There were two or three sofa chairs placed along one of the walls. But the two leaders chose to keep standing as they had been sitting in the assembly hall for three or four hours at a stretch. The only other person present was Khrushchev's interpreter.

Khrushchev asked the prime minister how well he knew Macmillan. But before pausing for an answer, he added that he didn't like him: 'He is a warmonger; he is not for peace and friendship. He came to Moscow, but our meetings achieved nothing, because all the time he was playing games, issuing threats. He is a liar. Is he the West's leader?' He then picked up a bottle of vodka and slowly poured three small vodka glasses with that elixir of Russian life. While the filled glasses lay at the table Prime Minister Nehru told Khrushchev that he knew Macmillan well enough, that he had visited India in 1958 for talks on bilateral relations and on the world situation. Macmillan had wanted to know whether in India's view it was a good time to start talks with Russian leaders to reduce Cold War tensions, and he had told Macmillan that any time was good time to talk peace and friendship. Mr Nehru added that Vice President Radhakrishnan had given him similar advice. Khrushchev intervened to say that during his visit to Moscow, Macmillan did not talk peace and friendship; he held out threats.

Khrushchev then picked up a vodka-filled glass and handed it to Mr Nehru. He looked at me and picked up the second glass, and as he took a step towards me I hung back thinking I might ask for orange juice. My prime minister said to me in Hindi: 'Peetey ho to le lo.' (If you drink, take it.) So I took the glass from Khrushchev, and following the prime minister I started sipping it drop by drop.

Khrushchev knocked down his vodka, but mercifully there was some more talk before he poured the second round. He looked at me and then at Mr Nehru and said: 'When I offer a glass of vodka to a young man in Russia, he knocks it down like this (he made the gesture) even before I pick up mine.' He looked at me and said, 'Come on young man.' Khrushchev was quite relaxed now and laughed a little at his own remark; so did Mr Nehru.

He then asked the prime minister what he should do. 'You know what Americans have been doing; the U-2 flights and other violations of Russia's borders and international law. Eisenhower refuses to assure me that he will put an end to this mischief. Without such an assurance, what is the use of talking with him? I thought he is a man of honour and peace; he has gone through a big war, seen so much death and destruction. But this is what he does by way of preparing for a meeting with me. U-2 is not the only violation; there were two more this year.'

The prime minister said that war was not an option for the world's two most powerful countries. The world wanted peace. He (Khrushchev) and Eisenhower in particular carried a heavy responsibility; the whole world looked to them to strengthen peace. What had happened—U-2 and the rest—was bad, but from his (Nehru's) meeting with Eisenhower, he had formed the impression that the President wanted to talk with Khrushchev but seemed inclined to let some time pass, the situation to cool and then look for a way out of the present impasse. Mr Nehru said he could not see how U-2-type activity could now continue. As a friend he would say that when the time is right, Russia, in pursuit of its traditional policy of peace and friendship, should be ready for talks.

'You, Mr Nehru, are the world's hope for peace, said Khrushchev, and filled three fresh little glasses with vodka. He left the prime minister's second glass at the table as he saw that he was not even close to finishing his first. He noticed that I was holding an empty glass, took it from me and handed me a freshly filled one.

The substantial part of the talk was over but while Khrushchev and I were holding our respective refills, there was a little inconsequential chit-chat: 'How long are you staying in New York? We should meet again'—that sort of thing. Hammarskjöld's name was mentioned rather disapprovingly by Khrushchev. 'He is pro-West, hurting African and

Russian interests in Congo.' Mr Nehru said that Hammarskjöld was no favourite of Britain or America, that in fact they were creating many difficulties for him in the UN's Congo operation.

The talk between the two leaders was slow because of the interpretation from Russian to English and from English to Russian. We had been with Khrushchev for about forty-five minutes. Khrushchev saw me looking at my watch; our eyes met, he raised his glass and drained it in one long swallow. I did the same. I looked at the prime minister and he nodded and I said to the interpreter that it was time for the prime minister to leave for his next appointment, which he communicated in Russian to Khrushchev who, then, accompanied the prime minister to the car, shook hands with him, then with me and we left for the Carlyle.

Panic gripped me, and also shame, for having been guilty of a serious breach of etiquette and good manners in the presence of my prime minister. He had graciously told me to accept the vodka glass from Khrushchev by way of courtesy to the host, and I should have sipped it slowly as he, a non-drinker basically, had done. I apologized to him for my folly. He smiled and asked, 'Are you all right?' I replied in the affirmative, but to test my level of inebriation further he asked what his first two appointments were the following morning. My answer must have reassured him somewhat. Then he said, 'There is something you had mentioned for later this week?' 'Yes, Sir, a thirty- to forty-minute walk in Central Park; it is all arranged.' I gave the date and time, and he was satisfied that vodka had not affected me much. He was not angry or unhappy about my conduct; he was worried about me! 'Tum kitna pee sakte ho, bhai?' he asked. (How much can you drink, dear fellow?) 'Not much, Sir: The minimum necessary in such circumstances,' I replied and apologized once again.

We had reached the Carlyle and I escorted him to his suite. Before taking leave, I apologized once again; he must have seen guilt on my face, and he placed a forgiving hand on my shoulder and said: 'Khrushchev was feeling dejected and embarrassed about hitting the desk with his shoe to disrupt Macmillan's speech. Our company seemed to lift his spirit somewhat.' Then the usual 'goodnight' and 'I will see you at breakfast tomorrow morning'.

The great man never mentioned a word about my impudence to anyone. Had Foreign Secretary Dutt heard of it from the prime minister, I am sure I would have been summoned for a well-deserved comeuppance.

The following day, Mr Nehru loved his walk in the park. At one point he noticed a few squirrels and remarked on their size. 'More than double our Indian squirrels in size.' As one or two kept dancing around him with hope in their little eyes, I gave him a handful of unshelled peanuts to throw at the squirrels one by one. They shelled and ate them with amazing skill and speed and turned to him for more. That amused the prime minister. I handed him a small paper bag full of peanuts and suggested that he empty it a little distance off the walking track. The lovely little animals jumped at the loot, leaving us alone to proceed on our walk.

One Sunday I took him out on a long drive in upcountry New York, where leaves were just beginning to acquire their gorgeous autumn hues. Another free morning Kadambari and I accompanied him to the recently opened Guggenheim Museum of Modern Art. There, Kadambari, who had walked up and down the display ramp of the museum several times, acted as his guide, drawing his attention to special features of some of the works displayed. He needed and appreciated this kind of relaxation and a change from sitting long hours in the assembly hall.

THE NAM INITIATIVE TO EASE TENSIONS IS UNSUCCESSFUL

The 15th session was going badly insofar as the grand summit was concerned; it only seemed to add to the intensity of the Cold War. So, Nasser, Nehru, Nkrumah, Soekarno and Tito met on 30 September to take counsel together, and they decided to jointly sponsor the following resolution:

The General Assembly, deeply concerned with the recent deterioration in international relations which threatens the world with grave consequences,

Aware of the great expectancy of the world that this assembly will assist in helping to prepare the way for the easing of the world tension,

Conscious of the grave and urgent responsibility that rests on the United Nations to initiate helpful efforts,

Requests, as a first urgent step, the President of the United States of America and the chairman of the Council of Ministers of the Union of Soviet Socialist Republics to renew their contacts interrupted recently, so that their declared willingness to find solutions of all the outstanding problems by negotiation will be progressively implemented.

Prime Minister Nehru moved the draft resolution at the end of a short speech in the General Assembly on 3 October. The speech, which I thought was the most constructive of all in that whole session in content and spirit, was received well because it was in tune with the sombre mood of the session following Macmillan's performance. Apart from highlighting the world's concern over the Cold War and its desire for peace, he emphasized the special responsibility of the two great powers and their leaders to halt the drift towards confrontation and conflict. On the question of disarmament, to which he attached great importance, he uttered a prophetic warning; in the event of the leaders' failure, he said, to take effective measures in the next three or four years, all hope for disarmament would be lost, with grave consequences.

On 5 October, when the debate began on the five-power resolution, Prime Minister Menzies of Australia moved an amendment to the operative paragraph that would substitute for the US–USSR summit, a meeting of the heads of government of France, Britain, US and USSR. It was a trivial attempt to sabotage the five-power resolution—Mr Nehru condemned it as such—and the amendment was rejected by the assembly.

Meanwhile American lobbyists were busy arm-twisting delegates and their governments in their respective capital cities. As a result, the Argentine delegation tabled another amendment which would have the two governments of the USA and the USSR, instead of the

President of the USA and chairman of the Council of Ministers of the USSR, resume contact. This was supported from the speaker's rostrum by the US Secretary of State Christian Herter, and was approved by the assembly. The sponsors saw little merit in the amended resolution, for the two governments, through their embassies, were in contact any way. The amended resolution was put to vote and was lost for want of the requisite two-thirds majority of members present and voting.

This was all Macmillan's work. A few days later, a friend from the British mission said to me: 'How could you guys leave out our prime minister from a summit meeting with the Russian leaders? You may not think so, but he believes he is at the very top of world leadership!' A day or two before the voting session of the assembly, Macmillan and Menzies had gone to Washington to dissuade President Eisenhower from responding positively to the non-aligned nations' appeals and pressures.

The 15th session had assembled quite a few orators, such as Sékou Touré of Mali (in French), Macmillan (in English) and Castro of Cuba (in Spanish). In a four-hour-long oration Castro used every possible combination of words to castigate the United States as a dangerous, colonial-imperialist, aggressive power. President Soekarno mounted the rostrum in a field marshall's uniform with two ADCs covering his right and left flanks. The one on his right would hand him a sheet of paper from which he would read his prepared speech, and then pass the same to the ADC on his left. The burden of his oration, which he repeated several times, was: 'Colonialism is a wounded tiger, more dangerous now than before; the world should be on guard.' He had little to say on the present and real danger which had brought thirty heads of state government to the UN General Assembly.

The prime minister of recently independent Nigeria, Sir Abubakar Tafawa Balewa gave one of the four or five best speeches in that session with a lot of information about the conditions prevailing in his country—little education, great poverty and a stagnant economy. He laid no blame on the administering power—Britain—but highlighted the myriad tasks confronting him for which Nigeria, like other newly independent countries, needed peace. He highlighted, in particular, a countrywide programme he had launched, involving the use of television, to promote universal primary education.

NEHRU ON INDIA'S NEEDS AND THE KASHMIR PROBLEM

Before leaving for New York, Prime Minister Nehru had inaugurated an experimental TV station in Delhi. While travelling back to the hotel, after Sir Abubakar's speech, I said to him, while India after thirteen years of independence was just beginning to experiment with TV, Nigeria, independent only for a year, was using TV for its countrywide educational programme! I can never forget the few words he said in response to my thoughtless taunt. 'I have many things to do,' said Mr Nehru, 'and very few resources to do them with for 400 million people. What I am trying to do is to lay the foundations in all areas of our country's present and future needs. As more resources become available, your generation can build on these foundations. My priorities could be wrong, but priorities can be reviewed from time to time and changed if necessary.' The great man never showed the slightest annoyance or impatience with my queries.

On another occasion, Pakistan came up in one of our casual conversations while travelling from one appointment in the city to another. I asked whether there was a solution to the problem of Kashmir and what it might be. His answer was brief and prophetic: 'There are problems in human affairs to which there are no solutions.' He paused for a moment and added, 'except Time.' That was wisdom of the ages in a nutshell.

Occasionally, Mr Nehru too had questions for me. He was greeted very warmly wherever he went by ordinary people. If his car stopped at a traffic light, the vehicle would be surrounded by admirers wanting to shake his hand or ask for his autograph. One day he said to me, 'People of this country are so good, so friendly and warm-hearted. What is wrong with their rulers whom these same people elect to high positions?' 'Power, Sir. Consciousness of the immense economic and military power they wield when in office,' I replied. 'That's it, I suppose,' said the prime minister.

chapter eleven

INDIA'S LEADERS AT THE UN

~

R.VENKATARAMAN: FUTURE PRESIDENT OF INDIA

During the annual UNGA sessions, we had opportunities of meeting
and working with comparatively young members of the Indian
Parliament who formed part of the Indian delegation. Among them
there were some future leaders of the country and quite a number of
men and women who would achieve distinction as cabinet ministers,
ambassadors and leaders in other fields. Mr R. Venkataraman, finance
minister in the Congress government of Tamil Nadu at the time, was
a man of sound parliamentary and ministerial experience. He was
a prominent member of India's delegations to the UNGA sessions
successively for a decade or more, and rose to become India's defence
minister, vice president and President successively. A popular figure
in UN circles, he was known for his experience and wisdom in
financial and administrative matters. I do not think it ever occurred
to anyone in Delhi to put him up as a candidate for the secretary
general's post following Hammarskjöld's death in 1961. Neither
Ambassador Arthur Lall—whom Krishna Menon was inclined to
sponsor—nor our ambassador to the USA, B.K. Nehru, whom the
Americans would have preferred as an acceptable Indian candidate for
the post, had a decent enough chance. The Americans were opposed
to Lall and the Russians were not enthusiastic about B.K. Nehru. An
Asian secretary general was favoured and Ambassador U. Thant, a

decent, non-controversial gentleman, who was Burma's permanent representative to the UN, soon became the obvious choice for the post and was elected.

ATAL BIHARI VAJPAYEE: FUTURE PRIME MINISTER OF INDIA

Of the Indian parliamentarians I met in the UNGA sessions of 1958–61, Mr Atal Bihari Vajpayee left the deepest impression, by virtue of his easy informality and friendliness, his sense of humour, his probing intellect and pragmatic wisdom and his keen interest in diverse aspects of international relations. He was a young man in his early thirties with a lean figure and attractive personality that made its presence felt equally in big gatherings and in small friendly company. Mr Vajpayee had been elected to the lower house of the Indian Parliament (Lok Sabha) in 1957, and his New York visit was perhaps his first appearance abroad. A day or two after his arrival in New York, I got a telephone call from an official in Prime Minister Nehru's house to say that Panditji (Nehru) wanted me, personally, to take special care of Mr Vajpayee, a young man of great leadership potential; that I should introduce him to young leaders at the UN and help him in every way. Mr Vajpayee was not only very pleasant company, our numerous informal chats were also my education in Indian politics.

While in the UN premises, he would spend most of his time listening to speeches in the assembly plenary, rather than declaim in committees speeches written for him by bureaucrats in the permanent mission. Nevertheless, I took him round to all the various committees, introduced a lot of delegates from different parts of the world to him, showed him round some sights in the city, took him home to our apartment on Central Park West now and then and gave a big dinner for him at home with a number of UN luminaries. Vajpayeeji never forgot the dinner at our residence. When we met in Delhi eighteen or twenty years later—he was foreign minister in Prime Minister Morarji Desai's government—he specifically recalled the dinner at our residence saying: 'I do not remember much from those days, but that dinner in your home was special.' I myself had many happy memories of the time I spent with him in New York, but I had totally forgotten about the dinner!

Much later during my appointment as foreign secretary, and subsequently, I saw a little more of him and had occasions to hear his spellbinding speeches in Parliament or in public meetings elsewhere, and my admiration and respect for him grew with every encounter we had. His speeches in Hindi were a fiesta of wit and wisdom, with solid substance, gently biting humour and an occasional self-deprecatory barb, all woven together in a combination hard to match. In my long life I have not known a more powerful and persuasive speaker in simple, easily understandable Hindi.

INDIA'S NUCLEAR TESTS

In the summer of 1995, I was doing some work on nuclear disarmament at the Rajiv Gandhi Foundation, Vajpayeeji was then leader of the Opposition, having been foreign minister between 1977–79 in the Janata government. Professor M.L. Sondhi, a confidante of Vajpayeeji's, called on me to say that the great man was remembering me. A day or two later Sondhi accompanied me to his residence. After a bit of small talk our conversation veered round to various aspects of disarmament and Vajpayeeji suddenly asked, 'Bharat ka ek dhamaka aur hona chahiye.' (Rasgotraji, what do you think? Isn't it time for one more Indian nuclear explosion?) I responded, 'Vajpayeeji, one dhamaka (explosion) had taken place way back in 1974. It did not lead to India's recognition as a credible nuclear-weapon power. So if you want to do it, one "dhamaka" will not be good enough. It will land the country in more trouble.' He asked, 'Toh hamein kya karna chahiye?' (Then, what is it that we should do?). 'Only a series of half-a-dozen explosions will win respect for India as a credible nuclear-weapon power.' He nodded. 'Yes, a series,' commented Vajpayeeji. I came away from the meeting convinced that he was readying himself for the assumption of the country's prime ministership and for conducting nuclear tests.

The BJP's election manifesto preceding the 1998 election had clearly stated that if the party came to power, it would conduct nuclear tests. But no one took the one or two sentences on the subject in the manifesto seriously. Some of my friends in the diplomatic corps, including my good friend the ambassador of France, Claude Blanchemaison, had asked what I thought of the 'brag' about nuclear tests in the manifesto. I remember telling him, in particular, that since the manifesto could not have been issued without Mr Vajpayee's approval, all indications of future policy in it must be taken as carefully considered and seriously meant. I myself, I added, was convinced that the few words about conducting nuclear tests were a statement of firm intent.

None of the ambassadors who had spoken to me, not even the ambassador of France, took the manifesto, or me, seriously. After the event, Blanchemaison was full of regrets for not having reported to his government what I had said. He wanted to know why I, an advocate of nuclear disarmament and not even a member of the BJP, had taken that declaration at its face value. I have known the man, I said; he is someone who never utters a word he does not mean.

After the brouhaha following the Indian nuclear tests of May 1998 died down, the USA and other Western powers started to engage with the Vajpayee government. They began to recognize not only the decisive quality of the prime minister's leadership, but also his quick grasp of international problems and the wisdom and profundity of his thought processes. After a meeting of an Indo-French group, co-chaired by President Jacques Chirac and myself at the Élysée Palace, President Chirac mentioned a recent international event where he had met Prime Minister Vajpayee. The Indian prime minister, he said, had struck him as a sage-like statesman of superior wisdom. 'When you talk to him,' said President Chirac, 'make an observation or ask a question on a complex problem; he is slow in responding, but when he speaks, he has said something.'

ORATORY AT THE UN

In 1958, India's future prime minister was not much impressed by the speeches he had heard in the UN. He thought the speeches in the assembly plenary mostly were argumentative without being persuasive, and read from texts in dull monotones they bored the listener. In some cases there were flashes of bitterness, even anger and fire, but there was no humour, he had observed.

Actors on the UN stage do often treat it as an arena for rhetorical flourishes to hide the truth at the core of an issue. A combination of lung-power, logorrhoea and logomachy are the tools used to create an effect and befog straightforward issues. Sir Muhammed Zafarullah Khan of Pakistan commanded a rare mastery of this particular genre of verbal diarrhoea. Although he had a bad case to defend on Pakistan's aggression in Kashmir, he took the offensive and spun out an oration of six or seven hours, suppressing true facts and inventing new ones. It was not a convincing performance. He lacked the light touch and habitually shunned brevity even when economy of words might better serve his purpose. But his committed supporters in the Security Council, delegations of the US and Britain, lapped up his tale about an 'injured and defrauded Pakistan'.

KRISHNA MENON

Krishna Menon's oratorical inventory was superior to Khan's, and he also had wit of the biting, sardonic kind, which would make his audience laugh at his opponent and make him run for cover. Also Menon could be disarmingly brief when brevity served him better. To the force of his words he could add the artistry of changing facial expressions, a dramatic pause accompanied by a roaming, inquiring glance on his audience to drive home a point. And, if need be, he could convincingly feign exhaustion, or even throw a fit to win the sympathy of his admirers back home, if not of his present audience. Menon was always strong on facts and impeccable in his choice of words. His coruscating asides could be devastating.

On an earlier occasion in the Security Council, the British delegate had the temerity to pick holes in some of the words Menon had used in his speech in the council. Menon interrupted him, 'Sir, I can understand your difficulty in understanding what I have said; you picked up your English on the streets of London, I devoted several years of my life to learn it with the care and respect it deserves!'

Derisive laughter silenced the man, Sir Pearson Dixon, for the rest of the session. At the same meeting when Sir Muhammed Zafarullah Khan had repeatedly emphasized the urgent necessity of a plebiscite in Kashmir, Menon turned to the chair and exclaimed, 'Plebiscite, Plebiscite, Plebiscite! Sir, ask this gentleman whether his country has ever seen a ballot box!'

In 1961, after a term as a judge at the International Court of Justice (ICJ), Sir Muhammed Zafarullah Khan had returned to New York as Pakistan's permanent representative to the UN. One of his very first acts was to launch a campaign for another discussion of the Kashmir question in the Security Council. He must have thought that his having been on the ICJ would lend greater credence to his old tale of concealments, half-truths and plain falsehoods. Under US pressure on Pakistan's behalf, a meeting of the Security Council was scheduled for May–June 1962, which would see another confrontation between Khan and Krishna Menon. In Khan's long and rambling harangue there was just one new element. He had said that in the event of an armed conflict between India and Pakistan in the prevailing situation of unrest and uncertainty in and around Kashmir, a great power (China presumably) might be drawn into the 'vortex'.

Menon was fully prepared for a long rebuttal of all that Khan might say. I was sitting behind him with the papers he might ask for. He turned to me and asked whether Khan had said anything new. 'Not a word Sir, except the vortex thing,' I said. B.L. Sharma, the MEA's expert on Kashmir who had come from Delhi for the meeting and was sitting by my side, gave him the same answer. 'He has uttered a threat, hasn't he?' asked Menon. 'What exactly did he say about a big power being dragged into the vortex?' I gave him the sentence in which Khan had used that word.

Khan had exposed himself to a tongue-lashing because of the threat he had uttered. In his reply, to begin with, Menon made three important points, namely: That Kashmir was an integral part of India and India's sovereignty in J & K was non-negotiable; that the UN resolutions envisaging a plebiscite had become inoperative because of Pakistan's failure to withdraw its forces from Kashmir, a condition stipulated in the UNCIP Resolution of 1949; and, finally, because of the lapse of time and changed circumstances surrounding Kashmir, the UN's resolutions of an ad hoc nature had become un-implementable. He asserted that no matter how many meetings the council might hold, there was no question of a plebiscite in Kashmir any more.

Then, Menon picked on the word 'vortex' and Khan's improper use of it, and what followed was an attack on Khan for uttering a threat of war in the Security Council, a forum for peaceful resolution of disputes! Then he chided him for threatening involvement of some third country, a great power, in a bilateral India–Pakistan issue. 'Which great power?' he asked, and left the question hanging in the air. For that impropriety, he quietly said, it was for the Security Council to chastise Khan.

Menon said he was deeply disappointed, for he thought that after having been a judge on the World Court for several years and having been the court's vice president for three years, Khan had chosen to return to the council to express regret for all the lies, untruths and half-truths he had uttered in earlier debates, and to apologize—not to India—but to the august council for those misdeeds. It hurt to think, he said, that Khan should have learnt nothing of fairness, justice and probity in all those years at the ICJ! What, he asked council members, was there for him to say about Khan's same old web of lies that had not been said before the council earlier? 'Is the council really ready and willing to hear me in detail for a few hours?' Silence followed, and on a member's request the vote was called on a Western resolution not acceptable to India. It was vetoed by the Russian representative, Ambassador Valerian Alexandrovich Zorin. Three or four more meetings were called in later years, but they all ended without the Security Council taking any specific action.

KRISHNA MENON AND THE USA

There was a fairly widespread view in India that all of America hated Krishna Menon and that Krishna Menon hated the Americans. His interventions in the debates in the UN were noted in the American media with a slant which did not always faithfully reflect the substance of what Menon had actually said. The media provoked him, and he hit back.

Menon had been feeling unwell for some time. He needed surgery in the head to remove a blood clot, and after much hesitation, he had it done in a hospital in New York in the late summer of 1961. The news of his hospitalization was flashed by America's print and electronic media all over the country, perhaps not without some unexpressed malevolence. But Menon did have his admirers and well-wishers in America! From the following morning till the day he was discharged from hospital, messages of good wishes and prayers for his quick recovery poured into the permanent mission of India. The corridor outside his hospital room was filled with fresh flowers every day. It took me weeks to acknowledge, with Menon's personal thanks, every message of good wishes received by us by letter, telegram, telephone or a gift of flowers. The man was known all across the United States, and not everywhere as a dangerous, malefic figure, as made out by the ruling elite and the media of the United States.

In the mid-1950s, Menon had proposed acquisition, on payment, of F-104 fighter jets from the USA, but the request was turned down by the latter because it would tilt the India–Pakistan military balance in India's favour. The rejection was repeated in the wake of the China–India war of 1962 on the grounds that an F-104 was much too costly a weapon system for a country like India. The British were even worse in this regard; they impertinently turned down India's request in the 1950s for the supply, on payment, of a couple of submarines saying India did not need submarines!

BRITISH HOSTILITY TOWARDS INDIA

This, despite the fact that we had retained British naval officers in command of the Indian navy for eleven years after Independence. That was a serious mistake on the part of Nehru's government, for it unduly delayed the development of the Indian navy commensurate with India's security needs. When we turned to Russia for jet fighters and other military hardware, the British resented it, and the USA dubbed Menon a communist and India a pro-communist country!

In the early years of India's independence Britain's professions of friendship were but a veneer for its scarcely concealed dislike of India.

After China's attack on India in 1962, President Kennedy was in favour of strengthening the Indian army against China by supplying a variety of modern arms to it. Macmillan successfully opposed the move because, he argued, it would upset Pakistan and the India–Pakistan military balance. It was the British representative in the Security Council, Sir Philip Noel Baker, who in a masterly play of hypocritical British diplomacy had inveigled the Security Council into sidetracking the basic issue of Pakistan's aggression in Kashmir. 'Let us forget the past and work for a better future for both countries,' he would say to the Security Council in meeting after meeting. 'The need of the hour is a plebiscite. The condition the UN had stipulated about withdrawal of Pakistan's army from Kashmir has little relevance to the future,' argued Sir Philip, posing all the time as a man of peace with tender feelings for India! In 1965, Pakistan had committed aggression first in Kutch and then in Kashmir, but Prime Minister Harold Wilson lost no time in declaring India the aggressor. But we Indians have a weakness for the Brits, and the Brits know it.

A TIFF BETWEEN NEHRU'S TWO FAVOURITES

In the summer of 1961 Menon was in New York, as usual in connection with some routine meeting at the UN. Before leaving Delhi he had arranged a White House meeting with President John F. Kennedy through the American ambassador in India. India's ambassador in Washington, B.K. Nehru, who was a good friend of President Kennedy's, had not been informed. He got to know of Menon's scheduled meeting with the President two or three days before the event, when a White House official telephoned him to find out whether he would be accompanying the defence minister to his meeting with the President, B.K. Nehru was understandably annoyed at being bypassed. He tried to speak to Menon but the minister would not take his calls. So, Ambassador Nehru rang me up, asking me to tell Menon that the White House had informed him of the meeting, and he, the ambassador, would be accompanying the defence minister to the meeting with President Kennedy. When I conveyed this to Menon, he hit the ceiling. In that case, he said, he would simply not go to Washington and let Panditji—Prime Minister Nehru—know of his reason for cancelling the meeting. There wasn't much love lost between Krishna Menon and B.K. Nehru. Both were close to Panditji. Prime Minister Nehru was very fond of his nephew, B.K. Nehru, whom he also respected for his proven ability as an economic policy thinker and as an accomplished and highly successful diplomat.

After he had vented some of his fury at the ambassador's obstinacy on me, Menon suggested that I talk the ambassador out of it. I was in a real dilemma, but I had a long talk with Ambassador Nehru. He was adamant on accompanying Menon to the White House. The tongue-lashing my pleading to the contrary provoked was not part of my past experience. Tell Menon, he said, that if he insists on going to the White House alone, the meeting with the President will be cancelled. I then pleaded with Menon to follow the established practice in these matters.

The arguments I had made about embarrassment being caused to Prime Minister Nehru by cancellation of the meeting, and an ungainly situation created over a trifling matter had some effect. The ambassador's friendship with the President was well known in Washington, therefore in any case, the White House itself would let him know what had transpired at the meeting. So, I said to the minister, why not take the ambassador along? After dubbing me a member of the Pandit mafia and calling me B.K. Nehru's stooge, he relented.

The following day His Excellency even spared his official car to fetch the minister from the airport to his residence for breakfast, and together they went to the White House for the meeting with President Kennedy, and all was well for the day.

NEHRU'S LAST MEETING WITH PRESIDENT KENNEDY

From all accounts, Indian as well as American, Prime Minister Nehru's own meeting with his long-time admirer, John F. Kennedy, later in the year 1961, did not go well at all. On his way to Washington, the prime minister had spent a couple of days in New York and had delivered an address at the UN General Assembly, and we had all noted that health-wise he was not the man we had seen a year before. He had slowed down a great deal and the verve and spark that used to animate the environment around him were missing.

Ambassador B.K. Nehru, who had accompanied the prime minister to his meeting with Kennedy, described the meeting to me as a disaster. The prime minister, he told me, just did not react to Kennedy's repeated pleas for his advice as to what he should do, or not do, in Vietnam; there were pressures on him to rush in there with military force, he did not know Asia well and he wanted the great Asian statesman's personal advice as a guide for his action. The President never received the word of advice directly from the prime minister that might have prevented America's disastrous involvement in Vietnam.

However, the following day the prime minister did instruct Foreign Secretary M.J. Desai to meet his counterpart in the State Department or the secretary of state and tell them that the US should not get involved in Vietnam; that they will get bogged down there with no good result. This was sound advice, which might have saved the US a long war and a morale-shattering defeat. But American bureaucracy was not inclined to accept from Desai what the prime minister himself had failed to convey to the President.

C.S. JHA: GOA IN THE SECURITY COUNCIL

Ambassador C.S. Jha, India's permanent representative at the UN, was an able, hard-working, far-sighted and experienced diplomat. He made friends easily and his ability to quickly get to the core of a complex problem, and his negotiating skills were the envy of his peers in the UN. When a situation demanded firmness to defend India's national interest, Jha could be tough and defiant. In my experience, Jha was one of the only two men who, while working under Menon, could stand up to him, and not only survive but also prevail. The other was Sardar Khushwant Singh who was the public relations officer in the Indian High Commission in London.

In December 1961, when India used force to expel the Portuguese colonial administration from Goa, Portugal's permanent representative to the UN, Vasco Garin, with the active support of the American delegation headed by Governor Adlai Stevenson, asked for an emergency meeting of the Security Council on the grounds of India's aggression against Portugal in Goa. At the meeting he launched a vicious attack on India and Nehru accusing them of naked aggression. He had repeatedly referred to the sanctity of the UN Charter and its various provisions which, according to him, India had violated. He urged the Security Council to compel India to withdraw its forces from Goa.

We had received no advance alert from Delhi about military action to liberate Goa. A Security Council meeting was bound to be convened in 'an emergency', on a complaint of aggression by one UN member against another. Delhi did not anticipate this and we had no brief or instructions for the Security Council meeting. So, with whatever information I could gather locally I prepared a briefing note for Ambassador Jha and a set of papers for distribution to members of the Security Council. In reply to Garin's outbursts, Jha patiently explained the fruitless negotiations India had held with Portugal over the years to peacefully vacate its colony on Indian soil, as Britain and France had done from their respective colonial possessions earlier. He explained the history of the bit-by-bit colonization of India by Europeans, who came as traders and embarked on a course of conquest by pitching one Indian ruler against another. He rejected the idea of a colonial power's sovereignty over its colonial possessions. India, he said, could no longer tolerate a remnant of European colonialism in India. Finally, recalling Garin's numerous references to the UN Charter and the Security Council, Jha asserted that no provision of the charter could make a part of Indian territory an integral part of a far-away European power. He concluded his remarks with a sentence which resonated in the halls of the UN for months: 'Charter or no charter, Security Council or no Security Council,' said Jha, 'India will not tolerate a vestige of colonialism on its territory.'

India was supported by the representatives of Sri Lanka, Liberia, United Arab Republic and Ambassador Zorin of Russia who vetoed the resolution sponsored by Britain, France, the United States and Turkey, calling for immediate cessation of hostilities and withdrawal of Indian forces from Goa. Adlai Stevenson, leader of the US delegation, spoke up in support of Portugal while explaining his vote in support of the vetoed resolution. Normally a pleasant and persuasive public speaker, he launched a vitriolic tirade against India, accusing India of hypocrisy and violation of the UN Charter. He went on to threaten further action against India. He warned the council of dire consequences of India's military action. India's attack on Goa, he said, was the 'first act of the drama' which might lead to the death of the UN! The occasion also gave him the opportunity to condemn Russia for its 100th veto in the council.

The reason for Stevenson's intemperate criticism of India and Nehru is hard to understand. The US had been warned at the highest levels that India's patience was running out, and in fact, at the height of the Goa crisis, Dean Rusk had given some good advice to the Portuguese. He had 'urged them to act promptly, even more, dramatically—in accordance with the historical imperatives of the day—in offering self-determination to their colonies,'[1]

Ambassador Jha listened to Stevenson's angry taunts and deprecations with exemplary forbearance. His vehement condemnation of India and impassioned support of Portugal were shocking. When his pontification about the immorality of the use of force and the sanctity of the charter became unbearable, Jha asked for the floor for a brief intervention in which he reminded the governor of his own country's history and its war of independence.

A colony by any other name remains a colony, and colonial rule, Jha said, was repugnant to human nature, man's dignity and his innate sense of freedom. The elimination of colonial rule from all parts of the world, he reminded Stevenson, was declared objective of India's foreign policy. He then bluntly asked whether Stevenson and the US government wanted the perpetuation of Portuguese colonies in Africa? To that the he sheepishly responded by saying that the United States' position on colonialism was well known. The end result of this confrontation was that Jha rose in prestige and popularity in the UN and Governor Stevenson lost some of his sheen.

After the May–June Security Council meeting on Kashmir, the defence minister wanted to make some calls on a few friends before returning to Delhi. As usual I accompanied him on these calls. During his long meeting with Russian Ambassador Zorin, I learnt for the first time about armed clashes on the India–China border. We had no information on the subject in our mission. Menon said to Zorin, 'Your Chinese brothers are causing trouble on the India–Tibet border. Please do something to restrain them. Otherwise we will be forced to take action which they won't like!' Zorin's response was equally surprising to me and perhaps also to the defence minister: 'Mr Menon, what makes you say that their behaviour with us is brotherly?'

Four months later, China launched a massive attack on India for which they had been assembling men and materials in Tibet for months. Obviously Indian intelligence organizations had no clue about what was going on across India's northern frontier. Equally shocking was the state of the Indian army which just disintegrated under the unexpected Chinese attack, and the defence minister's delusional confidence in the army's capacity to inflict punishment on the invader.

THE BRITISH COMPLAIN AGAINST ME TO NEHRU

In the month of July, a few days before my family and I boarded the luxury liner—it was one of the queens, Elizabeth or Mary—for our return voyage to India, the Decolonization Committee held a meeting which would be my last in the UN as an Indian delegate. I had not intended to speak in the meeting as the agenda was of a routine nature and I had already said my farewells to my colleagues in the preceding days. To my surprise, an African delegate took the floor, thanked me for my contribution to the cause of the liberation of colonies in Africa and requested a parting message or advice regarding the future work of the committee, for the creation of which I had done so much! Others also joined in urging me to speak to them, however briefly.

I was not prepared for this and it was not without hesitation that I took the floor. In my remarks I thanked members for their friendship, and expressed my deep gratification at the arrival of a score of newly independent African countries as UN members who would give fresh impetus to Africa's decolonization. The movement for Africa's liberation, I said, was unstoppable and even Portugal will not be able to resist it for long. South West Africa needed the committee's special attention, though I myself was convinced that the racist regime of South Africa would have to let go of that mandated territory.

The greater danger, I emphasized, lay in what was happening in the British colony of Southern Rhodesia. What the white rulers of the colony were doing there, under British watch, was to divide the territory into two, making the richer and more developed part a white majority area by relocating its black inhabitants to the poorer parts, thus making the latter a black majority area which could opt for independence after a popular consultation of some kind. The white majority part would then be free to declare its own independence or merge with South Africa! Southern Rhodesia, I said, is a black majority country and it should become independent as such.

To conclude, I said, I had a question for the British representative concerning this matter. Sir Hugh Foot, who was leading the British delegation at that meeting, was a man of liberal views but of uncertain credentials as a decolonizer. I looked at him and asked, 'Why, Sir Hugh, is your government doing this? Isn't one South Africa enough trouble for Africa and the world?' Sir Hugh chose not to answer the question. But there was an amusing sequel to this of which I learnt only on reaching Delhi.

The British high commissioner in Delhi, under instructions from his government, sought a meeting with Prime Minister Nehru to protest against the question I had addressed to Her Majesty's representative in the Decolonization Committee!

Prime Minister Nehru asked Krishna Menon to find out what I had said and dispose of the matter. After ascertaining what I had said, Menon sent for the British high commissioner and said to him laughingly: 'That boy Rasgotra is too much of an anglophile. Lot of trickery is going on in Southern Rhodesia. He only gave you a friendly warning; I would have said much more.'

So, amid much thumping of the desks, I thanked members for their cooperation and friendship during my four-and-a-half years in the Fourth Committee and the Trusteeship Council, wished them well and took leave. I was leaving behind a large number of friends, many of whom I would not see again and a few would even become tragic victims of the tumult and turmoil of politics in their countries following independence.

chapter twelve

BETWEEN TWO WARS: INDIA AND
ITS NEIGHBOURS, 1962–65

~

Working in the UN had given me an overview of the world of the 1950s and the 1960s. It had also made me aware of the problems and concerns of different countries, the impact of the Cold War on international relations and the possibilities and limits of India's role on the world stage. On issues like General and Complete Disarmament and Nuclear Arms Control, our legitimate concerns and constructive ideas exerted only marginal influence. I personally had the satisfaction of actively witnessing the implementation of an important plank of India's foreign policy; namely, the liberation of colonies in Africa and other parts of the world ruthlessly suppressed and exploited by small European countries. Decolonization was a heartening development in a world dominated by the USA and the European colonial powers who enjoyed its support—Britain, Belgium, France, Portugal and Spain. It would change the lives of people and international relations in unpredictable ways.

Nuclear weapons had already rendered obsolete the old concepts of warfare, victory and defeat. Russia's sputnik, circumambulating in outer space, marked a huge leap in science and technology. A few years later, the world witnessed an even more daring leap into the future with US astronaut Neil Armstrong taking his first tentative steps on the moon's surface! India too was making progress in consolidating its democracy, in spreading education among millions of its illiterates, in expanding its base of science and technology, in improving its agriculture and in laying the industrial infrastructure for its future growth. Though the country was still dependent on imported food grains, the economy was growing steadily at around 4 per cent of GDP per annum. This so-called Hindu rate of growth was not something to be jeered at considering that the Indian economy had been regressing for decades before Independence. China's economy was not doing as well and the GDP growth rate in Britain, still one of the world's leading powers, was around 2 per cent.

With Nehru's declining health and the slow erosion of his hold on Parliament, parliamentary debates had become noisier and more contentious, revealing increasingly a growing deficiency in calm and constructive reasoning. There was little awareness in our political circles of the war clouds gathering on the country's northern horizon. It passes understanding that the fairly large and costly intelligence apparatus we maintained should have failed so miserably to detect China's war preparations, spread over a period of a year or two, before it launched a massive attack on India in October 1962.

CHINA'S WARNING OF WAR

There was a diplomacy lapse also. Exactly one month after His Holiness the Dalai Lama crossed the border to seek political asylum in India, the *People's Daily* of Peking wrote threateningly: 'We give a solemn warning to imperialists and Indian expansionists—you must stop at once. Otherwise you will be crushed to pieces under the iron fists of 650 million Chinese people.' Then, on 16 May 1959, the Chinese ambassador, Pan Tsu-li, called on Foreign Secretary Subimal Dutt and insisted on reading out a written statement in which he accused India of encouraging the 'Chinese rebel'—the Dalai Lama—and in that context criticized the warm welcome accorded to His Holiness and Prime Minister Nehru's talks with him. The ambassador concluded his démarche with a plea and a warning: 'Enemies of the Chinese people,' he said, 'lie in the East—the American imperialists. China does not want India as a foe in the southwest of China. Friends, it seems to us that you too cannot have two fronts . . . Will you please think it over?'

These were serious warnings from a country which had traditionally relied on the use of force as first recourse in 'diplomacy' vis-à-vis its neighbours—Tibet, Sinkiang, Mongolia, Manchuria, Vietnam. China's occupation, by stealth, of a large chunk of our territory in Aksai Chin in the days of bhai-bhai relationship should have been enough of a warning. But there is no evidence to show that we thought of any of it as warnings of a future war, or took steps, diplomatic or military, to avert the threat or deter it.

Dutt acknowledges that 'the ambassador's reference to two fronts was significant. The obvious suggestion was that it would be unwise for India to have unfriendly relations with both Pakistan and China'.[1] But the Government of India, he adds, could not pay the price which the Chinese government were demanding for friendly relations with China. But he does not mention 'the price' China was demanding. Presumably, China wanted India to handover the Dalai Lama to them which would be impossible for the Indian government to do. That being the case, prudence demanded that New Delhi seriously explore ways and means of neutralizing the threat so deliberately uttered by the accredited representative of a big and powerful neighbour.

New Delhi was content, instead, to reply to China's protest stating, naively, that India did not regard any country as its enemy, that it only wanted to cultivate China's friendship and avoid interfering in China's internal affairs—but India would not change its policies under foreign pressure!

Prime Minister Nehru was already disillusioned with China's cynical disregard of Panchsheel. During his visit to Nepal in 1960, he had said in reply to a journalist's question that China had trampled all over Panchsheel, and Panchsheel could not be implemented by one side alone. During the 1962 war, in a radio interview to a reporter of the Kenyan Broadcasting Corporation in New Delhi, he had expressed similar sentiments. The reporter, Chamanlal Chaman had asked the prime minister to 'throw light on the future of Panchsheel'. Nehru replied, 'Throwing light is now difficult, as the Chinese have spread darkness all over. How can I throw light on Panchsheel?

By this war they have totally acted against the spirit of Panchsheel. Panchsheel cannot take place in the air or [be] implemented by one side alone. It can only work if both countries agree to follow it; if the Chinese don't want to follow Panchsheel, it is finished.'[2]

To make matters worse, in September 1959, His Holiness, in defiance of Nehru's strong advice to the contrary, sent a long cable to the UN headquarters requesting the General Assembly's intervention to restore Tibet's autonomy and respect for the fundamental human rights of the Tibetan population. In October, the General Assembly adopted a resolution sponsored by Malaysia and Ireland calling 'for respect for the fundamental human rights of the Tibetan people and their distinctive religion and culture'. India's abstention in the vote on that resolution did not lead to any lessening of Beijing's suspicions and distrust of India.

During his visit to India in 1960, Zhou En-Lai frankly told Morarji Desai, then a senior member in Nehru's Cabinet, that the grant of asylum to the Dalai Lama was the cause of deterioration in India–China relations. His talks with Nehru failed to find common ground on any point of dispute. Even earlier Nehru had become totally distrustful of Zhou En-Lai, but after his meeting with the Chinese premier in 1960, Nehru had written—in one of his letters to chief ministers, if my memory serves me right—that Zhou En-Lai had told him so many lies that he did not feel like meeting him again.

The only result of the Chinese premier's visit was the creation of a committee of officials of the two countries to examine historical documents and other traditional evidence in support of their respective stands on the border. The joint committee held three meetings in Beijing, New Delhi and Rangoon over the next four or five months. The Indian side, led by Jagat Mehta, deputy secretary in the ministry of external affairs, presented solid documentary evidence in support of India's case, whereas the Chinese team at each meeting only produced a new map showing even more areas of India as parts of Tibet, in Ladakh and in the central sector of the border, than they had claimed in their maps given to India in 1956. In addition to this creeping cartographic aggression, the Chinese team tried, without success, to persuade the Indian team to accept certain Chinese positions on the border issue which Nehru had already rejected in his talks with Zhou En-Lai.

The officials' joint report, so-called, was in fact a document containing two separate reports, with little common ground for further negotiation between the two countries. An impasse had been reached and, with the state of relations as it was, there was little hope for a future breakthrough. For reasons best known to it, the Chinese government did not publish the report for eighteen months! India published the report immediately and placed it before the Lok Sabha in April 1961.

INDIA SPURNS PRESIDENT KENNEDY'S EXTRAORDINARY GESTURE

At around the same time, the United States' President, John F. Kennedy, made an extraordinary gesture towards India. American intelligence had learnt that China's nuclear programme was progressing towards a weapons' detonation in 1963. Kennedy, who was an admirer of India's democracy and held its leader Jawaharlal Nehru in very high esteem, felt that democratic India, not communist China, should be the first Asian country to conduct a nuclear test. So, it is said, that the President sent a letter, written in his own hand, to Nehru offering help to India to conduct a nuclear test, and that accompanying the Kennedy letter was a technical note from the chairman of the US Atomic Energy Commission setting out the assistance his organization would provide to Indian nuclear scientists to detonate an American device from atop a tower in the Rajasthan desert.

A detailed paper on this subject was circulated at a meeting which I chaired in 2014 to honour G. Parthasarathy[3] on his 100th birth anniversary by his son, Ashok Parthasarathy. According to Ashok, Nehru shared the letter with only two persons, G. Parthasarathy (G.P.),who had returned from China on completion of his tenure as India's ambassador on the very day Ambassador Galbraith had personally handed Kennedy's letter to Nehru, and Dr Homi Bhabha, whom Nehru had urgently summoned from Bombay to discuss Kennedy's offer. In his letter Kennedy had said that he and the

American establishment were aware of Nehru's strong views against nuclear tests and nuclear weapons, but emphasized the political and security threat China's test would spell for Nehru's government and India's security. 'Nothing,' Kennedy's letter emphasized, 'is more important than national security.'

Ashok's paper also stated that Bhabha was for immediate acceptance of Kennedy's offer, and Nehru himself was not disinclined to it; for he promptly instructed Bhabha to 'work out a plan of action on a most urgent basis, should we finally accept Kennedy's offer'. G.P., on the other hand, wanted a couple of days to mull over all the various implications of the offer, and he utilized the time for long talks with Galbraith and B.M. Mullick, India's pretentious intelligence chief, but ignored their advice favouring acceptance of the offer. In the end what he told Nehru was in line with Nehru's own convictions and perhaps also what Nehru wanted to hear. So, good friend Kennedy's well-meaning offer of a lifetime was gently and thankfully turned down.

What puzzles me is that the prime minister chose not to consult in this case of vital importance his closest adviser in the Foreign Office, Subimal Dutt, for whom he entertained great esteem and affection. Equally, the two main arguments advanced in favour of rejection also do not sound very convincing to me. First, that the seismic and other signatures of the test would have traced it to American origin by Moscow which, then, would have isolated India totally! Surely, the Americans themselves would have wanted to do the utmost to conceal the seismic and other signatures of the test. And, at any rate, plain denial of truth was the common diplomatic practice in the days of Western dominance of the art. As for Moscow isolating India, Soviet Russia, having already fallen out with China, was itself in a despairing state of isolation and in great need of India's friendship. Failure of diplomacy again. Our embassies in Moscow and Beijing had failed to gauge the intensity of the strains in China–USSR relations.

The second argument for rejection was that the test would have dealt a mortal blow to India's foreign policy of Non-alignment. Kennedy had not asked India to join the Western camp. There were no strings attached to his offer. An Indian nuclear test at that stage would have empowered both India and its policy of Non-alignment, and we would have been spared the pain of sanctions which followed the nuclear test of 1974.

Non-alignment had become a way of life and of looking at the world to such an extent that we had come to regard it as an effective instrument of safeguarding India's national security. Did Prime Minister Nehru's pathetic letter of 19 November 1962 to Kennedy, requesting twelve squadrons of F-104 jet fighters, two squadrons of B-47 bombers, radars and C-130 transport aircrafts—all operated by American military personnel—make the slightest dent in our sanctimonious belief in the infallibility of Non-alignment? Or, was its sanctity sullied by our security treaty with the Soviet Union in August 1971?

Of course, all this is hindsight wisdom, but one thing is certain that India's acceptance of Kennedy's offer would have deterred China from launching its war of 1962 and even imparted a note of caution to Field Marshal Ayub Khan's plans for war in 1965. Nothing deters an aggressor more than a couple of big bombs in the armoury of the target of his hostility.

As the Chinese attack began in October 1962, I was designated the MEA's war book officer, and also given charge of the northern division of the MEA, which dealt with Nepal, Bhutan and Sikkim, the Dalai Lama's establishment in Dharamshala and the problems relating to the resettlement, in appropriate vocations and in climatically suitable locations in India, of some 1,10,000 Tibetan refugees. This turned out to be a highly engrossing and satisfying assignment in that I got to know and enjoy the blessings and affection of His Holiness. In the next two years the Tibetan refugees were resettled in Tibetan handicraft production centres in several locations in India's northern hills and in agricultural, industrial and cultural projects in places in central and southern India. A prestigious Cultural Centre (Tibet House), under His Holiness's chairmanship, was set up in Delhi and major Tibetan studies centres were established in Varanasi and Sikkim. In a short course of time impressive Tibetan monasteries burgeoned in Tibetan settlements.

The most important centre for the preservation and dissemination of Tibetan arts, culture and philosophy is, of course, at Dharamshala, the seat of His Holiness and his self-proclaimed 'government in exile'. The Tibet House in New Delhi has acquired an international reputation for its most valuable collection of Tibetan manuscripts, artefacts and sacred objects and for its manifold activities in the dissemination of knowledge of Tibetan arts, religion, philosophy, culture and medical lore through its publications, lectures, seminars and short course studies—organized in Delhi and, from time to time, in other places in India.

ANGLO-AMERICAN PRESSURES ON NEHRU

In response to Nehru's appeals to the United States and Britain for arms, ammunition and communications equipment to fight China's aggression, the first installment of small arms and ammunition arrived in Calcutta in the first week of November 1962. Over the next few weeks, arms worth about US$ 60 million for our troops deployed on the Himalayan frontier areas were received. But the supplies dried up to a trickle within a week or two of China's unilateral ceasefire in November. Instead, an American team led by Ambassador Averell Harriman and a British group led by Duncan Sandys, secretary of state for Commonwealth Relations in Prime Minister Harold Macmillan's government descended on India to tell our authorities: a) to enable them to continue further arms supplies, India should settle the Kashmir problem with Pakistan; and b) that while the US and Britain wanted to strengthen India to better defend itself against China, their arms support was not intended to strengthen the Indian army to a point where it might feel encouraged to embark on a campaign to expel the Chinese from Aksai Chin! Macmillan had personally urged Kennedy to limit arms supplies to India to avoid alienating Pakistan. There was suspicion in some quarters in India that Britain might have been privy to Pakistan's plans to attempt another war to snatch Kashmir by force, before the Indian army got fully re-equipped with supplies of modern Western or Russian arms.

I was one of the notetakers at the talks between Foreign
Secretary M.J. Desai and Commonwealth Secretary Yezdi Gundevia
on one side, and Harriman and Sandys on the other. On our critical
needs, the Western attitude was negative. We wanted to pay for the
arms and equipment we needed but we were told, 'India does not
need F-104 jet fighters; C-130 transport aircraft are too expensive
for India.'

Duncan Sandys, a political lightweight in British politics, ran a
shuttle between New Delhi and Islamabad to resolve the Kashmir
problem. He thought he could pressurize Nehru to give a part of the
Vale of Kashmir to Pakistan! It must be said to Nehru's credit that,
arms or no arms, in that time of trial for India, he resolutely rejected
Western pressures. All that India agreed to was to engage in bilateral
talks with Pakistan at the ministerial level, followed by a summit
meeting between Prime Minister Nehru and President Ayub Khan
of Pakistan.

INDIA–PAKISTAN TALKS AND THE 1965 WAR

Between December 1962 and May 1963, six rounds of talks were
held alternately in Pakistan and India. The Indian delegation was led
by Sardar Swaran Singh, a tall, imperturbable man of inexhaustible
patience whom nothing and no one could ever provoke into an
angry response in negotiations. A remarkably patient and pragmatic
statesman, he was resourceful in ideas and argument. He could, if
need be, repeat himself endlessly in an impasse in talks without batting
an eyelid, leaving it to the other party to end negotiations. Jawaharlal
Nehru was of course in a class of his own, but Sardar Swaran Singh
outshone all other Indian foreign ministers who had followed Nehru
in the job. His long spell as foreign minister was totally free from
mistakes or flawed approaches to contentious bilateral or international
issues.

The Pakistan delegation to the talks on Kashmir was headed by
Zulfikar Ali Bhutto, Pakistan's mercurial minister of industries. A
talented and ambitious young man, Bhutto hated India but was a self-
proclaimed admirer of the Indian prime minister and his economic

and social policies. The talks ended in failure. India had offered to Pakistan an additional 1500 square miles of territory in Kashmir on the Indian side of the ceasefire line, the new line being treated as the international border in Jammu and Kashmir. Bhutto rejected the offer; he wanted virtually the whole of the state, leaving India in possession of the Kathua district of the Jammu province bordering Himachal Pradesh. The failure of the talks in 1963 resulted, under Pakistan's pressure, in the total stoppage of Western arms supplies, forcing India to turn to Russia as a reliable, future supplier of the arms needs of India's army, air force and navy.

Neither Ayub Khan nor Bhutto had any intention of settling the Kashmir issue through negotiation on the basis of the partition of the state along a mutually agreed line, behind which both sides would feel secure.

Soon after Nehru's death in May 1964, the Pakistan army started putting war paint on its tanks. In the spring of 1965 it launched a diversionary attack in Kutch in the western Indian state of Gujarat over a minor territorial issue. The international community stepped in with arbitration and that initial bout was satisfactorily resolved. The big show commenced in August when hundreds of Pakistani soldiers disguised as Kashmiri mujahideen infiltrated into Kashmir across the Haji Pir Pass. Field Marshal Ayub Khan expected Kashmiris to rise in revolt against India; instead, Kashmiri Muslims started capturing the invaders and handing them over to the Indian army. The Operation Gibraltar had failed.

Field Marshall Ayub Khan then launched a major tank attack across the international border in Jammu, which threatened to cut India's roadlink with the Kashmir valley. To blunt this manoeuvre, Prime Minister Lal Bahadur Shastri ordered the Indian army to go for Lahore in Pakistan's Punjab. As the Indians reached the outskirts of that great city, the UN stepped in to save Pakistan. A ceasefire was agreed upon, and we learnt never again to allow the UN or anybody else to intervene in a brotherly India–Pakistan imbroglio.

Another lesson we learnt was that in an India–Pakistan conflict over Kashmir, Britain and the United States will always side with Pakistan. Therefore, at the end of the war we made sure that neither would have any role in peacemaking. The Peace Agreement was negotiated and signed under Soviet Russia's aegis at Tashkent. Many of us in the MEA were not happy with the agreement to return to Pakistan, as an unwarranted gesture of goodwill, the Haji Pir Pass, a strategically important mountain feature in Kashmir which our army had captured in the war. Pakistan has never shown the least appreciation of such gestures. Indian peace negotiators in those years seemed to suffer from a malady called the Versailles Syndrome. Having won the war, they would go all out to lose the peace. We would see an even worse recurrence of this kind of peace negotiation in 1972.

India suffered a tragic national loss in the death, at Tashkent, of Prime Minister Shastri a few hours after signing the Peace Agreement with Pakistan. In his small mortal body Shastriji carried the mind and heart of a hero. His tenure as prime minister was short, but there was much of historic value in it. Regrettably, so far the nation has not celebrated his achievements and honoured his memory in a manner worthy of the man.

REACTIONS IN NEPAL

As the old saying goes, victory finds a 100 fathers but defeat is an orphan. Of all our neighbours, I found the behaviour of the Royal Nepal government of the greatest interest. Soon after the end of the 1965 war, King Mahendra sent his prime minister Dr Tulsi Giri to Delhi to tell Prime Minister Shastri how much he had admired his courage and leadership to take Pakistan head-on in such a decisive manner. This was in sharp contrast to Nepal's behaviour in the wake of the debacle of October–November 1962.

In February or March 1963, Prime Minister Nehru had sent Lal Bahadur Shastri, minister without portfolio in his office, to pay a goodwill visit to Nepal. I had accompanied Shastriji to Kathmandu and was present at all his meetings with Nepalese leaders; they couldn't be colder!

On the first evening of our three-day stay in Kathmandu, there was a low-level official dinner in the minister's honour, followed by a cultural show the central feature of which was a dance by a group of a dozen or so Nepalese young men. As they danced, they waved their unsheathed khukris and sang a song the refrain of which was: 'We'll wash our blood-stained khukris in the Ganga!'

It was an uncouth show of malice and provocation, and Shastriji said to me, 'Rasgotraji, we have got the message. Should we leave now?' I advised against a walkout and we sat through the programme. At the end, while we were leaving the hall some friendly gentlemen expressed their unhappiness, but the Nepalese minister who was our host said nothing when Shastriji politely took leave of him. The affront, I was sure, could not have been staged without approval of the highest authority of the country.

The pro-China tilt in Nepal's foreign policy that had begun in 1960 now became more pronounced and its overtures to Pakistan more open. Nepal's demands for all manner of concessions in its trade with India, the number of transit points for its trade with third countries and its propaganda as a country, disadvantaged because of being 'India-locked', became provocatively strident. The only positive or friendly feature in Nepal–India relations, in the wake of the 1962 war, was the huge number of Nepalese Gurkhas rushing down from their hamlets in the hills to the recruiting depots in India to join the Indian army to defend brother India against China. It must be said to Nehru's credit that, in the face of crude provocation, he maintained his poised interest in and friendly attitude towards Nepal.

Sometime in the third or fourth week of April 1964, Foreign Secretary Gundevia showed me a short minute by Prime Minister Nehru in his own neat handwriting saying that he had 'made a date with the king of Nepal' for the latter to lay the foundation stone of the Gandak barrage at Bhainselotan in his (Nehru's) presence, which had been delayed by his recent illness. He instructed that the date for the function should now be fixed to suit the king's convenience, and the necessary arrangements taken in hand for his own travel to the barrage site. The prime minister was still in a very delicate state of health and Gundevia tried to dissuade him, without success, from undertaking an arduous air journey of about three hours in the hot summer month of May in a small aircraft. There was no gainsaying the prime minster, who was determined to fulfill the commitment he had made to King Mahendra of Nepal.

The king and the prime minister met for tea and light conversation before proceeding to the barrage site on the Gandak River's west bank, where a huge raised platform had been erected for the king and the prime minister to address a gathering of some 3,00,000 men and women, who had walked miles to see and hear their beloved leader, Jawaharlal Nehru. That journey had taken its toll; the prime minister was an exhausted man when we left for the public function, but the sight of that massed humanity seemed to energize him. After King Mahendra had laid the foundation stone and read out his written speech, the prime minister delivered a long and lively speech in a strong, well-modulated voice. All of us who had accompanied him were relieved to see our ailing prime minster back home safely. India lost its hero exactly twenty-two days later.

Before leaving Bhainselotan, King Mahendra left a letter for the prime minister, allegedly a record of their conversation over tea. In fact it was a narration of Nepal's perennial grievances, none of which had any validity—the shortcomings in the Kosi project which the king's father had approved, inadequacies in the Gandak project agreement which he himself had approved and, indeed, everything else India had done to help Nepal. He had not mentioned any of this in his hour-long talk with the prime minister. Mahendra now made a practice of this—after very friendly talks with an Indian prime minister or President, he would leave a letter, before leaving the venue, allegedly a record of the talks but in fact a list of unfounded grievances about India's injustices etc. against poor, helpless Nepal!

SIKKIM

Sikkim and Bhutan were also part of my charge in the ministry of external affairs. The maharaja of Sikkim, Palden Thondup Namgyal, started showing unwelcome ambitions in the wake of India's debacle in 1962. During British rule in India, the ruler of Sikkim was a member, like other rulers of Indian states, of the Chamber of Princes. Namgyal was not pro-China, but he had married an ambitious American young woman, Hope Cooke, who soon developed a passion for her state's independence and UN membership. Unfortunately for them, the Namgyals were not a popular couple because the ruling family belonged to the Bhutia–Lepcha ethnic group, which accounted for no more than 8 or 10 per cent of Sikkim's population, the rest being of Nepalese and Indian origin. The people wanted democracy and absorption of the princely state into the Indian Union. But for the Indian government's protection, the maharaja would have been ousted from power long ago.

New Delhi had retained this feudal relic as a semi-autonomous entity in the hope that it might be of some use in dealing with a genuinely autonomous Tibet. But that hope was dashed after China's occupation of Tibet. However, the exposure of New Delhi's weakness in the war had spurred Thondup Namgyal's ambition. He now did not wish to be called maharaja or addressed as 'His Highness'. He took the title Chogyal (meaning 'king' in the Bhutia language). During Maharani Hope's visits to New York and Washington, her friends and gullible American journalists and officials guilelessly pandered to her vanity and regal ambition by addressing her as Her Majesty. In Sikkim, she wanted to be called Gialimo (queen). All this went to the heads of the young couple and they began to indulge in intrigues to make Sikkim independent of India and a member of the United Nations! Meanwhile, the couple's alienation from the people of Sikkim had been growing. Political parties revolted against the ruler and appealed to New Delhi to integrate the state fully into the Indian Union.

BHUTAN

Bhutan was different from both Nepal and Sikkim. The King Jigme Dorji Wangchuck, who ruled the country from 1952 to 1975, was apprehensive about China's expansionism and wanted India to strengthen its defences by reorganizing, rearming and training its small army. On the king's request, a programme of building a network of roads and of strengthening the administration was undertaken on an emergency basis soon after the China–India war of

October–November 1962. A decision had been taken in New Delhi in the late 1950s to help develop Bhutan's international personality and, at a mutually agreed time, to sponsor Bhutan's application for UN membership.

One episode stands out in my memory of my dealings with Bhutan in those days. While the Wangchucks were the reigning monarchs, the Dorji clan held the prime ministership of the country. Jigme Dorji, an able and affable man, who apparently commanded considerable influence in the country was the prime minister. He and his younger brother Lhendup Dorji, who also held a high position under his brother, were frequent visitors to Delhi for a variety of negotiations and I saw a good deal of both during their talks with our authorities and also socially. Lhendup Dorji, who was more or less my age, became a good friend of mine. Because of the power Jigme Dorji wielded as prime minister, he had made enemies in the country. On 6 April 1964, he was shot dead by an assassin who made good his escape after committing the crime.

Lhendup Dorji, who immediately took over as Bhutan's prime minister, suspected, quite unjustly I believe, that in some indirect way the king was responsible for his brother's assassination. So, one day without prior intimation, one of Lhendup's confidants showed up at my residence to say, in a roundabout way, that Lhendup wanted to avenge his family's loss by ousting the Wangchucks, 'one way or another', and that he was hoping for my support! I was shocked by the message, and bluntly told Lhendup's friend that the Government of India, or I personally, were not in that kind of business. And I advised him to leave Delhi at once and tell Lhendup to get on with his sovereign.

On hearing my response, Lhendup must have thought that the news of his improper approach to me might leak; he panicked and chose voluntary exile in Nepal. Two or three days later, when the news broke that Bhutan's prime minister had fled his country and found asylum in Nepal, Secretary General M.J. Desai asked me to look into this sudden development in Bhutan. I told him what had happened, and explained that I had avoided asking Lhendup's friend to wait in Delhi till after I had spoken to him (Desai) or to Foreign

Secretary Gundevia, because I did not want to give the impression that anyone in Delhi would give such a nefarious idea even a moment's consideration. Desai said I had done the right thing and I should now just forget all about it, and he would find a way of alerting the king about his security. He advised that I should keep a discreet eye on Lhendup's activities in Nepal. Lhendup did not receive any encouragement from any quarter in Kathmandu and settled down to a quiet, unpretentious life as an expert chicken farmer.

Nine or ten years later, when I was India's ambassador in Nepal, he came to see me. He was a very repentant and saddened man, terribly homesick for Bhutan and asked me to do something to enable him to return to his own country where he wanted to live peacefully as a loyal citizen. When an appropriate occasion arose, I did the needful. The new monarch Jigme Singye Wangchuck graciously allowed him to return to Bhutan where he lived in mildly restricted freedom, did some farming, played a lot of golf and died peacefully in 2007.

Bhutan's monarchy is a stable institution commanding respect, loyalty and affection of the people. Without ambition for direct autocratic personal rule, King Jigme Singye Wangchuck, in order to accustom his people to the responsibility of self-rule, took the initiative to institute an elective assembly and the cabinet government responsible to it. There was no demand or pressure on him from any quarter for those important political reforms. After the system became fully functional under his benign watch for some time, he voluntarily abdicated in favour of his son Jigme Khesar Namgyel Wangchuck, who is following the path charted by his father and is a popular king with a modern outlook. This is a rare example of an all-powerful monarch guiding his people to democratic self-rule under a constitutional monarchy. All this bodes well for Bhutan's progress, prosperity and stability.

chapter thirteen

A DIPLOMATIC WRANGLE WITH CHINA

~

In the India–Pakistan war of 1965, the Indian army and air force had inflicted heavy damage on Pakistan's armoured units of US-built Sherman tanks and its air force equipped with American Sabre jets (F-86s), F-104s, radars and other equipment supplied by America to its CENTO and SEATO ally. India's air-warriors in their little Gnats had virtually chased Pakistan's F-86s and F-104s out of the skies, and IAF bombers had raided and destroyed targets in faraway places like Peshawar and Karachi. In a huge tank battle, our gunners had knocked out numerous supposedly invincible Sherman tanks and also captured a few in good working condition. The army wanted to install one of these trophies in the green area in the middle of Connaught Place in New Delhi; but our higher authorities were persuaded by the US embassy to save them and their arms captured in battle such disgrace.

Throughout the two-week India–Pakistan war, China kept flinging threats and ultimatums on India from across the northern border. We treated these with cool indifference as empty threats. All this helped restore somewhat the Indian army's reputation and India's prestige and influence in Afro-Asian circles which had been badly dented by the debacle of 1962. In British and American military circles there was surprise at the speed of the recovery of India's political morale and military confidence. But Peking still thought that it could push India around and diplomatically humiliate and maul it at will.

One of the more interesting developments in that context during my time in New Delhi was a move by the China–Indonesia–Pakistan triad to convene an Afro-Asian Conference on the tenth anniversary, in 1965, of the Bandung Afro-Asian Conference of 1955. In March 1964, President Soekarno of Indonesia took the initiative to invite nineteen countries, including India, to send their foreign ministers to Djakarta for a meeting to consider the convening of a second Afro-Asian Conference. At Bandung itself, in 1955, Nehru had become aware of the many ideological divisions and other serious rifts among Afro-Asian countries, and of the ambitions of some Bandung participants to use the conference for the promotion of their own national interests or for their own projection as world leaders. It had taken a huge personal effort on Nehru's part to achieve consensus on the declaration that was issued at the end of the conference. The ten principles enunciated in the declaration were but a rehash of the five principles of coexistence (Panchsheel), and Nehru was already totally disillusioned with China's cynical disregard of Panchsheel in the conduct of its relations with India and in its foreign policy generally.

We found out that before issuing invitations to the preparatory meeting in Djakarta, Soekarno had consulted only two countries, China and Pakistan, and that China's main objective was to dominate the Afro-Asian Conference and isolate and humiliate India in that forum. Nevertheless, Nehru somewhat reluctantly gave the go-ahead for India's participation in the Djakarta meeting by a three-member delegation led by Sardar Swaran Singh (a senior cabinet minister), with Azim Hussain (special secretary in the MEA), and myself in tow for legwork usually indispensable in any conference.

In a discussion of our strategy in the forthcoming conference, C.S Jha, commonwealth secretary in the ministry of external affairs, recalled that in the Bogor preparatory meeting preceding Bandung, the idea of inviting the USSR to the Bandung Conference was mooted but not pursued. The question under discussion was whether we should revive the idea and make a formal proposal that Russia be invited to the second Afro-Asian Conference. Nehru instructed that Moscow should be consulted in the matter beforehand, and our delegation should make the proposal only with Moscow's consent. Gromyko told our ambassador that Russia would not ask for an invitation but would attend the Afro-Asian summit if invited. In other words, we were free to propose at the Djakarta meeting that Russia be invited to the conference.

The agenda of the preparatory meeting convened by President Soekarno of Indonesia was simple: venue and dates etc. of the next summit—Algiers in June 1965 was agreed without difficulty—and approval of the list of countries to be invited to the summit in Algiers.

When the second item came up for discussion, the chairman read out names of countries to be invited. The list did not include Malaysia, an Asian country which had recently achieved independence. This was odd, and in answer to my query a middle-level Indonesian official told me that Soekarno simply would not have Malaysia in the conference. Lobby gossip further revealed that Pakistan and China had also agreed to this. When I mentioned it to Sardar Swaran Singh, he said, 'That is very strange, but good! We shall see what happens.' Then he asked Azim Hussain and myself whether we should also take it upon ourselves to propose the addition of Malaysia to the list of invitees even though Malaysia had not asked us to do so. We both supported the idea.

So, when Sardar Swaran Singh's turn came to address the meeting, he thanked the chair, expressed his appreciation of Indonesia's important initiative to convene the second Bandung Conference and the solid work Djakarta had done for the preparatory meeting, which he felt deeply honoured to attend. He profusely thanked the Indonesian government for its generous hospitality, and referred, in a very soft and gentle voice, to what he thought were one or two omissions in the list of invitees. The world, he said, had been changing very fast, thanks to decolonization and other developments. For example, Malaysia had recently become independent, and Russia (he recalled Bogor) had been actively supporting Afro-Asian causes. Besides, 65 or 70 per cent of its area lay in the Asian land mass along the borders of another huge Asian country, China, and along the borders of a South Asian country, Afghanistan. Furthermore, Soviet

Russia had fully adopted the Bandung policy of peaceful coexistence in its external relations. And finally: 'Mr Chairman, I feel that these two Asian countries fully deserve to be taken into the Afro-Asian community's fold. Therefore I formally propose that Russia and Malaysia be included in the list of conference invitees.'

If there is a thing called 'political bombshell', this was it.

For several minutes there was stunned silence in the conference hall. Then I noticed that China's Marshal Chen Yi looked at the leader of the Indonesian delegation, Ali Sastroamidjojo or Foreign Minister Subandrio—I am not quite certain which one of the two—who looked at Bhutto. Bhutto fixed his questioning gaze on Chen Yi sitting next to him.

Two participants in the meeting spoke briefly; one to say the Indian proposal deserved serious consideration, and the other—an African (perhaps the delegate of Guinea)—supported invitation for both countries. I was watching Bhutto, a frown on his face, anger in his eyes, and Chen Yi, sweat streaming from his agitated face, fanning himself furiously. It was a hot, summer day in Djakarta—the conference hall was not air-conditioned and the ceiling fans whirring above us were only circulating hot air—but never before had I seen a man sweat so profusely on the face.

Sensing that the Indian proposals might gather compelling support, the Indonesian chairman proposed a short recess of fifteen or twenty minutes for informal consultations among delegates. The triad, China–Indonesia–Pakistan, met behind closed doors for half an hour or so, while we relaxed in our seats, awaiting resumption of the meeting.

Neither Indonesia nor Pakistan, not even China, seemed inclined to openly oppose Russia's inclusion in the draft list of invitees to the second Bandung Conference. Pakistan, in particular, was put in a great Islamic dilemma by Indonesia's allergy to the newly independent Islamic Malaysia. China's plan to dominate the Afro-Asian Conference and isolate India had come up against an unanticipated hurdle. And three friendly Indians sat there with solemn visages hiding their satisfaction at the turn of events and wondering what the conspiring triad would come up with next.

The chairman came to Sardar Swaran Singh to say that Chen Yi and his delegation would like to have a meeting with the Indian delegation after dinner that night and he, therefore, was thinking of adjourning the meeting for the day. Sardar Sahib made a show of consulting his two colleagues and gave his consent.

In the two or three early decades of Independence, we Indians were a guileless and very gullible lot. Witness the following account by Subimal Dutt, foreign secretary who was with Nehru at the Bandung Conference:

> The friendship and understanding established between Nehru and Zhou En-Lai was further strengthened by the discussions they had during the Bandung conference . . . Nehru took him (Zhou) as a younger brother. During midday recesses the two used to walk hand in hand along the streets of Bandung with crowds cheering on both sides.

There was no awareness of what was happening behind the scenes. I asked an Indonesian friend about the origins of the China–Indonesia–Pakistan hook-up we were witnessing at Djakarta; when did it take place? 'At Bandung, in 1955,' he said. 'When you guys were gloating over India–China friendship. Nothing secret about it. You guys were sleeping when all this was going on!'

To go back to the Djakarta scene of action, at 9:45 p.m. sharp that evening the two delegations sat face-to-face across a narrow table in a small room, where I had quietly arranged a map of Asia to be hung on a wall showing the mass of China held in tight embrace by the mass of Asian Russia on its northern and western flanks. No handshakes and no greetings were exchanged, despite Sardar Swaran Singh's remark in the air, as it were: 'I am happy to meet Marshal Chen Yi again.'

Chen Yi (CY) opened the meeting: 'The Afro-Asian Conference is very important,' he said.

Sardar Swaran Singh (SSS) said, 'Yes of course; very important. Your Excellency, we attach very great importance to Afro-Asian solidarity and to China's role in strengthening it. As you said, this conference we are planning will be of very great importance. I fully agree with Your Excellency.' (This is a very, very short precis of what SSS had spun out over four or five minutes.

CY: Then why are you doing this?

SSS: Doing what, Excellency?

CY: Wrecking the conference. By trying to bring Russia in it. Russia is not an Asian country.

SSS: Field Marshal Chen Yi, I have only submitted a proposal for discussion. Decision on it rests with Your Excellency and others in the meeting. In the view of many countries, Russia is both a European and Asian country.

CY: Are you doing it because Russia is a great power? (He thumps his chest.) We, China, also a great power.

SSS: I know, Excellency. China is a great power, a very great power. But thank you for telling me. I agree with you.

CY: Then why are you doing it? You do not want the conference.

SSS: We are very keen to have a second Afro-Asian Conference, Excellency. More countries have become independent since Bandung, like Malaysia in Asia; and many more, twenty or more African countries have become independent since 1955. Excellency, you asked why I proposed Malaysia's inclusion.

CY: No, No. Malaysia is not important. Why Russia?

In answer to this, Sardar Sahib launched off on a long explanation, very much on the lines of the arguments he had adduced in the morning in support of his proposal, repeating each important point a couple of times.

Then he looked at his watch; it was eleven o' clock. Without rising from his chair, he mentioned that he had to take some medicines at a particular hour, and that he had not brought the medicine to the meeting.

CY: What you are doing is not wise.

Chen Yi rose from his chair. He looked flustered. Sardar Swaran Singh also rose saying to Chen Yi that if he wanted to leave, their deputies could continue the discussion. Then he specifically instructed Azim Hussain to continue the important discussion with His Excellency's delegation.

He lingered, hoping Chen Yi would leave first. Chen Yi obliged after signalling to his delegation to continue, and saying to Sardar Swaran Singh: 'This is not good; you will not gain anything by doing this. Not wise,' and he left the room.

A line in Aeschylus's *Prometheus Bound* came to my mind: 'Sometimes a wise man gains his point by being thought unwise.'

The same old ding-dong argument continued for the next hour and a half between Azim Hussain and Chen Yi's deputy. Finally, to disarm his interlocutor, Azim Hussain drew his attention to the map on the wall: 'Look there, Sir, China's longest border with a foreign country is with Russia, three-fourths of Russia's territory lies in Asia in close proximity to China. Look at that central Asian region of Russia bordering Afghanistan, Turkmenistan and your own Sinkiang province! All Asian lands, Asian people!'

There was a guarded hint at a 'compromise'—China could perhaps agree to invite Malaysia; India should compromise and not press for Russia's inclusion!

Azim Hussain said Mr Chen Yi could propose that in the meeting the next day.

The Chinese saw through the trick. They sulked, looked angry, spoke harsh words. Azim Hussain and I relaxed, listened, argued back politely and enjoyed doing all that hugely.

No compromise; and we dispersed after midnight!

The following day the conference decided to transfer this issue, along with some other minor routine items, to Algiers, where these would be considered in March–April 1965 in succession by the standing committee, the preparatory committee, and the foreign ministers' meeting in advance of the summit on 29 June 1965.

A strong Indian delegation comprising five or six MPs, led by India's veteran of UN conferences, Foreign Secretary C.S. Jha, frustrated all attempts by the triad and their five or six supporters to shelve the issue of invitations to Russia and Malaysia. On two or three occasions, Algerian organizers arranged meetings of the preparatory committee with only China and its supporters present to approve the list of invitees (excluding Russia and Malaysia), by obtaining a rump consensus behind the backs of India and its more numerous supporters. But Jha would somehow find out and turn up at those secret locations, as if on a magic carpet, to frustrate their attempts. The end result was that the China–Indonesia–Pakistan triad could not achieve their purpose and were on the defensive. On their initiative the summit was postponed to November 1965.

At every stage of discussion of the issue, support had grown for invitations being extended to both Russia and Malaysia to the Summit Conference. China was isolated in regard to the invitation to Russia. Indonesia did not have enough support, not even from Pakistan, for excluding Malaysia. Pakistan could not openly oppose the exclusion of Malaysia or Russia from the conference. Therefore, at the preparatory meeting in November, Indonesia let it be known that President Soekarno would not attend the summit. China, now, in any case, did not want the summit. So, in November, the summit was adjourned sine die. End of farce.

chapter fourteen

IN GRIEF: A LEAP INTO
THE BIG WORLD

~

I had been in post in the ministry of external affairs for four years when in mid-1966, pressures of postwar workload began to ease somewhat and Foreign Secretary C.S. Jha asked me whether I was keen on an immediate posting abroad. He advised that I should stick around at headquarters for another eight or ten months, for two or three posts of head of mission would fall vacant and he would, then, consider me for an ambassadorial appointment. Meanwhile B.L. Sharma, who was doing the specialist job of officer on special duty (Kashmir) in the MEA since 1947, was to retire shortly and Mr Jha wanted me to join that post. The post was outside the IFS cadre and its emoluments were substantially higher than those of the director's grade in the IFS. I readily agreed to move over to the office of OSD (Kashmir) on B.L. Sharma's retirement. Mr Jha advised me to keep to myself the matter of my likely elevation to ambassadorship in 1967.

I was forty-two at that time; promotions were slow in the Foreign Service and there was a lot of frustration in the ranks of competitive recruits in the service. I had not expected such luck for another four or five years, or more. It was thrilling news which filled me with feelings of excitement, humility and gratitude to the powers on high. I did not have enough words to thank Foreign Secretary Jha.

The work in my new job was of great interest to me, but it was not without a pang that I moved off my old desk. For though the area of my charge as director (north) was limited to Nepal, Bhutan, Sikkim, His Holiness the Dalai Lama and his offices in Dharmashala and New Delhi, resettlement of Tibetan refugees and the war book duties, the area was in the news all the time. In Delhi's diplomatic corps there was a lot of interest in the region and in the problems I was dealing with. Therefore, many foreign ambassadors were in regular touch with me to discuss the situation on the northern border, the ongoing build-up of our defences in the Himalayas or simply to exchange views on the ever-changing hue of India–Nepal relations—a fair number of ambassadors resident in Delhi were concurrently accredited to Nepal.

The ambassadors of Nordic countries and Switzerland, in particular, were interested in our experience of resettling Tibetan refugees in different parts of India. Their visits to my office gave me the opportunity to observe how an ambassador walks, how he sits, how he talks, how he greets you when he comes to call on you or takes leave, how he comports himself when he visits the Foreign Office to call on a minister or the foreign secretary or to have a chat with a comparatively junior official like myself.

As head of the northern division, it was also a part of my duties to control visits of foreigners to India's northeastern region. For visiting Sikkim and other northeastern states, foreigners required an Inner Line Permit, which was issued by a designated authority only after clearance from me. Normally I would accommodate foreign dignitaries and diplomats resident in Delhi, if they were a friendly sort and not likely to sniff around for secret information or cause some other mischief. I would give the clearance after consulting the concerned military and civil authorities in Delhi and the designated authorities in the region. But quite a few requests had to be turned down for security reasons.

A case of particular interest was that of Sir Olaf Caroe of the former ICS, who wanted to visit Sikkim, Bhutan and Assam. The gentleman, I knew, was not well disposed towards India. In Sikkim, I was certain, he would only incite the international ambitions of the maharaja who, I was told, had invited Sir Olaf to Gangtok. The area was not open to tourism; Sir Olaf could not possibly have any legitimate business there. Besides, he was governor of the North West Frontier Province of Pakistan when, under his indulgent watch, tribals were armed and trained by Pakistan's army to invade Kashmir. So, I rejected his request for an Inner Line Permit. The British high commissioner then made approaches on his behalf to high quarters in the Foreign Office and in the prime minister's office, but they upheld my decision and Foreign Secretary Jha told the high commissioner that the procedure for the issue of Inner Line Permits was a complicated one, requiring prior consultation with a number of concerned authorities by the director (north), whose decision was final and could not be countermanded.

KASHMIR: THE LAND OF MY ANCESTORS AND MY DREAMS

During my stint as OSD (Kashmir), I travelled frequently to Jammu and Srinagar and to some vulnerable areas on the Line of Control, and got to know well leading Kashmiri leaders of all the various political parties in the state. Most Kashmiri politicians are a cultivated, charming and witty lot, scintillating conversationalists and hard to beat in argument almost on any subject. My interactions with them were always an enjoyable and enlightening experience.

Over the millennia, Kashmir had been a favoured destination of invaders from Iran, Afghanistan and central Asia. Conversions to Islam, forced as well as voluntary, in the last six or seven centuries of the Hindu (mostly Brahmin) population, had changed the Valley into a Muslim majority area. Kashmiri Islam is of the liberal, tolerant variety. I have met some Kashmiri Muslims who still proudly carry the Hindu honorific 'Pandit' as their surname! Long before the subcontinent's Partition, when Dogra rule was firmly established, Kashmiri Muslim leaders approached one of Maharaja Hari Singh's[1] ancestors for their reconversion from Islam to their original Hindu faith. The ruler, it is said, sent for Brahmin priests from Banaras to perform the conversion rituals. In the discussions with the priests that followed, a dilemma arose about the caste to be allotted to the converts. The issue could not be resolved, and the matter was dropped!

Kashmiri men, Muslim or Hindu, are known for their intellectual eminence and political pragmatism. Kashmiri women are renowned in the world for their beauty and other feminine allures. Kashmiri traders are among the most suave and accomplished bargainers. Kashmiri handicrafts—woollen and silk carpets, hand-embroidered shawls and other garments, decorative papier mache articles and carved walnut wood furniture are the prized possessions of connoisseurs in India and faraway countries of the world. Kashmiri cuisine, especially its non-vegetarian content is rich in variety and taste and in life-shortening calories.

The verdurous slopes of snow-capped mountains, which stand guard around the valley, nurtured all year round by glittering streams pouring out of hidden springs, are still a poet's dream; but the two great lakes—Dal and Nagin—have diminished in size and their waters are without the pristine clarity of earlier times.

The Valley is overpopulated and overcrowded, and ungainly structures of brick and stone have encroached on the Jhelum River's course resulting in disastrous periodic flooding of Srinagar city.

My vision of paradise is a place sparse in population, with foaming silver streams flowing unhindered in their natural courses and young maidens singing old ditties of far off romantic times while grazing their herds of goat and sheep, their songs echoed by the sweet warbling of bulbuls and other heavenly birds. In paradise divine law exiles crafty shopkeepers and noisy politicians, and bans violence of word and deed.

Kashmir is not that kind of paradise any more, alas; it is beautiful nevertheless and tourists flock to it from all over the world to savour its charms. The hills of the Jammu region also have their scenic spots of rejuvenating natural beauty. Since our week-long honeymoon in Srinagar in October–November 1956, I had not been back in the land of my ancestors, and I availed of my four or five visits to the state to greedily fill my eyes, mind and heart with its manifold attractions. It was a very happy time of my life.

DEATH OF OUR LIFE'S STAR

Then tragedy struck to make the rest of our lives a benighted region of sorrow. On 18 March 1967, our elder son Yatish Krishna, was run over by a military truck and instantly killed in front of our residence at the end of Wellesley Road (now Subramaniam Bharti Marg), facing Purana Qila.

Eight or ten boys of the locality, including Yatish, were playing cricket in an open space near our residence. The boy with the bat hit a boundary way across the main road running nearby. Yatish, a fielder, crossed the road to pick up the ball, alas to be brought back home wrapped up in a white sheet, dead. That evening I took him to the cremation ground and placed him on the funeral pyre with a heavy heart, which wanted to burst and die but was fated to live and grieve. I did not have the courage to bare his face for a last look at that visage of innocence and love which had filled our home and our lives with so much laughter and joy. I had no tears for now; only silent rage against life's errant companion, Death.

Yatish was ten years old with the maturity of a teenager of fifteen. A brilliant student of the Junior Modern School on Humayun Road, Bahrisons bookshop in the nearby Khan Market was his favourite haunt. He had built up quite a collection of his own, and appropriated some of my books, and serially numbered them all! One of the latter was a coffee-table book of coloured reproductions of famous paintings exhibited at the Louvre in Paris. Having gone through the book, he showed the Mona Lisa portrait to his mother and said that he wanted to see that painting whenever we were in Paris. From me he extracted a promise to take him to the Louvre to see the Mona Lisa when we visited Paris. When asked why he had chosen that particular painting, he answered: 'because that is the best of the lot!'

Yatish's sudden and tragic death had shaken us all to the very core of our lives. His younger brother, Dilip Krishna, aged seven, would ask every now and then when his brother would come back, bringing a fresh flood of tears in our drained out eyes. Grief had so broken Kadambari that she became suicidal. She began to hate Delhi, the

city she once loved. I, a practising Hindu since childhood, became
an agnostic. My Foreign Service colleagues, our friends, relatives and
well-wishers rallied around us with emotional support in our time of
black despair. Touching support and solace came from an unexpected
quarter: Dr Zakir Hussain, vice president of India, walked into our
residence unannounced, and held us both in his arms till our sobbing
stopped. His words were those of a kindred spirit; they soothed and
comforted us. Dr Hussain became India's President in May 1967 and
after my appointment as India's ambassador to Morocco and Tunisia
was announced in September 1967, he honoured us with a big lunch
at the Rashtrapati Bhavan. He complimented us on our choice of
Morocco; he had visited the country and loved it. He gave us very
useful advice as to how we should conduct ourselves in Morocco and
Tunisia.

Days passed somehow, but at night grief filled the home of our
absent child. It took five years and an unplanned meeting with Sri
Sathya Sai Baba of Puttaparthi, his love, grace and revelatory teaching
to recover my faith. He was a God-man in the true meaning of the
phrase.

I tried hard to hold myself together to be able to look after my
wife and our disoriented child, Dilip Krishna. What, in an unusual
way, also helped me in my struggle was a nagging voice that had
haunted me throughout Yatish's life of ten years. Stop grieving, it
would say, you were forewarned; what was fated has happened, now
be a man!

An astrologer and horoscope caster in our village, which his
family and mine had left behind in Pakistan in 1947, had turned up
at our residence a few weeks after Yatish's birth wanting to know the
exact date and time of the boy's birth. His family had been preparing
the horoscopes of my forebears for generations. 'Your son is a blessed
soul, a favourite of the gods. He will be a brilliant and affectionate
child, but do not get too attached to him,' he had said in a sombre
and subdued voice. I asked why, but he would say no more. After a
great deal of my urging and coaxing him, with a face darkened with
unhappiness, he stammered out a few words: 'I have tried very hard,
but I do not see his life after nine or ten years.' He gave me the boy's

horoscope which said as much. I had not the heart ever to share this deadly knowledge with Kadambari. Thereafter, even in the happiest of our times together, that same voice within me would say, as if to itself: 'I wonder how long he will be with us.' And I would try to suppress that voice, but without success.

In July 1967, Azim Hussain, the MEA's administration boss at the time, walked into my room in the MEA to tell me that on the Foreign Service Board's recommendation, Prime Minister Indira Gandhi had approved of my appointment as ambassador, and that I had a choice of three posts which would fall vacant in the next month or two: high commissioner for India in Australia, ambassador to Turkey, and ambassador of India to Morocco with concurrent accreditation to Tunisia. We needed time and a calm environment for more family time together to get over the trauma we had suffered and to put our lives together again. After weighing the pros and cons of each post we chose Morocco and Tunisia, largely for the reason that Rabat and Tunis were close to London, Paris, Rome and Geneva, just in case Kadambari or I might need medical attention in an emergency.

Ankara would have been busier and, in some ways, a more interesting post work-wise, but our choice was also influenced by our civilizational and historical interests. Carthage of yore had always held much fascination for us both. What weighed with Kadambari even more was the likelihood of a leisurely pace of life in Morocco, and also the pleasant memories we had of our association with the friendly delegates of Morocco and Tunisia at the United Nations in New York.

We left New Delhi by air for Morocco in October 1967 with three or four days' halt each in Moscow, Stockholm and Paris to spend some time with friends I had worked with during my five years in the Foreign Office. Ever since Yatish's death, both Kadambari and I had dreamt of our departed darling child virtually every night. In the dreams during this journey, in particular, both of us saw him as a happy, smiling and somewhat excited little boy. During our first night at 5 Rue du Général Lambert, the ambassador's residence in Paris, I had a particularly vivid dream in which he said to me: 'Remember? You had promised to show me the Mona Lisa painting in Paris.' We went to the Louvre the following day and had a good, long look at that famous masterpiece by Leonardo da Vinci. His wish fulfilled, from that day on I had no more dreams of my little boy.

Our dreams in this case, I felt, were a palpable medium of contact and communication with our child's disembodied spirit every night for months till that day in Paris. That experience raised many questions in my mind about the nature of the soul to which I have not found the answers. When the soul casts away the body's garment, does it have a form and a voice, eyes to see and ears to hear? And are such dreams real, or just vain imaginings of our minds, or echoes of our thoughts stored in memory? Does the soul retain a memory? Or nurse human feelings, hanker for fulfillment of a wish or desire formed during its earthly existence? And what happens to it once that wish or desire is fulfilled? What is its shape after it has shed its body?

The Bhagavad Gita, in its most profound and expressive definition of the soul in verse twenty of its second chapter says:

It is never born, nor does it ever die,
Nor having come to be, will it cease to be;
It is unborn, eternal, permanent and primeval.
It is not slain when the body is slain.

But even this does not answer any of my questions. My own personal search for answers to these questions has been in vain.

FRIENDSHIP AND GOODWILL IN MOROCCO AND TUNISIA

On arrival at Rabat we made ourselves comfortable in our residence, a well- furnished, spacious, two-storey homely building with well-maintained lawns in front and back. The house was flanked by the residence of the Swedish ambassador on its right and a very friendly French physician whose little son of seven or eight, Xavier, instantly struck up a friendship with Dilip when the family came over to greet us with flowers the day after our arrival in Rabat. Our other neighbour, the Swedish ambassador, Lars Petrus von Celsing and his wife were a charming couple and we enjoyed a very friendly relationship with them throughout our stay in Morocco.

On the afternoon of 22 November, I presented my credentials to His Majesty King Hassan II. The king spoke very warmly of India, of India's leadership of the Non-aligned Movement and its strong support for Morocco's independence from France. He fondly recalled his meetings with the late Prime Minister Jawaharlal Nehru and his daughter Indira Gandhi during his visit to India as crown prince. He said I would have his and his government's strong support in anything I wanted done to further strengthen India–Morocco relations. With its forty or so embassies, the diplomatic corps in Rabat was a very friendly and informal group and soon we were drawn into that friendly circle's social activities. To my very pleasant surprise, access to high authorities, including Prime Minister Benhima, Foreign Minister Ahmed Laraki and other cabinet ministers was easy and there was a general desire in Morocco's policymaking circles to strengthen relations with India.

The credentials presentation ceremony in Tunis was much simpler than the one in Morocco, where the whole cabinet was standing behind the king when he received me. In Tunis, as soon as Foreign Minister Habib Bourguiba Junior and the Chief of Protocol Taher Braham led me into President Bourguiba's spacious office, he rose from his chair behind his large table and took a few steps towards us. Braham formally presented me to him, I bowed my head slightly in respect and gave him my 'lettres de créance'. He asked me to sit in the chair next to his, saying, 'Let us talk instead of making formal speeches,' and I took my seat after the President sat down in his chair.

After the usual exchange of greetings, the President said how much he had admired Gandhi and Nehru and that he had keenly followed the struggle led by them for India's Independence. He did not know much about Nehru's daughter, Indira Gandhi, he said, and asked me to tell her that it would give him great happiness to see her in Tunis. In an aside he added he himself was getting on in years and did not like to travel—the President was looking a bit frail. 'Like her father I am trying to stabilize secular democracy in my country. Tunisia is much smaller than India but that does not mean I have no problems. Give Mrs Gandhi my best wishes. I want to see India strong and prosperous; all of us derive strength from India's strength.'

I respectfully complimented him as a great leader of a country with a fabulous inheritance of history and a blend of two ancient civilizations, Carthaginian and Roman. That seemed to please him and he said, 'India has even a larger civilizational heritage. What do you think? Is it an advantage or a disadvantage for a nation to have such an inheritance?' In reply I said that he was by far the better judge in the matter; but in my opinion, for what it was worth, a great civilizational inheritance stimulated and enhanced the scope of a nation's intellectual powers and historical memory and adds value to its arts and culture. But it could also tether the national genius to the past and become an obstacle to change which could be a serious disadvantage. 'You are right ambassador; there are advantages and disadvantages,' said the President. To conclude a short but very lively discourse that followed on the affairs of the Maghreb, he said, 'There is not much cooperation among us.' Finally, in an informal personal note, President Bourguiba said, 'Mrs Rasgotra has come with you. Why didn't you bring her here?' 'She would have loved to pay her respects to you, Mr President, but protocol does not allow that on such occasions,' I said. 'Ah, protocol! Well I invite you both to attend the pony races day after tomorrow as my guests.'

We attended and enjoyed the pony races in which one of the President's own ponies was running. At the races he was a young enthusiast, encouraging and urging his own pony, which however lost the race. I came out of my meeting with President Bourguiba with the impression of a big-hearted man of great wisdom and moderate views who, as the leader of a bigger country, would have been a major figure on the world stage. Size does matter; would there be a Churchill without the Empire? Lee Kuan Yew of Singapore is an exception to the rule.

In the seven days I spent in Tunis, I met a lot of Tunisian men and women in meetings and receptions organized by the chief of protocol and my very energetic and popular deputy, Zaman who, in my absences from Tunis, acted as the chargé d' affaires. There was a general atmosphere of freedom and good cheer in the country. I saw very few women wearing veils. Well-spoken educated young women seemed happy working in offices and large establishments like hotels and tourist centres. In human development, Tunisia was way ahead of its neighbours and other African and Arab countries. That the recent phenomenon of the Arab spring began in Tunis and many young women were the leading figures in it did not surprise me. The fizzling out of that new dawn in the Arab world has puzzled me much.

Tourism was a major contributor in the economy of both Morocco and Tunisia. I do not recall seeing beggars or other signs of distressing poverty in the towns of either country. The trade of both countries was mostly with Europe. President Bourguiba had said to me that geography had tied the country and its economy to Europe. Tunisia's only export to India was phosphates, with the balance of trade very much in Tunisia's favour. A textile industry, winemaking and some other small enterprises were doing good business with Italy and other European countries.

Morocco's trade with India in those days was also limited to exports of phosphates and its derivates for our fertilizer factories. Moroccans drank lot of green tea (imported from China) with fresh mint. During a golf game with King Hassan, I persuaded him to direct his government's tea importing department to look at India also as a source of tea imports. The following day the director of the department—a very pleasant Jewish gentleman whose name I have forgotten—called on me to say that the king had directed him to go to India to explore the Indian market for the department's tea imports. I advised him to visit the Kangra district and the Amritsar tea market for green tea, and Darjeeling and Assam for other brands. Within a couple of weeks he was in India and soon returned with a load of samples. I was unable to pursue the matter further as within weeks of these happenings I was transferred to Washington DC as deputy chief of mission over my unavailing protests and pleas to leave us in Morocco for at least another year, to enable us to get over the trauma of our first child's tragic death in Delhi.

In my first meeting with Prime Minister Mohamed Benhima, he mentioned that a summit meeting of Islamic states was to take place at Rabat in a couple of years, and added that he had heard there were more Muslims in India than in Pakistan. That, I said, was a fact and I gave him the figures. 'India's President is also a Muslim,' he said and I confirmed that too, and added that President Zakir Hussain had visited Morocco some years ago and loved the country and had advised me in particular to visit Fez—a most colourful and attractive city. Then the prime minister said something which surprised me: 'Wouldn't it be wonderful if your President were to declare India an Islamic state!'

I said to him that Indian democracy was governed by elected officials under a secular constitution, and that no single authority had absolute power to make declarations of the kind he had suggested. The great majority of the population of 400 million were Hindus. Muslims were the next largest religious community numbering about 50 million, and then there were millions of Christians, Sikhs and Buddhists. They were all equal citizens of the state, each perfectly free to practise his or her faith. The Indian state was not a religious entity; it was the protector of all religions and of freedom for all its citizens to practise the faith of their choice.

After he had heard me out, Benhima said he felt India's Muslim President should attend the Islamic States' summit, and asked whether he would be allowed to attend the summit if he were invited. I said I could not visualize anyone standing in the way of his attending the summit if invited. I do also clearly recall mentioning that if there was an objection at all, it might come directly or indirectly from Pakistan. Benhima's reaction was: 'Why should Pakistan object if India has a larger Muslim population than Pakistan? After all, it is a meeting of top Muslim leaders in the world!'

I reported this conversation to my government in considerable detail, with the recommendation that the government carefully consider their response should the Moroccan hosts finally decide to invite President Zakir Hussain to the Islamic countries' summit. As preparations for the conference got under way, I was not in Morocco to watch developments and advise New Delhi. To my regret and my wife's profound unhappiness, I was transferred in an emergency to Washington DC in February 1969 after a short stay of sixteen months in Morocco.

A few months later Morocco did send an invitation to President Zakir Hussain, and the invitation was accepted. When the Pakistan President General Yahya Khan discovered this on arrival in Rabat in October 1969, he kicked up a shindy. Our delegation was late in arriving in Morocco and the Indian chair at the conference table was occupied initially by an Indian embassy official, which riled Yahya Khan all the more. He told the conference organizers that if an Indian was present in the conference he would not attend it. So, when the Indian delegation arrived in Rabat, an embarrassed Morocco advised it to stay away from the conference. The affair ended in a fiasco, bringing little credit to Pakistan, India or the conference's several participants who, in addition to Morocco, had supported India's participation.

Indian films and film music are popular in Morocco. I was invited to a quiet dinner at home by a Moroccan friend. When I entered the house I was greeted by a lovely little girl of six or seven years. With her parents standing a few feet away behind her, the girl greeted me with folded hands and sang three lines from a catchy little rhyme from an old Indian film:

Akhiyan mila ke
Jiya bharma ke
Chale nahin jana

(Having linked your eyes with mine,
Having sent aflutter my heart
Do not go away ever)

And then she did a little jig Bollywood style followed by 'Namaste'.

I picked up the little angel and kissed her on the forehead and both of us walked over to her parents. I thanked them for such a touching welcome. My hostess said: 'Ambassador, you are now a part of our family!' There is nothing on earth to match 'poulet aux citrons' and 'poulet aux olives' made in a Moroccan home. Moroccan cuisine and the warmth of Moroccan hospitality, from the feasts in the royal palaces to meals in middle-class homes, are in a class of their own. Kadambari and I had enjoyed both in good measure.

For Kadambari, an exciting occasion came soon after the mother of the king's children (that is the description of the lady who in other countries would be called the queen) gave birth to a son—the present Mohammed VI. As a part of the celebrations, the king invited the wives of some local dignitaries and a few ambassadresses, including Kadambari, to the harem to see and bless the mother and the child and enjoy a lavish dinner with the ladies of the harem. The king himself spoke with each invitee and was a most warm-hearted and charming host. For the invitees this was a once-in-a-lifetime treat: nearly half a century later Kadambari still recalls the occasion with nostalgia.

Morocco is one of the most scenic countries in the world with snow-clad mountains, lush green plains with their palm groves and orchards, and deserts juxtaposed together in an abundance of countless cultural, historical and architectural attractions for tourists of all ages. The cities of Fez and Marrakesh in central Morocco and Agadir down south in the desert were my favourites. Marrakesh had a golf course lined with orange trees. I played a game of golf there with some Moroccan friends. To quench our thirst on a sunny afternoon we plucked and ate juicy oranges while walking on the course! In the 1960s, Morocco had a population of 8 million, and it was regularly hosting 9 to 10 million tourists every year—that number must have grown larger still. Morocco's scenic golf courses are among the country's major tourist attractions.

In December, I received orders transferring me to our embassy in Washington DC as deputy chief of mission. I was told that our ambassador in Washington, Ali Yawar Jung was seriously ill, that Nixon had been elected President, and Prime Minister Indira Gandhi felt there would be new difficulties in India–US relations and she wanted me there to deal with the situation. When I returned to Delhi for a short holiday and consultations, Prime Minister Indira Gandhi said to me, 'Richard Nixon means trouble for India. He dislikes India and he hates me. You know America; I want you to be there to deal with the problems that might arise and hold Ambassador Jung's hand. I don't want to withdraw him while he is under treatment there.'

Kadambari was disturbed and unhappy again, but there was no way I could argue with the prime minister. My normal tenure of three years in a post had been cut short by half. We were not happy to leave Morocco and Tunisia. But this short posting had a therapeutic effect on our lives and prepared us for exacting times during the next eight to ten years. A long meeting Kadambari had with Indira Gandhi helped her calm down, and off we went to Washington DC in April 1969.

chapter fifteen

INDIA AND THE NIXON WHITE HOUSE

~

We reached Washington in May 1969 after a couple of months of leave and consultations in New Delhi. In Morocco Kadambari had met and made friends with King Hassan's sister, Lalla Aicha during the king's dinner for a few ladies in the royal harem to celebrate the birth of Prince Mohammed. Princess Lalla's husband, Moulay Hassan al-Yaqoubi was Morocco's ambassador in Washington. A day or two after we reached Washington, I called up the Moroccan embassy to request an appointment for Kadambari and myself to make a courtesy call on the ambassador and Princess Lalla. Almost immediately, we received an invitation to a welcome dinner for us at their elegant residence the following week.

A MEETING WITH DR HENRY KISSINGER

A surprise awaited us at the embassy. Of the assembled guests, the very first Princess Lalla introduced to us was Dr Henry Kissinger, President Richard Nixon's assistant for National Security Affairs! The introductions over, I walked over to him and said: 'Sir, this is a dream come true. Ever since I read your book, *A World Restored* in 1957 I have been wanting to meet you. That book is the most lucid account of a critical period in European history and of conference diplomacy where the interactions of three or four statesmen succeeded in giving a constantly feuding Europe a century of peace.'

This was not flattery; I meant what I had said and Dr Kissinger liked it. After dinner he sat down with me for a chat. It was then that I told him that after reading the book from cover to cover in 1957 I had made a summary of it in about ten pages and circulated it to all my colleagues in the ministry of external affairs, and recommended the book as a must-read for IFS officers. I also told him that his pioneering work, *Nuclear Weapons and Foreign Policy* had greatly helped me to understand the complex issues involved in nuclear arms control when I was dealing with disarmament issues at the UN in 1961–62.

Dr Kissinger was pleased by what I had said and before taking leave of the host and hostess that evening, he walked over to Kadambari and myself and said, 'I know you were ambassador to Morocco and Tunisia before coming here, and here you are deputy chief of mission (DCM) with personal rank of ambassador. I do not meet many ambassadors, but whenever you have a problem or wish to see me just call the White House number, give your name and ask the operator to put you through to me and we shall meet.' This was a very special favour and in my own embassy Ambassador Ali Yawar Jung and other colleagues were surprised, puzzled, impressed that within a few days of his arrival in Washington the minister for political affairs (that was the Indian DCM's official designation) had managed to meet with the inaccessible Dr Kissinger. I never abused the access he had given me, but the word spread that I had met Dr Kissinger and that facilitated my access to high authorities in the State Department and other wings of the US government.

From that book of 332 pages, *A World Restored*, its author emerges as a historian of rare understanding of the forces at work in international relations in Europe, of the tenets of diplomacy and of the special attributes and limits of European diplomacy and statesmanship of the time. His intellectual powers and his great command of the English language are manifest in his writing and in the nuggets of encapsulated political and diplomatic wisdom which fill the book's pages. Savour, for example, the following:

The acid test of policy is its ability to obtain domestic support.

Policy may be based on knowledge, but its conduct is an art.

History is greater than the individual, but although it teaches its lessons surely, it does not do so in a single lifetime.

Not only geography and the availability of resources trace the limits of a statesman, but also the character of the people and the nature of its historical experience.

Although men can conquer ideas, ideas outlast men.

Diplomacy (is) the art of restraining the exercise of power.

Diplomacy in the classical sense, the adjustment of differences through peaceful negotiation, is possible only in a legitimate international order.

An intelligent man can make up the lack of everything except experience.

My next meeting with Dr Kissinger was on 16 July 1969 in response to a call from him, not a request by me. President Nixon was going to visit a few countries in Asia, including India and Pakistan, and Dr Kissinger said to me he was not getting a clear picture of the prevailing political scene in New Delhi. The Congress party had split and Prime Minister Indira Gandhi was faced with the prospect of running a minority government. 'What is the turmoil in Delhi about? Is there a threat to the stability of Indira Gandhi's government? He asked. I assured him New Delhi was perfectly stable and that the tussle was about the election of the next President of the country. The result would present no threat to government even if Indira Gandhi's candidate lost, but I expected him to win. Meanwhile the acting President would host the banquet in honour of President Nixon. 'Are you sure Prime Minister Gandhi's government will be firmly in position, when the President visits New Delhi?' he asked. 'Absolutely,' I answered.

That seemed to satisfy him and he said the White House chief of staff also wanted to see me for information on some routine matters pertaining to the visit and called in an assistant to escort me to the gentleman. But before leaving him I asked whether the US was planning to give 100 tanks to Pakistan—there were rumours to that effect in Pakistan and in Washington. He said there was no truth in the rumours; the US government had no such proposal under consideration. Dr Kissinger added that the whole question of the supply of arms was under a policy review, and he personally had reached the conclusion that, by and large, the arms supplied by the US government to various countries had not been used by them for the purposes for which the arms were given.

I was still finding my way about the town which had changed a great deal since I had last lived in Washington in the early 1950s. Washington in 1969 was a far bigger, wealthier and busier city, with a more cosmopolitan flavour to it than before. The African American population in the city had increased substantially and Washington DC now had a popularly elected black mayor. Shopping facilities were impressive with good-looking, young, educated, black and white girls on the shop floor in super markets and other big shops. They greeted you with a 'Hi' and 'Can I help you Honey?' which was not an invitation to a rendezvous. It was strictly a business tack inducing you to stay around and buy more than you need. They were taught to treat the customer as king.

Social activity in the town was much greater and far more varied and sophisticated than I had known in the 1950s. A few rich, well-endowed society hostesses helped newly arrived diplomats to meet and mix with the city's high society. There were more bars, restaurants, hotels and other entertainment facilities. American University and Georgetown University had grown in repute and profile. I was invited to both institutions a number of times for talks which was a new experience for me; for among student groups there was curiosity about Indian spirituality, yoga, gurus and meditation. The people I met, and old acquaintances were warm-hearted and friendly as ever. The number of foreign missions had grown to 100 and the diplomatic corps had more than doubled in size. The State Department people dealing with India were not unfriendly but were somewhat sceptical about our country.

A score or more of the senators and congressmen I met in the first two or three months were mostly interested in knowing whether the Indian economy, under democratic governance, was doing as well as Pakistan's economy under dictatorship. Pakistan's rate of growth was higher at the time mainly because of the generous military and economic aid it was receiving from the USA. Per capita foreign aid input in Pakistan was several times higher than in India. Occasionally I would ask my interlocutors whether they would be happier to see India as a dictatorship and they would throw up their hands in horror. 'So, help us,' I would tell them, 'our problems are huge; we are doing our best with our own resources which are insufficient.'

KRISHNA CONSCIOUSNESS IN AMERICA

One day after lunch in a small restaurant near Dupont Circle, I was taking a leisurely stroll on Connecticut Avenue when I heard familiar drum beats and the clanging of cymbals accompanied by chanting of 'Hare Rama Hare Rama, Rama Rama Hare Hare; Hare Krishna, Hare Krishna, Krishna Krishna Hare Hare.' Soon a group of about thirty persons came into view, mostly white, dhoti-clad American young men with shaven heads, a couple of black young men and two or three brown Americans of Indian origin also with shaven heads—all wearing Indian style, loose white and saffron coloured garments. The lead party included three or four white American girls in saffron saris playing the cymbals and an equal number of American young men clad in dhotis and short upper garments were rhythmically beating the oblong Indian drums (dholak) hanging from their necks. Seemingly lost in devotion, they were all chanting the Hare Krishna Hare Rama (HKHR) devotional mantra given to them by their guru, A.C. Bhaktivedanta Swami Prabhupada, the leader of a spiritual movement called 'Krishna Consciousness' (Awareness of the Supreme Lord).

Swami Prabhupada resided in an unpretentious ashram, a few kilometres outside London in Britain. From there his followers were carrying the message of a devotional approach to God in different parts of the West. They were all strict vegetarians and practised total abstinence from alcohol and drugs. The movement had originated in Lord Jagannath's Temple in Puri in the coastal Indian state of Orissa. Its foreign adherents who wanted to go to the Puri Temple for pilgrimage faced difficulties in obtaining Indian visas, because our intelligence authorities had decided that the HRHK people were agents of the CIA! When I saw the faces of those thirty persons glowing with devotional fervour, I felt no such suspicion. In fact after I had absorbed the scene I said to myself, 'Well, finally India has arrived in America!'

Many young Americans were disenchanted with society's almost total preoccupation with money and material aspects of life and the ruling elite's ambition for world dominance. There was hunger among them for a taste of the spiritual dimension of life, the quest for which was turning them to India's sacred music, the Bhagavad Gita and other Indian scriptures, and a simple, contented life of devotion and prayer, meditation and yoga. Young Indians, on their part, were looking to America for entrepreneurship, wealth generation and humanitarianized materialism. The Indian population in the United States (mostly students and young professional immigrants) had grown in 1969 to around half a million or more, as against about 3000 or 4000 in 1950. A slow, quiet blending of two civilizational streams was taking place in two liberal democratic societies.

That day I followed the HKHR procession in order to observe the reaction to the phenomenon of small groups of busy Americans who would stop by out of curiosity to understand what that group of Americans were about, and then move on, a bit puzzled, perhaps even amused. To my surprise the procession turned into the short street—an offshoot of Massachusetts Avenue on which the Indian Chancery is located. I wondered whether they were heading for our Chancery to lodge a protest against our government's policy of denying the HRHK movement's foreign followers entry into India. But about a block away from our building they entered a three or four storey brick building, which was their base in Washington. Here they sang devotional songs, practised meditation and studied Indian scriptures—especially the Bhagavad Gita and the Bhagvatam, the story of Lord Krishna's life.

A few weeks later, three young men turned up at the Chancery with applications for visas for a two-week visit to Puri. The embassy's consular attaché rejected their applications and in despair, they asked for a meeting with the ambassador. After consulting me on the phone the attaché brought them over to my office. I had a long chat with them following which I authorized the issue of visas to them, ignoring instructions concerning prior consultation with the home ministry in New Delhi. The trio went out of our embassy dancing with joy. I followed up by writing to our home ministry, and the head of our Intelligence Bureau to say that the CIA had many other, far more sophisticated and subtle ways of gathering intelligence in or about India, that these boys and girls were spreading India's name and its message of human brotherhood and spirituality without costing us anything. Therefore, government should remove the Krishna Consciousness movement from the list of suspects. I also expressed the hope that the government would honour my action to grant visas to the three HRHK young men to visit the spiritual centre of their movement—Lord Jagannath's Temple at Puri in Orissa. Government approved my action and also accepted my recommendation to remove the movement and its followers from its list of suspected foreign agents.

AMERICANS ON THE MOON

The third week of July brought dramatic evidence of the strides American science and technology had made in the preceding decade. In a wonder moment on 21 July 1969, I saw spectacular pictures on TV of two Americans, Buzz Aldrin and Neil Armstrong, in some kind of a fancy dress, standing on the moon's surface in front of a weird-looking contraption which had carried them to that distant celestial body. It was an astonishing feat not only of America's technological prowess, but also of human daring and endurance.

The United States I had come back to in 1969 was indeed very different from the country and the society I had known in the early 1950s. Perhaps the most important change was in the fraying of the family ethic and the beginnings of the young generation's revolt against family disciplines: indulgence in drugs and in free sex was spreading fast among the youth. The youth's opposition to the war in Vietnam and protests against the draft were widespread and would gain strength.

American popular music was undergoing a change for the better in quality and power. Rock music, popularized by the Beatles, was good but it wasn't all that much of a sex stimulant, nor was its influence on American music as deep as it was made out to be at the time. American jazz had a quality and a resonance all its own. Duke Ellington's orchestra had lifted jazz into a classic art form with worldwide appeal. Blues music, confined to church halls frequented by Black Americans only, was fast gaining national and international acclaim.

There were some wholesome Indian influences also at work in Western societies. In Britain for example, Indian curry in general and kebabs and chicken tikka masala were gaining popularity in middle-class homes. Indian restaurants, though small in number, did brisk business in New York. Yogurt, which was unknown in America in the 1950s, was now a breakfast staple. Those of us living in America in the 1950s and 1960s used to make our own yogurt at home and serve it to curious American invitees. In the intervening years enterprising American visitors to India or the Balkans had picked up the recipes, and set up production chains in their own country. In 1969, I was amazed to see yogurt in different colours and flavours arrayed on the shelves of supermarkets in Washington DC. Indian 'dal' (lentils), a staple of every Indian meal, was also on sale in supermarkets in cans labelled 'lentil soup'. I doubt that there was any acknowledgement of the millennial parentage of the recipes of these high-quality nutrients of Indian origin.

Classical Indian instrumental music and dance, Transcendental Meditation (TM) and yoga were changing Western artistic and cultural tastes. I saw enraptured Western audiences listening to Ravi Shankar's sitar recitals, or joint recitals by him and the master violinist Yehudi Menuhin in pin-drop silence for hours in New York. In London, in 1989 as India's high commissioner I was chief guest at a concert by Ravi Shankar in which he was accompanied by a leading orchestra of the country in a huge auditorium packed to capacity. Ravi Shankar's solo performances were described to me by an

American friend as a spiritually uplifting experience. The Beatles had freely acknowledged Shankar's influence on their later innovations. They had even spent some time with the Transcendental Meditation (TM) guru, Maharishi Mahesh Yogi in Rishikesh on the banks of the sacred Ganga in meditation. However it wasn't all a one-way flow of cultural influences. Zubin Mehta had taken Western orchestras and popularized Western classical music in our country. American painters, sculptors and architects were exerting notable influence on Indian arts and architecture. Hamburgers, Kentucky fried chicken, pizza and Coca-Cola were fast becoming favourites among the Indian youth.

NIXON'S FOREIGN POLICY

The year 1969 passed peacefully without any trouble of the kind New Delhi had apprehended from the Nixon Administration. Even President Nixon's twenty-four-hour visit to Delhi had gone off without any mishap, though also without the slightest lift in relations. In his report to the nation on his Asian tour, the President mentioned with appreciation, a remark by acting President Hidayatullah, about the world's need for a 'generation of peace' and added that he wanted to work for that modest but important goal. All that Dr Kissinger said to me was that it was good to see Prime Minister Indira Gandhi's authority in government and her pre-eminence on the Indian political scene well established.

On the other hand, Secretary of State William Rogers' talks in India seemed to have gone off really well. Assistant Secretary Joseph Sisco, who had accompanied Rogers, was full of praise for the frank and friendly talks they had with Prime Minister Gandhi, Foreign Minister Swaran Singh and Foreign Secretary T.N. Kaul in New Delhi. Our embassy's working relations with the State Department were good. On learning of my frequent visits with congressional leaders, Assistant Secretary Sisco had said to me that there was aid-fatigue on the Hill, and in my talks with senators and congressmen I should impress on them the importance of American economic and technical assistance to strengthen the only working democracy in Asia. My talks, he said, would reinforce the State Department's efforts on the subject.

TOWARDS RAPPROCHMENT WITH CHINA

In an article of 6000 words in the *Foreign Affairs Journal* of October 1967, Nixon had in broad outline indicated the foreign policy he would pursue if elected President. He had dealt at some length with what he called the 'reality of China'. While ruling out early recognition of the Beijing regime by the US and its admission to the UN, he had stated that the world 'simply cannot afford to leave China forever outside the family of nations, there to nurture its fantasies, cherish its hates and threaten its neighbours . . . There is no place on this small planet for a billion of its potentially most able people to live in angry isolation; the world cannot be safe unless China changes.' And there were indications that if elected President he would 'open dialogues' to change China and pull it back into the world community, 'but as a great and progressing nation, not as the epicentre of world revolution'.

There were enough hints in the *Foreign Affairs'* article and in the later Presidential remarks on various occasions that serious moves were contemplated towards US–China reconciliation. In a discussion in January 1970 with Assistant Secretary of State Marshall Green, a most intelligent and respected American diplomat, he had advised me to stop worrying about Vietnam and watch out for developments in American policy towards northeast Asia. He had added that the most difficult problem the US would face in the years ahead was that of the Washington–Tokyo–Beijing triangular relationship, and in that context he had drawn my attention to Japan's deep-rooted fears of the Washington–Beijing relationship which, he emphasized, was bound to affect Japan deeply.

Turning to South East Asia, Marshall Green had said that what the US was aiming at was the emergence of a group of stable non-aligned states in the area, and to that end the US was winding down the war. Green had added that the United States wanted to see South Vietnam evolve as a non-aligned country! All this was news to me. For in my two previous assignments in the country I had only known of Vice President Nixon's visceral hostility to the very idea of Non-alignment. After his visit to New Delhi in 1953, Nixon had told Selig Harrison that he suspected the Indian prime minister, Jawaharlal Nehru, to be 'a secret communist'! Secretary of State Dulles was equally suspicious of Nehru and had taken strong umbrage at Nehru's view that the communist block was not the 'monolithic threat' the Americans believed it to be at the time.

I had asked Green whether the President now really believed that Non-alignment was good for South East Asian countries. Green had affirmed that what he had said on the subject fully reflected the President's thinking, that President Nixon was a realist and pragmatic statesman whose views had been evolving in the light of changing realities in Asia. For instance, the President now recognized that the South East Asia Treaty Organization (SEATO) had little relevance to Asian security and his hope was that the Asia Pacific Council (ASPAC), an organization for cultural and economic cooperation, would acquire a security dimension because of the China threat and that India, having itself been the target of overt Chinese aggression, might be persuaded to support it.

What Green had said about the President's hope for ASPAC and India's support for it is actually stated in Nixon's article in the *Foreign Affairs Journal*. In that article Nixon was no longer contemptuous of, or hostile towards India. After describing India as a 'staggering giant both challenging and frustrating; challenging because of its promise, frustrating because of its performance', he had gone on to remind those who were pessimistic about India's future that in the past five years India had fought two wars and faced two catastrophic droughts, and that on both the population and the agricultural fronts India's leaders were trying. He had stated that the essential factor, from the standpoint of US policy was that a nation of nearly half a billion people was seeking ways to wrench itself forward without a sacrifice of basic freedom, and in exceedingly different circumstances the idea of evolutionary change was being tested:

> For the most populous representative democracy in the world to fail, while communist China . . . succeeded, would

be a disaster of worldwide proportions. Thus the United States must do two things: (1) continue its aid and support for Indian economic objectives; and (2) do its best to persuade the Indian government to shift its means and adjust its institutions so that those objectives can be more quickly and more effectively secured.

This sympathetic and friendly view of India was a good enough basis for a serious exchange of views between Nixon and Indian leaders; but such a dialogue never took place because of Washington's lingering suspicion and worry about New Delhi's deepening relations with Moscow and India's unfading memories of Nixon's past hostility and the anti-India feelings Nixon had tried to spread in American political circles after his 1953 visit to Delhi. Poor personal chemistry and mistrust between him and Indira Gandhi also came in the way of a rapprochement when the two elected leaders were in power in Washington and New Delhi.

PROTESTS AGAINST THE WAR IN VIETNAM

The youth protest movement against the Vietnam War began to look like a permanent feature of the Washington scene in the summer of 1969. Thousands of young men and women were doing day-and-night sit-ins in the open grounds around the Lincoln Memorial, specifically against the Vietnam War and the draft for compulsory military service in Vietnam. I personally mingled with the crowds at the Lincoln Memorial for an hour or two on several days. The protest was perfectly peaceful and the boys and girls at the memorial site were a serious and sombre lot. There were no drugs there, nor sex; there were serious discussions questioning why America was fighting wars in faraway Asian lands, first in Korea and now in Vietnam. The most popular slogans were: 'No to War, No to Draft; Yes to Friendship and Peace; We Want Our Brothers back from Vietnam'.

There were no joyous faces in that crowd; there was silent anger over the deaths of young Americans in the jungles of Vietnam. There was defiance of government and the determination to change its policy. I was not a witness to the event but there were reports that one late evening, President Nixon had visited the protest site and tried to explain to the protesters what he was doing to wind down the war, but he was shouted down and left the place feeling angry and frustrated.

It was on one such day that Dr Kissinger had asked me over to the White House for something unconnected with the protests, but protests against the Vietnam War came up in our conversation and he said, 'There is a declaration every day from New Delhi criticizing us over the war in Vietnam. We want to end the war. What do you think we should do?' I said, 'Dr Kissinger, the intensified bombing campaigns have made no impression on the Vietnamese. In my judgement, neither Madame Binh nor Hanoi want a coalition government with Thieu in Saigon, which is the linchpin of your policy. Therefore, a coalition government in Saigon as a precondition to American withdrawal from Vietnam is not going to work. My honest opinion as a friend of the United States is that you should negotiate a ninety- or hundred-day ceasefire, declare victory and withdraw your forces from the country. The sooner you do it the better.'

Dr Kissinger looked at me in utter disbelief and asked, 'What kind of thinking is that?' 'Indian,' I said and I could see that he was not amused.

So, I added by way of amplification that I did not think there was going to be a victory for the US on the ground in Vietnam, that modern war against a millennial civilization accustomed to fighting periodic aggressions made no sense, that the Vietnamese would perish but not accept defeat from China or the United States or any other power. That was their identity. Therefore, it would be best for the US to declare victory and come out with its honour intact.

'That is what our Vietnamization policy is about,' he said. 'Why don't you Indians try to understand?' In fact, Vietnamization was not about that; it was about saving Thieu and perpetuating the division of the country. But we left it at that.

However, Dr Kissinger had a point about New Delhi's daily criticism of America over the war in Vietnam. Overall, official

Washington's mood in relation to India was not unfriendly, and in the Senate and the House of Representatives there was even some sympathy and support for India's viewpoint on the war. In both Houses there was strong opposition to intensified bombing campaigns and when the secret extension of the war to Cambodia and Laos was discovered there was an angry uproar among the public, and in the media and the Congress. India's denunciations of the war were neither necessary, nor were they going to hasten the war's end. We were only causing avoidable irritation in official circles whose goodwill we needed.

Richard F. Pedersen, counsellor for the Department of State, a very senior official with a White House base, was known to be a bit cynical about India. One day in the course of a conversation with him I asked American style, 'My friend, we are a democracy; there is so much common between our two countries. Why don't you like us?' His reply, delivered with a smile, was equally straightforward and honest, 'Ras, your people are too preachy. Also in most things what you people tell us, about Asia in particular, you turn out to be right, and that hurts, you know.' We shook hands on that. There was no rancour, just plain, honest truth!

On another occasion Pedersen had accused India of having made 'those communist bastards respectable'! In American freestyle diplomacy discourse, the word 'bastard' carries different meanings in different contexts. Sometimes the word is used to show affection and endearment. Everyone knows how much the Americans love the British; so, in a moment of deep emotion General Haig, Henry Kissinger's very likeable and able deputy, had publicly called the Brits 'those duplicitous bastards'!

In 1971, in a conversation with President Nixon, who was frustrated over some Indian action or India's failure to conform, Kissinger had soothed him by saying: 'Indians are bastards anyway'. 'I had a hard time convincing my Gandhian foreign minister, Sardar Swaran Singh not to feel offended because all that Kissinger had meant was that Indians are OK guys in need of a little rough up.

When Dr Kissinger was secretary of state in President Ford's administration, he remembered he had been partial to the Indians in conferring on them his favourite epithetical distinction—bastards; and so, to be even-handed between India and China in a conversation with the President, he endearingly called the Chinese, for whom he had so often proclaimed his love and respect, 'cold, pragmatic bastards'!

All that was by the way. When I visited New Delhi in 1970 for consultations, I asked the concerned authorities why it was considered necessary to criticize and condemn the United States through press briefings or formal statements by government officials every other day. All that, I was told, was by way of expressing sympathy for the underdog! Underdog? The Vietnamese, underdogs! They were already teaching the Americans a thing or two about waging war in Asian jungles.

Anyhow, I took up the matter with Foreign Secretary Kaul, with Principal Secretary P.N. Haksar and finally with Prime Minister Indira Gandhi. They all agreed that our opposition to the war was well known and there was no gain in unnecessarily provoking the United States. The mischief did not end completely but the frequency of official utterances on the subject did register a notable decline.

I had been chargé d'affaires (CdA) for some months when President Nixon sent his foreign policy message to the Congress in February 1970. There was an almost impenetrable overlay of verbiage on its important core content: reunion of Europe and the necessity of reconciliation with China. The American media was highly critical of the message. The *Washington Post* had described it as 'a finely phrased brochure on foreign policy'. The *New York Times* called it 'banal and wordy'. The burden of reactions in the diplomatic corps was that the message really did not say anything new!

No doubt, there was much rhetoric and dissembling in the message, but under the overlay of the treacle of peace, just peace, lasting peace, cooperation and partnership, there was the hard core design to forge a world balance of forces favourable to the United States. Rivalry with, and concern over, the growing power and influence of the USSR ran through it all. Japan and China had therefore to be yoked into the design of a US-dominated power balance. The President was not yet ready to talk openly about the China initiative he was planning;

he was waiting for the Beijing–Moscow rift to deepen and come out in the open. There was a good deal of pampering of Japan, a sort of pre-emptive sop against the shock that awaited Tokyo in Dr Kissinger and President Nixon's visits to China in 1971 and 1972 respectively.

The message referred to the Chinese as a 'great and vital people', whose basic interests were not in conflict with American interests. There were positive references to China as a nuclear weapon power— the spectre of 'a billion Chinese armed with nuclear weapons' had vanished. Now the Chinese were not to be feared, for they were 'a gifted and cultured people' and 'an exploited people'! Clearly the US–China talks in Warsaw, and in Bucharest, were making progress.

While the message gave a lot of space to Asia, its core concern, other than China, was Europe. The 'reunion of Europe,' said the message, 'will come about from an extended historical process' of the erosion of Moscow's power in eastern Europe, which would be hastened by the Soviet Union's conflict with China. President Nixon was well ahead of his time in his visions of Europe and Moscow–Beijing relations.

The message had little in it about India. We were back in the bracket with Pakistan. A cursory sentence raised the expectation of India and Pakistan together making a contribution to peace. New Delhi's imprecatory pontifications on the Vietnam War had taken a toll on Nixon's somewhat positive appraisal of India, to which he had given expression in his *Foreign Affairs* article. In a relaxed moment, my counterpart in the Pakistan embassy told me that his country was unhappy with both Nixon's article and his first Presidential foreign policy message to the Congress.

In regard to the great problem of American foreign policy, the war in Vietnam, the message sought to reassure the public that the President 'would make use of the nation's wisdom to reach the end of the problem'. The message described Vietnamization of the war as a spur to negotiations for a peace settlement. A coalition government in the South was considered the key to ending the war.

My overall assessment of the policy was that Washington's hope for a coalition government in Saigon as a negotiated end to the war was a mirage, and that while Nixon intended to continue the planned reductions of American troops from Vietnam, no one in Washington had a clear idea about how the conflict would end. But clearly our parroting about the unconditional withdrawal of American forces from Vietnam as the only likely solution to the conflict was not going to cut any ice with the White House. Therefore, after my talks on the subject with Dr Kissinger and Pedersen, I too thought it best to leave Vietnam alone.

However much one may dislike or disagree with American officials and their government's foreign policy, if one gets to know the country and its common people, their simplicity and warmth, their childlike desire to be liked, their easy, friendly ways and their generous humanitarian instincts as I had over the years, one learns to respect and love them. In the years that followed it saddened me no end to see American casualties mount in a futile war and its ultimate end in American's defeat and humiliation.

chapter sixteen

GENOCIDE IN EAST BENGAL

~

In the elections held in Pakistan in December 1970 Sheikh Mujibur Rahman, head of the Awami League, the most popular Bengali party, had campaigned vigorously for East Pakistan's autonomy. Pakistan's policies hitherto were dominated by the country's west wing and pursued largely in the interests of West Pakistan. Leaders of the country's Bengali majority population had many grievances about the exploitation of their region's resources for the benefit of West Pakistan. The six-point platform for autonomy, on which Sheikh Mujib's election campaign was based, included the restoration of democracy in the country and autonomy for both East and West Pakistan with the Central government's role restricted to foreign policy and defence. In addition, Sheikh Mujibur Rahman wanted East Pakistan to have the freedom to conduct its own trade and aid negotiations and to raise a militia to assist the police to maintain law and order.

A recent cyclone had caused enormous loss of life and property in large areas of the east wing, and while foreign governments had rushed in with relief and rehabilitation assistance, there was no effort on the part of Pakistan's government to provide succour and comfort to its Bengali population in its hour of need. This callous indifference to their plight had angered the Bengalis and lent poignancy to Sheikh Mujib's campaign for autonomy. In the event, the Awami League swept the polls in East Pakistan winning 167 National Assembly seats out of 169, which gave Sheikh Mujib an absolute majority in the country's National Assembly and, if the democratic process was to be respected, the right to form the government at the centre.

In West Pakistan, Zulfikar Ali Bhutto, a former foreign minister and leader of his newly founded Pakistan People's Party (PPP), had conducted an equally vigorous and populist election campaign for democracy and against military rule. The PPP and its coalition partners had won a good majority in the west wing but Bhutto's vaulting ambition to rule the entire country as its President or prime minister was frustrated by Sheikh Mujib's triumph in East Pakistan. A clash seemed unavoidable. Equally, the election of two leaders with strong popular support in the two wings of Pakistan frustrated General Yahya Khan's hopes to retain his hold on power by playing different groups against one another. Yahya Khan's dislike of Bhutto was well known, but he shared with Bhutto a deep suspicion of Sheikh Mujib's demand for autonomy and for the right to pursue trade and aid negotiations with foreign countries. They feared that he might even declare East Pakistan's independence and seek the friendship of India, the country both hated.

When their protracted negotiations with Sheikh Mujib, mainly to persuade the latter to give up the demand for autonomy, collapsed, Yahya Khan postponed, indefinitely, the National Assembly's meeting scheduled for 3 March 1971. On Sheikh Mujib's call the people in East Bengal launched an indefinite general strike. Shops and markets closed down and masses of people—young and old, men and women—took out processions shouting 'Jai Bangla' (victory to Bengal). In Washington DC, we saw it all on television and in newspapers. There were minor cases of violence but by and large the protests were peaceful and disciplined. However, Yahya Khan's response to this exhibition of democratic fervour was to use force to maintain law and order. Before leaving Dhaka for Islamabad he ordered the army to restore order, and on 25 March 1971 the military, beginning with a massacre of students and teachers, unleashed a brutal reign of terror on the Bengalis, radicalizing a peaceful movement for a people's civil and political rights into an uncompromising revolt for independence.

As I look back on the happenings of the next nine months, I am convinced that this was a moment when Washington's advice to both Sheikh Mujib and Yahya Khan to moderate their positions, avoid violence and the use of the army to suppress a popular movement and reach a compromise on a large measure of autonomy through patient talks, might have averted the bloody genocide that followed and saved Pakistan as a state.

Yahya Khan was dependent on Washington for arms and financial support; he would have paid heed to Nixon's counsel of moderation and survived the crisis. What better reward could there be for his help in Washington's China opening! The fiercely ambitious and pro-China Bhutto, whose intense dislike of the US and implacable hatred of India were well known, would have been isolated. It passes understanding that for their futile inactivity at such a critical and potentially creative moment, Henry Kissinger and President Nixon should have taken shelter behind a shibboleth: 'Why should we tell others how to manage their affairs?'

There was no danger of the Pakistan channel to China becoming defunct. Yahya loved his role of bringing two great powers together and the benefits that would accrue from that role. Nor was the Pakistan–China channel the only contact Washington had with Beijing. As Kissinger himself later wrote: 'To say that we tilted toward Pakistan because of the opening to China is an over simplification. We might have done that anyway.'[1] The Romanian channel was available and the Chinese were as keen on an opening to the US as Nixon and Kissinger were on the opening to China.

The Chinese were apprehensive of an attack by the Soviet Union whose one million heavily armed troops were deployed on the border. Paul Kreisberg, a policy planner in the State Department, had told me that in the event of war, Russian forces would easily detach Xinjiang and Tibet from China and the Chinese knew that. Bravado apart, the Chinese were in panic and in the absence of an approach from Washington, Beijing itself might have deployed a conciliatory approach to Washington. But Kissinger did not want that; it would have deprived him of the fun and excitement of a cloak-and-dagger secret mission to China.

At the time of his visit to China in July 1971, because of the Pakistan army's atrocities, six million Bengali refugees had come into India. By November the number would grow to ten million. Despite our warnings to Washington that India would never acquiesce in that situation and agree to resettle them in India, the White House seemed to think that with some financial help for refugee relief and rehabilitation, India would be persuaded to resettle Bengali refugees in India. Worse still, Kissinger chose to practise on us the nineteenth-century diplomacy of threat.

On the evening of 13 July, after his return from China, Kissinger phoned the residence of the Indian Ambassador L.K. Jha, who was out of the house attending a reception somewhere in the city. The call was taken by the security guard at the residence. Kissinger had given the guard his name and asked him to tell the ambassador to call him back in California on a telephone number he left with the embassy guard—a semi-literate, junior police official from India. When Jha came home from the evening reception, the guard dutifully informed him that one Kishen Singh had called from California and gave him the telephone number which, fortunately, he had noted down with care for the ambassador's return call.

It did not take Jha long to understand who the caller was. He asked me to join him at his residence immediately; he wanted me to be there when he spoke to Henry Kissinger. We had a good laugh over the security guard's Kishen Singh goof. When Kissinger came on the line at around 8 p.m. Washington time, after a quick exchange of greetings he said to Jha that he was one of the four or five ambassadors to whom he was giving the advance information about his return earlier that day from a visit to China. He added that President Nixon had accepted an invitation to visit China the following year. So far so good, and Jha suitably complimented him. But then Kissinger added, quite unnecessarily, what in diplomatic parlance would be considered a threat: 'I hope,' said Kissinger, 'the Indian government will say something nice about this. Any criticism from India will not go down well with us; we will not understand it!' And the line went dead. As Kissinger's China visit was yet to be announced—it was announced by President Nixon on national television on 15 July we sent a brief confidential telegram on the subject to Foreign Minister Swaran Singh.

I had listened to the conversation on a parallel line; Kissinger sounded excited and triumphant, but Ambassador Jha was puzzled by the peremptoriness of the last part of his remarks. I thought Kissinger did not want an immediate response from the ambassador and any probing by the latter into the nature of the secret mission. Or, he might have thought that a prolonged conversation on an open phone line might lead to premature leakage of the news. Or, perhaps, a longer chat would result in diminishing the effect of the words he had uttered.

Ambassador Jha was always inclined to see and interpret Kissinger's words and deeds in the most positive light, and he was somewhat suspect on that account in the MEA in Delhi. But Kissinger's unfaltering support for Yahya Khan, and his callous indifference to the ongoing massacre of innocent Bengali men, women and children in East Pakistan, were hard to explain away. Both Kissinger and President Nixon were contemptuous of India and Prime Minister Indira Gandhi. Their utter lack of concern about the disastrous effects of the influx of ten million Bengali refugees on Indian politics, economy and security was becoming a serious issue between India and the US.

The Indian embassy's effort to persuade the Nixon administration to ask Yahya to stop the Pakistan army's campaign of violence in East Pakistan, release Sheikh Mujibur Rahman from prison, enter into negotiations with him on the question of autonomy and stop the ongoing exodus of Pakistani nationals into India, was getting nowhere. So, we focused our information dissemination efforts on the Congress and the general public. The American media was receptive and helpful and either Ambassador Jha or I was on national TV networks every other day to expose the Pakistan army's atrocities on unarmed Bengalis and its use of American arms for the purpose.

My younger colleagues in the embassy and I travelled to several major cities, leading universities and colleges to inform willing listeners of the ongoing genocide in East Bengal. Despite widespread appreciation of Nixon's China initiative, the country had no sympathy for his South Asia policy.

Everywhere people asked me, 'Why doesn't India use its army to end the genocide in East Bengal and liberate that country?' A retired general of the US army, in a discussion with me and a senior official of the Pakistan embassy on a national TV channel in Chicago, exhorted me: 'Ambassador, it will be a ten-day job for your army to end the genocide and liberate Bangladesh. Why are you allowing this?'

Our publicity and PR efforts had taken care not to violate any American law. Nevertheless, Kissinger took a dim view of our activity, and the burden of his ire fell on Ambassador Jha. He issued a directive that the Indian ambassador should not be received by any American official above the level of a desk officer. However, he himself kept the doors of his office open to occasional visits by Ambassador Jha.

One day, Jha asked me to accompany him to a meeting to which Under Secretary John Irwin, a lean, desiccated, unsmiling figure, rather conscious of his high position and quick to anger, had summoned him. In one of my spells as chargé d'affaires, I had met Irwin and my impression of the man had left me a bit uneasy; our brief meeting had not gone well. But Jha and Irwin were on first-name terms and the meeting began pleasantly enough. Jha told him that the number of Bangla refugees had reached eight million and more were still pouring in; the situation was becoming intolerable for India. Irwin acknowledged all that somewhat grudgingly and added that Indian war preparations did not bode well, that training and arming of Bengali guerrillas for war in East Pakistan was not in accord with international norms. Then for the fifth time in the course of a conversation lasting twenty minutes, Irwin urged that as a responsible power India must exercise the utmost restraint!

Jha looked at me as if to ask whether there was anything more to say, and I took the liberty of addressing Irwin: 'Sir, India is exercising restraint. Nevertheless your counsel for more restraint is welcome. But it will help if the Pakistan government and its army are also advised to exercise restraint and stop killing innocent people so that the influx of refugees into India stops.'

That infuriated the choleric gentleman. Nostrils flared, forehead furrowed with contemptuous surprise, and with anger in his eyes, Mr Irwin, under secretary of state turned upon not me but Ambassador Jha and said: 'Your Excellency, we are doing what is in our national interest, and we shall continue to act in our national interest. We do not need advice about what we should or should not do!'

Jha did not want to respond to that outburst, and we stood up to take leave. Irwin calmed down as quickly as he had flared up, we shook hands and left. As soon as our car left the State Department, I apologized to Jha for ruining not only the meeting but also his friendship with Irwin. 'I suppose you would now want to have me moved out of Washington!' I said. Jha burst out in uncontrollable laughter; so did I. He said, 'You know Krishna, there is a deep sense of guilt lying hidden somewhere in that man; you triggered it. 'Jha had a sense of humour. We differed on some issues of policy but we got on well together and made a good team during that most trying time in India–US relations.

The other under secretary, Mr Alexis Johnson was a very different man: thoughtful, urbane, a good listener, tolerant and considerate towards a viewpoint different from his own. Jha and I had met him in his office two or three times for very constructive and enjoyable conversations. In the meetings of the Washington Special Action Group (WASAG), chaired by Henry Kissinger in the White House, he spoke up against illegal actions under consideration in the group, such as Kissinger's idea to persuade Jordan and Iran to transfer American fighter jets to Pakistan in violation of American laws. I had played a couple of rounds of golf with him, courtesy my good friend Assistant Secretary of State Marshall Green. He was very pleasant company on the golf course and very easy to talk with on any matter whatsoever.

Almost from the day in March 1971, when the Pakistan army launched its brutal crackdown in East Pakistan, the State Department, the staff in the American embassy and consulates in India and the American consulate general in Dhaka were in strong dissent from the Nixon–Kissinger policy towards East Pakistan and the duo's all-out support for General Yahya Khan. In the White House too, Kissinger's two staffers dealing with South Asia, Sam Hoskinson and

Hal Saunders and Kissinger's special assistant, Winston Lord saw the dangers in the policy and had repeatedly, but in vain, advised Kissinger to reconsider the policy.

The consul general in Dhaka, Archer Blood, was also reporting daily by telegram to the State Department the gory details of the crackdown and the Pakistan army's use of American equipment, such as C-130 transport planes, F-86 jet fighters, M-24 tanks and other arms and ammunition in massacring its own nationals. But the White House paid no attention to the ongoing genocide in East Pakistan. Instead Nixon and Kissinger were angered by the consulate general's objective reporting of the ground reality in Dhaka.

In an act rare in the annals of bureaucracy, American officials of the consulate general drafted a telegram of dissent from their government's East Pakistan policy. The telegram was sharply critical of Washington's moral bankruptcy and its failure 'to denounce the suppression of democracy, atrocities and genocide'. The consul general, Archer Blood himself did not sign the telegram but in forwarding the same to the secretary of state endorsed its content and supported the right of the signatories 'as professional public servants' to express their dissent with current policy.

The secret telegram received far larger circulation than its senders might have intended. A day or two after it was received in the State Department I was shown a copy of it in a senator's office. In the State Department's middle and lower ranks, there was a lot of support and admiration for the courage of the young foreign service officers who had staked their careers to uphold the honour and humanitarian ideals of their nation. But President Nixon, Kissinger and Secretary of State Rogers were enraged and they took it all out on Archer Blood who was recalled from Dhaka, shunted into a nondescript job in the State Department, denied promotion and deprived of the ambassadorial appointments which would have been his in the normal course.

Another target of contempt and abuse from Nixon and Kissinger was the American ambassador to India, Kenneth Keating, a former Republican senator from New York. He was a highly respected and influential political figure in Washington who could not be bullied.

His recall from Delhi would have caused a furore in political circles in Washington DC. He was an outspoken critic of US policy in East Pakistan and forcefully supported Dhaka's 'Blood Telegram'. He described the situation in East Pakistan as a 'massacre and selective genocide' and repeatedly warned Washington DC of the danger of war inherent in the ceaseless flow of Bengali refugees into India.

The official capital was leaking like a sieve in those days and Ambassador Keating's cables had the effect of turning influential congressional circles, the media and the civil society against Nixon's policy. American diplomatic personnel in Lahore and Karachi were also agitating against Washington's studied indifference to the gruesome happenings in East Pakistan, but their dissenting voices were suppressed by Ambassador Joseph Farland, the only senior American diplomat in the region to toe the Nixon–Kissinger line that the reign of terror in East Pakistan was strictly an internal matter for Pakistan!

So far as the influx of refugees in India was concerned, my impression from my talks with White House officials and Assistant Secretary Joseph Sisco in the State Department was that, at least, Nixon and Kissinger believed that given a few million dollars for refugee relief and rehabilitation India would be mollified into resettling ten million Bengali refugees in India. In a bizarre conversation with me one day, Sisco cited to me India's history of 'taking into its fold' waves of foreign migrants of diverse origins. The Bengalis from East Pakistan, he said, were people of Indian origin, therefore, it might not be difficult for India to absorb them. The United States, he added, would help India in that humanitarian task with financial support.

I reminded Sisco that the United States, far more than India, was a nation of refuge seekers; it had a much larger area and more vast open spaces than India. So perhaps we should consider a deal: we should go fifty-fifty. America, I said, should accept 50 per cent of the total number of refugees and India would consider accepting the rest for rehabilitation in its territory. Sisco threw up his arms in horror. I then rubbed it in saying, 'You gentlemen have no idea of the gravity of the situation. You have not paid attention to Prime Minister Gandhi's repeated declarations that every single refugee will have to return to his home in East Bengal. She means it.' The thought never came up in our conversations again.

Henry Kissinger's two very able and conscientious staffers on South Asia, Hal Saunders and Sam Hoskinson clearly saw the consequences of the tragic happenings in East Pakistan to US–India relations. But Kissinger was deaf to their prognostications about the growing inevitability of an independent Bangladesh and the impending estrangement of India. I had kept in touch with them about India's likely responses to the deteriorating situation in East Bengal. They became very good friends of mine and we met, often for lunch, to exchange information and views. Young Sam was particularly upset and angry over the Nixon–Kissinger policy, which he considered un-American in its gross disregard of American humanitarian ideals and natural good sense. *The Blood Telegram*, by Garry Bass, fully vindicates these two exemplars of the best in the American tradition of foreign policy and diplomacy.

Because of my personal involvement in the Indian embassy's publicity effort, which had incurred Kissinger's disapproval, I had thought it best to stay away from him. However, a situation arose in July 1971 necessitating my approaching him for the favour of a meeting with an Indian political leader, Jayaprakash Narayan, a well-known Gandhian of socialist orientation. Though a professed pacifist, he was so roused by the Pakistan army's brutality in East Bengal that he had been openly urging Prime Minister Indira Gandhi to declare war and liberate Bangladesh. He was also advocating India giving all financial and arms help to the Mukti Bahini guerrillas. Narayan believed in the moral force of truth and was keen to visit a few foreign countries to bring their leaders round to his own viewpoint on the issue of Bangladesh. In Delhi, where the reasons for caution and patience were better understood, he was making life difficult for Prime Minister Indira Gandhi with his emotional outbursts. So, she sent him out on a tour of foreign countries to 'convert' world leaders to his viewpoint.

Narayan was in Washington DC for a week. He was made comfortable by Ambassador Jha at his residence and I organized his meetings with leading American figures in public life, and with members of the House Foreign Affairs Committee and the Senate Foreign Relations Committee. In addition, I had requested Sisco, who knew Narayan, to arrange meetings for him with Henry Kissinger and senior State Department officials as well as himself. Narayan's sincerity and genuine concern for human rights, his impassioned pleas for an end to the genocide in East Pakistan and for that region's independence had impressed his interlocutors and he felt encouraged by their sympathy and support for his mission. There were only two more days left before his departure for India and the one meeting on which he was most keen, had not come through.

So, Narayan said to me, 'Rasgotraji you have done so much to make my visit fruitful, but the main purpose for which I came here remains unfulfilled.' I asked what exactly he wanted me to do and he said, 'I must meet Henry Kissinger; I want him to know the truth, and I want to convert him to my understanding of the stark reality and how it should be dealt with.' I told him that a meeting with Kissinger had been requested through official channels but he had not responded. I promised that I would do my best to get some time for him with Kissinger before his departure for Delhi.

A while later I called the White House number, gave my name and requested to be put through to Dr Kissinger. When he came on the line I said that I had sought an appointment for Jayaprakash Narayan with him, through the State Department, and asked whether he could spare some time for the Indian leader. 'Why through State? Is it important?' 'Yes, he is very keen to meet you,' I answered. 'He is a most important and influential figure in India. He has come here all the way especially to meet you.' 'How long is he here?' asked Kissinger. 'Just two more days,' I said. He asked me to stay on the line while he looked at his diary. Then he said that with great difficulty, he could only spare twenty minutes in the late afternoon of the following day and asked whether I would be accompanying Narayan. I confirmed that and thanked him for his kindness.

The following day at the appointed hour, Kissinger welcomed Narayan in his office in the White House basement. He complimented India for its patience and restraint in dealing with the difficult situation created by the influx of refugees. Narayan told him that the situation was becoming intolerable for India and only the US could now help prevent an India–Pakistan war by asking Yahya Khan to end the reign of terror in East Pakistan; that region had nothing in common with West Pakistan, it wanted independence from the latter. In the name of humanity and human rights, for the sake of truth, morality and human decency and to safeguard the future of democracy in the world, Narayan repeatedly appealed to Kissinger to intervene directly and effectively in support of freedom and independence for the people of Bangladesh.

Repeatedly, Kissinger assured Narayan that the US and India had the same objective though the approaches of the two countries might be somewhat different; that autonomy of East Pakistan was a foregone conclusion and in the prevailing circumstances even secession might become unavoidable. He hoped that India would continue to exercise restraint and avoid going to war over the refugee problem. That counsel of restraint provoked a repeat of the facts, arguments and appeals that Narayan had invoked earlier.

It was ten minutes past our allotted time. Out of respect for the older man Kissinger did not cut him short, but looked at me pathetically, so I whispered to Narayan, in Hindi, that we were long past our allotted time and to please thank Kissinger and take leave. Narayan took another five minutes to do that and make an 'earnest heart-to-heart appeal' to a man of 'high moral stature and global responsibility to put his great weight behind Truth, Justice, and Human Rights and Freedom of the Bengali people'!

On our way back to the ambassador's residence, I noticed that Narayan was mentally going over his talk with Kissinger and I did not disturb his contemplation of an important, recently concluded meeting. After a few minutes he asked, 'Rasgotraji what do you think, how did the meeting go?' I said, 'The meeting has gone off well enough; you explained all the various implications and dangers in Pakistan's military action in East Pakistan and Henry listened to you attentively.'

'It was a good meeting, Sir, don't you think so?' I asked. 'Oh yes, I am happy with the meeting,' and a long pause followed. 'I think I have converted him to my viewpoint, and we can expect a policy change. Don't you think Rasgotraji?'

I kept quiet and he asked again what I thought but repeated, 'I think I have converted him!' I said, 'Sir, we should wait and see. My experience is they do not always mean what they say, and Nixon and Kissinger are so deeply committed to Pakistan and General Yahya Khan personally that I do not see that a change in policy is likely.'

'No, no, I think I have converted him. Rasgotraji, why are you so cynical?' said Narayan and I thought it best not to say more on the subject and disappoint that God's own good man. When I saw him off at the airport two days later, he thanked me warmly and said, 'When you come to Delhi you must come home for a meal and we will have a long talk; don't forget Rasgotraji.'

The India–Pakistan war for Bangladesh's liberation ended in the Pakistan army's surrender in Dhaka on 16 December 1971. The war over, I was summoned to Delhi for consultation in February 1972. I had asked for time to call on Narayan, but he hosted a dinner party for me with a few other guests, including three or four notable political figures. When I knocked at the door of his residence in Friends Colony he opened the door himself, gave me a warm hug and said in Hindi:'Rasgotraji, yeh Washington ke log bade badmash hain, jhoot bolte hain.' (Rasgotraji, the people in Washington are very wicked, they tell lies). 'Not everybody Sir, only a few. There are many good people there,' I said and we went in to meet other guests.

Throughout 1971, Kissinger had been talking to India in two voices. On his way to Pakistan and China in July 1971 he had stopped in Delhi for a couple of days where he offered unsolicited assurances to Prime Minister Indira Gandhi, Principal Secretary P.N. Haksar and Foreign Secretary T.N. Kaul, to the effect that if China attacked India the US would back India. To Defence Minister Jagjivan Ram he gave a pledge that the US would take a very grave view of any Chinese move against India. All this was said in the context of the likelihood of war between India and Pakistan over Bangladesh.

However, in China he had contracted a malady from Zou En-Lai—the infectious India-animus. So, on his return from China, he admonished Ambassador Jha: 'You people cannot go to war over refugees.' And he issued a threat and a warning: 'In the event of war between India and Pakistan, if China intervenes in Pakistan's support, India should not expect help from the US.'

Kissinger's threats and warnings were taken seriously in Delhi. We guessed that the matter had been discussed during Kissinger's visit to China, and New Delhi was convinced that Kissinger had forged a Sino-US alliance in Pakistan's support on the issue of Bangladesh. So, the India–USSR talks that had been going on for a couple of years were quickly concluded in the Friendship Treaty of 9 August 1971.

US REACTIONS TO THE INDIA–USSR FRIENDSHIP TREATY

I remember the shock in Washington's official circles when the news broke of the signing of the treaty on 9 August 1971. Kissinger described it as a bombshell; Nixon was equally shocked. If Kissinger and Nixon had the wisdom and statesmanship, which Kissinger has claimed for both in his memoir, *White House Years*,[2] they should have foreseen this development and been warned. The American public and media had a clearer and more sympathetic perception of India's action and recognized that the White House policy towards South Asia was responsible for driving India into signing the treaty with Russia.

During Foreign Minister Swaran Singh's visit to Washington a few days after the treaty signing, I was witness to a rather unpleasant meeting between him and Secretary of State William Rogers to which I had accompanied my minister. Without the usual courtesies on such occasions, Rogers launched an intemperate attack on India's 'security alliance' with the Soviet Union and on Indian's 'Non-alignment' which, he said, had been exposed as a sham. Rogers was irritated, aggressive, even impolite; not even the usual cup of tea was offered during the twenty-minute meeting. He repeatedly asserted that the treaty marked a military alliance between India and Russia and that its language about mutual consultation was stronger than the wording in the NATO treaty.

Sardar Swaran Singh, his demeanor unruffled, sat there listening to the diatribe unperturbed, patient, calm and attentive. He was a perfect picture of a man of transcendental wisdom—yogi—described in the Bhagavad Gita.[3] He simply would not react to the tirade, and suddenly Rogers fell silent, exhausted, and perhaps feeling a bit foolish about his outburst. Silence seemed unending, as if Swaran Singh was waiting for Rogers to resume.

I must say I thoroughly enjoyed that hilarious scene of two very distinguished personages sitting there, as if in deep, silent, spiritual communication. I had a hard time controlling the laughter bubbling up in my stomach. Finally Rogers broke the silence to tell Swaran Singh: 'Well, why don't you say something?'

With a fleeting smile Sardar Swaran Singh thanked Rogers for the courtesy of receiving him; for there must have been very heavy pressure on him because of the war in Vietnam and the deteriorating situation in East Pakistan. He had wanted to brief Rogers about the tragic situation in the subcontinent, but that could wait for another occasion.

As for the treaty, he was wondering what in it had so upset His Excellency. 'Unlike NATO arrangements, there is no provision in the treaty to station armed forces in each other's territories. It is a treaty of friendship.' Then the clincher: 'Your Excellency, my prime minister has authorized me to sign an identical treaty with Your Excellency's government. I am ready to do so at your convenience in the next two days, or any time later if you prefer.'

This again left Rogers speechless and a little bewildered. Swaran Singh thanked Rogers for the time he had given him and stood up to take leave, giving the latter no chance to prolong the meeting. In the event the meeting ended more civilly than it had begun.

A lunch hosted by Secretary Rogers for the Indian foreign minister, the following afternoon at the State Department with the department's top brass present, was an infinitely more pleasant occasion. There the minister, duly aided by Ambassador Jha and myself, briefed them in detail about the refugee problem—their numbers had crossed eight million by then—and the deteriorating India–Pakistan relations.

Kissinger was understandably upset about the treaty and Ambassador Jha decided to go to the presidential residence and office in San Clemente, California, for a quiet, friendly meeting with him.

Upon his return he told me that he had had a good talk with Kissinger, during which the latter had spoken critically of Foreign Minister Dinesh Singh for having thought up and proposed the treaty, and said that Prime Minister Gandhi's two main advisers, P.N. Haksar and T.N. Kaul (foreign secretary) were pro-Russia and it was under their pressure that she had given the go ahead for signing the treaty. He said he had also availed of the occasion to settle some details about Prime Minister Gandhi's visit to Washington in November 1971. However Jha had also noted that in their meeting on 25 August that Kissinger was not the warm and friendly person as before, and that he was somewhat sceptical and defensive about US–India relations. He was very critical of Foreign Minister Dinesh Singh; he thought Singh was beholden to the Soviet Union and suggested he might have taken money from that country.

When the secret American documents of the period were recently released I was shocked to read the following very different account of Jha's meeting with Kissinger. It was a one-on-one meeting between the two and the following account of it must have been recorded by Kissinger himself:

Dr Kissinger said he did not really know what India wanted. If India wanted to become an extension of Soviet foreign policy, then inevitably the American interest in India was bound to decline and India would have to look to the Soviet Union for the greater part of its economic and other assistance. He could not understand why India would want to be drawn into the Sino-Soviet rivalry, or why it would deliberately antagonize the one country that had no national interest in the subcontinent except an independent and healthy India and an independent subcontinent.

Ambassador Jha replied that the situation in India was very difficult. First of all, Madame Gandhi was not at all pro-Soviet. She had for a long time resisted the proposal— that had first been thought up by Dinesh Singh, the former foreign minister—of this treaty of friendship. In fact, Jha said on a personal basis, he wouldn't be a bit surprised if Dinesh

Singh actually received pay from the communists. At the same time he also thought that Kaul and Haksar were very much under Soviet influence. In short, for both these reasons Madame Gandhi was under great pressure. The project had been going along for about a year, and recently Madame Gandhi felt she needed some dramatic foreign policy, so she picked it up, but Dr Kissinger could be certain that she did not have her heart in it.

That might be so, Dr Kissinger said, but the problem is how she would carry out the policy. Dr Kissinger could tell her that from our selfish point of view it did not hurt us to have India pursue such a pro-Soviet line in relation to our China policy, nor should the ambassador have any illusions that it was possible to stir up any basic American public support on the Bengali issue. Still, in order to score temporary points, India was running a tremendous risk of permanently alienating the United States.

Jha himself did not prepare a record of this meeting, or, perhaps, he kept one in his private papers. I did not see it. But if there is a modicum of truth in Kissinger's record, there is a lesson for future practitioners of the art of diplomacy in his curt dismissal of Ambassador Jha's denigration of his foreign minister and of the two senior-most advisers of Prime Minister Gandhi as virtual agents of a foreign power, as well as the implication that the iron lady was a puppet in their manipulating hands.

As if that were not enough, Kissinger also sounded a personal warning to the ambassador and a threat to India!

While it is advisable for a diplomat to keep up the search for common ground between two opposing sides, letting down your own side brings neither respect nor reward.

chapter seventeen

BANGLADESH: THE FAILURE OF NIXON–KISSINGER DIPLOMACY

~

The most important part of my tasks in Washington DC was to cultivate congressional leaders, the intellectual and academic circles of the country and its media. The underlying idea was that in the event we ran into problems with the Nixon administration, there should be friendly people in those circles to speak up for India. I had met and befriended a few congressional personalities at the United Nations when I was representing India in the Trusteeship Council and the General Assembly's Fourth Committee in the 1960s. I had listened to a few more during their meetings with Mrs Pandit in the 1950s and Prime Minister Nehru in 1960. The impression I had formed was that senators and congressmen were not unfriendly or indifferent towards India, but they were not well informed about our country, and in most cases, were eager for authentic information and discussion, and willing to change their mindset on Indian policies and problems. Another very clear impression I had was that those who had been to India, seen our country first-hand, warts and all, and met and talked with our leaders, had returned with a very good overall impression of the country.

In the preceding two years, 1969 and 1970, I had personally met and talked with forty or fifty senators and a somewhat larger number of members of the House of Representatives. Under an arrangement agreed with the ministry of external affairs, we had sponsored the visits of several such influential public figures to India, where they were our government's guests. They were impressed with the way India—a democracy—was grappling with its economic, and other, problems with noteworthy success. In Washington I remained in touch with them and they became India's friends and gave us much strength and support in the crisis year of 1971. The more notable visits we had sponsored in 1971 were those of Congressman Gallagher, chairman of the House Foreign Affairs Committee's subcommittee on South Asia and senators Frank Church, William Saxbe and Edward Kennedy. The evidence they saw in the refugee camps of the Pakistan army's atrocities had moved them deeply and their speeches in the House of Representatives and the Senate, condemnatory of the Nixon–Kissinger policy, caused much chagrin and discomfiture to the President and his national security adviser. What stung Nixon in particular was the hero's welcome Kennedy received in India, including an address to a joint meeting of members of the two houses of Parliament.

I had been working with Kennedy's experienced and energetic staffers for two years for the senator's visit to India. In 1971, there was a special reason for him to do so as he was chairman of the Senate's subcommittee on refugees. In India, at great risk to his health, in rain and sunshine and in the intense heat of an Indian summer, he visited several refugee camps to talk with victims of the Pakistan army's atrocities. On return from India his speeches in the Senate and his public declarations elsewhere were devastatingly critical of Nixon's South Asia policy. In a speech in the Senate on 1 November 1971, he severely indicted the Nixon administration:

Nothing is more clear, or easily documented than the systematic campaign of terror and its genocidal consequences launched by the Pakistan army on the night of 25 March . . . Hindus are being systematically slaughtered and in some places painted with yellow patches marked 'H' . . . . America's heavy support of Islamabad is nothing short of complicity in the human and political tragedy of East Pakistan.

Kadambari said to me one day, 'You spend a lot of money on entertaining congressional leaders and others in restaurants. You can do some of your working luncheons in restaurants, but if you want to cultivate enduring friendships, home entertainment is the thing.' 'Why?' 'Because Americans are family-oriented people.' She said in women's groups, there was always talk about families, their children and their husband's jobs and work.

Our house on Foxhall Road had enough bedrooms, a grand sitting room, but a dining area which seated only ten persons. We needed a bigger room for larger formal dinners for which black tie was de rigueur in Washington high society in those days. The house had a large, well-aired room in the basement opening out on the swimming pool and a lawn sloping towards a wooded area going down to Rock Creek Park. Kadambari wanted some money to clean up the room, carpet the floor, and suitably decorate the space to serve as the dining room for seated power dinners for eighteen to twenty-two guests, and to activate the swimming pool for informal family entertainment.

Our first dinner in that elegant basement room was in honour of Senator Keating, whom I had been meeting now and then since 1969. We had an excellent Indian cook and a well-trained Indian maidservant as our permanent household staff. Additional professional help for service at the table was available in Washington. As a rule, the food served at our parties was mostly Indian, with an occasional soufflé and a Western dessert prepared by Kadambari herself. Soon 'the Rasgotras' was known among our congressional and other friends as the place for Indian food in town.

In the embassy's publicity and public relations work, I was assisted by three very able and energetic colleagues. George Victor Shukla, the information officer, had established excellent contacts in all the various radio and TV networks, the country's print media and the universities. He kept Ambassador Jha and me busy, appearing on national and regional TV channels, in meetings with senior editors and columnists for backgrounders and in visits to academic centres for lectures all over the country. He had a big hand in the preparation of printed material on the situation in East Bengal for distribution in interested circles. He was a very likeable companion and when I was transferred to London as acting high commissioner, at my request, Shukla was also posted as counsellor (information) in the High Commission.

Two young members of the Indian Foreign Service, First Secretaries Vinay Verma and Kiran Doshi, talented professionals with pleasant personalities, were well versed in the sophisticated arts of diplomatic functioning. Both had a good sense of humour and created a good impression in the circles in which they moved with their dignified presence, ability, knowledge and an aptitude to make friends easily. Their wives, Geeta Verma and Razia Doshi, good-looking, well-educated, cultured and accomplished young women, were great assets to their husbands. They kept good homes and, at their level, entertained well. The two couples had cultivated friendships in fairly large and diverse circles of the town. Both Vinay and Kiran were held in respect by their counterparts in the State Department and in the diplomatic corps generally. From April or May onwards they went on speaking tours to academic institutions and groups of young social and political activists to spread information about the Pakistan army's campaign of brutal violence in East Bengal, and about the problems created by the ceaseless flow of refugees into neighbouring Indian states. Their contacts with young congressional staffers proved most useful in that period of crisis in US–India relations. Vinay and Kiran were of great help to me in preparing notes and sometimes texts of speeches which the staffers wanted for their bosses in the Senate and the House of Representatives.

This was the small team of four, whose PR and information dissemination work had attracted the adverse notice of President Richard Nixon, who had complained to Kissinger about the Indian embassy's 'huge public relations campaign'.

At one of Kiran Doshi's wine and cheese parties, a young officer of the State Department took me aside to say, in strict confidence, that there was talk in high circles of the government to declare me persona non grata because of my criticism of Washington's policy on TV networks. 'Sir, you should be careful lest your career be harmed; many of us in State are concerned for you.' I warmly thanked my young American friend and said to him, 'I am not afraid of being declared persona non grata. I shall go back home a hero, get elected to Parliament and perhaps even find a place in the cabinet. But the US would have lost a friend and well-wisher.' The young man was visibly relieved of his anxiety. 'Do me a favour,' I said, 'spread the word, but don't say you met me and I said this to you. Say you picked up this gossip at an Indian friend's house.' There was a smile on his face when we parted. I do not know whether he actually spread the word or not, but I did learn from another source that there was no more talk of declaring the Indian deputy chief of mission persona non grata!

THE WAR FOR BANGLADESH

In June, five Bengali diplomatic officers of the Pakistan Foreign Service, posted in Washington, walked out of the embassy of Pakistan and became free citizens of a new, independent nation in the making in East Bengal. We were instructed by New Delhi to give them all necessary assistance and support. The senior-most, Inayat Karim, was minister in the Pakistan embassy, Mohit and Kibria, both brilliant economists, were counsellors, Anwarul Haq Chaudhary and Moazzam Ali were first and second secretaries respectively in the political section of the embassy. Because of their undetermined diplomatic status, they had to be careful in how they conducted themselves and what they said in public about the unspeakable atrocities being perpetrated on their people in East Bengal. But they were in demand; people wanted to meet and speak with them. Their voices lent a special force and poignancy to the publicity and propaganda several American organizations were now doing in support of the independence of Bangladesh.

Three steps were needed to restore calm in East Bengal: i) Sheikh Mujibur Rahman's release from prison, followed by negotiations with him about Bangladesh's autonomy or independence; ii) the Pakistan army's return to the barracks and its negotiated withdrawal from the region; and iii) the return of refugees to their homes which was an imperative necessity to avert the danger of an India—Pakistan war. The action to implement all these steps rested with Pakistan's military dictator, who apparently had failed to grasp the gravity of the situation. He was amenable to advice on the lines mentioned above only from Nixon and, perhaps, also Kissinger. Had they done the needful, they would have saved their friend Yahya Khan and his country. Having seen the archives of the time recently released by the US, I am convinced that neither Nixon nor Kissinger had quite realized that after the Pakistan army's brutal campaign of violence, the Bengalis would no longer be satisfied with anything less than independence, that the burden of refugees had become intolerable for India, and, because of the lack of suitable action by the US, war between India and Pakistan had become unavoidable.

This regional conflict in South Asia was not something to be viewed and dealt with in the context of the global balance of power. Kissinger, it seems to me, was misled into a wrong policy course by his obsession with the doctrines of linkage and global balance of power, which treated every local conflict as capable of causing repercussions on faraway international horizons. There is a soaring metaphysical quality to Kissinger's prodigious intellect which seemed to prevent him from seeing the reality below a certain level of vision and dealing with it at that level.

It passes understanding why Kissinger should have been so easily persuaded that in the event of an India–Pakistan war, China would militarily intervene in Pakistan's support. How did so rational a man get so emotionally touched as to lose his sense of history? The Chinese had done nothing of the kind in the India–Pakistan war in 1965. And when did China, in its long history, fight another country's war? It did not do so in Vietnam, nor even in Korea, until the arrogant and short-sighted General MacArthur took the war to China's frontier. The Chinese were quick to see through Kissinger's game; he wanted China to do what the US wanted done but could not itself do. They were not going to oblige. Kissinger must have been a chastened man when the Chinese told him in December that they did not want to; that they would not intervene in the war even to save their friend Pakistan.

Throughout the period of six months, from mid-July to the end of the war in December, Kissinger's diplomacy was inconceivably flawed and dangerously adventurous—threats to India, exhortations to China to attack India, baseless assertions that after routing the Pakistan army in East Bengal, India had plans to invade and break up West Pakistan and was only prevented from carrying out that plan under Russian pressure, exerted because of Washington's ultimatum to Moscow to restrain India! All this was nineteenth-century European diplomatic mishmash.

Kissinger had been catapulted from his professorship in Harvard into a position of immense power. He had no training in or experience of diplomacy and, as he himself says in *A World Restored*, 'an intelligent man can make up the lack of everything except experience'. He knew nothing about diplomacy. Till recently, when I read a book titled *Restless Empire: China's America*, I did not know that in my poor assessment of Kissinger's diplomacy I was in the great company of Mao, who told the North Vietnamese: 'Kissinger is a university professor who does not know anything about diplomacy.'[1]

His advice to Nixon to act tough with Indira Gandhi (and be rude to her by keeping her waiting for forty-five minutes) only served to undermine the last chance of a joint search for solutions to the crisis created by Yahya Khan's military action in East Pakistan. Nixon's own perceptions of the Indian prime minister were the emanations of a tortured imagination. The archives of Nixon–Kissinger conversations about the Indian prime minister reveal Kissinger's role, in Dr Premen Addy's words, as that of Iago to Nixon's Othello.

The Indian prime minister's visit to Washington was doomed to failure from the start and it began badly on the White House lawns on the morning of 4 November. Poor chemistry between the two leaders was on view for anyone who had eyes to see it. To make matters worse, in his welcome remarks Nixon referred to the floods in Bihar but avoided any mention of ten million Bengali refugees in India! Gandhi's reply then dwelt at length on that particular subject and the ongoing massacre of innocent men, women, and children in East Bengal. The first encounter of the two leaders at a ceremonial public event was a bad augury for the talks to follow.

The White House banquet that night was another disaster. In his toast the President actually tried to be nice, and said some flattering things about India and about the prime minister. After complimenting her on her massive victory in the midterm elections earlier in the year, he asked how she did it! Gandhi's reply was a long lecture on how elections are won. As a member of the prime minister's delegation I had a seat at the head table; there was no humour, no smiles, no conversation at the table despite the excellent fare served and the effort that had been invested to make the occasion a relaxed and felicitous event.

The one amusing incident that caught Foreign Secretary Kaul's attention was the President trying to tell Kadambari: 'You know Ma'am, I love India'. 'Then why don't you do something to stop the killings in East Bengal so that ten million refugees can go back to their homes, they are such a burden on India,' shot back Kadambari and the President rejoined: 'That is what we are trying to do. I am discussing all this with Prime Minister Gandhi.

Kadambari then told the President how much she had enjoyed 'the banquet, the company, the music and everything. I had an interesting talk with Dr Kissinger; he is a charming man. I was honoured to be sitting next to him at the table.' 'Oh, great. I'll tell Henry that,' said the President. Kadambari thanked the President again; they shook hands, I joined them and shook hands with the President, and we took leave. The man could be gracious when he wanted to.

The talks the following day did not go well at all. The prime minister repeatedly told the President that the refugee burden had become intolerable, unacceptable; tensions were high in West Bengal, in other northeastern states of India and there was serious threat of communal riots breaking out. She said she had been very patient, but all political parties, the Parliament and the general public in India were clamouring for war as the only way to resolve the problem which was threatening India's stability. She added that perhaps even at that late stage, the President could help restore calm by persuading Yahya Khan to stop the massacre, release Sheikh Mujibur Rahman and negotiate a settlement with him.

President Nixon, not in the least willing to grapple with the real issue, said he would ask the Congress for some more money for refugee relief. He spoke of what Yahya Khan had already done under

American pressure and persuasion: he had promised not to execute Mujibur Rahman, he had appointed a civilian Bengali gentleman as the eastern province's governor, and the governor had appointed a cabinet of Bengalis. In other words, a civilian regime had been set up by Yahya Khan! He promised that the US would continue to press him to do more but there were limits to American influence in Islamabad.

To justify the continuing military supplies and other assistance to Pakistan, the President said that had been 'retained in a most limited fashion to enable the US to continue a dialogue with Pakistan's government'! He added that the US would continue to discourage military action by Pakistan. He recognized that Mujib was a core factor in the situation, but he still thought the issue was one of autonomy and that 'in the long run Pakistan must acquiesce in the direction of greater autonomy'. He conceded that Mujib 'will have to play a role in East Pakistan's future'. Clearly there was little inclination to recognize the ground realities!

And finally the threat; the one infallible weapon in the Nixon–Kissinger armoury of diplomacy reserved for India since Henry Kissinger's China visit. The President spelt it out:

i) India's treaty with the Soviet Union was understood by his government but India must recognize that it was not popular in the US;

ii) The initiation of hostilities by India would be almost impossible to understand; and

iii) It would be impossible to calculate with precision the steps which other great powers might take in the event of war.

On the basis of what Zhou En-Lai had said to him in July, Kissinger had assured President Nixon that 'China would not stand idly by if India attacked Pakistan'. But the Chinese had realized that the India of 1971 was not the India of 1962. Besides, India had taken measures to hold the Chinese in the north if they militarily intervened in the war. China's dilemma was resolved when the Pakistan Air Force initiated the war by launching surprise attacks on 3 December on a number of bases of the Indian Air Force in the northern states of Punjab, Rajasthan and Uttar Pradesh, and the following day Yahya Khan declared war on India.

From the start, the twelve-day war went badly for Pakistan. In fact the war would have ended in nine or ten days but for the American advice to Yahya Khan to hold out for the expected military intervention by China, which did not materialize. Nor did the dispatch of the Seventh Fleet to the Bay of Bengal intimidate or deter India, and on 16 December the war ended with the Pakistan army's unconditional surrender at Dhaka with 90,000 Pakistani troops as prisoners of war.

In the afternoon of the day President Nixon gave the order for the fleet to sail, an Indian gentleman with access to important persons in the White House, asked to see me urgently. He came to my residence within hours of the event to tell me of the President's decision: 'Mr Rasgotra, I cannot tell you how I got to know this, but the war is going to get bigger, and as a concerned Indian I thought I should warn you.'

I thought it was a plant, but the fact of the Seventh Fleet having been ordered to the scene of conflict was there. The White House must have thought India would panic, ask for peace and Pakistan would be saved. A few hours later, a friendly source confirmed to me the order for the fleet to sail to the Bay of Bengal, nominally to 'evacuate American citizens' but actually to 'pose a threat to the ongoing Indian military operations in East Pakistan'!

I telephoned Foreign Secretary T.N. Kaul, who was in New York in connection with a Security Council meeting, to give him the news, and he suggested I speak to P.N. Haksar in Delhi, which I did immediately. Haksar's response: 'Okay, how long will it take the fleet to reach our shores?' I said I would check and call back. I called him again to say that seven to eight days was the estimated time. Haksar said to me, 'Maharaj, it is all right. Let it come; the war will be over before that. But let me know if there are any further developments.'

That evening, Victor Shukla, the embassy's information counsellor, called five or six journalists to talk to me about the developments, which were still not in the public domain. The news was splashed across American electronic media later that night, and in print media the following morning in banner headlines highly critical of the administration. In the media, the Congress and the general public there was anger over this latest move against India.

In India there was shock but no panic. Prime Minister Gandhi summoned the chief of the Indian navy, Admiral Nanda and asked what he planned to do. Nanda said he would take command of the lead Indian vessel in the Bay, and he would ask the commander of the nuclear armed fleet to come over to his ship for a drink and offer him all necessary assistance for evacuation of American personnel! The morale of the Indian Armed Forces rose higher when the Indian defence minister, Babu Jagjivan Ram declared two days later that if the Seventh Fleet came too close to India or interfered with Indian military operations in East Bengal, he would take action to damage, if not sink, the fleet!

When I met Babuji in February 1972, I asked him how he had planned to sink such a formidable nuclear armed armada. A leading figure in the Indian National Congress hierarchy, Babuji had held several cabinet posts and was an experienced administrator. He was a cool-headed, soft-spoken man who never got ruffled in a crisis and was always careful in choosing his words in whatever he wanted to say. He said the day after the news broke, scores of naval officers and men volunteered for suicide attacks on the offending American ships. They had told him they would wrap themselves up in limpet mines and swim deep underwater towards the ships from all directions. Whether it succeeded or not, it was a practical strategy. What is more, it showed the determination not to submit to America's threat. My own guess, which I shared with Babuji, was that American public opinion was so roused against Nixon's move that, the threat apart, he would not find it possible to initiate hostilities against a sister democracy. In any case, the fleet reached the Bay of Bengal too late and lingered there in idleness for some time, a monument of shame to the President of the United States and his national security adviser.

In the last four or five days of the war, Kissinger conjured up another ruse to divert attention from the failure of his (and Nixon's) East Pakistan policy. It was said that after the war in the east was over,

India had plans to transfer a couple of divisions, or more, of its battle-hardened troops to the western front and launch a major invasion to destroy the Pakistan army and undo that country completely. West Pakistan had to be saved; therefore there were daily summons to the Russian ambassador to transmit fevered messages to Secretary General Brezhnev to stop the Indians from invading West Pakistan! It was a charade. The Soviet's laughed and went through the motions; the Indians were not amused.

The assurances the White House wanted had been given to Ambassador Keating by Prime Minister Gandhi and Foreign Minister Swaran Singh. In Washington, Ambassador Jha had given the required assurance to Kissinger and to Under Secretary John Irwin. I had repeated the same to Joseph Sisco. Besides, American intelligence itself had reported to the President and Kissinger that the Indian army had adopted a defensive posture against the Pakistan army's fierce attacks in the west. Regardless of all that, after the Pakistan army surrendered in Dhaka on 16 December and Prime Minister Gandhi ordered unilateral ceasefire in the west on 17 December, Kissinger exulted in his (and Nixon's) success in saving Pakistan! Having failed to involve China in the war, he was now assigning a role in ending the war to Russia under heavy American pressure! How obtuse could one be!

But Henry knew (and so did President Nixon) that their policy was in shambles. There were rumours in Washington that Dr Kissinger was in a state of deep depression and that for three or four days, even President Nixon had shunned him.

I felt sympathy for the man and prayed for his quick recovery from the shock of the failure of his policy. He had been under immense pressure lately because of the Vietnam War and his inconclusive, protracted peace negotiations with Hanoi's representatives in the bistros of Paris. He had alienated the entire State Department, lost congressional support and incurred disapprobation of the media and the public. All that must have taken its toll.

The acid test of policy, Kissinger had written in *A World Restored*, 'is its ability to obtain domestic support'. His policy's starkest failure lay precisely in its total lack of domestic support.

The emergence of an independent Bangladesh was not failure of Washington's India–Pakistan policy alone, it had demonstrated the irrelevance of Kissinger's doctrine of Linkage. Even his Chinese friends thought Linkage was a strategic trap, disavowed it and stayed a safe distance from it.

American policymakers were used to the willing submission of leaders of European democracies and other countries such as Pakistan to their dictates. Where American national interest came in conflict with another country's interests, the former had to prevail. In Europe, only General Charles de Gaulle's France dared pursue an independent foreign and security policy despite being a member of the North Atlantic Treaty Organization (NATO). In the post-World War II situation, Britain was the United States' most loyal and obedient ally, except during Edward Heath's prime ministership.

Therefore, for Nixon and Kissinger it was a novel, and unpleasant experience to be defied by an Asian leader, the prime minister of the world's largest democracy, who was conscious of her responsibility to safeguard her own country's security and stability, and of her answerability in that regard to her Parliament and people. In their frustration Nixon and Kissinger heaped insults and abuse on the Indian prime minister. She bore all that with unwonted sang froid, but left no doubt in her talks with Nixon in November 1971, that Pakistan's pushing ten million of its nationals into India was tantamount to an invasion of her country and it would be dealt with as such. She ignored their threats of aid cuts and made it clear that if the United States were to embark on a course of hostility, she would live with that too and explore other options.

US–India relations had reached their lowest point ever at the end of 1971. There was neither the mood, nor any move from either side to mend relations. Nixon made a gesture by way of making amends in his annual report of 1973 to the Congress by saying that 'India emerged from the 1971 crisis with new confidence, power and responsibilities . . . The United States respects India as a major country. We are prepared to deal with it in accordance with its new stature and responsibilities on the basis of reciprocity.' To allay India's anxiety over Washington's new relationship with China, the

President had added a reassuring sentence in the same report saying, 'The United States will not join in any group or pursue any policies directed against India.' But he commanded little credence in India. Nevertheless pro forma high-level contacts were resumed in early 1974 when Foreign Minister Swaran Singh met with Secretary of State Kissinger in New York in April, and the establishment of a joint commission was agreed to promote economic cooperation between the two countries. Kissinger's own return visit to India that year did not help advance the relationship because of the lack of trust in him in India due to his past hostility and unreliability.

Also the policies and actions of the two countries kept creating new hurdles in the way of an improved relationship. India's underground nuclear test (the PNE, so-called) in 1974 sent shock waves around the world and attracted American sanctions. New legislation by the Congress put an end to American fuel supplies for the Tarapur nuclear power plant, which had been gifted to India by President John Kennedy. Disputation about the rights and wrongs of this act of the US continued to hamper progress in relations till 1982, when Prime Minister Indira Gandhi's state visit to the US at President Ronald Reagan's invitation gave them a positive turn.

In Delhi, D.P. Dhar was in charge of developing the framework for peace negotiations with Pakistan. My opinion was invited in that regard during my consultations visit to Delhi in February 1972. The 90,000 Pakistani prisoners of war had been brought over to India for their safety. The Indian army had also occupied some strategically important areas of Pakistan, especially the entire sub-district of Shakargarh on the southern border of the Indian state of Jammu and Kashmir, from where the Pakistan army had threatened to cut our road link to the Kashmir Valley in 1965 and again in 1971. Foreign Secretary T.N. Kaul was present at my meeting with D.P. Dhar in a secure room at the Ashoka Hotel in Chanakyapuri. Two or three other persons were also present, representing the Defence ministry and our intelligence agencies. Kaul did not say much at that meeting; the others, including D.P. Dhar, were of the view that we should vacate the Pakistan territory we had captured and hold the prisoners as a sort of leverage for a good peace agreement.

My view was that 90,000 prisoners of war were no leverage but a huge liability. We would have to feed them and look after them under the Geneva Protocol. By handing them over to Pakistan we might earn the goodwill of their families in Pakistan's Punjab and Frontier provinces. Back home in Pakistan, they would be an embarrassment for Bhutto's government. On the other hand the areas we occupied in Pakistan were of strategic importance and should be handed back to Pakistan only after a satisfactory peace agreement was reached, especially on Kashmir. The goal in regard to Kashmir should be recognition of the new ceasefire line as the international border. Everyone agreed to the last point, but on the other two points I was overruled.

Nevertheless, I do not agree with those who say we won the war and lost the peace; that in my view is only partially true. Indian leaders wanted a bilaterally negotiated peace agreement without a third party's good offices. Since the Simla Agreement, the UN and all other meddlers in Kashmir have acknowledged that the issue is now squarely for India and Pakistan to settle between them. That was some progress, even though on the question of the new Line of Control (LOC) being treated as the international border in Kashmir, Bhutto had duped our negotiators, stricken by the Versailles Syndrome.

We were in a position to clinch the issue and we failed to do so for fear of a breakdown of negotiations. Haksar, D.P. Dhar and P.N. Dhar wanted to be generous to the defeated enemy. Heavens would not have fallen if Bhutto had gone back empty-handed. He or someone else would have come back to Shimla to agree to a final division of Kashmir along the LOC as the international border. The wily Bhutto agreed orally and promised he would persuade his people to support his agreement, but went back and reneged on the unwritten commitment he had given to Prime Minister Gandhi.

Many years later I asked Haksar why he had placed such trust in Bhutto's oral promise. He said Bhutto had sought a private meeting with him, fallen at his feet and begged him not to send him back to be butchered by his enemies, trust him and his word of honour about the LOC being treated as the border; he wanted time to sell the idea to his countrymen. Haksar then persuaded Indira Gandhi that Bhutto deserved her understanding and sympathy.

chapter eighteen

RENEWAL OF FAITH

~

There wasn't much more for me to do in Washington; so while in Delhi for consultations, I had asked for transfer from Washington DC to an ambassadorial post. But Foreign Minister Swaran Singh had something else in mind. He wanted me to go to London for a year or two to reorganize the 'vast railway junction' i.e. the Indian High Commission, into a diplomatic mission. On my return to Delhi from Washington in May 1972, I spent two busy weeks in the ministry of external affairs in consultations etc. concerning the task awaiting me in London. No one could give me the exact number of persons working in the High Commission. Guesses ranged from 1200 to 1400 employees, but no one had a clear idea of what this large group of men and women were doing in an Indian diplomatic mission in a foreign country of declining international importance. Foreign Minister Swaran Singh's final instruction to me was: 'Go there, see things for yourself and decide what needs to be done. After a couple of months when you have settled down I will send an inspection team which will work with you to formulate a plan of action to accomplish the task I have given you. The report of the inspection team will arm you with government's authority to implement it.'

Meanwhile, for a week or ten days my friend Rai Bahadur Sohan Lal had been urging me to visit his home in Golf Links for the benefit of a divine personage's darshans, an avatar named Bhagwan

Sri Sathya Sai Baba who was staying with him. I just ignored his pressing invitations for four or five days. Since the tragic death of my elder son in 1967 I had lost faith in God and gurus, and I kept putting off Sohan Lal by saying that I would spend some time with him after his divine guest left Delhi, and before my departure for a month-long golfing holiday in Srinagar and Gulmarg in Kashmir.

However, one early afternoon I was suddenly gripped by the curiosity to at least see the 'great spiritual being' Sohan Lal had been talking about, and I made my way to my friend's residence. The gate was locked and two volunteers on duty there, politely, with folded hands, firmly refused to let me enter the house. They said they were not even allowed to carry a message from anyone to the master of the house.

Disheartened, I walked away from the gate, but instead of heading for my car I turned into the open ground next to the house where Baba had been giving his discourses to assembled devotees in the mornings and evenings. The morning gathering had dispersed a couple of hours earlier but there were still a few men and women standing or sitting around the stage from where Baba gave his discourses. Some were reverentially touching the ground on which Baba had walked or stood, picking up a few grains of dust and rubbing it on their foreheads.

I stood away from all that, nearer the open side of the ground adjoining the road on one side and Sohan Lal's house on the other, contemplating what the scene might have looked like during the bhajan sessions preceding Baba's discourses. It was a hot day, the sun was bright and as I suddenly looked up in the direction of Sohan Lal's house I saw on the roof of the house a small radiant figure with an Afro bouffant head of jet-black hair, looking towards me. That must be him, I said to myself, and automatically my folded hands went up in salutation.

Then I noticed a gesture of his right forearm and hand as if to ask me to go into the house. I looked around; there was no one within ten or fifteen metres of where I was standing and I looked up at the roof again. He was still there and this time I noticed a luminescence around him and that he was wearing a sleeveless green vest. As I absorbed the scene, he repeated the beckoning gesture and suddenly vanished from the roof. Surely, he wanted me to go into the house, I said to myself; but what about the locked gate and those two unobliging volunteers with orange scarves round their necks? 'Let us try,' I said to myself, and made for the outer gate of the house.

The same argument ensued between me and the volunteers, but not for long. A short distance away the main door of the building opened and Sohal Lal's son, Rajji Kumar came towards the gate. Surprised to see me there, he ordered the gate opened and together we went into the house and into the small, open, inner courtyard where twenty or thirty persons were sitting on the floor awaiting a chance for Sai Baba's darshan in the evening. Sohan Lal greeted me with a friendly chiding: 'You have come, but too late. You have missed so much. Now stay here till Swami comes down for the evening bhajan session. At least you can have his darshan. It will be about three hours from now.'

I said I would, of course, stay but I had had Baba's darshan already. 'What! You have had Baba's darshan? Where, when?' he asked. 'On the roof of your house,' I answered. 'Those volunteers at the gate would not let me in. I was about to leave but I decided to take a look at the stage in the open ground next to your house. I happened to look up and saw Baba standing on the roof. He beckoned me into the house. I returned to the gate when Rajji came out and had the gate opened for me.'

Sohan Lal was surprised, puzzled: 'Really! Are you sure?' Baba, he said, was resting in his room and he himself had been sitting in the balcony outside the door of Baba's room. 'Are you sure it was Sai Baba on the roof of this house, out there in the sun? What did he look like?' And I described to him the jet-black Afro bouffant and the strange luminescence surrounding him, and the green sleeveless vest he was wearing. 'Green sleeveless vest? I have never seen him wearing such a garment. But the jet-black Afro head of hair is surely him. And that light! Yes I have heard people say that Baba's body sometimes radiates light! But Baba is sleeping and I was sitting up there in the gallery. I did not see him come out of the room and mount the stairs to the roof.' Intrigued, but no longer sceptical, he fell silent for a while.

After a few moments of silence, he said, 'Well, you did not want to come, now he has summoned you, and he has begun with you with a miracle! You are very, very lucky, my friend. You should wait here now. When Baba comes down, he likes to move about among the devotees sitting in the courtyard before going out to the bhajan session outside from where you saw him. He may want to say something to you.'

At around 5 p.m., Baba came out of his room to the balcony overlooking the courtyard where we were sitting on the floor. There again as I looked up and raised my hands folded in salutation, a beatific smile covered Baba's face. After a few minutes he came down and walked among the devotees, saying a word or two to one, touching another on the head, stopping in front of the third to let him touch his feet. Finally I saw him heading in my direction, but before I could turn around to face him, I felt his hand on my shoulder and he said three words in Hindi: 'Kuch parwah nahin,' meaning 'Do not worry, have no fear.' And he moved on out to the ground for the last bhajan session of his visit to Delhi. I saw no more of him that day.

It was time for us to proceed to London for my next assignment as deputy high commissioner of India. My wife was spending time with her parents in Trivandrum, where her father was stationed as governor of the state of Kerala. To fetch her back to Delhi, on the morning of 1 July I took an Indian Airlines flight to Trivandrum which had a brief scheduled halt in Bangalore. The plane had developed some trouble while approaching Bangalore, but it landed safely though the flight had to be terminated and the passengers were given a free night's halt in hotels in Bangalore. Another plane at the scheduled time would ferry us to Trivandrum on 2 July.

While heading for a hotel in the city, on an impulse I said to the taxi driver that I had heard that Sai Baba had an ashram near Bangalore. How far was it, I asked, and could he take me there? He said the ashram was fourteen or fifteen kilometres away and he would be happy to take me there: 'Sir, because of you, perhaps, I shall also have

Baba's darshan,' and he made a U-turn in the direction of Brindavan, Sathya Sai Baba's ashram. The ashram looked deserted and a friendly resident told us that Baba was in his ashram at Puttaparthi, the village where he was born, about a100 miles away.

Somewhat disappointed, we sat down for a cup of tea in a tea stall outside the ashram gate and to confer together about what to do next. The driver, Nandan, looked at his watch—it was 4 p.m.—and he said if I so wished he would be happy to take me to Puttaparthi—a journey of three hours. 'Sir, we can spend the night there in the ashram, have Baba's darshan in the morning and drive back to the airport well in time for your flight to Trivandrum tomorrow.' 'Good idea,' I said and gave him the money for filling the taxi's petrol tank, and soon we were on the road to Puttaparthi where we reached as the evening worship rituals were being concluded in the small old mandir, with a room at the back which was Baba's residence.

But Baba was not in Puttaparthi either and a resident devotee told me that only one man knew where Baba might be and he led me to a most kind, soft-spoken, elderly gentleman, N. Kasturi, Baba's most dedicated devotee, his biographer, interpreter of his discourses and translator of his writings from Telugu into English.

I introduced myself to Kasturi and explained the circumstances that had brought me to the ashram in a thus-far-futile quest for Baba's darshan. 'Not futile,' he said, 'you are here because Baba has called you. You are the first Indian diplomat to come here. It must be because he wants to see you and bless you.'

Baba, Kasturi said, was at Anantapur, another thirty kilometres away and suggested that I spend the night in the ashram and drive out to Anantapur early the following morning. He was certain Baba would give me an audience. Kasturi escorted me to a simply furnished comfortable room with bath. A while later, he sent up a delicious south Indian meal for me. I spent a restful night in the ashram's quiet and spiritually energizing environment. Nandan was also looked after in the ashram. The following morning, after an appetizing breakfast of dosas and idlis, we hit the road for Anantapur.

At 8:30 a.m. on 2 July I saw Baba at the site of an auditorium, which was under construction under his personal supervision in the premises of the Sathya Sai College for Girls. I approached him and the moment he saw me, I folded my hands in the usual Indian salutation, he smiled and said (in Hindi): 'So, you have come; good.' Baba asked me to wait for him in the drawing room adjoining the principal's office and added, 'baat karna hai.' (I shall talk to you.)

When he came into the room and sat down on a two-seater settee, he asked me to sit next to him on the sofa, but instinctively I sat down on the floor facing him. Communication would be better this way, face-to-face, I mumbled. To begin with, he recounted four or five very significant past happenings in my life as if my life was an open book in front of him; then he recalled the tragic death of my first child Yatish and how deeply it had affected me—'You are still sorrowing for the boy. Be strong for the tasks awaiting you,' he said very gently while placing his hand on my head. That was followed by a soul-soothing twenty-five minute spiritual teaching about life and death, work and duty, failure and success, spirituality and the relationship between man and God, Nature and its laws and the importance of the values of truth, love, peace, compassion and righteousness in life.

Each word spoken by him, infused with overpowering love and compassion, went straight to my heart. Then to my utter surprise he said, 'The job in London is going to be difficult, very difficult; you will have many enemies there. But you will be high commissioner there and you can deal with all that.' I interrupted him and said, 'Swami, I am going there as deputy high commissioner,' and asked 'What should I do about the enemies? I have not done anything to make enemies in London, in India or anywhere else.' He calmed my doubts and fears: 'You will be deputy only for a short time! You will be India's high commissioner in London.' And then he spelt out a brief code of conduct for me to follow in the years ahead:

When you are confronted with a difficult problem, do what you think is right and do it fearlessly as duty that has to be done in the spirit of service.

Where human beings are concerned, act with love, sympathy and compassion.

Never act in anger; nor consciously harm anyone.

Have no fear of enemies; treated with kindness, enemies will become friends.

Let love, truth and compassion be your guide in your actions.

I am with you always.

'You do not do meditation,' he said, 'only physical yoga, the exercise part. You will not have much time in London to do meditation, but whenever you can find a few minutes of calm, sit in a quiet room and concentrate on any divine image or thought'—and he instructed me how to do it. 'This will help your concentration and stop your mind from wandering hither and thither.' A few years later he gave me a mantra to be repeated mentally to aid concentration, which I have practised ever since.

It was in this marvellous way, with an abundant shower of Baba's grace and blessings on the morning of 2 July 1972, that I started my journey into a phase of high responsibility in my working life. That was also the day when I began to recover my faith. I came out of the audience with Sri Sathya Sai Baba a changed man from the one I had been, and with a set of instructions that would be my guide in what remained of my life and work.

Some people talk in wonder of Baba's miracles such as the materializations of things from the air, others deride them as the works of a magician. Baba's real miracles are worked in the hearts of human beings who approach him with open minds.

Those who are lucky enough to be granted an audience come out of it deeply changed, better human beings, shorn of their anger and ego. This, his greatest miracle, is transforming human beings and societies in virtually every country of the world. In India, he has revolutionized education and set up model educational institutions, from an esteemed university in Prasanthi Nilayam to colleges and schools in all parts of the country. He has established super-speciality hospitals where all services are free of charge, huge piped water supply projects for hundreds of villages and instituted a village integration programme benefitting millions of hitherto marginalized villagers.

These are examples for our Central and state governments to follow to serve the common people.

Like teachers and reformers of earlier ages, Baba also had his critics and detractors. But in the common man's age, Sathya Sai Baba was the common man's messiah. His miracles may be forgotten after the generation that witnessed them passes, but his message of one humanity bound in love and service will continue to resonate in the world in times to come, and the common man will remember and worship him for the monumental institutions and social service programmes he created for their well-being and upliftment.

From July 1972 onwards, I made it a practice to visit Sri Sathya Sai's ashram at least once, sometimes twice a year, and every time there was a new teaching and a fresh insight into life's myriad mysteries. My experiences of those years of Sathya Sai's love and grace would fill a book or two. Here I will narrate only one event, which was his last gift to me—a revelation of his own divinity and a vision of the nature of existences.

After my retirement from government service in 1990, I had been seeing a lot more of him. Apart from short visits, every year I would spend a month in the summer in Brindavan or Puttaparthi, attending his discourses, and spending time with the faculty of his university and giving lectures to students on international relations. In 1988, and a few years later for the second time, he had honoured me by asking me to deliver the convocation addresses at the university of which he was the chancellor. In all these visits I saw a good deal of Bhagwan Baba and on several occasions talked with him and received his guidance on spiritual matters. Four decades had passed since my first meeting with him. He must have thought that all those years of meditation and my effort to live my life in accordance with his precepts had readied me for the revelation which I attempt to describe here.

In Prasanthi Nilayam (old Puttaparthi), on the afternoon of 20 June 2009 and the following day, I saw Baba along with others assembled in the temple verandah for his darshan. I was scheduled to leave Prashanthi at 1 p.m. on 22 June and was hoping for an audience with Baba that morning. But Baba did not come to the temple and, instead, I received instructions to postpone my departure till after a meeting with him that afternoon, which in effect meant that I would be able to take a flight to Delhi only on 23 June. I willingly complied with Baba's command and changed my travel arrangements accordingly.

In the private audience with Baba, he graciously granted me at around 4:30 p.m. on Monday, 22 June. I gave expression to my gratitude for the honour he had bestowed on me earlier in April that year to make me a member of his Central Trust's Management Council, and asked for his guidance as to any particular service I could render as a council member. He changed the subject with a smile by informing me of a large sum of money he was giving to the Sathya Sai International Centre in New Delhi—I am chairman of the management committee of the centre. The centre's activities were expanding and, in particular, the work of the Sathya Sai Primary School and the School for the Study of Human Values attached to it was attracting notice in educational circles in India and abroad. I took Baba's generous gift as indication of his appreciation of the centre's work. Baba then said he would see me in the mandir at 8 a.m. the following day.

I reached the mandir at 8 a.m. on the morning of Tuesday, 23 June, and sat in the chair reserved for me in the outer verandah. The chair was provided out of respect for my age—I was eighty-five— and its placement was strategic in the sense that from where I sat, I got a clear view of Baba's arrivals and departures and of much of the rounds he used to make in the mandir's compound to give darshan to devotees assembled there. From my seat I could see Baba almost as he left his residence to begin the short journey to the mandir. He usually took three minutes to reach the gate of the compound, the area adjoining which was reserved for women devotees.

My eyesight was still good in those days. I could read a newspaper's small print without spectacles. Everything seemed normal that morning. But a moment after Baba came out of his residence, and my eyes caught sight of him, things started to happen the likes of which I had not experienced before. All of a sudden, I felt a surge of warmth in my body and a change came over my vision. All that was static and stable a moment earlier—the boundary wall, the buildings beyond, the serried rows of women devotees in their multicoloured saris, thousands of male devotees assembled in the hall—all became a sea of gentle waves of multi-hued light.

Instinctively my right hand went to the pulse in my left wrist. The pulse beat was normal. My eyes opened wide in wonder at the panorama unfolding before them. My gaze turned towards the gate of the mandir compound, a few yards beyond which I could still clearly see, for a few fleeting moments, Baba in the wheelchair, with four companions walking behind him, slowly advancing towards the gate. Momentarily the scene began to change and in a trice it was all light everywhere—the purest of pure white light enveloped all. It looked as if nothing else had ever existed there, nothing except the heavenly radiance I now beheld. Whichever way my gaze turned, I saw only light, an all-enveloping luminescence everywhere. Boundary walls topped by iron grills, solid buildings beyond, the gate where I had had a clear view of Baba and his companions, and a few thousand women devotees seated on two sides of Baba's route to the temple, Baba's party of four—all had dissolved into that splendour of divine effulgence. I could still see Baba moving slowly forward on air, as it were, no wheelchair under him, on his usual course of giving darshan. But now, he and his orange robe had also become a translucent white entity, yet clearly distinguishable in outline, afloat on the sea of light around it. All landmarks of the area with which I had become so familiar over the years had vanished or become part of that light. There was no solid substance in sight anywhere around.

How long did all this last? I cannot say with certainty. Perhaps not more than three or four minutes. While beholding that marvel, I remember saying to myself: 'I am fully conscious and in possession of my senses. This is strange, the light is so bright but it is not harsh on my eyes; no heat radiates from it!' I also observed how remarkably calm I was as my eyes feasted on that cool, bright light which had transmuted everything into itself. The supernatural spectacle had not unnerved me. And then suddenly the thought came to me, 'my Divine Teacher is giving me a vision of who he is and of the reality of existences. I am a blessed recipient of his grace.'

In a moment, as it were, the scene began to change again. The light swiftly receded from all sides to a point about forty or fifty yards from the gate into the temple compound, where Baba and his party had then reached. I could now make out Baba, in his orange-coloured robe, on the wheelchair with his four companions behind him at the centre of a quickly shrinking glow and, then, the normal everyday scene of Baba on his round to bless the assembled devotees. My eyes blinked and were filled with tears of joy and gratitude. Bedazzled by the transfiguration I had witnessed of Baba and the surroundings into a sea of light, I sat in my chair in the verandah, oblivious of what was happening around me.

A few minutes later, someone nudged me and I saw Baba's wheelchair advancing towards me in the verandah. Quickly I rose and touched his feet. As I looked at him, he beamed his usual beatific smile and raised his right hand in blessing. No words passed between us; none were necessary. The avatar had blessed me with a revelation of his reality and of the Divine Light called God.

Baba did not stay in the temple long that morning. Before leaving the temple he blessed me again and said, 'All is well; you can go back to Delhi today.'

Every detail of that experience is etched in my mind and in my memory. Looking back, I wonder how I could behold that marvel of indescribable brilliance without any sense of bewilderment or awe overwhelming me. It was also a wonder that no heat emanated from that sea of light. The mild warmth felt by my body before the transfiguration began, was due, I imagine, to what Baba had done to impart strength to my body and a supernatural vision to my physical eyes so that I could withstand the powerful impact of the divine revelation, behold and absorb it.

On two previous occasions, I had witnessed a self-revelatory act on Baba's part, which linked him with light. The scale of those manifestations was much smaller and my normal eye was good enough to view them. Rai Bahadur Sohan Lal's house was the venue of both occurrences. The first I have described earlier in this chapter. The second vision was that of a halo around Baba's head at a dinner in his company in the dining room. When others were concentrating on the plates laden with delicacies before them. I happened to look up and catch Baba's eye, suddenly a halo of grainy brilliance of an early winter morning sun had formed round his head, which vanished instantly but only after I had had a good look at it. That it was an act of grace on his part for my benefit was clear. When the feast ended and I took his leave Baba smiled and said, 'You saw!' and walked away without waiting for an answer.

For many years I had longed for a sight of that halo once again, but Baba had been preparing me for a much larger vision of his divine reality. In a discourse in the mandir compound in Prasanthi Nilayam, Baba had said, 'The avatar comes not only to proclaim the eternal virtues but also to shower his love on all mankind. But each one will get the benefit according to the size of the vessel he holds.'

On 23rd June, he gave me a vision of the Supreme Light, which the Upanishads describe as Narayana, the Supreme Reality also designated in the Upanishads as Brahman. Guru Nanak, founder of the Sikh faith, speaks of 'one supreme light (noor) from which the entire universe was born.' A vision of that noor was Sri Sathya Sai Baba's last gift to me before he went into mahasamadhi.

chapter nineteen

DIPLOMACY IN BRITAIN

~

When I met Foreign Minister Swaran Singh before leaving for London in July 1972, he said to me that he realized it was not going to be an easy task and to do it I would need to be in total charge of the mission. 'You are not senior enough to be designated high commissioner, but after you have settled down in London in a month or two I shall transfer High Commissioner Apa Pant to another post. You will be acting high commissioner until the day you tell me you have completed the High Commission's reorganization. I shall then give you a big ambassadorial post.'

Two months after my joining duty in London as deputy high commissioner, Apa Pant was transferred to Rome. He did not like it but having completed his normal term in London, he could hardly demur. Soon after, I had taken charge as acting high commissioner. Minister (administration) in the High Commission, A. Madhavan, a brilliant IFS officer, and I carried out a thorough inspection of all the various branches of the High Commission, spread over six or seven different locations in London. Yezdi Gundevia, a former DHC and foreign secretary had described the Indian High Commission in his book, *Outside the Archives* as an 'inglorious archipelago from Aldwych to Edgeware'.

In Gundevia's days in the 1950s, the sanctioned staff strength of the High Commission was 1100; a couple of hundred more posts seemed to have been added in the next two decades. But neither

Gundevia, nor the five or six DHCs who succeeded him, were able to do anything to cut the High Commission to size because public figures who occupied the high commissioner's office were averse to staff reductions for fear of becoming unpopular locally and also incurring the displeasure of their ministerial friends in Delhi whose protégés in India House would lose their sinecures. Besides London offices of their ministries would be closed down.

My room by room inspection of the main premises of the High Commission, India House in Aldwych, gave me the idea that in that building, around 400 persons could be accommodated and if we could reduce staff strength to that number, we could dispense with fairly expensive rented spaces in other parts of the city. A compact mission of that size will make for greater efficiency in its functioning and also result in substantial savings in the mission's annual budget.

TERRORIST ATTACK ON INDIA HOUSE

The inspections also revealed worrisome shortcomings in the security of India House. After the 1971 war, we could not take the security of any of our missions for granted. In London, in particular, there were a number of settlements of Pakistani Muslims and my fear was that a group of fanatic hotheads might decide to launch a terrorist attack, kill some of our employees, take a few prominent hostages, or explode a bomb in the building to avenge Pakistan's defeat in the 1971 war. India House would be an obvious target for such an attempt.

I shared my concern in this regard with Ved Marwah, a thoughtful and highly competent police officer who was the High Commission's security officer. He was conscious of the gaps in the building's security and was feeling a bit frustrated because higher authorities in the past had not wanted the public's access to the High Commission hampered in any way. When given the authority to do the needful, he did an excellent job of plugging the gaps in the building's security.

Other than the main entrance on Aldwych, there were several entry/exit points in the building's rear. Checks were installed on these points and Ved immediately took several steps to sensitize the staff to be watchful of likely security threats to the mission. The one arrangement that proved of critical importance when an attack on India House actually took place in the summer was the establishment of a direct emergency link with the police station nearest to India House. But other than positioning an unarmed security guard at the main entrance, we failed to set up in time foolproof security checks there, such as a couple of physical barriers and identity checks which took time to put in place.

About 400 persons worked in the building, and at the opening time of the office, perhaps 250 to 300 staff members used that particular entrance. It was at such a time in the morning in the press of people wanting to enter the building that four young Pakistani men gatecrashed into the building, pulled masks over their faces, took out their pistols and in the centre of the circular reception hall, set up a mechanism to spray acid on anyone who tried to approach them.

They asked where the high commissioner's room was and a guard shouted that the high commissioner was in Rome and he tried to engage them in conversation. Meanwhile, another security man called the police on the emergency link. Within minutes three or four policemen came into the building from a side door, raised their guns and their leader shouted at the intruders to drop their guns and surrender. The masked young men did not respond to the senior police officer's repeated warnings. In the absence of compliance, his men shot all four masked men dead. I wasn't in the building that morning as I was at our supply mission's premises in Edgeware. The bodies were being removed by the police when I arrived at the High Commission an hour later.

It turned out that the pistols the Pakistani intruders were carrying were toy guns looking very much like the real, lethal stuff. When the story broke, we in India House and the London police feared that the killing of four young men carrying toy guns might attract criticism, but nothing of that sort happened. In fact there was widespread condemnation of the terrorist attack on the High Commission.

For a while, there was much concern in London's official circles about my personal security. The drill the police chief prescribed made my life difficult. I had public engagements to fulfill, but the moment I got out of my car at the venue of a meeting four constables would surround me, link arms and escort me to my seat; I was embarrassed and felt like a prisoner. After a week or so I invited the police chief to India House and after many protests and pleas persuaded him to just give me an armed security officer in mufti to accompany me in my movements in town. He did that, but I gathered some additional personnel in mufti were also deployed discreetly here and there in support of the lone gunman who accompanied me everywhere. But I did not see them and that was fine. I felt like a normal human being again and could resume my walks between my residence and India House.

PAINLESS STAFF REDUCTION IN INDIA HOUSE

The inspection team from India which the foreign minister had promised, arrived in due course. After numerous inspections of all our offices and personal interviews with employees, it included in its report as an important objective of the reorganization exercise to reduce the staff strength to around 400. The team left the implementation procedures to the mission. Another idea of mine which the team approved was that the discharged personnel should be compensated with a golden handshake such as several months' pay, in addition to any other entitlements, such as pension due to them.

Before initiating action to reduce staff, we took care to take India-based personnel numbering around 150 into confidence and they assured me they would be happy to take over any amount of additional workload and see to it that public services, such as passport and visa work would not suffer the least interruption.

Madhavan, my deputy, then called a meeting of the locally recruited staff—India-based personnel had been asked to remain in their seats to avoid overcrowding in the meeting room. In the group that attended, there were around seventy-five locally recruited old, loyal people, good workers deeply attached to India House. I had privately told them I wanted them to stay with us and I would take steps to enhance their salary cheques after the reorganization was completed. The only one in this group to let me down was Besant, my chauffeur, who had loyally served a succession of high commissioners and was a most likeable man. He found the golden handshake too attractive to miss.

In a brief address to the gathering I made the following points:

1. The government's instructions to me to relocate some of the mission's current functions in India necessitated fairly large reductions in locally recruited staff.
2. Tentatively, the government had fixed the mission's strength, including, India–based personnel, at 400.
3. I was under orders to carry out these instructions in the next three to four months.
4. I assured them there was no reason for anyone to panic, that I was determined to ensure that no one would leave India House without an equal or better job firmly in hand, and all departures would be voluntary and we shall part as friends.
5. I asked them—all of them, I emphasized—to consider themselves on paid leave for three months w.e.f. first of the following month, look for an equal or better job, come back to India House when they have one firmly in hand and we would give them all that they were entitled to under their terms of appointment plus a golden handshake, the details of which Madhavan spelt out at the meeting.
6. Finally, I said I would be willing to consider extension of the period of paid leave by a month or two if necessary.

There were still a few Englishmen employed under some dispensation by the former secretary of state for India. They objected, and rudely too: 'High Commissioner, you are wrong; you are not aware of the rules or our terms of appointment,' under an act or order governing the secretary of state's employees.

I ignored the impertinence, and shouted to their leader sitting in the back row: 'There is no secretary of state for India any more, and you must remember India House is a diplomatic mission of a foreign country. But as I said we shall fulfill every obligation India House has undertaken in letters of appointment issued by it. You haven't heard me; I also said no one is under compulsion to leave. Stay on if you like.'

'You work in this building?' I asked the objectors. 'Yes, right here in India House,' shouted those who had raised objections. I said to them that in the last couple of months, in my several rounds of inspection of all floors I had not seen any of them even once. 'I would like to see more of you in the coming months.' A ripple of mirth swept the hall and I closed the meeting by saying anyone who had any questions or doubts should feel free to see me or Madhavan for clarification.

Those secretary of state's men were among the first lot of about 150 or so to leave at the end of the first month of paid leave. Unemployment in Britain was not high at the time and opportunities were available in London for educated persons with work experience. Also for middle-class salaried employees, a cash handout of a few month's salary was a bounty not to be scorned.

So, another 300 exited voluntarily the next month. And in another month or two, we had reached down close to the number we had in mind. However, towards the end of the exercise we were left with a score or two of unwanted local staff, including protégés of previous high commissioners, underlings of powerful persons in Delhi and relatives of some members of the Indian press corps in London—all sinecurists used to a good life at the expense of India House.

We got rid of them too, but they created a stink in London and in Delhi. Indian press correspondents wrote long articles against me. *The Hindu* was the worst culprit in this regard. But its management later made amends by fully publicizing what I had done to make the High Commission a tightly organized and efficient diplomatic mission of India. There were criticisms and questions in Parliament, but throughout Foreign Minister Swaran Singh silenced critics by saying Rasgotra was doing what he had been asked to do, and he was doing it in the gentlest way possible.

Some critical stories were circulating in the British media also about 'India House sacking employees without good reason'. Another rumour had it that India had downgraded its London mission and posted a junior official to head it as chargé. On appropriate informal occasions, I briefly informed Foreign Secretary Sir Alec Douglas-Home and Prime Minister Edward Heath about the specific task my government had given me and how I was doing it, and that as soon as that task was completed New Delhi would appoint a senior figure as the high commissioner. Both Home and Heath said they were happy to have me as the head of India House. The prime minister added that he understood and appreciated what I was doing and how I was doing it, and that he was thinking of asking Prime Minister Gandhi to loan my services to his government for a couple of years to do a similar job on some of his embassies and high commissions.

Five or six rented premises were vacated. The spacious building in South Audley Street, hitherto occupied by the three service attachés and their support staff, was converted into residential accommodation for three or four senior diplomatic officers. The loyal local employees were rewarded with a raise in their emoluments. It took us another couple of months to redistribute the workload over different sections within the building. A good deal of the workload, such as purchases of various kinds or auditing, which could be carried out efficiently in India, was transferred back to the concerned departments of government in Delhi. At the end of it all, the entire High Commission personnel, numbering 410, were under one roof in India House.

In September 1973, I reported to the foreign secretary and the foreign minister that the task allotted to me had been accomplished. In October, the ministry announced my appointment as India's ambassador to Nepal, one of India's ten or twelve most important and prestigious ambassadorial posts. I handed over charge of the mission in November 1973 to High Commissioner B.K. Nehru to take up the post in Kathmandu.

COUNTERING RACISM: THE INDIAN COMMUNITY IN BRITAIN

Great and taxing as my preoccupation had been with the High Commission's reorganization, there were tasks of a political nature

1982, Delhi: Foreign secretaries of the seven SAARC countries meet to draft the SAARC charter.

July 1982: Giving President Zia-ul-Haq a draft of the Treaty of Good Neighbourly Relations including a No War Pact.

1983: At a meeting with US Vice President
George H.W. Bush in Delhi.

1983: Signing an agreement with the Finnish foreign minister, with
the two prime ministers standing behind. Afterwards,
Mrs Gandhi said, 'Foreign secretary, you are losing hair!'

1981, the author with the Indian minister of HRD in a meeting with
M'bow, Director General of UNESCO.

1983, Mauritius: Signing a cultural agreement with the
foreign minister of Mauritius in the presence of PM Indira Gandhi
and PM Sir Anerood Jugnauth.

With other officials at the opening session of the
Commonwealth Summit in New Delhi.

With His Majesty King Jigme Singye Wanchuck after the
king gave his consent to the Chukha Hydroelectric Project.

January 1985: Greeting President Julius Nyerere
of Tanzania at the Six Nation Summit in New Delhi.

October 1988: Kadambari and myself about to board the Royal Coach to proceed to the Buckingham Palace to present credentials to Her Majesty the Queen Elizabeth II.

Kadambari and myself welcoming PM Margaret Thatcher to India House to unveil a sculpture of Indira Gandhi.

Welcoming Prince Charles to the dinner to celebrate
PM Nehru's birth centenary.

With Mother Teresa and the Duke of Edinburgh at an
exhibition of photographs of Mother Teresa's charity
works in London.

1989: Kadambari hosted a special event at India House to promote the Indian
beautician Shahnaz Husain's products. Barbara Cartland was present.

November 1989: With Sathya Sai Baba and vice chancellor
of the Sathya Sai Institute of Higher Learning,
Prashanti Nilayam, after my convocation address.

With former foreign minister (and future prime minister)
Narasimha Rao at a function at the Rajiv Gandhi Foundation,
with Mrs Sonia Gandhi looking on.

March 2000: With President Bill Clinton in New Delhi
at PM A.B. Vajpayee's reception for him.

Group photograph taken at the Élysée Palace in Paris after a meeting of the Indo-French Forum, co-chaired by President Jacques Chirac and the author.

Yatish Krishna Rasgotra, aged 10, who lives in our memories and hearts.

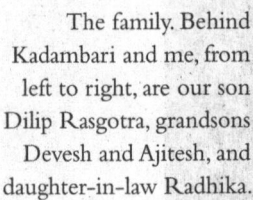

The family. Behind Kadambari and me, from left to right, are our son Dilip Rasgotra, grandsons Devesh and Ajitesh, and daughter-in-law Radhika.

which could not be overlooked. The post–World War II era was a time of unprecedented rapidity of change in the world economy and in the social and cultural environment of countries. The growing shortage of labour in Britain had encouraged immigration, legal as well as illegal from India, Pakistan, Bangladesh and other commonwealth countries. In the 1960s and 1970s, there was substantial migration into Britain of people of Indian origin from east Africa and from India. Most of the migrants from Uganda held British passports and were entitled to entry and permanent residence in Britain. A well-off and enterprising lot, they settled down quickly in a variety of big and small enterprises making a solid contribution to the growth of Britain's economy.

At another level, a number of legal and illegal, skilled and unskilled immigrant workers from India were helping to meet labour shortage in the country. Nevertheless, the Indian immigrant community as a whole was faced with social prejudice and racial discrimination on the part of the white population in matters of housing and wages. All this led to the emergence of a new dimension in India's diplomatic work in Britain, and it was feared that it might lead to new cultural and economic problems in UK–India relations.

Racism was not British government policy, but it was part of a not-easy-to-shed traditional practice. Hotheads in the extreme-right political groups were spreading fear of the country being swamped by 'coloured immigrants'. A diehard Tory leader, Enoch Powell was predicting race wars and 'rivers of blood' drenching his lily-white land!

Throughout 1972 and 1973, I personally and some of our senior officers maintained frequent contacts with the Indian community to allay their fears and to have their grievances of racial discrimination and low wages redressed. In the eighteen months I was acting high commissioner, I visited every cluster of Indian immigrants in central and southern England to inquire after their welfare, to join in their celebrations of an Indian festival or to attend a community centre's annual function etc. These contacts helped to raise the community's morale, self-esteem and confidence in their future in Britain.

At one such gathering of immigrants from Punjab in Birmingham, the leader of the community, a young man of forty or so, in his speech to thank me for my presence at their annual function said: 'Sir, whether these white English people like it or not, we are here to stay and we want to be friends with them. We can live with their prejudices and, when the time is right, we will even fight their subhuman racism. We are deeply obliged to you, high commissioner, and your officers for your support and encouragement. Now, there is only one thing we want you to do, and that is to tell these white people not to be so proud of their colour. White is no colour. Their society was dull and colourless before we Indians came here; we have added colour to it and made it much more interesting!'

Much laughter and applause followed the man's remarks. There was humour in them which also revealed high morale, courage and determination to succeed, and a flash of deeper wisdom: one colour does not make the rainbow of a diverse humanity.

MARGARET THATCHER

The annual conferences of the two main British political parties, Labour and Conservative, are occasions for the rank and file to assert themselves and approve or reject policies proposed by their leaders at these lively gatherings. These are also occasions for heads of foreign diplomatic missions to make friends in high political circles of the country and to get to know constituency leaders. In my two tenures in London, I made it a point to attend both conferences in 1972–73 and 1988–89. I had friends in the leadership ranks of both parties and it was both an education as well as fun to watch them in action and to mix with a majority of British politicians.

At the annual conference of the Conservative Party in 1972, Edward Heath, the prime minister, was clearly the much acclaimed leader. Another person who left a deep impression on me was the comparatively young Margaret Thatcher, the education minister. She was good-looking, confident and self-assured, well spoken and clearly a potential future leader of her party. François Mitterrand, the French socialist leader, was to say of her that she had the mouth of Marilyn Monroe and the eyes of Caligula. She had a striking, action-oriented personality with a magnetic quality to it which was hard to describe. She oozed strength, determination and power. She had very precise ideas about Britain's political, social and economic problems and their likely solutions. She struck me as a born leader and prime ministerial timber.

Thatcher did not know much about India, but when I paid a courtesy call on her in her office a couple of weeks after the party conference, she evinced particular interest in Indira Gandhi, her politics and personality. When I asked her whether she would like to visit India, her response was quick and decisive: 'Oh, yes, high commissioner, but only if you can also arrange for me to meet with Madam Gandhi.' A day or two later I sent a handwritten note to Prime Minister Gandhi giving my impressions of Thatcher's personality and her likely future role in British politics. I suggested that an invitation to visit India should be sent to her by the Indian minister of education. I also mentioned Thatcher's keen desire to meet with her when she visits India.

An invitation arrived within a couple of weeks and in the spring of 1973 Thatcher was in India on a week-long tour of our country. In New Delhi, a half-hour scheduled meeting with Indira Gandhi stretched into a ninety-minute interaction of two soulmates in the course of which they talked, in Indira Gandhi's words to me, 'about everything in the world and especially our children'. A deep bond of mutual respect and affection grew between them, and I too became a beneficiary of Margaret Thatcher's friendship.

PRIME MINISTER HEATH LEADS BRITAIN INTO THE ECM

Prime Minister Edward Heath, whom I had been meeting off and on, was an outstanding figure on the European scene. An independent minded Oxford graduate, he was a very likeable, warm-hearted person of friendly disposition. He was a good sportsman, an eloquent public speaker and an excellent parliamentarian. In the company of friends, his impish sense of humour, revealed in casual asides, was always a source of much mirth.

Heath believed that Britain's future was in Europe. He was not anti-American but unlike most other British leaders—Labour as well as Conservative—he was not inclined to follow the United States' line in foreign policy issues. During Harold Macmillan's prime ministership, Heath was the principal negotiator for British entry into the European Common Market which was blocked by General Charles de Gaulle's veto on account of Britain's closeness to America. During his tenure as prime minister he was determined to take Britain into Europe. In 1972 and 1973 he was busy mobilizing parliamentary support for Britain's entry into the common market.

One day, a prominent Labour MP, a good friend of mine, rang me up to say that he and four or five of his colleagues wanted to meet me to discuss an important matter, and a time was fixed for them to come over to India House the following day. They told me that they represented a group of sixty or seventy Labour MPs who were uncertain as to whether to support or oppose Britain's entry into the common market in an impending vote on the issue in the House of Commons. They said Labour MPs were divided on the issue of entry and their group's collective vote would decide the issue one way or the other. What effect would a decision to enter the common market have on the commonwealth countries, especially on India's continued membership thereof, they asked. As a friend of the Labour Party, they wanted my personal opinion/advice as to which way they should vote!

My own view was that the European option was the best for Britain. The alternatives were splendid but powerless isolation from Britain's natural partners and to become America's obedient, poor cousin. I mentioned this view to my friends. On the commonwealth aspect I said that Britain's influence in Europe could be helpful in obtaining better terms in trade and other matters for commonwealth countries. I did not see any damage accruing to the commonwealth as such, or to Britain's bonds with India or other members of the commonwealth. This, I told them, was strictly my personal view; none of it should be ascribed to the Government of India. They said they only wanted my personal opinion as a friend of the Labour Party.

Later that day I spoke to Foreign Secretary Kewal Singh on the phone to let him know what I had done and asked whether the government had a different standpoint. He said the government had not taken a position on the issue, that it was a matter entirely for Britain to decide, but it was all right for me to give my personal opinion or advice to my friends.

Two or three days later, the House of Commons voted in favour of British entry into the common market. My friends in the Labour Party maintained total silence about their meeting with me. Whether Prime Minister Heath got to know of what I had done, I had no way of knowing. He never said a word about it to me. However, our future contacts were marked by greater cordiality and warmth. In my second term as high commissioner in London in 1988–90, he was out of power but our friendship deepened. In eighteen months, my wife and I were guests at his residence for luncheons and dinners five or six times, and he graciously attended every function to which I invited him at India House, including my farewell reception in February 1990.

Though Labour governments, headed by Clement Attlee and Harold Wilson had been rather unfriendly to India, we had very strong bonds with the Labour Party's rank and file. The Parliament's curry group numbering some hundred MPs—a majority of them Labour MPs—came to India House for a curry lunch and briefing by the high commissioner twice a year on UK–India relations and world affairs in general. That mechanism kept us in close touch with Britain's parliamentary politics.

I personally visited the constituencies of some of the group's members. Michael Foot, a very dear friend of mine, had invited me to Ebbw Vale, the constituency he had inherited from Aneurin (Nye) Bevan on his death, on an occasion in 1973 connected with Nye's life. Jennie Lee, Nye's wife, was there in the huge hall which was packed to capacity. A local leader welcomed me and thanked me for visiting Nye's constituency. 'How could I not visit Ebbw Vale? In my student days in Britain, Nye was my guru in political thought. Jennie I adore, and Michael is a dear, dear friend.' My visit, I said, was of the nature of a pilgrimage.

I had barely finished that sentence when the entire audience stood up in a thundering standing ovation. What I said later about India–UK relations or anything else was lost in repeated cheers and applause. Michael's words of thanks, offering to vacate the constituency for me, were again lost in an unending standing ovation.

LORD MOUNTBATTEN'S OBSESSION

One day, early in 1973, Lord Mountbatten asked me over to his office in Mayfair for a chat and came to the point straightaway: 'High commissioner, what will the Government of India do when I die?' I instantly responded by saying, 'My Lord, I do not think you will ever die, and I am sure my government has given no thought to that kind of an eventuality.' We both had a moment or two of laughter over this, but then he became very serious and said, 'Jokes apart, high commissioner, seriously, I want to know whether the Government of India will do anything when I die, and if so, what? Please find out and let me know.'

In the next three months, I wrote two or three letters to the concerned officials in the MEA but failed to elicit a response. Lord Mountbatten kept reminding me every fortnight. I was really at a loss as to what to say to him. Finally, when we met one day he said he was puzzled at the lack of response from New Delhi to his query and asked whether I personally had any thoughts as to what India might do when the time comes. I said to him that I myself had a fair idea of what would happen: 'You, Sir, as governor general were the first head of state of newly independent India. So, on your passing the flags will be lowered at half mast, all entertainment and celebrations will be cancelled for seven days and all else that goes with state mourning at the loss of a head of state will follow; some prominent Indian personage will be present at the funeral, and a mixed detachment of the Indian Armed Forces will march in Your Lordship's funeral procession.'

Mountbatten was visibly pleased to hear all that from me, but he asked, 'Well, then why doesn't your government say so?' 'My Lord,' I responded, 'even I was reluctant to spell this out for you, and it did not give me joy to do that. Our people do not like to talk, even think, about the death of a person they like and hold in respect and affection. Indians haven't forgotten you were in the Rashtrapati Bhavan as governor general of independent India.' A few months later he came to my farewell reception decked up in full regalia of his high status. When he came to Kathmandu to attend King Birendra's coronation in February 1975, the very first thing he did on the day of his arrival was to call at my residence in the company of Prince Charles!

Countless Indian VIPs—ministers, members of Parliament, politicians and others—flock to London in the summer months of May and June on one pretext or another, and it's the high commissioner's prerogative to meet with and entertain them to a meal and organize some useful meetings for them. Two such visits stand out in my memory. Field Marshall Manekshaw came on an official visit. He and I had studied in the same college in Amritsar. The entire military brass of the UK turned up in their uniforms and decorations to greet him at the reception I hosted for him at 9 Kensington Palace Gardens.

Among the Indian ministers I hosted, the most dignified and least demanding was Defence Minister Babu Jagjivan Ram. He had come to London on a private visit at the invitation of his community, the Dalits, whose numbers had grown considerably in the preceding three or four years. We had a dinner for him and a few other guests at our small residence in Park Street, which he appreciated. He did not want any meetings with government officials, but I persuaded him to call on the British defence minister. As the news spread about his presence in London, I got word from the foreign and commonwealth office that Foreign Secretary Sir Alec Douglas-Home was interested in meeting him. At their meeting Sir Alec treated the minister with great deference; he had two of his junior ministers and four or five top bureaucrats with him to listen to the minister's expose of Indian policies and some incidents in the 1971 war.

A MODEL SUMMIT MEETING

Prime Minister Indira Gandhi, on her return journey to India from a meeting in New York in 1973, spent a day in London for talks with Heath. I had given 10 Downing Street the list of four or five senior advisers, including Principal Secretary P.N. Dhar, who were accompanying her. Their opposite numbers were present at 10 Downing Street that sunny afternoon on the lush green back lawn of the building. Twelve chairs were arranged in a circle on the lawn, but Heath and Gandhi sat down in two chairs and Heath said to me, 'I am sure you gentlemen have a lot to tell each other,' which indeed we did. And so had the two prime ministers. They talked for an hour and more without any aides and walked over to us in another part of the lawn, and Heath said to us with a smile: 'We have talked about everything in the world and satisfactorily resolved all problems. Do you have any problems on which you want our advice or help?' The meeting broke up in laughter. This was the best, the most pleasant summit meeting I had seen in my long career in diplomacy.

Over the years I had noticed a curious fact: British–Indian relations were at their best during the Conservative Party's rule in Britain. Under most Labour prime ministers relations lacked warmth and often were adversarial. They touched their nadir when Harold Wilson was prime minister in the 1960s. This was a strange phenomenon considering that while the Conservative Party and its leaders, especially Winston Churchill, were opposed to India's Independence almost till the last moment, the Labour Party had always lent support to India's freedom movement, and the transfer of power in 1947 actually took place when Labour-led Prime Minister Clement Attlee ruled Britain. At the time of Indian Independence, Attlee's foreign minister, Ernest Bevin, was busy putting together a security grouping of Muslim countries against 'Godless Russian communists'. In that Cold War endeavour they found Pakistan cooperative. On the other hand they found Indian leaders and their policies much too independent for their liking. Besides, under the Labour government, London's partisan support for Pakistan on the Kashmir question in the UN Security Council also badly affected relations between the two countries.

chapter twenty

NEIGHBOURHOOD DIPLOMACY:
NEPAL DURBAR'S DURAND SYNDROME

~

The briefings and instructions I received in India about Nepal were far from encouraging. Everyone I talked with in government spoke of the hostility of Nepal's ruling elite and of King Birendra himself. Prime Minister Indira Gandhi's instructions to me were clear and characteristically laconic: 'Nepal's rulers cannot be trusted,' she had said. 'They say one thing and do the opposite. I do not like that. They are not our friends. I am sending you there, because you know them. See what you can do to mend matters. But be firm in dealing with them.'

The 'Panchayati Raj' system instituted by the late King Mahendra in 1960, after dismissing an elected government, gave his autocratic regime only a thin veneer of democratic governance which was already cracking in places. The local administrations in the zones and districts, headed by commissioners and bada hakims respectively, received their orders from and were directly responsible to the Palace Secretariat. As a result, in the public the king was already regarded as being directly responsible for acts of misrule or failures of economic policy.

It did not take me more than two or three weeks after arriving in Kathmandu to realize how far the royal regime had tilted towards Beijing and that it actively encouraged anti-India propaganda. The regime's violations of the provisions of the trade treaty were blatant and confrontational. Despite the generous transit facilities granted by India, official circles and the media were disgruntled and critical of India. They no longer described their country as landlocked; they ascribed Nepal's economic woes and other difficulties to Nepal's misfortune of being 'India-locked'!

Much had changed since I had last lived in Nepal in the mid-1950s, but two things struck me in particular. Of Nepal's 32,000 sq. miles of dense forests, now only about 8000 sq. miles were left; and the monarchy, which was a popular and respected institution in the country, had become controversial. How had so astute a man as Mahendra, and also his two well-educated and widely travelled sons Birendra and Gyanendra, failed to discern that a fake democracy—in the guise of Panchayati Raj—was not a system that could endure for long in the world of the late twentieth century?

In jettisoning democracy, Mahendra had actually shortened the life of his dynasty. His son Birendra, after direct rule of eighteen years which had seen periods of unrest and widespread rioting by students, terminated the Panchayati Raj system in 1990, restored democracy and regained people's respect and affection for himself and his dynasty. But that gain was squandered by his brother Gyanendra, who ascended the throne after Crown Prince Dipendra massacred his family and killed himself on the night of 1 June 2001. King Gyanendra's assumption of direct rule in 2005 sounded the death knell of monarchy in Nepal.

The city of Kathmandu, a small town in the 1950s, had grown in size and wealth. New educational institutions, hotels and restaurants had come up, some of international standards. Prestigious new buildings and modern housing were coming up in once seedy localities. Industry had not progressed much, but tourism was thriving and it was a substantial foreign exchange earner. The trade deficit with India was rising.

Every luxury item, the import of which was banned in India, was imported in large quantities and smuggled into India openly in violation of agreed provisions in the India–Nepal Trade and Transit Treaty. One of His Majesty's ministers said to me in confidence, 'Sir, exports to India of luxury items imported from third countries are our bread and butter. India, our friend, should not take too much notice of this thing!'

Nepal had become a popular destination for Indian tourists the year round. The casino in Kathmandu's best hotel, the Soaltee, was the favourite haunt of rich Indian gamblers. One late evening, after dinner with my friend Prabhakar Rana, the Soaltee's owner, I walked into the casino out of curiosity. The large, semi-dark room was packed to capacity and heavy betting was going on. There wasn't a single free table or chair for Kadambari and me to take. As we stood there absorbing the scene someone recognized us and instantaneously a whisper went round the quiet room: 'Indian ambassador'. And all of a sudden, much to my embarrassment, the entire gathering stood up. I apologized for disturbing them, asked them to carry on with what they were doing, wished them a good holiday in Kathmandu and made a quick exit.

Kathmandu's young, educated elite were an impressive lot. Some of its members, educated in Britain and America, had acquired an anti-India bias, but most were well disposed towards India and altogether they were a cultivated and likeable lot. But Kathmandu had also become the world capital of hippie culture. A scenic part of the city around the Swayambhunath Temple had become a place of pilgrimage for the world's hippies. Living expenses in that complex were unbelievably low and drugs were freely available. So lots of them, male as well as female, came there from Europe and America for unfettered drug use and a spell of peace, friendship and free love. They did not create any law and order problem and the Nepalese authorities wisely left the harmless young kids to enjoy themselves in that tranquil natural environment. They smoked grass, played music, danced, sang and lived happily in that little heaven on earth of their imaginations. Dev Anand, a well-known Indian film star made a popular film on them with a catchy title, *Hare Krishna, Hare Ram*, which was also the burden of the film's hit song which went as follows:

Dum maro dumm . . .
Mit jaaye ghamm . . .
Bolo subho sham . . .
Hare Krishna Hare Ram.[1]

It says something about the strong cultural moorings of the Nepalese youth that they remained unaffected and uninfluenced by the hippies and their way of life.

OFFICIALLY INSPIRED ANTI-INDIANISM

During the calls I made on Prime Minister Nagendra Prasad Rijal and Foreign Minister Karki, I detected an undercurrent of undefined grievances about India-aided development projects. Prime Minister Rijal had mentioned a particular project about which there was much brouhaha in the media, about work on the project being slow and not as good in comparison with Chinese projects. After a few days when I visited the project site I found that work was progressing satisfactorily and everything was neat and tidy as it should be. Confidential inquiries revealed that negative propaganda on the project was instigated by people within the government at the behest of the Chinese embassy. The Indian embassy had given all relevant facts and figures to the media, the Foreign Office and other concerned departments of Nepal government, but they had all chosen to ignore them.

I sought a meeting with Prime Minister Rijal and reported to him what I had seen at the project site and also gave him copies of the information material on the project which Harish Shukla, the embassy's able and energetic information officer, had supplied to all concerned. Clearly the propaganda was motivated to malign India. I told Prime Minister Rijal that India's aid programme in Nepal was not conceived to compete with China or any other country. 'Mr prime minister, India itself is a developing country with many needs and insufficient resources; its aid projects in Nepal, undertaken at your government's request, involve a considerable sacrifice of the needs of our own people. If you are not satisfied with our aid, I shall immediately stop work on the project and send the Indian personnel back to India. You can hand the project over to China. Derogatory treatment of India, inspired by Nepalese officials or by a foreign embassy in Nepal is not acceptable.' We heard no further criticism of that or any other Indian project.

Gyanendra Bahadur Karki, the foreign minister, was a smug little man of extreme leftist views and my first impression of him, which would be borne out by subsequent meetings, was that he was China's man in Nepal's Foreign Office. General Padma Bahadur Khatri, the foreign secretary, was a soft-spoken, wise and thoughtful gentleman of friendly disposition, and it was a pleasure dealing with him on day-to-day matters and larger policy issues. His deputy, Uday Deo Bhatt, who succeeded him as foreign secretary in 1975 or 1976, was an equally amiable, able, considerate and friendly person with an open mind and clear appreciation of the importance of Nepal–India relations.

A few weeks after the presentation of my credentials, I invited the king and queen to a private dinner at the embassy. While Kadambari and the wives of my two senior colleagues kept Queen Aishwarya Rajya Laxmi Devi Shah engaged in another room, I had a long talk with the king over drinks. The king opened the conversation by saying that Queen Mother Ratna Rajya Laxmi Devi Shah had asked him to convey her regards to me. I requested him to kindly convey my respectful regards to Her Majesty. In the course of our general survey of India–Nepal relations, the king mentioned the activities in India of Nepali Congress leaders which adversely impacted Nepal–India relations, and I asked his advice as to what should be done about it. We would like, I said, to see a harmonious situation in Nepal in which Nepalese politicians did not have to seek refuge in India. The king, I suggested, should invite B.P. Koirala and others back to Nepal, and allow them to pursue peaceful political activity. I mentioned unjustified and false anti-India propaganda in Nepal's official media and he said he would speak to Prime Minister Rijal about it.

As for the 1950 treaty, he said there was agitation among the public from time to time and I said if he and his government had any serious problem with it, they should talk to our government frankly and propose alternative arrangements. Public agitation only vitiated the friendly atmosphere needed for talks on such complex matters. Gurkha recruitment in the Indian army—an issue raised by anti-India elements from time to time—was not a serious problem, he said.

Altogether it was a pleasant evening; but I was not convinced that the king's attitude towards India would change for the better.

PROTESTS OVER SIKKIM'S INTEGRATION

In April 1974, when I was in New Delhi for a few days to report my first impressions of Nepal to the authorities in the MEA, I picked up whispers about the changes under consideration in Sikkim's status from protectorate to an associated state or state of the Indian Union. So, I sought a meeting with Prime Minister Indira Gandhi to ask whether something was in the works concerning Sikkim's integration. 'But you are in Nepal,' she said, 'how does it concern you or Nepal?' I told her that the event was bound to provoke a wave of anti-India protests, prolonged agitation, abuse and attacks on Indians and on our information centre and library in the town. The Chinese will be active in instigating and financing protests and anti-Indian propaganda. 'In that case, ambassador, I shall expect you to deal with the situation as you think best,' she said. 'Be firm and don't take any nonsense from them.' I asked her whether I should talk to the foreign secretary or anyone else on the subject. 'Not necessary,' she said, 'and if it all happens as you say it might, do not ask for instructions; just deal with it all as you think best.'

In the next five months, in three long meetings with King Birendra, I brought the conversation round to Sikkim and told him that the Maharaja Thondup Namgyal had totally alienated the non-Bhutia-Lepcha population which constituted the state's overwhelming majority; and that his American wife Hope Cooke was lobbying in America for Sikkim's independence and UN membership. Sikkim, I repeatedly mentioned, had always been a member of the Indian Chamber of Princes, but when other princely states were integrated, Sikkim's distinct status was maintained in the belief that it might be useful in cultivating contacts with Tibet, but that situation had changed after China's occupation of Tibet. There was complete breakdown of law and order and India would be compelled to respond to the people's demand for the state's closer association with India. Generally the king would nod agreement, and on one occasion—when I had clearly said that Sikkim was a princely state of India and what we do there, I hoped, would not be allowed to affect India–Nepal relations—he had said that Sikkim was not Nepal's business.

In similar terms I had also spoken to Prime Minister Rijal, Foreign Minister Karki and Foreign Secretary Khatri. They all knew of the happenings in Sikkim in the preceding year or two and their only worry was that disturbances and agitation and protests against the Sikkim ruler should not percolate into Nepal! Only Foreign Minister Karki had demurred: 'What will India do with Sikkim?' he had asked; to which I had replied: 'The same, as we did with other princely states: Give the people the right to vote and govern themselves through their elected representatives.' He did not say anything, but there was a frown on his forehead.

Regardless of all my efforts to forewarn the king and others, the day New Delhi accepted the demand of Sikkim's recently elected assembly for closer political and economic association with India and declared Sikkim an associate state of India, Radio Nepal and other official and unofficial media launched virulent attacks on India. The following day, 2000 or 3000 students gathered in an open ground close to our embassy, shouted anti-India slogans and burnt Indira Gandhi's effigy. Later that day we observed that meals were being served to the crowd in an organized way, and Chinese and Pakistani diplomats were mingling with the protesters.

On the third day of protest, a group of students stoned our popular information centre and library in the town, shattered its large glass windows and broke some furniture. Insults were flung on Indian tourists by student protesters. Later that day, I lodged an oral protest with Foreign Secretary Khatri and warned that it was time to call it all off. Meanwhile, we kept receiving information from reliable friendly sources that the whole thing was being managed by the valley commissioner's office, who could not possibly be acting without a nod from the palace.

I was still in hopes that the protests might end through exhaustion or by government action. But the following morning the goons attacked Indian shops, damaged their goods and disrobed the shop owners in public, heaping insults all the while on them and on India.

The gathering in the open ground burned an effigy of Jawaharlal Nehru and shouted anti-India slogans—India murdabad (death to India), Indira Gandhi murdabad, independent Sikkim zindabad (long live free Sikkim). We could see Chinese and Pakistani officials freely mixing with the crowd and cheering the slogan shouters and other miscreants.

Meanwhile, resident Indian journalists' reports of all this activity were appearing in Indian media, causing anger in Delhi. That afternoon when I met my senior colleagues, I was told that the Indian press representatives were asking why throughout the crisis, I had avoided talking to them or issuing a statement condemning the officially inspired agitation. The deputy chief of mission, N.N. Jha, told me that anti-Panchayati Raj politicians were accusing the ambassador and the embassy of being royalists etc. My own patience was wearing thin but I thought we could wait another day or two to see whether the Nepal government would pay heed to the protests I had lodged without making public noise about them.

On the morning of 3 September, the fifth day of the protests, the agitation in the ground close to the embassy got louder and the protesters burnt an effigy of Mahatma Gandhi, the father of our nation. That roused my ire and I wondered whether a regime which allowed the perpetration of such an act could be considered friendly. So I decided to go to the Foreign Office to lodge a strong protest personally with Foreign Minister Karki who, I knew, was in close touch with the palace clique; and later, asked for an urgent meeting with the king.

Karki's office set the meeting a couple of hours later. To make matters worse, an hour later, apparently on advice from some Nepalese official, a crowd of about 300 protesters blocked the main gate of the embassy to prevent me from going out. My residence and the chancery were under siege.

NEPAL GOVERNMENT IGNORES MY PROTEST

The Nepalese authorities had gone too far and I felt that our acquiescing in this kind of behaviour by the Nepal government, might encourage them or other unfriendly elements in the country to make Sikkim a long-lasting issue between our two countries. So, I spoke to Foreign Minister Karki on the phone to tell him what had happened and that I was determined to drive through the crowd for my appointment with him, and if my car was stopped I would disembark and speak to the students about India's action to dislodge an unpopular, autocratic ruler and introduce democratic government demanded by the Sikkimese population, the majority of whom were of Nepalese origin.

I also told Karki that his government would have to face the consequences of an assault on me by the mob, or any damage it caused in the embassy's compound. And that he should also be mindful of the consequences of Nepal's demonstrated hostility on an issue which was an internal matter for India. Within minutes, two truckloads of policemen arrived and made a baton charge on the crowd blocking the embassy gate, and then turned on the larger gathering in the open ground. When I drove out of the embassy to go to the Foreign Office, there wasn't a protester in sight anywhere.

Foreign Minister Karki pretended that the whole thing was a simple, spontaneous show of disappointment by Nepalese youth over India's takeover of Sikkim. I was blunt with him. 'What is your interest in Sikkim, Mr minister?' 'Oh,' he said, 'you know, ambassador, the majority of the population there is of Nepalese origin.' 'Those very people and their elected representatives,' I said, 'had been pleading with India to liberate them from Chogyal's autocratic rule and make Sikkim a state of India, equal in every way to all the other Indian states. Have those people ever asked for merger with Nepal that you should be feeling so concerned about them?'

Karki insisted that it was only a small, friendly remonstrance and asked me not to read too much in it. I bluntly told him that according to my information the protests had official encouragement, which was something totally unacceptable and that his remarks were tantamount to adding insult to injury. 'Mr minister, day after day, the valley commissioner's men have been feeding the protesters; your police calmly watches Chinese and Pakistanis exhorting and cheering them on to heap abuse and insult on India and Indian leaders. This may look to you as innocent fun, but under the gaze of your officials, they burnt an effigy of Nehru who liberated the monarchy from the Rana stranglehold. Worse, they burnt an effigy of Mahatma Gandhi this morning. Nepal, Your Excellency, is the only country in the world where Gandhiji's effigy has been burnt. My embassy was under siege; Indian shops were looted and their owners disrobed in public in broad daylight; our information centre was attacked and our property damaged. And you, Sir, are telling me that all this was "small friendly remonstrance". I have not come to argue with you but to lodge the strongest protest against these offensive actions and to demand:

i) A public apology by your government for unwarranted interference in a domestic matter of India's—Sikkim.
ii) A clear declaration by a high authority that Sikkim is none of Nepal's business.
iii) Compensation for damage to property of Indian nationals.
iv) Immediate repairs to the embassy's information centre and library.'

Karki was flustered and silent. So, I took his leave and returned to the embassy.

That evening I sent a long telegram to Foreign Secretary Kewal Singh describing the events of the five days and the action I had taken. The prime minister approved of my actions and I received instructions to ask for an immediate meeting with King Birendra, lodge a protest with him in even stronger terms, and demand immediate action by his government on the lines I had spelt out to Karki. I was also instructed to tell the king that my government was recalling me by way of the strongest possible protest against the treatment meted out to their envoy, and that the embassy would remain under a chargé d' affaires, pending the requisite apology and amends etc.

The king received me the day I had asked for a meeting and I informed him of our government's decisions. Two days later I returned to New Delhi to engage in an exercise under the prime minister's instruction to chart out a new Indian policy towards Nepal, based, largely, on the fundamental principle of international relations—reciprocity.

Action by the Nepal government to meet our demands was swift. A public apology was voiced on three occasions by Prime Minister Rijal; he also paid a day's visit to Delhi as a conciliatory gesture. Accompanied by me, Prime Minister Gandhi received him at the airport but in her talks with him she was forthright in letting Rijal know of her anger over Nepal's behaviour. Among other professions of friendship, he asked for the restoration of normality in relations and my return to Kathmandu.

Nearly two months passed before the prime minister agreed to let me go back to my post. Karki was not the foreign minister any longer.

A DIPLOMATIC MISSTEP BY NEPAL'S FOREIGN MINISTER

But obviously, it was not all over yet. Karki on his way to Moscow asked for a meeting with Foreign Minister Swaran Singh at the airport in Delhi. When they met, he complained to Singh that I had unnecessarily got angry over the spontaneous and harmless protests over Sikkim, and that I was responsible for spoiling the relations between the two friendly neighbours. Swaran Singh heard him out patiently and then rather gently ticked him off: 'Your Excellency, we know exactly how innocent and spontaneous demonstrations in Kathmandu were! Now, you are complaining against my ambassador! What kind of diplomacy is this? Our ambassador had simply carried out the instructions my prime minister and I had given him. India will not accept this kind of behaviour from Nepal or any other country.'

The Nepalese ambassador, who was present at Karki's meeting with Swaran Singh, must have reported the event to his government. For, soon after his return from abroad, Karki was sacked and the king appointed Professor K.P. Aryal, a friendly gentleman, as foreign minister.

A few days after my return to Kathmandu to resume my post, the king invited Kadambari and me to a drinks party at the palace to meet the entire royal family with no outsiders present. It was a conciliatory gesture and we availed of the opportunity to pay our respects to the

Queen Mother Ratna Rajya Laxmi Devi Shah, whom I had known since the 1950s. A few weeks later the king and queen, with some other members of the family, came to the embassy for dinner and we resumed our dialogue on problems which tended to sour Nepal–India relations; among these, B.P. Koirala's activities in India were on top of my list.

Understandably, Koirala's exile in India was causing some concern in the royal circles in Kathmandu. At the same time his activities in the states of Bihar and Uttar Pradesh were causing annoyance to the Congress party circles in Patna and Lucknow. In New Delhi, Prime Minister Indira Gandhi was unhappy at his hobnobbing with George Fernades, for whose politics and personality she felt an intense dislike. At one of my meetings with her, Indira Gandhi had asked me to do something to ensure Koirala's return to Nepal.

B. P. KOIRALA'S RETURN FROM EXILE

It so happened that a few weeks later, B.P. Koirala's younger sister, Vijaya Laxmi was in Kathmandu and wanted to see me. I was delighted to receive her, a very lovely and elegant woman, who as a young beauty had made my heart leap up into a rumba dance when I saw her briefly at a social occasion in Kathmandu in 1954 or 1955. But she was already engaged or married to a Pakistani diplomat, and I had to hold myself back to avoid adding one more irritant in India–Pakistan relations.

I explained to Vijaya Laxmi that B.P. was wasting his life in exile in India. For various reasons the possibility of a war from Indian soil to topple the regime in Kathmandu was out of the question. In Nepal, on the other hand, he would always enjoy the people's respect and affection. The presence of Nepali Congress leaders in Nepal, in whatever condition, would help advance the prospect of democracy under constitutional monarchy in the country. I requested Vijaya Laxmi to go to Varanasi and convey a message to B.P. from me that he should write directly to King Birendra expressing his desire to return to Nepal to lead a peaceful life as a loyal citizen, and repeat his request two, three, or four times as necessary.

Vijaya Laxmi's fear was that on return to Kathmandu B.P. would be incarcerated, perhaps even tortured. I told her that I would try to persuade the king to accept B.P.'s pleas, keep him in detention or under surveillance for a while and then free him. I asked her to keep in touch with me and advise B.P. to take the leap only after I had given her an indication of a softening of the king's attitude. Political circumstances could change in Nepal and B.P. might still have a constructive leadership role in the country.

During dinner at my residence in April or May 1976, the king mentioned that he had received two letters from Koirala asking for permission to return to Nepal, and he wondered why he was doing that. I told him that B.P. seemed to have realized that in power or out of power as an ordinary citizen his place was in his own country; that B.P. was a sick man, and deserved the sympathy and care of his relatives and friends; and in Nepal he could pose no threat to the government and it would be a gracious gesture to let him return to a peaceful life in Nepal.

Later in 1976, in a similar conversation the king mentioned that there were some charges against Koirala; the law would have to take its course, but if on return to Nepal he behaved well no harm would come to him. I conveyed this to Vijaya Laxmi for communication to B.P. So, after a few months B.P. landed up in Nepal after letting the king know of his plan to do so in advance. There was a trial on charges of treason while B.P. was under detention in reasonable conditions for more than a year but he was absolved of treason and set free. There was bound to be a struggle for the revival of democracy in Nepal and it was best carried out within Nepal.

THE ZONE OF PEACE PROPOSAL

Earlier, in the beginning of 1975, rumours had reached me about a plan being hatched in the palace to fire an 'amogh astra'—an infallible missile—on India. This came in the shape of Nepal's desire to become a Zone of Peace. In a speech to conclude the ceremonies of his coronation in February 1975, King Birendra proposed that Nepal be declared a Zone of Peace to ensure that Nepal's 'freedom and independence shall not be thwarted by the changing flux of time when understanding is replaced by misunderstanding and conciliation is replaced by belligerency and war'. Clearly, Zone of Peace was a metaphor for neutrality.

Nepal's neutrality would require a complete overhaul of its political, economic and open-borders relationship with India. But India had not been consulted. China and Pakistan promptly supported the proposal, which indicated a prior consultation with them.

The trouble with Nepal's ruling elites is that they are not reconciled to the geography of their country. When a country's internal and external policies are conceived in disregard of the dictates of geography, the resulting failure is bound to generate complexes, which render even India's friendly embrace as a source of discomfort. Both Nepal and India have to find a better modus vivendi between them.

In 1890, after a three-year stint in Kathmandu, the British Resident, Major E.L. Durand, reported to Foreign Secretary H.M. Durand in Delhi, that 'despite the fact of liberality of (British-Indian) government the settled policy of the durbar is to play off China against us and to make use of pretended subordination to that power as a safeguard against the spread of our influence over this country'.

Durand's observation echoed my own feelings as I approached the end of my tenure in Nepal. The Nepal durbar was actually trying to reduce, if not eliminate, India's interests, role and influence in the country.

Months after Sikkim was settled, in a long evening of candid talks at a private dinner at my residence in circumstances of moderate inebriation, a close adviser of King Birendra, in a slight variation of Major Durand's complaint, said to me: 'Your Excellency, we are not anti-India, we know China cannot do for us what India has been doing to help Nepal; and our social, cultural and economic links with India are much deeper. But if we expose ourselves as too pro-India, we shall have to forget about our northern areas!' It was the Nepal Durbar's Durand Syndrome all over again!

The 'amoghastra', so-called, was easily diverted, but India would have to learn to live with the Nepal government's Durand Syndrome.

I advised the government to neither accept nor reject the Zone of Peace proposal and keep asking the Nepalese what its implications will be for India–Nepal relations, to the rights Nepalese nationals enjoy in India in matters of residence and employment and to India's security and other interests. The proposal died a natural death a few years later when a democratic government unceremoniously abandoned it.

However, other than this act of flamboyance, the royal government's behaviour was impeccable. There wasn't a word of criticism from any quarter when Sikkim was finally integrated in India in May 1975. Nepal's official and non-official media even lauded Indira Gandhi when she imposed the emergency in mid-1975. They described it as a step which prevented India's drift towards anarchy. Even under the Panchayati Raj system, the appointment of Dr Tulsi Giri as prime minister helped improve relations further.

My own relationship with the king remained smooth and friendly during the rest of my tenure. The criticism of India and Indian aid projects ceased completely. Under the king's direction, without the usual bickering by Nepalese negotiators, the Trade and Transit Treaty was accepted and signed as it was offered by India.

When I finally returned to India, Indira Gandhi asked how long this happy state of affairs might last. 'For ten to fifteen years,' I said, citing the logic of Nepal's Durand Syndrome.

chapter twenty-one

AN AMBASSADOR'S DILEMMAS

~

I. HOLLAND

At the end of my three year term in Nepal in October 1976, I requested the prime minister for a European posting where Kadambari could recoup her health which had suffered a setback in Kathmandu. The ambassador's post in Holland was the only one available in Europe and I thankfully accepted it and joined duty at the Hague in early November.

There were no serious problems between India and Holland except the strident personal attacks on Indira Gandhi by Holland's socialists and media because of the Emergency she had imposed in India. When I called on Prime Minister Joop den Uyl in early December 1976, he said tauntingly: 'Ambassador, we in Europe respected India, especially for its democracy; now you have a dictatorship. Has India given up democracy for good?' It wasn't a pleasant opening for our talk, but I politely said to him that he would soon revise his opinion about India and the Indian prime minister, that the Emergency was not a popular measure and opposition to it was growing even in the prime minister's own party. Indira Gandhi was not going to go down in history, I assured den Uyl, as the killer of democracy in India; the Emergency would end soon. He asked when, in my view, that would happen and I answered that he would not have to wait long, only a few months.

The talk then turned to Holland–India relations in general and I took the opportunity to convey India's appreciation of Holland's economic aid and also indicated our need for more. I also stressed the need for more Dutch cooperation in trade, industry and science and technology. He said after the Emergency was lifted, his government would certainly consider all that and meanwhile, I should talk to Ruud Lubbers, the finance minister, and to Jan Pronk, the young minister of economy, who was already a respected figure among the world's leading economists.

Why was I so confident about an early end to the Emergency? Before leaving for The Hague, I had a fairly long meeting with Prime Minister Indira Gandhi in which she had expressed unhappiness about the attacks on her in Holland's political and media circles. She had asked me to do what I could about all that and, in that context, I had said that the Emergency could not possibly go on indefinitely and asked her how long it was likely to last. 'No, it cannot go on indefinitely; perhaps a few more months, not many months,' was her short answer. I had, then, asked her whether I could say that to the high authorities in The Hague and she had replied with a smile, 'Yes, you can say that.'

So I was speaking about an early end to the Emergency on the authority of India's prime minister. Still, I was putting my neck out a bit, just in case some unanticipated event came in the way of what Indira Gandhi had planned to do. And though my talks with the Dutch ministers were confidential, word was spreading in The Hague and even in neighbouring capitals about 'what the Indian ambassador had said to such and such Dutch minister'.

A predawn telephone call on 21 March 1977 woke me up: 'Congratulations Ambassador! Your prime minister has lifted the Emergency and ordered fresh elections. You told me three months ago that this would happen. Are you a political prophet or astrologer of some kind?' And we had a little laugh. It was Jan Pronk, the minister of economy, always well disposed towards India and already a good personal friend.

The Hague's ruling elite warmed up towards India and India's ambassador; aid was increased and the prospects of cooperation grew in other areas. But I could not achieve much progress in those fields, because my assignment in Holland was too short for sustained pursuit of initiatives. In February 1979, I was transferred to Paris as ambassador to France and India's permanent representative to UNESCO.

INDIA SPURNS THE CHANCE OF A MAJOR INDUSTRIAL ADVANCE

Philips of Holland was the largest electronics company in Europe at that time. When I visited its headquarters in Eindhoven, all the senior executives of the company were there to receive me. At the end of a very pleasant lunch the head of the board of directors surprised me with an offer. He said Philips, an electronics firm, was only making light bulbs in India; that he, along with me, would be ready to fly out to India in the company's aircraft at my convenience to meet Mrs Gandhi and tell her that Philips would set up a huge electronics research and production centre in India to cater to the entire electronics goods market of Asia. The offer, Mr Philips himself had assured me, was a serious one and if accepted India would become a leading electronics manufacturing centre in the world.

I wrote to Raja Dinesh Singh, a Congress leader close to Mrs Gandhi and former minister of commerce and industry, recommending the offer for favourable and urgent consideration and requesting him to arrange the date and time of a meeting for Phillips' chief executive with the prime minister. Singh, who was also a personal friend, did not even deign to acknowledge my letter.

When I met Dinesh Singh a few months later he said he did not want to hand over his country's electronics future to a Western capitalist! Mrs Gandhi told me that Dinesh Singh had not even mentioned the matter to her, and she chided me for not having spoken or written directly to her. 'People around me are showing themselves off as better socialists than myself,' she had said. Disappointed with the lack of India's response, Philips decided to set up the planned production centre in another more welcoming country. India missed the chance of making a big leap in electronics technology and manufacturing.

ANWAR EL SADAT'S BOLD INITIATIVE

Surprising events were occurring in different parts of the world, reshaping political geography and policies of countries. At a small dinner party at the residence of the Egyptian ambassador on 20 November 1977, I was talking to the host about the situation in the Middle East when, after answering a brief telephone call, he led me into his study and switched on the TV. The screen was filled with pictures of Muhammad Anwar el Sadat, President of Egypt, addressing the Knesset in Jerusalem about peace between Arab countries and Israel.

It was an extraordinary initiative and I praised Sadat for his courageous leadership. To begin with, it might isolate Egypt in the Arab World for a while, but eventually peace between Israel and a leading Middle Eastern country would open up possibilities of arriving at negotiated settlements of Israeli-Arab problems.

Two other guests, ambassadors of European countries, were also full of praise for Sadat's bold initiative, but our host seemed upset and apprehensive because he felt that Sadat had taken an enormous risk and he feared for his life. The Peace Treaty signed by Sadat and Israeli Premier Begin in March 1979 ended the state of war between the two countries and Egypt regained the Sinai peninsula which it had lost to Israel in the six-day war of 1967. But, as the Egyptian ambassador had feared, Sadat was assassinated in 1981.

In Holland's placid political environment, some excitement was caused by the three-day visit of China's Foreign Minister Huang Hua in the second week of June 1978. Immediately on landing in Amsterdam after a four-day visit to Zaire, he denounced the Soviet Union's 'undisguised and unbridled aggression and expansionism in Africa', and called on western Europe 'to unite against the danger of being outflanked and encircled by Moscow'. The Soviet objective, he said, was 'to divide, disintegrate and attack west European countries one by one'! His anti-Moscow rhetoric evoked no applause or response from the Dutch.

It was a special privilege to get to know the famous Dutch economist Jan Tinbergen, a soft-spoken saintly figure whose quiet manner reminded me of Albert Einstein. I called on him at his unpretentious residence twice simply for the honour of meeting the nobel laureate and to learn something from him. The founding trustee of Economics for Peace and Security, Tinbergen was a proponent of income distribution and a just social order. He was a strong supporter of increase in aid to India. A few years later, when at an NGO meeting in the United States I ran into an argument with an American economist over the insufficiency of international aid to India because of its per capita meagreness, Tinbergen supported me by saying that since the purpose of aid was to improve the lives of individual human beings its per capita evaluation was in order.

Both Kadambari and I loved Holland for its museums which house great treasures of works of art, especially paintings. The Mauritshuis and the Gemeente museum were our favourites. The former has a fabulous collection of the works of Van Gogh, Vermeer, Rembrandt, Frans Hals, Holbein and others. The Gemeente museum is known for its collection of modern art, including the works of Degas, Monet, Picasso and several modern Dutch painters. In my travels in the country I found that virtually every small town and village had a modest museum of its own, in some cases, a small room displaying no more than a dozen or so works of local artists.

In May–June, when tulips are in full bloom, the entire country is a multihued carpet of heavenly beauty. Holland's minister of tourism did me the favour of taking me with him on a helicopter ride over much of the country during the tulip season. The entire land was an indescribable picture of earth's beauty. I made a wish then, that the powers that be allow my soul in its final flight to some other destination to tarry a while over Holland in the season when tulips are in full bloom.

2. FRANCE

Paris, the city of architectural wonders of unfading beauty, grows on you with every fresh visit. The history of Europe is etched on its stone-paved boulevards and streets. How many times, across centuries, the armies of the great powers of Europe—Russia, Germany, Britain, Austria and also France—have marched up and down the Avenue de La Grande Armée and the Champs-Élysées! But Paris has also contributed a great deal to, and continues to be a prominent centre of Europe's artistic, literary and philosophical tradition. Above all it is the city of love and romance, of great treasures of ancient and modern art and of ambrosial food and drink of the bistros of Rive Gauche.

If you have eyes to see, a surprise awaits you at every turn of the street. On my way from my office at 15 Rue Alfred-Dehodencq, to my residence at 3 Rue du Général Lambert, at least once a week I used to stop my car to take a good long look at a seated sculpture of 'the Thinker' by Rodin. Even though distances are long, it is a city to be enjoyed and appreciated by walking along its wide boulevards and its streets pulsating with activity. For a diplomat there is no greater reward than a posting in Paris as his country's ambassador. Especially if you know the French language and can speak it reasonably well, you are a privileged guest of the country and many doors open for you.

Prime Minister Raymond Barre was pleasantly surprised when during my first call on him, I initiated the conversation in French. A few days later, at a dinner at Matignon, the prime minister's official residence, Mme Barre really took to Kadambari and the Barres became good friends of ours. Prime Minister Barre was a very far-sighted man. At that dinner, during a general exchange on Europe and Russia, he said, 'Russia's empire has become too large. Moscow will not be able to control it for long; soon it will start breaking apart. What will happen then? No one can tell. The world is changing so fast! New thinking is needed, but there are no new thinkers.' This was in April 1979.

HUMOUR WORKS WONDERS IN DIPLOMACY

When I presented my credentials to President Valéry Giscard d'Estaing on 23 March 1979, he spoke of his admiration for India and dwelt at considerable length on 'the excellent state of Indo-French relations'. When my turn came to speak I thanked him and agreed with him that our relations were trouble-free, and that we admired and appreciated each other's cultural attainments. 'However, Mr President, the impression I have is that our two countries with much to give each other have prematurely retired into the happy placidity of an old couple; there are no problems between them, but there is no action.'

The President burst out in laughter. He had enjoyed the quip, but soon he became serious and said, 'How right you are, ambassador! Why haven't we thought of joint ventures in industry, agriculture and several other areas in which collaboration can be beneficial to both countries?' Lest he should appropriate all the blame for neglect, I intervened to say that the fault lay equally with us because we too hadn't done much to put our planners, businessmen and industrialists together with those of France. In my presence, the President instructed the young minister of state in the Foreign Office, Olivier Stirn who was in attendance, to explore with me the areas of meaningful collaboration between the two countries, facilitate my meetings with other concerned ministers and leaders of business and industry in France and periodically report progress to him. A relationship was established which would bear fruit in the course of the next few months.

THE ROLE OF CONFIDENCE AND TRUST IN DIPLOMACY

In May or June 1979, I got a telephone call from Jacques Wahl, the President's secretary general, to say that the President wanted to see me and asked whether I could make it convenient to come to the Élysée Palace on the day and time he mentioned. The President received me in a private sitting room with no one else present. For a while we discussed the progress Minister Olivier Stirn and I had made in earmarking areas of Indo-French cooperation. But soon he came to the point, 'Strictly between us, man to man, not President and ambassador, I want your personal advice as a friend on an important matter. Prime Minister Morarji Desai has been pressing me to pay a state visit to India this year. But I am getting contradictory reports concerning the stability of his government. I do want to go to India, but as my visit will be the first by a President of France, I want solid results on which our two countries can build a meaningful and strong new relationship. I liked your candour about the emptiness of Indo-French relationship and I want to change that. Please be absolutely frank with me. Tell me, in your assessment, how stable is the government headed by Prime Minister Desai. I am asking you in strict confidence as a friend.'

Here was a dilemma the like of which I had not faced so far. Would I be letting down my side by sharing with the President of France the assessment I had formed of the situation in India? On the other hand, would it be right to spurn the trust and confidence Giscard d'Estaing had reposed in me 'man to man and as a friend'? And if I misled him into a futile state visit, would the chance of building a new relationship be lost forever? So, I said, 'Sir, I thank you for your confidence and friendship. Mr Desai is a great man, a true Gandhian, upright, honest and sincere, but the government he heads is a hotchpotch of several dissonant groups and factions. There are many fissures and much rivalry among faction leaders. Frankly I do not see this government lasting beyond the end of this year; it may even collapse earlier.'

'What will happen then?' the President asked. 'Fresh elections to Parliament will follow,' I said. 'The Congress, headed by Indira Gandhi has been regaining lost ground fast; it will win the elections and Indira Gandhi will become prime minister again for at least five years, possibly longer.' 'Thanks my friend. In that case I'll do the visit when she is back in power,' said the President.

As soon as election results were announced and Indira Gandhi returned to power with a majority in the new Lok Sabha, I conveyed to her the substance of my talk with President d'Estaing, and she authorized me to convey to him the invitation to visit India and be the guest of honour on our Republic Day, 26 January 1980. A formal invitation from the President of India followed, and President Giscard d'Estaing's four-day visit from 25–29 January 1980, transformed Indo-French relations. Eleven agreements, MOUs and protocols, covering cooperation in industry, telecommunication, energy, agricultural and rural development, coal mining, petrochemicals, ocean sciences, technology, environment and renewable energy were signed. High-power groups were set up to take cooperation forward in some of these areas. Financial arrangements to get projects going were agreed upon. Soon after the visit, Aluminium Pechiney of France started work on a big plant in Orissa and Alcatel entered the Indian telecommunications market.

These agreements and a long joint statement apart, the prime minister and the President broke new ground in issuing a separate declaration in which Russian military intervention in Afghanistan was criticized as being 'unacceptable'.

Before leaving for India, the President had said to me that on a free day in their programme, he and Mme d'Estaing were keen to do a quiet pilgrimage to Varanasi and Sarnath without any security or official escort, that they would fly to the sacred city in their own aircraft, and hire their own boat for riding the waves of the Ganga. He did not want any security or other arrangements to be made by the Indian government; the only concession he made was to let me accompany them.

Our authorities went as far as they could to comply with the President's wishes and everything went off well, and the President and the First Lady were happy and satisfied. The couple spent nearly an hour going up and down the river in their boat. His communications man put him through to someone in France and I heard the President shouting to him in excitement: 'Je suis sur la Gange; je suis sur la Gange!' (I am on the Ganga!) Later they took a walk in the streets of Varanasi to savour the city's air. Mme d'Estaing had herself prepared, at the French embassy, a meal of rice cooked with lentils and vegetables which we consumed, along with some fruit after the pilgrimage was over at Sarnath. The piety, humility and reverence with which the couple conducted themselves at the sacred sites was a deeply moving sight.

On return to Paris, in a long report to the nation, the President described India 'as a country charged with history (and a country) which possesses privileged relations with eternity' because of the 'exceptional permanence of the Hindu civilization'. He said the agreements that had been signed will 'establish economic relations between India and France on a level hitherto unknown'. A good deal of progress was achieved during the remaining year and a half of his presidency, and the momentum was carried forward during his successor François Mitterrand's presidency. Today, hundreds of French companies are engaged in a variety of business and industrial ventures in India.

INDIRA GANDHI IN PARIS

A few more agreements were signed during Prime Minister Indira Gandhi's state visit to Paris at the invitation of President François Mitterrand from 11 to 15 November 1981. She was received with extraordinary warmth and courtesy by Mitterrand, who was one of her severest critics during the Emergency. He broke protocol to make unscheduled appearances at a couple of places where the prime minister had public engagements. The talks between her and the President were most cordial and fruitful. The joint statement issued at the end of the visit demonstrated a significant congruence of views and perceptions of the two sides on international issues, such as détente, nuclear arms control, the worsening world economic crisis, the need for a new international economic order, food security for developing countries and opposition to block politics and ideological confrontation between power blocks. The declaration denounced 'conduct of international relations based on fear, dominance and arrogance'.

More agreements for cooperation in coal mining, environmental management, switchgear testing facilities and energy utilization were signed. An agreement in principle was reached whereby France would offer credit for the purchase of forty Mirage-2000 aircraft for the Indian Air Force, terms of the deal being negotiated in the following months. In a press conference on 15 November, Prime Minister Pierre Mauroy summed up the spirit and scope of cooperation in a few words: 'the areas of cooperation between India and France would include coal, steel, oil, telecommunications, everything'.

On 12 November the Sorbonne University conferred an honorary doctorate on Indira Gandhi in a most impressive ceremony. The huge hall was packed to capacity with the country's intellectual elite. Her forty-five minute long address in French was heard in pin-drop silence and she was given a thunderous ovation at the end. According to custom it was my prerogative, as ambassador of the country of the distinguished recipient of the honour, to accompany her to a small adjoining room to sign on a massive book which carries the names of all recipients of similar honour by the university. There was no one else in the room and I complimented the prime minister on her address of course but especially on the excellent delivery in good French pronunciation. 'Arre bhai (O, brother) I am sweating from head to toe; I was so nervous!'

There was a tender, human side to the Iron Lady!

chapter twenty-two

FOREIGN SECRETARY:
THE STRUGGLE FOR CHANGE IN
FOREIGN POLICY

~

Soon after Prime Minister Indira Gandhi's state visit to France in November 1981, I was asked to return to Delhi to take over as foreign secretary in the ministry of external affairs. The day I assumed charge of the post of foreign secretary I called on the prime minister and she asked me what I planned to do and what my priorities were. I said as head of the service my first priority was to clean up the work environment of our junior personnel and refurbish two important sections with modern equipment—the communications centre (called Telegraph section), where all incoming and outgoing traffic was centralized, and the Central Cypher Bureau, where officials were at work twenty-four hours a day. The services of these two sections are used not only by the MEA but also by the prime minister's office and other departments of government for confidential communications worldwide. She told me to go ahead with the cleaning up and modernization I wanted to do. I handed over this task to Joint Secretary V.B. Sony, head of the ministry's Establishment Division, with the authority to incur the necessary expenditure. He did a marvellous job of it all, and within months the ministry's performance showed marked improvement.

In the same meeting the prime minister had asked what else I planned to do, especially in connection with the MEA's external relations activity. I said if things were to remain as they were my task would be easy. 'We are in a situation of diplomacy stasis. We are not talking with countries with which we have problems. The foreign secretaries' talks with Pakistan are in suspension; with the world's most powerful country, the United States, we haven't had much to do since 1971; we are not talking to China about the border problem or, indeed, about any other important aspect of bilateral relations and world affairs in general. The only major active relationship is with Moscow which is of course of central importance to our foreign policy, but with the USSR we do not have any serious problems and a couple of visits to Moscow a year for consultations will suffice.

'No, that will not suffice,' said the prime minister. 'In the given situation what exactly would you like to do?' she asked.

I said I would like to open up in all directions, with the USA as my first priority, then restart foreign secretaries' talks with Pakistan, followed by a search for an opening to China. 'A country of India's size and importance cannot remain bound in exclusive friendship with only one major power. While our relations with France, Britain and Germany are in good shape, we need to strengthen ties with Japan, a front rank power of the coming decades. Next-door neighbours should be in our focus all the time without our being obsessed with them.'

'I like that approach,' said the prime minister, 'you can plan accordingly. That reminds me I received an invitation from President Reagan to visit the US some time ago; the American ambassador has been reminding us for an answer, but here they are all opposed to my accepting the invitation Foreign Minister Rao, policy planner G. Parthasarathy (G.P.) and my Principal Secretary P.C. Alexander are all opposed to my accepting the invitation. What do you think? Should I accept the invitation?' 'Of course Ma'am, you should go to Washington,' I answered and added, 'the sooner the better. It's not the Washington of Nixon and Kissinger any more. Reagan wants to mend relations with India. Why should you not respond positively?' She suggested that I take a look at the papers and talk to Narasimha Rao and Parthasarathy about the matter.

HOME DIPLOMACY

Home diplomacy is seldom the easy part of a Foreign Service officer's tasks. Foreign Minister Rao did not think a visit to the US would achieve much; and it might annoy the Russians. He approved of resumption of the foreign secretaries' dialogue with Pakistan, but was cautious about the timing of an initiative towards China.

Parthasarathy was opposed to any initiative towards any of the three countries. 'Indira is not popular in the US. She will get a bad reception there, only criticism of Non-alignment, the Emergency etc.' And then the clincher, 'Russians won't like it, and we'll lose the one friend we have in the world. Don't you see?' India's policy planning chief was content with India having just one friend in the world!

On China, Parthasarathy was frantically negative: 'Krishna, you want her to talk to the Chinese? Are you crazy? They killed her father, you know!'

I must say I was quite bewildered by this kind of personalization of foreign policy. But Parthasarathy was adamantly against any initiative towards China. When Prime Minister Rajiv Gandhi, Indira Gandhi's son and successor in office, decided that he did not want 'to remain mired in the past' and wanted to defreeze the India–China relationship, he had to dislodge Parthasarathy from the ministry of external affairs.

On Mrs Gandhi's advice, I had another round of discussion with Rao and Parthasarathy with no better result. And I was in a dilemma whether to give up the effort or persevere in the advice I had given to the prime minister and which she seemed to approve. 'What is the use of being foreign secretary,' I asked myself, 'if I cannot make a contribution to foreign policy and pull it out of its one–friend-policy-freeze?' So I recorded a long note on US–India relations, with all their ups and downs during the previous decades, highlighting the advantages of an improved relationship with the USA in the vastly changed world situation. The note concluded with the recommendation that the prime minister should accept President Reagan's invitation to visit the United States.

R.K. Dhawan, Indira Gandhi's perceptive and dedicated private secretary, told me that she did not like long notes but he thought the subject matter was important enough for her to read my note and he put it in her box for weekend reading.

Simultaneously I had sent copies of the note to Narasimha Rao and Parthasarathy. On the morning of the following Monday in April 1982, the prime minister's copy came back to me with her approval of the visit to Washington and I was told to convey to the US ambassador her acceptance of President Reagan's invitation for a visit in July. I was also instructed to take in hand preparations for the visit.

Foreign Minister Narasimha Rao took the prime minister's decision stoically and he, in fact, graciously wished me good luck with the visit. Parthasarathy, not having noticed that I had sent the note directly to the prime minister, walked into my room to chide me for misplaced enthusiasm for America and for putting at risk India's relations with Moscow. After a little argument I ordered coffee for him and showed him my copy with the prime minister's decision on it. 'Oh. Well, that settles it then,' he said; he gulped his coffee and left the room not pleased with the foreign secretary's independence and audacity.

The dates of the visit were settled—28 to 31 July in Washington and 1 to 5 August in New York, Chicago and Los Angeles—and the MEA began the preparatory work for the visit. In the course of the week, I sent to the prime minister, through Foreign Minister Rao, a list of members of her delegation for her approval; she struck out the names of both P.V. Narasimha Rao and G. Parthasarathy and sent the paper back to me with her approval of the rest. When I pleaded with her to include the two senior-most persons in the MEA, she said she did not want in her delegation people who did not understand the importance of normalizing US–India relations!

But a few days later the prime minister told me that Parthasarathy had called at her residence and expressed appreciation of her decision to accept Reagan's invitation! So, she said, I could include him in the delegation. Narasimha Rao did not ask for a reprieve and, to my deep regret, did not join the party.

THE TARAPUR IMBROGLIO

However, three or four weeks before the visit, the prime minister said to me that Parthasarathy had told her that because of the controversy in the Indian media about Washington's unilateral stoppage of fuel for the Tarapur nuclear energy plant gifted to India by President John F. Kennedy, the visit ran the risk of being marred by controversy. After India's nuclear explosion in 1974, the American Congress had adopted legislation prohibiting the supply of any nuclear materials to India. The US administration was helpless in the matter and India, instead of engaging with it in a joint search for a solution, was content to criticize and condemn it for reneging on its commitment to supply fuel for the Tarapur plant for its life. Mrs Gandhi asked me to do whatever was necessary or possible to sort out the Tarapur problem before her visit to the US.

My counterpart in the US State Department, Under Secretary Larry Eagleburger, an experienced diplomat and a great gentleman of friendly disposition, was keen to restore normality in US–India relations. I called him on the phone to tell him of the dilemma I now faced and asked him how keen Washington was on Prime Minister Gandhi's visit and whether he saw a possibility of finding a mutually satisfactory solution to the fuel supply problem. Washington, he said, was very keen on the visit and wanted to take US–India relationship forward. He said he would consult the concerned officials about my idea of an alternative supplier and suggested I visit Washington for a day or two for talks. I urged that there should be no publicity or leakage about my short visit to Washington because its failure might put the prime minister's visit at risk of cancellation. I was reassured by a vintage Eagleburger response: 'Come over quickly Krish; there are always solutions to problems.'

In Delhi, I took personal charge of the Tarapur issue and stopped the daily official briefings critical of the United States. In personal discussions with three or four leading journalists who were writing about the problem, including the formidable G.K. Reddy of the *Hindu*, I persuaded them to suspend speculation on the issue till after the prime minister's Washington visit. With her permission,

I quietly slipped out of Delhi by a foreign airline, stopped over in Paris for a day and landed in Washington for an unpublicized one-day visit. In Paris, my friend Patrice Pelat, through whom I had met François Mitterrand before he was elected President of France, was most helpful in getting an assurance from the President that France would be willing to supply fuel specifically for the Tarapur plant provided the US clearly indicated that it had no objection.

In Washington DC, Eagleburger had put together a team of five or six specialists headed by a very senior official, Ambassador Kennedy. After some argument and counterargument I mentioned that France should be immediately sounded by them as an alternative supplier of fuel. The modalities were discussed and it was agreed that the concerned US authority will send a 'no objection' communication to the concerned French authority. An agreement between France and India was signed when President Mitterrand visited India at the year's end. It took some more negotiations to remove hurdles to the supply of spare parts for the Tarapur plant by an alternative supplier, Germany. Tarapur did not figure during the visit at all. Even the American media took little notice of it except to mention that an 'agreement in principle had helped clear the air for a constructive visit by the Indian prime minister'.

From the day of her landing in the United States the country gave Indira Gandhi an enthusiastic welcome and the enormous media coverage was all most favourable and friendly. The prime minister herself had set the tone in her remarks on arrival at the White House in which she gave expression to her 'hope for friendship and cooperation with the United States'. In another sentence she refuted Western propaganda about her being pro-Soviet: 'One friendship does not come in the way of another.' At a press conference later she paid warm tributes to America and to its President:

> The endeavours of early pioneers, the struggle for human values, the coming together of different races, have enabled it (the US) to retain its élan and dynamism of youth. With dynamism and high ideals, it has grown into a great power. Today its role in world affairs is unmatched. Every word and

action of your President is watched and weighed for its global repercussions.

President Reagan was at his charming best and Prime Minister Gandhi was a relaxed and happy guest. The atmosphere at the banquet at the White House was a treat of warmth, informality, friendliness and congeniality. The following day, the talks between Reagan and Gandhi and between the two delegations for two hours covered in some depth US–India relations, the relations of the two countries with China and Pakistan, as well as the situation in Afghanistan and Lebanon. North–South and East–West relations and problems of economic development also figured in the talks. The general approach of both sides in this comprehensive exchange of views was to build a new relationship of mutual understanding, friendship and cooperation and to look for common ground on issues on which they differed. That agenda was shared by the two sides and in the prevailing bonhomie several important decisions were taken jointly to enhance cooperation between the two countries. For example, it was agreed to set up joint panels to strengthen cooperation in education, science and technology and to set up a fund for the promotion of democracy worldwide.

The friendly informality of the occasion is illustrated by a little negotiation between a close associate of the President, generally known as Judge, and myself. Judge walked up to me and said: 'You know, our President is a Californian, the state which produces the best almonds in the world. He will be mighty pleased if you were to buy some almonds; say one million dollars worth.' Since India was traditionally an importer of almonds I mentioned the request to the prime minister who told me to straightaway convey our agreement to the deal. Before long, Californian almonds became a regular item in India's imports from the US.

At the end of the scheduled three days in Washington I had to leave for Delhi to prepare for my first visit to Pakistan. The prime minister and her party would travel to New York, Chicago and Los Angeles. She had spoken to me intermittently about Pakistan but in the midst of fast-paced and extremely busy programmes of the last few weeks she could not find the time to give me detailed instructions.

When I saw her off at the airport she took me aside on the tarmac and said, 'I am sorry we haven't had time to talk about Pakistan. But you know it all and you can talk to them about any subject they want to talk about, including Kashmir and the No War Pact they are so keen about. What I will want to know from you on your return is whether there is a grain of sincerity in him (President Zia-ul-Haq).'

TALKS WITH PAKISTAN

My eight-day visit to Islamabad in August was for two purposes: to resume foreign secretaries' dialogue on the whole range of India–Pakistan relations and to give shape to the nascent South Asian Association for Regional Cooperation (SAARC). About the latter, Indira Gandhi had been informed by some highly reliable sources that SAARC was conceived as a move to gang up on India. When she mentioned that to me and asked my view I said that in the geographic conditioning of the subcontinent, I could not see any kind of gang up against India gaining anything for any one or all of our six neighbours. Therefore, our best course would be to neither exhibit enthusiasm for the plan, nor appear to stand in the way; we shall join the group if the others want us in. She agreed that in the Islamabad meeting I could adopt that posture and decide the issue accordingly.

Pakistan's initial reluctance to join the association was based on the apprehension that in decision-making, the smaller countries might be influenced by India to join hands with it to Pakistan's detriment. So, when the seven foreign secretaries met in Islamabad, the Pakistan Foreign Secretary Niaz Naik proposed that the decision-making should be by unanimity, and once all the others had accepted the unanimity principle, I indicated my agreement to the same.

Another provision agreed at Pakistan's initiative stated that bilateral issues (such as Kashmir) will not be raised in SAARC. The next three days were spent in discussing the areas of regional cooperation, and to draft working procedures and the rules of association for our future meetings. A considerable amount of time was spent in discussing the successes and failures of the EEC and ASEAN, and a group was set up to prepare a draft of SAARC's charter.

The draft charter was approved by the region's foreign ministers in 1984. It was adopted by the first SAARC summit meeting in Dhaka in 1985. Since then the summits have adopted numerous declarations, which have remained mostly on paper. Regional economic cooperation has not made much headway largely because of Pakistan's obstructionism. The member countries are now turning to bilateral cooperation or sub regional cooperation in order to make progress. Overall, SAARC has been a disappointment.

PRESIDENT ZIA-UL-HAQ ON KASHMIR

The resumption of the foreign secretaries' bilateral talks was big news in the Pakistan media and there was also some speculation that I was in Islamabad to discuss Kashmir. When I went to the President's residence to seek his guidance, Zia-ul-Haq was standing in the verandah close to where I was to disembark from the car, and as I approached him, he welcomed me with a big hug and introduced to me Niaz Naik, his foreign secretary who would be my very friendly interlocutor in the next three years. As the three of us sat down, I conveyed the prime minister's greetings and good wishes to him and requested his guidance as to what Naik and I should talk about. I mentioned the prime minister's instruction to me to leave it to my hosts to set the agenda for the talks. And since the Pakistan press had highlighted Kashmir for our talks, I said I would be willing to talk about Kashmir as well.

The President's response to my offer to discuss Kashmir is noteworthy: 'Rasgotra Sahib, what is there to talk about Kashmir? You have Kashmir and we cannot take it. I want you and Niaz Naik to work on a Treaty of Peace and Good Neighbourliness including a No War Pact.' The good general had learnt his lesson from the wars of 1947, 1965 and 1971. General Pervez Musharraf, a later military ruler of Pakistan, was without General Zia-ul-Haq's experience and wisdom; he learnt the same lesson but only after launching yet another war which ended in an ignominious defeat and much international opprobrium for Pakistan (see pp. 404–412).

In our bilateral talks in Islamabad from 11 to 14 August, the two delegations discussed the Indian draft of a Treaty of Peace and

Friendship and Pakistan's draft of a 'No War Pact' in a relaxed and friendly atmosphere, with the general idea of selecting the best and mutually acceptable ideas in the two drafts which could be merged eventually in a single document on Good Neighbourly Relations and Non-Use of Force between the two countries. The discussions also cleared a few differences on the issues of travel, tourism, visas and hostile propaganda etc. Some confidence building measures (CBMs), such as advance information being given by either country to the other about troop movements, were instituted.

PRESIDENT HAQ'S NEW DELHI VISIT

Perhaps the most significant event of this, my first visit to Pakistan, was a private conversation with me in which Niaz Naik said President Zia-ul-Haq would be going to Indonesia in November and naturally his aircraft would be flying over Indian territory. The President was wondering whether instead of greeting the prime minister and President of India from the skies, he should break journey in Delhi for a meeting with Prime Minister Indira Gandhi at the airport. Naik said the President had asked him to mention the idea to me and leave it to me to consider whether to take it forward and how. I told Naik that on return to Delhi I would mention the matter to the prime minister and get back to him within a week.

Prime Minister Gandhi's reaction to the suggestion was positive and after discussing the details with her, I conveyed to Naik that instead of a meeting at the airport, the prime minister would be happy to receive the President at the airport and bring him and his delegation to the Rashtrapati Bhavan for a friendly lunch followed by talks. He could then leave for Djakarta that evening or the following morning as convenient.

A couple of weeks later, after details of the visit were firmed up, an announcement was made about the day's visit by President Zia-ul-Haq on 1 November 1982. The news was welcomed in India generally, but P.N. Haksar, the prime minister's former principal secretary and her closest adviser at the Shimla negotiations in 1972 wrote to her, in her words, 'an extraordinary letter criticizing (her) decision to shake hands with Zulfikar Ali Bhutto's murderer'! I asked whether she would like me to speak to Haksar about it. 'Not necessary,' she said. 'He is living in the past.'

In the event, President Zia-ul-Haq's day-long visit produced much goodwill and a few solid results. The two leaders approved, in principle, the establishment of a joint commission. The list of goods traded between the two countries was expanded and in the following weeks information was exchanged about the nationals of either country held prisoner in the other. For the first time after many years a few Hindus from India were allowed to perform the pilgrimage to the famous Katas Raj Temple near Rawalpindi. The President's health adviser and a close friend attended a conference in Surat in India, and a senior minister, Mr Soomru attended the closing ceremonies of the Asian Games, including the final India–Pakistan hockey match in which the Indian team was soundly thrashed by the Pakistan team. We were making progress.

TREATY TALKS END IN FAILURE THANKS TO THE US

In our discussions on the treaty and the No War Pact in 1983, we succeeded in bridging some differences and bringing the two texts closer together to a point that in March 1984 Niaz Naik himself proposed that the two texts should be merged. When we met in Murree (Pakistan) in May 1984, negotiations led to full agreement on all the six or seven clauses in the draft treaty's preamble and also on nine out of the eleven articles of the treaty's operative part. Differences now related to article IV, which stipulated settlement of disputes 'exclusively through bilateral negotiations' and article V, which required the two governments to 'mutually undertake not to give to any great power . . . any use of their territory or area within their jurisdiction as a military base or any other facilities of a similar character, particularly those which adversely affect the security interests of the other party'.

Two days earlier, Naik and I had mentioned the differences on these two articles to President Zia-ul-Haq. With regard to article

IV he had advised that we substitute the language of the Simla Agreement for 'exclusively through bilateral talks' and I had indicated my agreement. In regard to the draft article V, he advised Naik to 'expedite as much agreement as possible', and I promised to do the same.

To conclude our talks in accordance with that directive from the President I gave Naik the texts of four or five pretty general declarations the Non-alignment Movement had made on the subject of alliances and bases, and suggested that he might rewrite article V reflecting, to some small extent, the spirit of those declarations in words acceptable to Pakistan. And I emphasized that I would accept whatever he wrote and had President Zia-ul-Haq's approval. I had even told Naik in the strictest confidence that if President Haq wanted the clause dropped altogether, I would try and secure my prime minister's agreement to that.

Accordingly Naik announced in the final plenary meeting of the two delegations that on clauses IV and V, he and I had reached an understanding to which he would obtain the President's approval on his return from the UAE and we would all meet in Delhi in July to initial or sign the treaty. That July meeting never took place.

Two things had happened which led to President Zia-ul-Haq's change of mind. While awaiting the President's return from the UAE, Naik had also telegraphed the text to Foreign Minister Sahabzada Yaqub Khan who was on a visit in Washington DC. Khan took the text around to his friends in the Senate Foreign Relations Committee and in the Foreign Affairs Committee of the House of Representatives, who strongly advised him against signing a treaty of that kind with India. I learnt of this development from a letter I received from a congressman friend of mine, member of the House Foreign Affairs Committee, asking me why we were coercing Pakistan into signing an anti-American treaty! This, I believe, was the primary reason for President Zia-ul-Haq's change of mind.

Another reason was our troubles in Punjab in which Zia-ul-Haq saw an opportunity to weaken India by supporting a violent secessionist campaign by Sikh extremist groups led by Jarnail Singh Bhindranwale, who had lodged himself, along with his heavily armed followers, in the most sacred Sikh temple in Amritsar, Darbar Sahib. Bhindranwale's depredations compelled Indira Gandhi to order the army to remove his occupation of the gurdwara. In the three-day battle that ensued, there was a bloodbath in the sacred premises. Bhindranwale and his armed followers were killed and a part of the temple premises was damaged.

Zia-ul-Haq's government started openly giving moral, political and arms support to extremist Sikh groups from the Indian Punjab and from the United States and Britain. The President himself started making public declarations about the alleged ill treatment of Muslims and Sikhs in India. To the Sikh hijackers of an Indian Airlines' passenger flight, who were without fire arms, Pakistani officials in Lahore gave a pistol and ammunition and sent them on to Karachi and the UAE where the flight was terminated with the help of the governments of the USA and the UAE, and the plane brought back to India along with the hijackers.

On frivolous grounds Pakistan refused to try in Pakistan, or handover to India, the hijackers of two other Indian Airlines planes. There was anger in India about this turn in Zia-ul-Haq's behaviour, and the talks on the treaty remained suspended for better times because Pakistan showed little interest in pursuing the foreign secretaries' talks on the treaty.

On return from my first visit to Pakistan, I had said to Mrs Gandhi that though at the moment Zia-ul-Haq seemed anxious to win India's goodwill, I had my doubts about his sincerity. For, I had learnt in my eight-day long stay in Pakistan that the general was training Kashmiris in armed jihad in Afghanistan to set them upon India at an opportune moment.

The troubles in Punjab were brought under control, though the unfortunate alienation of sections of the Sikh community continued for some time. Prime Minister Indira Gandhi was assassinated by one of her Sikh security officers on 31 October 1984, following which enraged mobs perpetrated another tragedy by murdering a large number of the city's Sikh residents. The next three months were the saddest period of my career in the Indian Foreign Service.

chapter twenty-three

FOREIGN SECRETARY:
DIPLOMACY AT SUMMITS AND WITH
A FRIENDLY NEIGHBOUR

~

INDIA-RUSSIA RELATIONS

Prime Minister Indira Gandhi had serious reservations about Russia's military intervention in Afghanistan and she had spoken to Russian leaders from time to time about the dangers of the jihad which the Russian army's presence in Afghanistan had provoked. Nevertheless, India–USSR relations had remained stable and she continued to advise Moscow to end its military intervention in Afghanistan. This matter came up, in a dramatic way, in the prime minister's state visit to Moscow in October 1982. When the two delegations met, after welcoming the prime minister, General Secretary Brezhnev said to her: 'Taraki[1] kept asking me for 10,000 troops; and I kept refusing. After much hesitation I sent 10,000 Russian soldiers to Afghanistan in 1979. Now there are 1,10,000 Russian soldiers in Afghanistan! I do not know what they are doing there. I want to get out of Afghanistan. Madam, you know that region well! Show me a way to get out of Afghanistan.'

Silence followed.Indira Gandhi did not show the slightest inclination to react to Brezhnev's plea. Brezhnev then repeated his little speech in Russian; the interpreter read out the English version from his notes. It was the same plea in the same words with emphasis on 'I want to get out of Afghanistan. Show me the way; show me the way.'

Indira Gandhi had an amazing capacity to hold her peace in such situations. P.C. Alexander, her principal secretary on her right, myself on her left, whispered to her to say something by way of advice to the Soviet boss. Reluctantly, she obliged with a nugget of wisdom born of long reflection: 'Mr general secretary, it is a good idea to withdraw your forces from Afghanistan. The way out is the same as the way in.'

There was much curiosity among the Russians about what she meant by 'the way out is the same as the way in'. The following day we were all going to Latvia or Estonia, but the prime minister asked me to stay on in Moscow and talk to Gromyko and other Russian officials and 'explain my meaning to them'. She did not explain to me the meaning of the aphorism she had uttered for Brezhnev's benefit; and I knew better than to ask her what she had in mind.

I met Foreign Minister Gromyko and senior officials in the Foreign Office the following day to tell them that Russia's military intervention in Afghanistan had done no good to Russia, Afghanistan or India. It had brought Pakistan, Saudi Arabia and the United States into play in that country. Their actions were radicalizing the local population, which was bound to have adverse consequences for the region. There was going to be no victory there for Russia. Moscow should simply declare that its intervention had achieved its purpose and start pulling out its troops from Afghanistan. Nobody was going to prevent or interrupt their retreat. The Afghans would then settle their problems in their own traditional ways.

We did not allow the differences on Afghanistan to affect close relations with Moscow. Foreign Minister Rao and I kept up a dialogue with our counterparts in Moscow. The joint commission of the two countries was active in exploring areas of cooperation.

In the morning meeting Andrei Gromyko had broken the spell of puzzled silence that had followed Mrs Gandhi's aphoristic observation by introducing some other insignificant topic, and the meeting had ended a half hour later. Brezhnev was in very poor health and it must have taken a strong effort of will on his part to sit through not only that meeting in the morning, but also to host the dinner in the Kremlin's ornate banquet hall for two hours in the evening.

Russia had developed a new advanced jet fighter, MiG-29. The Indian Air Force wanted it, but the Russians were secretive about it and denied its existence. Prime Minister Gandhi had asked me to try and find out whether the MiG-29 existed and, if so, why Moscow was reluctant to give it to us. At the high table at the banquet I was seated two places away from her on her left and facing me across the table was the Russian Defence Minister Field Marshall Ustinov. It was a golden opportunity to find out the truth and when there was a gap in the conversation I addressed the field marshall to say that I had seen a glowing account in an American journal of the performance of a brand new Russian jet fighter, MiG-29. India's air force needed an advanced jet fighter but we were told by the Russians that there was no such thing as MiG-29.

While the Russian translation was coming through, I saw Ustinov whispering to another Russian military officer at the table. When the interpretation finished, I heard Brezhnev asking his own people in a loud voice: 'Hey, what is he saying?' I took the opportunity to address him directly and repeat what I had said to Ustinov. And after the interpreter explained to him what I had said, Brezhnev turned to Ustinov and asked, 'Do we have the plane?' 'Yes, we have the MiG-29, but production is slow and numbers are not enough,' said Ustinov. 'Then we should give our friends what they need,' said Brezhnev. The decision was made; negotiating channels were activated and in due course we got the advanced jet we wanted.

In our recent efforts to improve relations with the US, New Delhi has allowed an impression to gain currency in the public of downgrading of Russia's importance in India's foreign policy considerations. I hope this is not so in reality. For this relationship remains of vital importance to India's security now and for the future. The Russians on their part, freely acknowledge the value of India's friendship. In all our crises since 1962, Russia's political and arms support has been the most critical factor in India's strength and growth as a world power. Which other country would loan us a nuclear submarine or help us build our own nuclear submarines? And why are we casting around for a multi-role jet, when Russian jets of the Indian Air Force had proved their superiority in the wars of 1965 and 1971? The Sukhoi series of jets are good enough for us. And of course, we must rapidly develop our own Light Combat Aircraft (LCA).

THE NON-ALIGNED SUMMIT IN DELHI

The seventh Non-aligned Summit meeting was due to be held in Iraq in early 1983, but because of its involvement in the ongoing war with Iran, the Iraq government had regretted its inability to host the summit. The current chairman of the Non-Aligned Movement (NAM), Cuba's President Fidel Castro, after consulting several NAM leaders, approached Indira Gandhi in June or July 1982 about the possibility of India hosting the summit. We were already committed to hosting the Commonwealth Heads of Government Meeting (CHOGM) in Delhi towards the end of 1983 and the prime minister was not sure that the ministry of external affairs would be able to handle at short notice the diverse preparatory work for a huge summit meeting in March 1983 in Delhi, of more than 100 non-aligned countries.

The ministry would have to undertake the pre-summit consultations with thirty or forty leading members of NAM, prepare the draft of the summit's declaration and complete a variety of other unavoidable tasks in the short time available a month or two before the summit in March 1983. At a meeting with Foreign Minister Rao and myself, the prime minister said she could not possibly turn down the request to host the summit but wanted to know whether we had the wherewithal to handle it competently. The maximum burden of the conference, she said, would fall on the MEA and asked me, 'Will the ministry be able to handle it?' I assured her that the MEA had the competence and it would discharge its responsibilities to her satisfaction. I suggested that the conference dates should be urgently decided so that we would then get on with the preparatory work.

Natwar Singh, my younger colleague in the MEA, the prime minister said wanted to be secretary general of the conference. I said that was fine. Natwar was already in charge of arrangements for

CHOGM; he should get busy with the more extensive arrangements for the NAM Summit. He will be given all the staff and all other help he might need.

Foreign Minister Rao said physical arrangements and protocol aspects were only one part of the conference. The preparation of briefs, prior consultations with leading members of NAM in their capitals, drafting the declaration and lobbying support for it on the conference floor during meetings and day-to-day contacts with the media and daily briefings etc., were other equally important tasks to be handled by the MEA. The prime minister looked at me and said, 'All that will be your responsibility and you will also be in overall charge of the operation.' I said to her and to Foreign Minister Rao that the ministry would rise to the task, and they would not be disappointed in its collective performance.

The seventh NAM Summit was taking place at a difficult time in international relations. In the early 1980s, detente had run out of steam. Nuclear arms control negotiations between the US and the USSR had reached an impasse; the nuclear arms race was accelerating and a fresh deployment of nuclear missiles in Europe was under consideration; and tensions were on the rise and conflicts were raging in the continents of Africa, Asia and Latin America, of which small non-aligned countries were the principal victims. The trends in the world economy were not favourable to the non-aligned and other developing countries and the North–South dialogue had not progressed. The development process was stagnating for want of necessary inputs of finance and technology; the Third World's debt had reached gigantic proportions and was mounting; and food scarcity was blighting vast areas of Africa. The rhetoric about a New Economic Order in UNESCO and in other international fora was not leading anywhere.

It was time for NAM to shed its outdated rhetoric of condemnations of imperialism, colonialism and the West generally, focus on economic issues and engage in a search for areas of economic and commercial cooperation among non-aligned countries themselves and also with the developed countries. Cuba's chairmanship of the movement in the preceding three years had further sharpened its traditional penchant for anti-West political rhetoric. There was a clear need to restore realism and balance in NAM's outlook on issues and shift the emphasis from hortatory politics to practical measures of global economic cooperation for development and poverty alleviation.

A team of MEA officers vetted the declarations of the six previous summits and any other material that was available concerning those meetings, including speeches of some of the more prominent NAM leaders, and after we had prepared the framework of the summit declaration and obtained approval of the same from the foreign minister and the prime minister, a few senior officers went out to forty NAM capitals to discuss with their high authorities our approach to the summit. I myself visited Egypt, Yugoslavia, Iran and the South Asian countries to talk with the high authorities about our plans for the summit. The leaders we consulted all agreed that the short, crisp statement of major issues with emphasis on economic problems we had in mind was the right approach and it would command greater international interest and attention.

However, when the advance teams of member countries, Cuba in particular, visited Delhi, almost everyone wanted some meaningless formulation added to the draft for them 'to take back home', The section on Palestine, for example, was restored to its usual sixteen paragraphs instead of the six into which we had compressed the issue without loss of content or emphasis. Much the same thing happened with some other sections. Fortunately, in my consultation with leaders on the conference floor I could get much of the fluff removed and the new economic context we had introduced remained intact.

As the conference drew to its close, it was decided that in addition to the usual conference declaration, there would be a short message to world leaders highlighting the world's pressing problems and inviting them to a meeting in New York during the UN General Assembly session to consider ways and means of resolving them. Fifteen or so heads of state, including President Mitterrand of France, Prime Minister Trudeau of Canada and King Hassan of Morocco, met in September under Mrs Gandhi's chairmanship in New York for consultations on NAM's appeal. Further action was left to the participants.

It was the Iran–Iraq war that caused us real heartbreak. Fairly early in the conference proceedings we had laboriously hammered out an agreement in consultation with Yasser Arafat who was keen on playing a role in ending the Iran–Iraq war. Arafat himself had sought Mrs Gandhi's support and approval of the effort. But a day later, Iraq suddenly withdrew its consent because it had achieved a victory of sorts in a procedural wrangle in one of the committees and demanded some more concessions. Arafat now lent vigorous support to the Iraqi delegation's unjustified action. I had always held Arafat in high esteem but his brusque jettisoning of a painstakingly reached agreement, which he had been instrumental in negotiating, surprised and disappointed me. His change of position was also a cause of embarrassment to the conference chairperson, Indira Gandhi. I had to take the issue back and forth to the concerned parties and then to the conference chairperson, all to no avail. On the whole, though, the conference organized at short notice was a magnificent achievement. The declaration and the message it issued, as well as Mrs Gandhi's chairpersonship, were acclaimed worldwide.

The week-long Commonwealth Summit in November 1983 was also a great success thanks to Natwar Singh's solid organizational work and the negotiating skills of Shridath Ramphal, the commonwealth secretary general. This conference was no small event by any measure. Forty heads of state government, including the British Queen who is a nominal head of the commonwealth, were in Delhi for the conference. The retreat in Goa—where the leaders talked among themselves in an environment of informality—went off well. Foreign Minister Narasimha Rao was proud of his ministry's performance and Prime Minister Indira Gandhi also let all concerned know of her satisfaction over the exemplary management of two major events in one year by India's small and compact Foreign Office.

GOOD NEIGHBOURLY SHENANIGANS

The NAM Summit over, I was due to visit Dhaka for a SAARC meeting of the seven foreign secretaries of South Asian countries.

When I called on the prime minister before leaving for Bangladesh she said both Dhaka and Kathmandu had been loudly complaining about India's alleged non-cooperation in building large water storage dams in Nepal. Foreign Minister Rao had told her that India had never been consulted in the matter. She asked me to find out what exactly the problem was. In Dhaka a day later I was greeted by articles in the press that were highly critical of India's obstructionist attitude in the matter of building water storage dams in Nepal to enhance the flows in the Ganga during the dry season of the year.

When I called on the Bangladeshi foreign minister, Aminur Rahman Shams-ud-Doha, he asked me why India was opposed to creating large water reservoirs in Nepal which Bangladesh and Nepal wanted. I protested that India had never been consulted, not even informed about any such plan. I informed Doha that for years we had been suggesting to Nepal to dam some of its rivers as a flood-prevention measure and also to generate electricity, but Nepal had been telling us that it did not want its fertile valleys inundated. I said to Doha that India would have no objection whatsoever to the building of any number of reservoirs in Nepal.

Doha was surprised. He asked whether I would be prepared to say in public to the Bangladesh press what I had just told him which I readily agreed to do. The same evening I made an authoritative statement repeating what I had said to Doha to a large body of Bangladeshi and foreign journalists, including some Nepalese journalists. A day later, Bangladesh's agricultural and water resources minister, Obaidullah Khan, a charming man who was also known as a great poet, gave a large evening reception for me at which I repeated what I had said to the press the previous evening. The minister said he was going to take up the matter with his Nepalese counterpart to ask why he had been led into making false allegations against India. I requested him to let me know the result of his demarche. A few days later he told me he was shocked by Nepal's attitude: the Nepalese minister, he said, had 'accused' him of 'giving up the game of keeping India under pressure'! Obaidullah Khan was not amused and he told the Nepalese minister that Bangladesh did not want to be part of such games.

TROUBLES IN THE LAND OF SERENDIP

In the late summer of 1983, violence erupted in Sri Lanka and following murderous riots in the capital city of Colombo, a large number of Sri Lankan Tamils sought refuge in the neighbouring Indian state of Tamil Nadu. The cause of the troubles in the land of Serendip was the denial, by Sinhala rulers of the country, of equal citizenship rights and opportunities of employment in the army and the police to members of the Tamil minority. Even in the two provinces in the country's north and east, where the Tamils were in majority, they had little share in provincial governance.

When their political agitation failed to achieve results, the Tamils began to take to arms and join the radical group called the Liberation Tigers of Tamil Eelam (LTTE), led by an extremist leader, Velupillai Prabhakaran. The LTTE was receiving arms and financial support from Tamil diaspora groups in countries like Norway, Germany, the USA, Thailand and others. As the flow of refugees increased, there was much public anger in the Indian state of Tamil Nadu and there were demands for action by the Government of India to ensure the security and safety of the Tamil minority in Sri Lanka. It required all of Indira Gandhi's patience, tact, political skill and authority to maintain calm in Tamil Nadu.

Indira Gandhi did not want to intervene in Sri Lanka, but was willing to use India's influence with the government in Colombo and with the moderate Tamil groups, such as the Tamil United Liberation Front (TULF), to persuade them to find a solution to the problem through peaceful negotiations, with Indian help if both sides wanted it. Two other important planks of our policy were maintenance of the unity and integrity of Sri Lanka, which meant rejection of the LTTE's demand for Eelam—an independent Tamil homeland in Sri Lanka—and the firm decision against direct Indian military or political intervention in Sri Lanka.

G. Parthasarathy was designated as the interlocutor for consultations with all concerned parties in Sri Lanka including President Jayawardene, and also to keep in touch with Chief Minister M.G. Ramachandran in Chennai. Parthasarathy succeeded in devising a formula which, while rejecting Eelam, provided for devolution of power from Colombo to the provinces (Annexure C to the constitution) which President Jayawardene agreed to, but failed to implement. This was the situation when Rajiv Gandhi became India's prime minister following his mother's death.

Both Parthasarathy and I, together and separately, briefed Rajiv in great detail on the history, nature and complexities of Sri Lanka's problems and commended to him the policy Indira Gandhi had followed. Rajiv said he agreed with the policy and even endorsed it in one of his interventions in the Lok Sabha. I retired from the Indian Foreign Service on 31 January 1985, Rajiv had already moved Narasimha Rao from the Foreign Office to the ministry of human resources development, and a few months later, due to some intrigue in the MEA or the PMO, Rajiv dislodged Parthasarathy also from his perch in the Foreign Office. Our young new prime minister was now without anyone around him with knowledge or first-hand experience of the problem in Sri Lanka and he was misled, by uninformed enthusiasts around him, to make one mistake after another in the next few months in dealing with the crisis in Sri Lanka.

Bypassing the TULF, the only effective Sri Lankan Tamil political formation, Rajiv invited Prabhakaran for talks in India and sent him back without the solution he wanted and without persuading him of the necessity of looking at solutions other than Eelam. The ego of that ruthless and vain man was wounded. Prabhakaran immediately embarked on a campaign of violence in the north. When his forces were besieged by the Sri Lankan army in Jaffna and ran short of food, Rajiv had food packets air dropped to save them an abject surrender to the superior Sri Lankan army. Of this action by the Indian prime minister, Jayawardene, in retirement in 1990, said to me that he had forgiven Rajiv for it but he could not forget that violation of Sri Lanka's sovereignty.

During his last year or two in office, President Jayawardene, face to face with a Buddhist Sinhala revolt in the south and the LTTE's armed rebellion in the north, inveigled Rajiv into sending the Indian army into Sri Lanka, first to peacefully disarm the LTTE, and when that failed, to use force to achieve that purpose. So now, when the Indian Peace Keeping Force (IPKF) was fighting the Tamils, Prabhakaran made a tactical alliance with President Premadasa, whose pathological dislike of India was well known, to fight and oust the IPKF from Sri Lanka. Its purpose achieved, the LTTE assassinated Premadasa, and Prabhakaran began to plan Rajiv's assassination which was successfully executed on 21 May 1991 in Sriperumbudur.

This was another tragic loss for India; for in a second term, I believe, Rajiv would have made a great prime minister. Since his defeat in the 1988 election, he had shed some of his ebullient young advisers and was critically examining the mistakes he had made during his five-year term as prime minister. The IPKF was hastily withdrawn by Prime Minister V.P. Singh who had succeeded Rajiv Gandhi, leaving the situation a good bit worse than before.

BHUTAN: SERENE LAND OF HEAVENLY BEAUTY

One of the happiest memories of my time as India's foreign secretary is a four-day visit to Bhutan at the invitation of His Majesty King Jigme Singye Wangchuck, the present king's father. Kadambari and I were His Majesty's guests and the royal hospitality we received was most enjoyable in its warmth, informality, friendliness and grace. Our days were filled with walks in the lovely wooded hills and dales around Thimphu or along a meandering stream which flowed close by, in witnessing Bhutanese dances and in my intermittent talks with His Majesty. Our talks were a treat of sincere, open-hearted, friendship-enhancing conversations. The king was an unusual monarch; he was a people's man and a democrat at heart. I was not surprised when a few years later, unasked he gave his people a parliament, introduced the electoral process and then abdicated in favour of his son.

Before my departure for Thimphu, Prime Minister Gandhi had mentioned that there was a shortage of electricity in West Bengal and we wanted to develop a power generation project on the Wang Chhu River in the Chukha district in Bhutan, but the king had not given the go-ahead despite several Indian requests. When I raised the matter with the king he said he was aware that Bhutan itself would get the electricity it badly needed in addition to the revenues from the sale of power to West Bengal, but Bhutan had neither the technical personnel nor labour for the project, and he feared that a lot of people from India—Bengalis, Assamese and even Nepalis—who came to Bhutan to work on the project, would settle down there permanently and become a source of tension in the future. I tried to allay his fear on that account by suggesting that from the start, untrained Bhutanese should be associated with our technical personnel, man to man, so that on-the-job training would qualify them to take over and run the project after it was completed. Indian project authorities, I added, would ensure that Indian labour returned to India on completion of the project. I requested his approval of one project on that basis, and he could decide on further projects to harness Bhutan's rivers for power generation in the light of that experience. If things worked well, Bhutan would become the richest country, per capita, in South Asia.

The king said, 'I trust you as a friend. I agree to the Chukha project that India wants to take up. But if I am betrayed . . .' and he made a sign of slashing my throat. I pledged my neck on the deal and added that in case of our failure to conform to what I had said, I would myself return to Bhutan to receive my punishment.

On return to Delhi I narrated to the prime minister what was agreed between the king and myself. She appreciated the king's desire to keep his country for his own people and approved of the undertaking I had given to His Majesty concerning the execution of the project as a means of building confidence and trust. The success of that experiment led to the building of some more projects, the requests for which came from the king's government.

Today, Bhutan is a wealthy country and its per capita income is the highest in South Asia. The country has plenty of power for domestic consumption and plenty more to sell to India. Wealth has not spoilt the Bhutanese people; they are the gentlest, most civil, courteous, contented and happy people on earth. The present King Jigme Khesar Namgyel Wangchuck continues the Bhutanese practice of measuring human well-being, not in terms of Gross Domestic Product (GDP) but in terms of Gross National Happiness (GNH).

INDIA–US AGREEMENT ON TECHNOLOGY

A noteworthy development during Indira Gandhi's visit to the USA in July 1982 was the creation of a joint senior scientific panel to promote India–US cooperation in science and technology and to make American high-technology accessible to India. A draft agreement setting out the modalities of transferring technology to India had been given to us by the Americans earlier, and Assistant Secretary of State Richard Murphy arrived in Delhi in November 1984, accompanied by four or five high-tech experts to finalize the agreement. My team for these negotiations included experts in priority areas of India's high-technology requirements, especially in nuclear energy and high-speed computers. The Americans had legitimate concerns about the security of their technology and its diversion to unauthorized Indian or foreign entities. We accommodated these concerns to the maximum extent possible. But they also wanted periodic 'on-site inspections by American personnel' of the use we were making of technology received from the USA and 'joint verification' in the event of violation. In regard to computers there was also the problem of end use. Under the guise of safeguards, the Americans wanted to prohibit the transfer of technology obtained from the USA even within the Government of India, from one wing to another. The motives underlying this last point were commercial and we rejected the demand outright. We were able to resolve most of the differences including our need for assurance of continuity of supply, but negotiations remained stalled for three days on the issues of on-site inspections, joint verification and some aspects of end use of American high-tech equipment.

At an informal gathering in a relaxed atmosphere, I asked the leading technology man in Murphy's delegation whether the US really wanted the high-tech agreement on which we had been bickering for three days. He said there was a technology surplus; it had to be sold, and for that they needed reliable partners and there were not many customers of that category!

Armed with that information, when the old arguments were renewed the following day, I suspended the meeting and took Murphy aside to tell him that we had gone to the limit to accommodate

American concerns and we could not go any further. Therefore, I would adjourn the meeting to allow his delegation to consult together and if they felt unable to accommodate our viewpoint I would announce failure of the negotiations in the evening. It all went very smoothly when the meeting was resumed after a short recess and we had an agreement which would be signed in Delhi or Washington after the Indian elections in December. The agreement was duly signed in April 1985.

BHOPAL GAS TRAGEDY

On 2 December 1984, the Union Carbide plant in Bhopal developed a gas leak causing widespread damage, including countless deaths and injuries to thousands of persons. The tragedy was truly horrendous. The American chargé d'affaires, Gordon Streeb, contacted me to say that Union Carbide's chief executive, Warren Anderson, wanted to visit Bhopal to see things for himself and form an idea of the damage, but he would come to India only if he was granted safe passage.

Prime Minister Rajiv Gandhi, who was also foreign minister at the time, was campaigning somewhere in central India for the general elections due at the end of December. I tried to contact him but he was not accessible. So, I consulted the cabinet secretary, the union home secretary and finally the home minister Narasimha Rao, whom I had known over the years when he was foreign minister, concerning grant of safe passage to Anderson. When the necessary clearance was received from the home ministry I conveyed the assurance of safe passage for Anderson to the US embassy. It was an emergency and all consultations and communications were done on telephone.

I had no idea of what transpired in Bhopal leading to Anderson's arrest and release and his flight to Delhi on a government aircraft. However, it is my firm belief that Anderson's arrest was wrong. Detaining him in India would have given rise to a complicated consular case leading to avoidable controversy and contention between India and the United States. India's image in the world would be badly sullied.

We were of course free to pursue our demand for compensation through legal action in India or the USA, but Anderson's imprisonment in India would not have strengthened our case; the action might well have prejudiced it. The prospect of foreign industrial investments in India would have been seriously affected.

The tragedy was truly enormous and all of us in Delhi found dealing with aspects of it even from a distance a shattering experience. Anderson called on me in my office in the afternoon of 7 December before leaving for the United States that evening. He must have been advised by the US embassy to do so. He was with me for twenty or twenty-five minutes. He looked bedraggled and saddened and said he was shattered by what he had seen; that what had happened could not be undone but he would do his best to ensure a generous package of compensation for those affected by the tragedy. I urged him to be truly generous, make the offer as soon as possible and remain open to negotiations.

On Prime Minister Rajiv Gandhi's return from his election campaign, he was informed of the grant of safe passage. I also spoke to him about other aspects of the case and he approved of what we had done. I had no further contact with the case before my retirement from service in January 1985.

INDIRA GANDHI: A COMPASSIONATE AND COURAGEOUS LEADER

At the time of her assassination on 31 October, I had worked with Prime Minister Indira Gandhi as foreign secretary for two years and eight months. I first met her in 1951, when someone presented me to her at the PM's house 'as a Hindi poet who is also a diplomat'. The description amused her and she remembered it. Thirty-two years later when I took over as her last foreign secretary, she asked me whether I still wrote poetry. In between I had numerous occasions to meet and work with her and those were all very pleasant and educative experiences for me. The times in which she was at the helm in India were fraught with challenges and difficulties, but nothing deterred her from pursuing the course her experience and instinct guided her to, and she dealt with them with courage and unwavering determination.

For several months during my tenure as foreign secretary she had held charge of the external affairs portfolio. Her handling of the most complex foreign policy problems was masterly. She had seen much of the world before becoming prime minister and she was always alert to happenings in far corners of the earth. She was a born diplomat with an unfailing instinct for the right word and the right action in any situation. A statesman of the highest calibre on the world stage, at home she was a patriot and a leader of strong will and steely determination. As a woman she was always kind and compassionate and her concerns for the human condition were genuine and deep.

Today, Indians are grudging in acknowledging the great legacy of India's early leaders. Indira Gandhi's rule spurred the industrial and intellectual revolution her father had begun to bring India into the modern age. Her contribution to those revolutions gave balance and stability to the country of which the generations that followed are beneficiaries.

Throughout my association with her as her foreign secretary, she showed me great consideration, respect and occasionally even a flash of affection. I was deeply saddened by her sudden, unnatural death at the hands of a personal security guard whom she had trusted. Life in government service was not going to be the same for me anymore. Fortunately the end of my career in the Indian Foreign Service was only three months away.

HOMAGE TO HENRY KISSINGER

In the midst of the hectic activity of my last month in office, I had the pleasure of hosting Dr Henry Kissinger and his wife Nancy for their four-day visit in Delhi in the third week of January 1985. I was glad to have that opportunity because even when US–India relations were at their worst, Dr Kissinger personally had been very kind to me. Henry and Nancy are a charming couple and we were happy to treat them as guests of our government even though he had no official position at that time. He called on me in my office and we went over old times. He explained to me that the real reason for the position the White House took in 1971 was not so much to save Pakistan as to protect Washington's newly forged relationship with China, and that there really was no hostility towards India in the White House! I was in Washington then and had experienced the hostility which was palpable, but I let that pass.

With his charm and sparkling wit and the versatility and expanse of his intellect and knowledge, Henry can cast a maya-like spell in which suspension of disbelief makes the unreal seem real and fiction as fact. He is a guru of modern world politics. He explores and interprets its intricacies as our Upanishadic teachers dwelt on attributes of the Divine—with mystic certainty. Dr Kissinger, I have often thought, is a modern, secularized avatar of one of those great sages of yore. I must have been an adoring pupil of his then as I am now.

chapter twenty-four

DIPLOMACY IN BRITAIN: A BASE FOR TERRORISM IN INDIA

~

Having retired from service on 31 January 1985, I was enjoying my freedom, travelling and lecturing in India and abroad when Prime Minister Rajiv Gandhi asked me to go to London as India's high commissioner. Britain, he said, had become the base of terrorism in Punjab and since I knew Prime Minister Margaret Thatcher, I might be able to persuade her to do the needful to put an end to the mischief.

A number of Sikh extremists from the Indian state of Punjab, having committed serious crimes in India, had successfully obtained 'asylum' in Britain, acquired British citizenship and joined the Conservative Party. They were illegally raising funds, acquiring arms and sending the same to extremist Sikh groups in Punjab for their terrorist activities in the state. With their help, other groups, who did not have British citizenship, were also moving freely between India and Britain to perpetrate terrorist violence in India. In their propaganda in Punjab, extremists were boldly claiming that in their anti-India activity they enjoyed the support of Margaret Thatcher and her government. My dilemma in Britain lay in confronting a friendly prime minister on that sensitive issue.

In February 1984, India's assistant commissioner in Birmingham, Ravindra Mhatre, was kidnapped and murdered by members of the

353

UK-based Jammu and Kashmir Liberation Front. It was a criminal act of the worst kind against a foreign diplomat. The murderer, Mohammad Aslam Mirza, a British citizen of Kashmiri origin, had moved to the USA, where he was arrested for overstaying the duration of his visa and as his finger prints revealed he was wanted for Mhatre's kidnapping and murder; so he was repatriated to Britain. However, the Birmingham Crown Court acquitted Mirza on 4 December 2005 on his plea that due to several problems he had no recollection of what happened in 1984!

Before leaving for London, I spent ten days in Punjab in July 1988 where I collected some printed propaganda material issued by extremist groups showing pictures of Mrs Thatcher shaking hands with some extremists who had committed murders and other crimes in Punjab and now were openly active in the Conservative Party. A day after my arrival in London, in accordance with the practice among commonwealth countries, I called on Foreign Secretary Sir Geoffrey Howe and explained to him at length the main purpose for which I had been appointed high commissioner in London. I was shocked at his cavalier response: 'It is your people who are creating trouble in India. What can we do about it? We cannot do anything about it. Not really.'

'That is not the answer I expected from you, foreign secretary,' I said. 'Sir Geoffrey these are British nationals of Indian origin, and of course also some Indian absconders from justice who have sought and been given "asylum" in your country on false grounds. They are collecting funds and arms here in your country for acts of terror in my country; surely you have laws against such activity. I hope after you have given thought to the likely consequences of these unfriendly actions from British soil, we can jointly consider ways and means of stopping this mischief.' Over the next twenty months we met often as friends, but I decided never again to raise the issue with him.

The following day I was received with great warmth by Prime Minister Margaret Thatcher. She spoke nostalgically of her first visit to India which I had arranged in 1973 and of her friendship with Indira Gandhi. She said Rajiv was like a son to her, and wished him well in discharging the heavy responsibilities that had fallen on him after Indira Gandhi's assassination. She thought Indo-British relations were progressing smoothly and offered all help to me in further strengthening the relationship.

I said I would indeed need her help and explained the reasons why Rajiv had summoned me from my retirement and sent me to London as high commissioner. I then spoke to her about terrorism in Punjab being supported with money and arms by extremists who had been given 'asylum' in Britain, and mentioned that some fugitives from justice in India were active in her party as well as the propaganda in Punjab alleging her support for their secessionist and violent activities in Punjab.

Thatcher looked genuinely shocked but to prove my point, I showed her a couple of photographs in Punjabi journals in which she was seen shaking hands with Sikh extremists against whom cases were pending in Indian courts for murders and other serious crimes. I said similar reports and photographs were in fairly wide circulation in Punjab. Now she was truly shaken. After moments of troubled silence she looked at me and asked, 'Tell me frankly, do you, you personally believe all this about me?' 'Of course not,' I said, 'and that is why I am here to talk to you frankly and in confidence. But something is wrong somewhere which needs to be set right. What are these criminals doing in your party? And why do they get the honour of being photographed with you?'

After another silence of a minute or so, she said, 'I get it. You know, I go to our constituency party meetings now and then. This has happened on several occasions: I see an arm stretched towards me for a handshake, beyond it I see a man with a turban and as I shake hands with him, there's a flash and the click of a camera. Could that be it? What do you think?' 'That's precisely it,' I said, and again asked why these criminals were in the Conservative Party. 'I know how strongly you oppose terrorism in any form anywhere. Why has India not heard you condemning terrorism in Punjab? Can you consider making a public declaration condemning such activities?' Without a moment's hesitation she agreed to do that and asked if I could provide an appropriate platform for her to speak on the subject, which I agreed to do.

On Dussehra or Diwali that year—I forget the exact occasion—I invited several friendly Punjabi groups to join the High Commission to host a big dinner to celebrate the occasion with Prime Minister Thatcher as the chief guest. They were enthusiastic and a dinner for some 300 persons was organized in the banquet hall of a hotel on Park Lane. Care was taken to ensure the presence of leaders from anti-India Sikh groups at the dinner. The occasion went off beautifully and Mrs Thatcher strongly condemned terrorism in Punjab and any activity to support it from British soil.

She declared that Rajiv, the son of her friend Indira Gandhi, was like a son to her and she would not tolerate any activity on British soil against him or the Indian government. She made similar declarations when she was in India House to unveil a bust of Indira Gandhi and at a banquet organized by the Bharatiya Vidya Bhavan. The targeted groups and persons got the message and disappeared from sight! The publicity of her declarations in Punjab helped calm the situation there. The main purpose of my assignment was achieved very largely in the first six or eight months of my second tenure in London.

RECONCILING AN ALIENATED COMMUNITY

Only one other important task remained and that was to tackle the alienation of the Sikh community from India House. From my earlier assignment as acting high commissioner I had friends in gurdwaras, especially the one in Southall, which I used to visit on holy occasions and on my birthdays. I was known in Sikh circles of the country to be a friend of the community. I genuinely wanted to make obeisance before the holy book—the Guru Granth Sahib—in the Southall gurdwara. A few days after my meeting with Prime Minister Thatcher I drove out to Southall. On arrival I left the big Daimler carrying the number plate IND-1 announcing its ownership at the gate and walked into the temple, bowed before the holy book, made the traditional offering of a small amount of money, prayed and came out. The granthis (priests) recognized me and greeted me with much warmth. They asked if I was on a visit to London and were pleased when I said I had just taken over as high commissioner. There was no untoward incident. The ice between the Sikh community and India House was broken, and word spread rapidly in the community about my visit to the gurdwara.

Day after day, a small group of Sikhs would assemble, across the road on the far side opposite India House, holding anti-India placards. One late afternoon, on a whim, I walked out of India House alone and crossed the road to where the protester group was. I introduced myself as the new high commissioner, in their language—Punjabi—and said to them: 'It makes me unhappy to see you standing here in inclement weather. If you have a problem with India or India House, please come to my office for a cup of tea and we can sort out the problem.' They did not accept my offer, but dispersed rapidly, never to assemble there again in protest while I was in the post in London.

By the time Rajiv Gandhi's government was defeated in the general election in December 1989 and I resigned, I had visited seven or eight other gurdwaras including the major ones in Glasgow, Manchester and Birmingham. Sikh men and women had started visiting India House for consular services and a friendly relationship between an important section of the Indian community and India House was established.

In all my activity to restore civility and warmth in Indo-British relations, apart from Mrs Thatcher's support I received the most valuable help from three others: her dedicated Private Secretary Charles Powell (now Lord Powell), a brilliant member of the British Diplomatic Service, from the permanent under secretary in the Foreign and Commonwealth Office, Sir Patrick Wright and Home Minister Douglas Hurd.

The London police had some anxiety about my security and had insisted on an armed security officer in mufti accompanying me in all my movements outside India House or 9 Kensington Palace Gardens. One of the police escorts attached to me, an Oxford graduate in geography, was a most pleasant companion. One day while walking in Hyde Park we passed by a dense cluster of tall bushes, and I asked John what he would do if a terrorist jumped out of the bushes and started emptying his Sten gun on me. 'Nothing very much, Sir, really,' he said, 'but I shall be able to make an excellent report of the incident!'

IMPORTANCE OF HOSPITALITY AND THE ROLE OF AN AMBASSADOR'S WIFE

In diplomacy, a great deal of delicate negotiations are successfully carried out at informal and formal dinners, luncheons and receptions. Being a good host is important for an ambassadorial couple everywhere. An ambassador who keeps a good table and entertains well—not only officials of the host country but also important Opposition leaders, media personalities, distinguished writers, artists and influential civil society figures—quickly gains respect and popularity in the host country.

Right from our days at the UN (1958–62), Kadambari had taken seriously to mastering the intricacies of purposeful and elegant hospitality, and from the day I rose to be ambassador she took full charge of this important aspect of my responsibilities. (See pp. 413–416 for a write-up on her qualities as chatelaine of 9 Kensington Palace Garden in a London society journal). In busy capitals like Paris, London and Washington, in particular, being a good housekeeper and hostess is a full-time job. Governments should find ways to monetarily compensate wives of diplomats for their unavoidable and hitherto unrewarded duties.

Even friendly entertainment (without a set purpose), apart from its enjoyment helps promote bonhomie and friendship. I had often met Princess Margaret, the queen's younger sister, at social functions and on royal occasions. A charming and exquisitely beautiful woman, she was my favourite among the young royals of London. We had invited her to dinner at 9 KPG, and since I knew she liked scotch whisky I had assembled several special brands of whisky and wines, and under Kadambari's supervision our two cooks had prepared a mix of Indian and Western dishes for her and other guests. The princess drank only Famous Grouse whisky and savoured a very small bit of every dish just to show her appreciation, but to the amusement of every one present concentrated on dal—lentils cooked the Indian way—of which she consumed a bowl filled to the top. She absolutely loved it, she said, and proclaimed it 'the best dish of all cuisines'! The royals can also be very human and very simple at heart. Kadambari and I wanted to call on her to bid farewell but she hosted a big seated lunch for us at Kensington Palace with the cream of London society at the table.

Before leaving London at the end of February 1990, Kadambari and I went to Buckingham Palace to take leave of Her Majesty the Queen. She received us in her small private drawing room where we had a delightful chat with her over tea for nearly an hour. The queen is highly knowledgeable and a most engaging conversationalist with a good sense of humour—just simple fun. She had recently returned from the Commonwealth Summit in Kuala Lumpur and I asked her how the summit had gone. With a merry twinkle in her eyes she said, 'What summit, High Commissioner! Rajiv did not come and Benazir was heartbroken!'

In the midst of some more lively talk triggered by Her Majesty's remark, we took leave of that most charming and venerable of monarchs. The closure to my career in diplomacy could not have been better.

chapter twenty-five

IMAGES OF A CHANGING WORLD

~

Throughout history advances in the means and speed of transport and communications were the cause of great social, economic and political transformations and changes in the nature of warfare. In the second half of the twentieth century the jet airliner, the chip, the computer and the cell phone were the agents of the most rapid changes ever in human history. A blending of cultures and arts of different regions and nations, greater social and political interaction among people and nations, rapid expansion of international trade and enhanced economic cooperation among countries were the special features of the resulting phenomenon which was baptized 'globalization'.

Trade and economic relations of nations had been an important part of foreign policy and diplomacy even in Kautilya's time, but their importance in diplomatic functioning was enhanced by globalization.

In Europe, the principal theatre of the Cold War tensions and confrontation, the period was marked by a major effort by thirty-four countries of east and west Europe, jointly with the Soviet Union, the United States and Canada to promote cooperation among them to stabilize peace and security in that continent. The two leading antagonists of the Cold War were obliged to devise and deploy initiatives to reduce nuclear arms and join in a search for detente. Continuing advances in technology are bound to further spur the process of change in the decades ahead.

In Asia the period was marked by the rise of new powers—China and India, Indonesia and the ASEAN and, of course, resurgent Japan. All this led to a significant shift in the world's economic and politico-military weight from the Euro-Atlantic region to the Asia-Pacific. But while an era of peaceful change ensued in Europe, Asia became the scene of tensions and conflicts. An angry China embarked on punitive expeditions against India in 1962 and Vietnam in 1979. Iran and Iraq fought a destructive war from 1980 to 1988. The United States' two wars in Iraq irrevocably altered power equations in the Gulf region and triggered unrest and civil conflict in other areas of the Arab region.

Russia's military intervention in Afghanistan from 1979 to 1989 gave rise to Islamist Jihad with Pakistan as its base of operations against neighbours and faraway countries. This violent religious movement was supported by American arms, Saudi money and Pakistan's jihadi troopers. The Afghan jihad was, verily America's war, with the Pakistan's army and intelligence as its proxies, against Soviet Russia. Two or three years after the withdrawal of Russian forces, jihadi Afghan groups with the Pakistan army's support had established an extremist fundamentalist regime in Afghanistan. The fanatics who called themselves Taliban disgraced the regime by destroying the centuries-old rock sculptures of the Buddha in Bamiyan. The regime also nurtured and protected al-Qaeda, the notorious terrorist organization headed by Osama bin Laden which organized the 9/11 air attacks on the citadels of American economic and military power—the twin towers in New York and the Pentagon in Washington. The regime was routed by American forces in 2001 but it found a safe haven in Pakistan from where the Taliban groups keep launching attacks in Afghanistan with the Pakistan army's connivance and support.

~

From time to time charismatic leaders have shaped history by guiding humanity towards new horizons of civilization. Mohandas Karamchand Gandhi discovered the power of truth and non-violence and brought down the world's largest empire. Jawaharlal Nehru, his most trusted followers laid the foundations and built the super structure of the world's largest democracy. Bhimrao Ramji Ambedkar gave hope and voice to India's downtrodden dalits. Similarly in the United States Martin Luther King liberated the community of Afro-Americans from white oppression. They were all leaders with a difference. Human freedom and equality and peace were their goals: Non-violence and truth their weapon in their struggle against the entrenched ranks of racists and imperial and feudal oppressors.

GORBACHEV

Mikhail Sergeyevich Gorbachev, who ruled Russia from 1985 to 1991, was a man of the same mould. His new thinking (Glasnost) and restructuring (Perestroika) led to the peaceful liberation of east European and central Asian nations.

I was invited to a one-on-one meeting with the great man at the Rashtrapati Bhavan during his visit to Delhi in November 1986. To my surprise he complimented me on an article I had written criticizing his views on Asian security. In a speech in Vladivostok, in which he had proclaimed Glasnost and Perestroika as the panacea for Soviet Russia's ills, Gorbachev had also proposed an Asian security arrangement on the lines of the Helsinki Accords. In an article in *The Patriot* of New Delhi, I had dubbed the proposal as premature and impracticable in the prevailing circumstances in Asia. For, the kind of patient preparatory work in the form of confidence building measures (CBMs) that had preceded the Helsinki consultations had not even been thought of in Asia. Besides, the many inter-Asian fissures that had surfaced in the Bandung Conference and the failed attempts ten years later to organize an Afro-Asian Conference had only deepened the differences and rivalries among Asian countries. Gorbachev said my article showed the kind of new thinking needed in the changing world and that was why he had wanted to meet and talk with me!

In a freewheeling discussion I said to him that during my travels in European countries, I had noticed an all-pervading fear and suspicion of Russia, and asked what he planned to do to change that unhappy situation. I had also drawn his attention to the dangerous consequences of Russia's military intervention in Afghanistan. His answer was brief and conclusive: 'Mr Rasgotra, I am going to change all that in the next two to three years.'

In regard to the secessionist urges in the central Asian region I had asked him whether a loose restructuring of the Russian state was part of his perestroika, and Gorbachev had said he had an open mind and that use of force was no solution in any situation. In a declaration signed by him and Rajiv Gandhi at the end of his Delhi visit he had renounced the use of force in international relations. He was the first communist leader to do so.

It seemed to me that Gorbachev had made two basic decisions: to change Moscow's policy of ideological confrontation with the West to one of peace and cooperation; and to abjure the use of force to suppress the aspirations for liberty within Russia's 'nationalities' and for sovereignty and independence in east European countries.

WESTERN REACTIONS TO GORBACHEV'S INITIATIVES

In April 1989, when the revolution he had unleashed from the top was about to lead to the unity of East and West Germany suspicions were rampant among western leaders about Gorbachev's flair for surprises and unconventional initiatives, such as unilateral reductions in the Soviet Union's army, withdrawal of Russian forces from east European countries and voluntary reduction of nuclear weapons. Slow, peaceful transformation of Soviet Russia into a democracy, albeit of a limited scope seemed to be his goal. All that was fine, but Margaret Thatcher in particular had apprehensions about the impact of Gorbachev's reconciliation to the idea of German unity.

'Can you trust eighty million Germans?' She had flung the question at me in a conversation with me in early 1989 which had nothing to do with German developments. She recalled the havoc the two world wars, initiated by Germany, had caused in Europe and how Britain, in particular, had borne the brunt of German militarism.

But German unity seemed unavoidable and would become a reality in a few months. So, I asked her whether Britain was in a position to do something to stop history in its tracks. 'Perhaps not,' Thatcher said, 'but eighty million Germans are a menace all the same!'

The only European statesman, other than Gorbachev, who was doing some new thinking was Chancellor Helmut Kohl. In his meetings with Gorbachev in June 1989 in Bonn, he gave assurances to the Russian leader that United Germany would not threaten Russia. He agreed to limit the United Germany's army troop levels below the West German army's present strength and to provide substantial credits to Russia. Kohl also agreed to forego nuclear capability and vigorously opposed the induction of new short-range nuclear weapons in Europe. He reassured another apprehensive neighbour, Poland, of Germany's acknowledgement of its present borders. As a result, on 31 August 1989, the two Germanys signed a state treaty on unification; on 3 October 1989, East Germany merged with West Germany, and on 9 November 1989 East Germany's government opened the Berlin Wall to the great rejoicing of people on both sides.

MARKET ECONOMY: THE MANTRA FOR PROGRESS

Political developments in Russia, Germany and east Europe had demonstrated the linkage between politics and economy.

In the West, Ronald Reagan and Margaret Thatcher were crusading for free market. In September 1983 in New York, I sat in at a meeting between President Ronald Reagan and Indira Gandhi. A brief remark by someone in the meeting led to an illuminating and inspired discourse by President Reagan on the 'magic of the market'. Even Indira Gandhi was unusually attentive and impressed.

In Britain, the decade of the eighties was a period of a veritable economic revolution. Thatcher had successfully fought and reduced the clout of the trade unions, privatized five major public-sector industries and modernized them. There was notable improvement in productivity in manufacturing and rising profits were leading to investment at record levels. Employment opportunities were increasing and standards of living were steadily rising. National debt was reduced to an acceptable, low level. Inflation was high but the retirement pension was protected against it.

Gorbachev was facing difficulties in reviving Russia's economy and was looking for help from the West. In a conversation with Thatcher in November 1989, I complimented her on the healthy state of the economy and suggested that she should help Gorbachev with credits as Helmut Kohl was doing. Her reaction was quick, short and sharp: 'Help Gorbachev! Why should I help Gorbachev? His country's evil system and its communist empire are disintegrating. I like that!' It was all said with a wry smile reflecting deeply felt satisfaction.

In Asia, the Indian economy's collapse around the same time demonstrated the failure of a controlled economy to make a dent in the poverty that still afflicts the country. Dr Manmohan Singh, as finance minister in the 1990s, and later as prime minister from 2004 to 2014, did implement several major reforms and initiate policies to eliminate wasteful subsidies, but had to give up the effort for want of political support from Prime Minister Narasimha Rao in the first instance and because of strong opposition from advocates of discredited socialist economics in the Indian National Congress hierarchy. Nevertheless, he succeeded in pushing through some basic economic liberalizing measures and laid the foundation for future reforms. But overall, the huge talent of one of the world's best economic thinkers was wasted on the country.

THE CHANGING LEXICON OF DIPLOMACY

Rapid increase in the number of independent countries, more frequent contacts among them and other far-reaching changes to which I have drawn attention were bound to influence the nature and idiom of diplomacy. Perhaps, because we as a nation were new to diplomacy, we felt no great difficulty injecting our own ideas and metaphors into the idiom of diplomacy required by a continuously changing world environment. Perhaps for the same reason old, established powers inured to their old ways of diplomatic functioning found our behaviour and speech, pretentious, moralistic hypocritical and preachy.

On the lighter side of it a fun change was also taking place in the lexicon of diplomacy. Khrushchev, perhaps, was the first statesman to introduce some picturesqueness and novelty in diplomatic utterance and protest. Addressing India and China in a speech in Moscow, when in the nineteen sixties we were skirmishing on the Himalayan frontier, the Soviet general secretary asked: 'What the devil are you two doing on those heights where shit gets frozen?' He was only a little gentler with American Vice President Nixon, who was in Moscow to discuss a new arms control proposal; Khrushchev told him that the American proposal smelt like horse dung!

Americans were also imparting new vigour, candour and clarity to diplomatic parlance. In Washington, an American diplomat and I were having a friendly argument about Washington's support for dictatorial regimes to the detriment of democracy. Suddenly he turned on me in exasperation to close the issue: 'You are right my friend. We know, as you guys do, that they are all bastards, those dictators. But they are our bastards, you know!' In a counter-attack he accused gullible Indians of having made 'those Red bastards respectable'. In their time, Nixon and Kissinger added a few more home-grown additions to diplomacy's new lexicon.

Perhaps not unjustifiably, our diplomatic parlance was dubbed argumentative, spiritually pretentious and hypocritical by western diplomats in the early decades of India's Independence. Pretentious we are not, nor hypocritical. Argumentative? Yes; our nobel laureate, Amartya Sen, has written a whole book on the subject.

Nor is our spirituality a pretence; it is in our DNA. Look at our tradition: the Vedas, the Upanishads, the Ramayana, the Mahabharata, the Bhagavad Gita, Rama and Krishna, the Buddha and Shukracharya, Ramakrishna Paramahamsa and Vivekananda, Gandhi and Sathya Sai Baba of Puttaparthi.

This is not to claim India's monopoly on spirituality and truth. Because of the divine origin of life, spirituality is inherent in every human being and it is manifest in societies all over the world.

Spirituality and Truth are two sides of the same coin: Spirituality expressed is Truth. Indians are no more spiritual than Americans or

Africans. But from our long history of suffering we perhaps have a deeper appreciation of the values of tolerance and peace, non-violence and respect for life and of the importance of righteousness, love and service in human conduct. We are not unworldly or other-worldly either. We live and work like all the others of our species, try to safeguard our interests and have managed to get by reasonably well in the world. But the lexicon of our parlance could not but echo our experience of a long history of deceit and discrimination, exploitation, violence and suffering under foreign rule.

Perhaps in our own telling of the truth, we need to mellow our speech, especially when the truth is bitter. In that respect the Bhagavad Gita offers sound advice. In discussing disciplines to be observed in life, in the matter of discipline of speech, Lord Krishna recommends the use of 'words which do not cause offence, (and yet) are truthful, pleasant and beneficial'.[1] Elsewhere he also commends 'maunam', meaning not silence so much as listening patiently and exercising moderation in speech.

But such speech does not come easy. It requires hard practice, study, control of anger and emotion and steady cultivation of the serenity of mind. For as the Mahabharata teaches us, the 'speaker and listener of what is both disagreeable and beneficial are hard to find'.[2]

chapter twenty-six

FOREIGN POLICY: PAST AND FUTURE

~

PART—I

NON-ALIGNMENT

The foreign policy of a state is a framework of principles and practical considerations in the light of which it seeks friendship and cooperation of other countries to pursue and strengthen world peace and to safeguard its security and other national interests on a reciprocal basis. Foreign policymaking is a dynamic process which must remain open to adaptation, adjustment and change in accord with changing conditions of the world.

The foreign policy of a state begins with its neighbours, but it must not remain trapped in the region to the neglect of the state's interests and role in the larger world. India will grow to greatness only if its vision and policies transcend the subcontinent's truncated geography.

In that overall context, Nehru had adopted the policy of the good neighbour. His engagement with neighbours was benign but watchful, which meant helping them if they asked for help and if India had the means to provide it. But he would not allow them to take liberties with India's security and other vital interests.

Nehru was also one of the few statesmen who realized that foreign policy, which earlier used to be bilateral, or regional, had became global after World War II because of the global reach of missiles and nuclear weapons and of the national power of the USA and Russia. Great advances in the speed and means of travel and communication and the activities of the United Nations are contributing to globalizing foreign policy.

India needed a world of peace and cooperation to stabilize its system of democratic governance and for its economic and social development. It passionately desired and worked for the freedom of colonies and for the elimination of racial discrimination and poverty in the world. While it wanted to cultivate the friendship and cooperation of all nations, it abhorred and rejected the role of a camp follower of one of the two power blocks engaged in Cold War. The independent policy of Non-alignment, which Nehru announced on 7 September 1946,[1] was a response to the condition of the world in which India had attained Independence.

Non-alignment was not a mere idealistic concept. It was a policy in which pragmatism, idealism and realism went hand in hand, and Nehru used one or more of these traits in his conduct of India's relations, at different times, with a neighbour or a great power or in the United Nations Security Council on issues which included Kashmir, the Suez Canal crisis, Goa's liberation or Soviet Russia's military interventions in Hungary and Czechoslovakia.

The very novelty of the concept of Non-alignment aroused curiosity, interest, bewilderment and hostility. But it also assured for India a distinct place in the councils of the world. That was no small gain for a country which had just emerged on the world scene. For the world in which India awoke to freedom was not friendly towards it. Within a few weeks of Independence, Pakistan launched its first war in Kashmir with the connivance of British officials in its employ.

Britain's resentment over India's Independence was palpable in bilateral dealings and in the UN Security Council's discussions on Kashmir. China was engaged in surreptitious encroachments on Indian territory. Stalin's Russia did not consider India truly independent. The United States disliked India's independent foreign policy opposed to military alliances, and would soon start arming Pakistan which would militarize that country's polity and lead to more conflicts with India.

The first decade of Independence was one of struggle to convince the world of the genuineness and sincerity of India's desire for world peace and its concern over prevailing tensions, the nuclear arms race and the problems of racism, poverty and deprivation of colonial possessions of Western powers.

The period of the 1960s and 1970s, when scores of newly independent countries endorsed and adopted Non-alignment as their foreign policy, was the heyday of Non-alignment. India received substantial financial and technical assistance from both superpowers to lay its industrial base, to meet its recurring shortages of food grains and to modernize its agriculture. From zero or negative growth in 1947, the economy grew at a steady pace of 4 to 4 ½ per cent of GDP per annum, and a base was laid for India's scientific, technological and industrial advance.

The institutions of democracy—universal suffrage, electoral process, Parliament, the cabinet system and an independent judiciary were firmly established. Despite its failure to prevent the two wars of 1962 and 1965 and China's growing hostility, the policy had proved its relevance in a world polarized in two opposing military alliances.

THE NON-ALIGNED MOVEMENT (NAM)

Nehru was not thinking of forming a third block, or even a loose group led by him. However, at the first summit meeting of non-aligned countries in Belgrade from 1 to 6 September 1961, attended by twenty-five countries, what hitherto was the foreign policy of individual countries was launched as the Non-Aligned Movement (NAM). Nehru was not impressed by the political rhetoric at the conference and in his address on 2 September, he drew the participants' attention 'to their inheritance of backwardness' and emphasized the need to develop and modernize their economies, which only led the conference to a rhetorical demand that 'all the gains of scientific technological revolution be applied in all fields of economic development to hasten the achievement of international justice'.

The summit also issued appeals to the USA and the USSR to stop nuclear tests and agree to ban nuclear tests as a step towards nuclear disarmament. NAM's campaign on the important issue of nuclear disarmament succeeded only partly in the adoption of a partial test ban. Its rhetoric on General and Complete Disarmament had little impact, and whatever reductions in the nuclear arsenals of the USA and Russia took place in the following decades were achieved through direct negotiations between them.

But from India's point of view, NAM's worst failure lay in the fact that despite the prestige and respect it commanded in the movement, in its three crises—China's invasion of India in 1962 and the India–Pakistan wars of 1965 and 1971—India's comrades in NAM chose to be non-aligned between the two non-NAM aggressors and India, their victim.

In 1962, solid political and arms support for India came from the United States. A semblance of India's non-aligned status was restored when the USSR also came in with generous military supplies on a sustained basis. But nine years later, to fight off the combined hostility of China and the USA towards India in the war for Bangladesh's liberation, New Delhi had to enter into a virtual military alliance with the USSR.

From 1971 till 1982, when our relations with the USA were in limbo, India's Non-alignment lacked credibility. The revival of friendly relations with the USA in 1982 at least enabled Indira Gandhi to host the seventh Non-aligned Summit in Delhi in March 1983 with a fair measure of credibility. Thereafter the movement kept withering till it became irrelevant in 1991 when the Soviet Union and the Warsaw Pact headed by Russia disintegrated.

PART–II

FACTORS IN INDIAN FOREIGN POLICY FOR THE FUTURE

1. TRADITION

In civilizational states like India and China, their millennial traditions dormant in the memory of succeeding generations, manifest themselves in transformational moments in the nation's life and exert an influence in the making of foreign policy. The remarkably rich and varied Indian tradition comprises Vedantic beliefs, the independence of spirit bequeathed to man by his Divine origin, the idea of the world as one family, Buddha's middle path, Emperor Ashoka's renunciation of war, Emperor Jalalud-din Muhammad Akbar's respect for and tolerance of faiths other than his own, and Mahatma Gandhi's truth and non-violence as the means for humanity's uplift to a higher level of civilization.

Kautilya's realistic contribution of pragmatic statecraft is also part of this tradition. 'Peace is to be preferred to war' is a critical principle of Kautilyan foreign policy. The choice of policy, he says, is dictated by the 'current condition of the states involved (the world)'.In another axiom he sums up the basic conditioning of international politics: 'Bilateral relations are determined by the power equation between the two states.' A mix of all these streams goes into the making of the country's foreign policy. What he says about neighbours is dealt with later in this chapter.

At a meeting of the Conservative members of Parliament in March 1936, Winston Churchill spoke of the 'wonderful unconscious tradition of British foreign policy':

> For 400 years the foreign policy of England has been to oppose the strongest, most aggressive, most dominant power on the Continent, and particularly to prevent the Low Countries falling into the hands of such a power . . . Moreover, on all occasions England took the more difficult course . . . we always chose the harder course, joined with the less strong powers, made a combination among them, and thus defeated and frustrated the Continental military tyrant whoever he was, whatever nation he led. Thus we preserved the liberties of Europe, protected the growth of its vivacious and varied society, and emerged after four terrible struggles with an ever-growing fame and widening Empire and with the Low Countries safely protected in their independence. Here is the wonderful unconscious tradition of British Foreign Policy.[2]

The cardinal principles underlying this 'unconscious tradition' were Britain's naval supremacy and a balance of power in Europe which favoured Britain. It was more a military strategy than a tradition which actually led to a succession of conflicts in Europe followed by two cataclysmic world wars. The principle of balance of power lies buried in the debris of those wars.

China, like India, is a civilizational state and while its culture and arts continue to evoke appreciation and emulation in faraway regions, the use of force to conquer and absorb alien lands and populations or assert suzerainty over them, which forms the dominant part of China's tradition, continue to put it at loggerheads with its neighbours. In contrast, the humanist, value-based Indian tradition places emphasis on relations of peace and cooperation with neighbours and others. And because of its inherent spirit of tolerance and its attitude of receptivity towards new streams of thought, it is in tune with modern times and a globalizing human society. Therefore today, when India is in its second transformational moment, the world around it, unlike the world of 1947, is well disposed towards it. This new world wants India to succeed and is even willing to help it achieve its goals.

SECURITY OF THE STATE

The first and foremost duty of a state is to ensure its security. An ancient text, Sukraniti, says: 'Without the Armed Forces the state, its wealth and power cannot survive. The strong control all, the weak have only enemies.'[3] Earlier, Kautilya had also emphasized the necessity of military preparedness to deter aggression by a powerful neighbour.

Nehru had taken several measures to expand and strengthen India's Armed Forces, especially the army and the air force. By 1960 the army's strength had been raised from around 2,00,000 in 1947 to 550,000. The strength of the Indian Air Force had grown from seven squadrons in 1950 to eighteen squadrons of fighters and bombers. The Indian navy had lagged behind because the emphasis at the time was on the defences on land and in the skies against Pakistan. But all this was not good enough for defence against

China in the north. So, following the tragic experience of 1962, Nehru enlarged the programme which he had launched in the 1950s for the creation of an indigenous defence industry. The results of that action, limited as they were, served India well in 1971 in the war for the liberation of Bangladesh.

But now in the new Asia Pacific security paradigm, it is India's defences in the vast Indian Ocean that demand special attention. Ancient India had a strong naval tradition. Emperor Chandragupta Maurya maintained a strong navy for protection of the empire's coastal regions and its foreign trade. The Indians of the peninsular half of the country, in particular, were a seafaring people. In later centuries the southern kingdoms maintained navies to protect trade and to undertake foreign expeditions. Later still there are accounts of the exploits of units of the Maratha navy. The Mughals had neglected naval power and the British rulers of India systematically destroyed whatever had survived of India's naval tradition and its shipbuilding industry. When the British were expelled from India, we inherited very little by way of the navy of a country a large part of which is exposed to the seas on three sides.

'The Indian Ocean is China's next frontier' is common talk in China these days. India needs to be wary of China's plans in this regard and be prepared for any eventuality. China's seemingly innocent One-Belt-One-Road (OBOR) strategy is a scheme to dominate the Indian Ocean by setting up naval bases around India. India should adopt all necessary measures to prevent any threat to India's security in the Indian Ocean. It should strengthen its traditional maritime links with the world's leading maritime powers.

Good as the Indian navy is, it needs rapid expansion to become a force capable of deterring China's trespass of India's security zones in the Indian Ocean. For the protection of its long coastlines in the Bay of Bengal and the Arabian Sea and its other vital interests in the vast stretch of the Indian Ocean, India must build a deterring naval force of some 300 warships, including four carrier groups, twenty-five to thirty conventional submarines and five or six nuclear submarines. China is bound to come into the Indian Ocean but its entry into waters, which are a virtual extension of peninsular India's land mass, should not be a source of international tensions and a threat to India's security.

2. NEED FOR A FIRM, STABLE AND UNWAVERING NEIGHBOURHOOD POLICY

The classic wisdom of East and West on neighbours and a state's foreign policy towards them is summed up in the words of Plato, Niccolò Machiavelli and Kautilya: The Greek philosopher Plato (fourth century BC) proclaimed that 'a world without neighbours is the ideal world'. Kautilya (third century BC) was of the view that 'neighbours are of three kinds: enemy neighbours, friendly neighbours and vassals', and 'an immediate neighbour is an enemy and that a neighbour's neighbour is a friend'. Niccolò Machiavelli (fifteenth century AD) advised that a ruling prince 'ought to make himself the head and defender of his less powerful neighbours, and to weaken the more powerful amongst them, taking care that no foreigner as powerful as himself shall, by any accident, get a footing there, for it always happens that such a one will be introduced by those who are discontented, either through excess of ambition, or through fear. . . The Romans were brought into Greece by the Aetolians'.[4]

For countries like India, for example, which hanker for the love of its neighbouring countries, Machiavelli has this advice:

Men have less scruple in offending one who is beloved than one who is feared, for love is preserved by the link of obligation, which owing to the baseness of men is broken at every opportunity for their advantage; but fear preserves you by a dread of punishment which never fails.[5]

Modern great powers—the USA, Russia and China—have followed a mix of Machiavelli's teachings in their policies toward their neighbours. The United States sent its forces to the Dominican Republic in 1965 and later invaded Guatemala to avert the establishment of another 'Cuba-like' hostile regime in the Caribbean. Earlier, at the end of World War II, the Soviet

Union established its dominance over its east European neighbours. China, as mentioned earlier, has traditionally gone out to conquer its neighbours or to make them tribute-paying vassals. Xinjiang was conquered in the mid-nineteenth century; Tibet was independent from 1911 onwards, but was reconquered in 1950. Almost till the middle of the twentieth century, Nepal used to send tribute-bearing missions to China.

Nehru's policy of benign but watchful engagement, which took into account the classic wisdom on the subject, is best for India. Unfortunately after Indira Gandhi, every new prime minister, including Morarji Desai, Rajiv Gandhi and P.V. Narasimha Rao, started off by declaring that his government's highest priority would be 'to improve relations with our neighbours'. As if the previous government had done everything to spoil relations! Inder Gujral, who was prime minister for a few months, even issued a doctrine bearing his name, which stated that India would do everything possible to give its neighbours whatever they wanted without expecting the least measure of reciprocity from them! This reveals an astounding innocence of the reality of international politics.

The Bharatiya Janata Party (BJP), presently in power under the leadership of Prime Minister Narendra Modi, has traditionally nursed a soft attitude towards Nepal because the country was a Hindu kingdom. Though the monarchy has gone, Nepal as a secular Hindu republic continues to generate much mawkish sentimentality in some quarters in India. This kind of emotional approach to foreign policy is not conducive to stable relationships. In this respect, Europe's two most outstanding foreign policymakers and diplomatists have some good advice for India. Bismarck was against basing policy on any kind of emotion; and Talleyrand strongly cautioned against excess of zeal in foreign policy and diplomacy.

Of course there are also lessons in our own history of betrayals by co-religionists. Prithviraj Chauhan, king of Delhi, and Jaichand ruler of Kannauj were both Hindus: the latter's collusion with the invader Muhammad Ghori resulted in Chauhan's defeat and the establishment of Muslim rule in north India. In an equally contemptible act of treachery Nawab Siraj-ud-Daulah was betrayed by his Muslim commander, Mir Jafar, in the battlefield of Plassey leading to the advent of British rule in India.

Having seen the evolution of India's relations with its neighbours since Nehru's time to date, I am convinced that the concessionist policy of seeking our neighbours' love will only bear the bitter fruit of disappointment. In particular, in relation to Nepal, Indian policymakers would be well advised to keep religious sentiment out of their calculations.

Recently, the high-handed action of Kathmandu's ruling elite to adopt a constitution which deprives the population of the Nepal Terai—nearly half of the country's total population—of its legitimate citizenship rights has given rise to a volatile situation which, if not dealt with wisdom and foresight, could degenerate into an avoidable, civil conflict for the Terai's secession. Kathmandu's ruling elite has always ruled the Terai as a colony. With the introduction of democracy and the spread of education and political awareness among the Teraian youth, the old system—the country half free and half colony—cannot work any more. The sooner Kathmandu's communist rulers realize this, the better for all concerned.

Towards the end of 2015, a widespread protest movement in the entire Terai resulted in the disruption of movement of goods from India to the Kathmandu valley. The Nepal government, instead of resolving an internal political problem through negotiations with leaders of the Terai population, launched a campaign accusing India of having imposed a blockade and turned to China as an alternative supplier of essential goods. These tactics should not cause anxiety in India. We should welcome China sharing some of India's burden in meeting Nepal's requirements of concessional transit and trade facilities. For Nepal is landlocked not only by India but also by China.

3. ASIA'S NEW SECURITY PARADIGM: TWENTY-FIRST CENTURY MANDALA

The shift of the world's political, economic and military weight from the West to Asia, which began with India's Independence and the communist victory in China's civil war, was accelerated by the Soviet Union's disintegration in 1991. The shift was completed with the

United States Asian Rebalance in 2011 and the transfer of a carrier group of the American navy from the Atlantic to the Pacific region. These developments have created an unprecedented, proximate constellation of five powers—China, India, Russia, the United States and Japan (see diagram on p. 395). The policies they pursue and their interactions will decide the questions of war and peace in Asia (and the world) in the twenty-first century. Around this constellation are clusters of smaller powers which are affected by and in some ways influence the policies of the big five. China occupies the centre of this constellation in contiguity or close proximity to the other four major powers. Its policies and actions, therefore, will act as a catalyst to the policies and reactions of the other four.

Though the globalized world is free from the ideological confrontation of the Cold War era, the rapid rise of China as a great military power is creating tensions in the Indo-Pacific region. China's rise is not taking place in a vacuum, nor is it entirely peaceful. China is building artificial islands in the South China Sea to reinforce its trumped-up claims on the waters which either fall in the maritime zones of its smaller neighbours or have traditionally been a thoroughfare of the world's commercial traffic.

The day President Xi Jinping landed in India on a state visit in September 2014, Chinese troops in Tibet staged a big intrusion across the Line of Actual Control into Indian territory to remind India of the bigger neighbour's potential to create trouble! A few months later the berthing of a Chinese submarine in the Colombo port was an even more provocative trespass of India's security zone. The then President of Sri Lanka, Mahinda Rajapaksa was apparently complicit in this action; he described that first-ever event of its kind as a normal thing!

The more I look at the Asian scene, the more convinced I am that Kautilya's concept that natural accretion of power centres in a circular formation—called Mandala—determines the nature of relations between them, is a verity of international relations. The diagram on p. 395 shows how geography has knotted together the five big powers into a Kautilyan Mandala with China at its centre. Though geographically the US is not located in the Asian land mass, it occupies a special place in the Mandala because it is a power of global reach, with political, economic and security interests and solid military presence in all regions of Asia and in the Pacific and Indian oceans.

Bilateral relations between the five countries offer a fascinating subject for a doctoral thesis. China's relations with the United States are characterized by extensive economic and commercial engagement on the one hand and serious differences over China's rapid modernization of its military and its aggressive claims in the Sea of Japan and the South China Sea on the other. Despite some improvement in recent years, China's relations with India are still marked by lack of trust because of the former's continuing nuclear and conventional military support to Pakistan, the unresolved India–Tibet border and Beijing's unfolding ambitions in the Indian Ocean. Japan and the US enjoy close relations. India's relations with both are undergoing a positive transformation. India has traditionally enjoyed friendly cooperative relations with Russia.

A close look at the Mandala diagram will show that with the exception of five bilateral relationships—India–Russia, India–Japan, India–US, US–Japan and China–Russia—all other bilateral relationships are of the antagonistic variety. And yet all are tied together in strong economic and commercial engagement. This presents an opportunity for forging a Pentagonal Equilibrium, which would rule out the use of force.

Such an equilibrium should be the goal of an Indian foreign policy of Engagement With All, with the degree and depth of India's engagement with any particular country varying according to the congruence of the interests of the two countries and India's requirement of investments and cutting-edge technologies. In the light of these requirements, engagement with the United States and Japan should obviously be India's top priorities. Geography. and history also dictate that Russia should never be discounted or ignored. India should invest all necessary effort to deepen its traditional bonds with Russia.

In the context of India's security, two factors should be given special weight in its foreign policy; namely that China and Pakistan, two nuclear weapon powers, are bound in a military alliance targeted specifically on India; and China's relations with India's neighbours, including Maldives, and its Indian Ocean policy are driven by a politico-strategic design to surround and isolate India. These factors highlight the necessity of a much closer political understanding and cooperation between India and the United States to deter or deal with any misadventure threatening peace and security of the region. After much reflection in 1999 Prime Minister A.B. Vajpayee, borrowing a phrase from Kautilya, had stated that America and India are 'natural allies'. Nevertheless, in cultivating relations with the United States of America, it should always be borne in mind that Washington has a proclivity in a crisis to act primarily and always in its own interests, and when a choice between India and Pakistan is forced on it by unforeseen circumstances, it opts for Pakistan.

PART—III

A SPECIFIC PROBLEM FOR INDIAN FOREIGN POLICY

PAKISTAN

Pakistan is a specific problem for India's foreign policy. I am all for a continual dialogue with Pakistan on all issues, including Kashmir. Our position on the issue of talks with Pakistan is not steadfast; it changes with every new government for reasons not of logic or good sense but of a passing sentiment.

The most recent dialogue was initiated in the time of Prime Minister Atal Bihari Vajpayee on a clear commitment by the President of Pakistan, General Musharraf, in a joint press statement (see annexure p. 396) issued by the two leaders in Islamabad on 6 January 2004, to reassure 'Prime Minister Vajpayee that he (Musharraf) will not permit any territory under Pakistan's control to be used to support terrorism in any manner'. Musharraf did stop terrorist attacks on India and secret talks made considerable headway during Dr Manmohan

Singh's prime ministership, till Musharraf's position weakened within Pakistan and even as a document was virtually ready for signing, he told Prime Minister Manmohan Singh that he was not able to carry the negotiations forward to a conclusion. Thereafter terrorist attacks have taken place in India with the ISI's support. So, we should either forget about Musharraf's commitment and engage in talks, or take a firm stand on it and wait for Pakistan to fulfill its commitment before resumption of talks.

Secret negotiations actually had led to agreement on many aspects of the Kashmir issue and there was a document ready for signatures. It was agreed, for example, that there would be no independence (azadi) for Kashmir and no change in the border (LOC), but there would be freedom of movement across it for Kashmiris of both sides. There was no reference to UN resolutions, and India had agreed to reduction of military troops in Kashmir subject to Pakistan ensuring the end of hostilities and terrorism (a vitally important condition). Finally, a joint mechanism of the two Kashmirs, for socio-economic subjects only, and autonomy for J & K, like all other Indian states, was also agreed on.

It was Pakistan, not India, that balked at proceeding to a positive conclusion of the negotiations. While President Musharraf was also the army chief, his deputy general Ashfaq Parvez Kayani and the ISI were on board; but as soon as Musharraf shed his role as head of the Pakistan army, the new army chief, General Kayani, withdrew his support compelling Musharraf to abandon the agreement.

The most recent ruckus was about the practice of visiting Pakistani delegations to meet with the Hurriyat people before engaging in talks with India. The Pakistanis, in their attempt to make Syed Ali Shah Geelani and his Hurriyat colleagues the true representatives of the Kashmiris, are, in fact, exposing them as Pakistan's show boys in Indian Kashmir. Visiting Pakistani delegations' insistence on such meetings is quite ridiculous. What surprises me is that someone as dignified and with such high religious authority as Mirwaiz Umar Farooq, submits himself to this kind of treatment.

It would be a great pity if such little difficulties were to oblige India and Pakistan to hold talks only in third countries. The present logjam has to be broken and the leadership in both countries should consider new informal initiatives. Prime Minister Modi's short visit to Lahore on the occasion of Nawaz Sharif's granddaughter's wedding was a praiseworthy act of statesmanship.

A basis for the resumption of comprehensive dialogue, including talks on Kashmir, exists. The efforts of Prime Minister Modi and Nawaz Sharif to restart the comprehensive dialogue, including talks on Kashmir, deserve support. It might help matters and eventually ensure success of the dialogue if representatives of the armed forces of the two countries are also involved in it or the two are encouraged to engage in a parallel dialogue of their own.

MISSING LINKS IN THE KASHMIR STORY

There are several mistaken ideas or ill-informed myths still in circulation about 'Nehru's blunders' in Kashmir. Some accuse him of unnecessarily taking the matter to the United Nations Security Council, others blame him for holding the Indian army back when it was poised to push Pakistan's forces from the areas they still occupy. The armed conflict would have attracted the Security Council's attention in any case, and the council might have taken a decision to inject an international force in J & K to enforce a ceasefire under Chapter VII of the UN Charter, which authorizes the council to enforce its decisions by taking 'action by air, sea, or land forces as may be necessary to maintain or restore international peace and security'. Failing a collective move by the Security Council, Pakistan, Britain or the USA would have inscribed Kashmir on the Security Council's agenda under Chapter VII to India's disadvantage.

India lodged its complaint under Chapter VI of the charter under which the council can only make recommendations to the parties 'with a view to a pacific settlement of the dispute'. When under Anglo-American pressures the Security Council ignored the basic fact of Pakistan's aggression, India rejected its recommendations. Britain and the United States exerted enormous pressure on Nehru to cede a part of the Valley to Pakistan in the wake of India's defeat in the 1962 war with China. Nehru, in weak health, resisted and rejected their pressures and blandishments with firm resolve, and Kashmir remains a part of India.

Not many people are aware that the armies of India and Pakistan were fighting in Kashmir under the overall command of British generals on both sides. General Douglas Gracey was chief of staff of the Pakistan army and General Sir Francis Robert Roy Bucher was commander-in-chief of the Indian army. The two commands were in touch with each other and regularly exchanged written reports—the Pakistan high command's communications to the Indian high command are in Indian archives[6]—and both were being directed by the British authorities in London.

When the Pakistan army had fallen back to a line which both Gracey and Roy Bucher thought would be 'adequate for Pakistan's overall defence', the latter, on one pretext or another, just would not use force to change that line. Nehru was keen to eliminate the Poonch bulge but Roy Bucher told him that the army was fully stretched and there were simply no troops available for the task. For similar reasons we failed to clear the Pakistani forces, commanded by a junior British army officer, from Gilgit and Baltistan, a region of high strategic value which is now being exploited by China for developing a road link to the Persian Gulf.

The basic mistake was to retain British officers in command of the Indian army after Independence. The retention of British admirals in command of the Indian navy for eleven years after Independence only delayed the development and expansion of India's navy; the British government even refused to sell a submarine to India when the USA had gifted one to Pakistan.

PART—IV

CONCLUSION

The conclusions that emerge from the foregoing analysis concerning India's foreign policy for the foreseeable future are:

1. In the prevailing world environment of goodwill for India, a foreign policy of Engagement with All Nations will best serve India's security and other interests. Within that template the closest political, economic and security relationships with the USA, Japan and Russia are recommended.

2. The military power of a nation flows out of its economic strength. Considerations of trade and economy must be given due weight in the making of foreign policy.

3. Benign but Watchful Engagement with neighbours should characterize the overall policy toward all neighbours. However, there should be no compromise on India's security; and zeal and anxiety to please implacable neighbours should be avoided. All neighbours are not alike; therefore within this overall framework, a differentiated approach for each is advisable.

4. Three neighbours—Bhutan, Bangladesh and Myanmar—are of exceptional value and significance for the future of India's relations with countries of east Asia and South East Asia. Along with the seven northeast Indian states, they constitute a compact sub regional hub for joint development activity and for trade, tourism and cultural exchanges between South Asia and South East Asia. A broad gauge railway line and/or a six-lane highway through the Siliguri neck to Myanmar will add vigour and substance to India's Act East policy and activate the full potential of the semi-dormant relationship of the two regions.

5. i) Conditions in Afghanistan are likely to remain muddled for quite some time. President Ghani has brusquely set aside the Afghanistan–India Strategic Partnership Agreement signed recently by his predecessor, introducing an element of uncertainty in the close traditional relationship. India should rapidly complete the projects under construction, hand them over to the Afghan government and withdraw its surplus personnel without delay. India should maintain regular policy consultations with Iran, Russia and Central African Republics concerning Afghanistan's future. Discreetly, India should also renew contacts with our traditional friends, the Pashtuns.

ii) In a Machiavellian move, the United States has not only manoeuvred India out of the Afghanistan peace process, it has also brought China in to placate Pakistan. India should carefully analyse and assess the damage this American act does to India's position in South Asia, to the US–India 'strategic partnership' and the trust building between Washington and New Delhi.

6. China is likely to remain a problem for Indian foreign policy because of its close nuclear military alliance with Pakistan. Nor is a solution to the border problem in sight in the near future. Nevertheless we should pursue border negotiations with patience. But, in view of China's nuclear-military alliance with Pakistan, suitable US–India strategic arrangements should be devised to deter any misadventure threatening peace.

7. In west Asia, India should cultivate the strongest possible political and security relationships with Iran at one end and Egypt at the other. This is not to suggest neglect of other countries of the Arab peninsula and the Gulf region. We have extensive trade and economic interests in the entire region, which requires further strengthening of our bilateral links with each of these countries.

8. Special relationships should be cultivated with countries willing to set up high-tech defence-related manufacturing in India. All political and bureaucratic resistance to foreign investments in this sector must be curbed. The habitual preference of the air force and the army for imported weapon systems should be discouraged.

9. The external security of the state is the foremost objective of foreign policy. Future threats to India's security are more likely to come from the seas than from land frontiers. The Indian navy should be rapidly developed into a deterring blue water force. Similarly the strength of the air force, which has depleted to a dangerously low level, should be quickly brought up to fifty squadrons. We should stop looking around for jet fighters in the West. The Russian Sukhoi's have served us well and we should acquire more of the same. The jet fighter that is good enough for Russia, should be good enough for India.

10. There is a world beyond the Asian Mandala: Africa, the EU and Latin America deserve India's closer attention. The following specific actions are recommended:

i) **Africa:** Following the India–Africa Forum Summit of October 2015, attended by fifty-four African states, India should substantially expand the facilities for the education of young Africans in India and also set up appropriate educational institutions, including those at the university level, in African countries.

Indian investment in projects of direct benefit to African populations—agriculture, small and medium industries and telecommunications—should be doubled. Health is another important area in which Indian assistance is much appreciated by Africans. Without in any way competing with China, India should set an example of a non-exploitative, genuinely sincere and cooperative partnership with African countries.

ii) **Europe:** The immediate conclusion of the bilateral India–EU investment agreement, which has been under discussion for eight long years, is strongly recommended. Maintenance of strong bilateral relations with Germany, France, Britain and Italy are an all-time necessity.

iii) **Latin America:** The region is bound to play an increasingly important political and economic role in world affairs in the coming decades. Cooperation with Brazil in IBSA (India, Brazil, South Africa) or BRICS (Brazil, Russia, India, China, South Africa) has not progressed much. Direct bilateral relations should be strengthened with Brazil and other major countries of the continent, such as Mexico and Colombia, Chile and Argentina. Associate or observer status for India in Mercosur—a subregional block of six countries, which seeks to promote free trade and free movement of goods and people among them—will help strengthen our economic, commercial and political links with the continent.

~

SUMMIT DIPLOMACY

The energy and time Prime Minister Narendra Modi has invested in getting to know the world and in making his own impact on it is a new experience in India's foreign policy and diplomacy. His initiatives to develop fresh links at the summit level with fifty-odd countries, big and small, through carefully timed visits abroad and hosting an equal number of return visits in his first year and a half in office as a prime minister is unprecedented in independent India's history.

There was a significant geo-economic content to each of Mr Modi's summit-level contacts. The absence of manufacturing has been a drag on the Indian economy. 'Make in India' may well prove to be a game changer for the country's economy.

When world conditions and times change, leaders can make a difference. One must not remain mired in the past. By reinforcing old friendships and cultivating new ones, Prime Minister Modi has already made a difference in India's foreign policy and relations with foreign countries. In his time, Prime Minister Manmohan Singh had made a difference by signing the US–India nuclear energy deal despite stiff domestic opposition.

Narendra Modi, a man who has risen to the top from a street tea vendor, is obviously a natural leader. He may well be India's man of destiny in this transformational time for the country. The massive majority the Indian electorate gave him in the general election of 2014 does great credit to Indian democracy. Will that election perhaps mark the beginning of a new era of the rise of the common man's leadership in Indian democracy?

India's strategic community, so-called, is already beginning the search for a doctrine in Prime Minister Modi's achievements; I hope he will not give them a chance to declare one on his behalf. The unpredictable advances in technology, knowledge and communications and the ever-widening range of international interactions dictate that India keep its eyes and ears, heart and mind open to stay abreast of unimaginable changes and unforeseen events which will require quick responses and adjustments in policy. A combination of principles and pragmatism makes for a successful foreign policy.

NOTES

~

CHAPTER ONE

1. Nehru's radio broadcast from New Delhi on 7 September 1946.
2. In Samskrita: *lokasamastasukhinobhavantu.*
3. In Samskrita: *Om SahaNau-Avatu, SahaNauBhunaktu, SahaViiryamKaravaavahai: TejasviNau-Adhiitam-AstuMaaVidvissaavahai*
4. In Samskrita: *Om SarveBhavantuSukhina, SarveSantuNir-Aamayaah, SarveBhadraanniPashyantu, MaaKashchid-Duhkha-Bhaag-Bhavet, Om ShaantihShaantihShaantih.*
5. Nehru, Jawaharlal. *The Discovery of India.* Penguin Modern Classics Edition. New Delhi: Penguin Books India, 2012, p. 17.
6. The principles of Panchsheel are: Mutual respect for each other's territorial integrity and sovereignty; Mutual non-aggression; Mutual non-interference in each other's internal affairs; Equality and mutual benefit; and Peaceful coexistence.
7. Sir Girija Shankar Bajpai ICS was agent general for India in Washington from 1942 to July 1947. As secretary general, he was the senior-most officer in the new ministry of external affairs.
8. Text of the letter is in annexure 1.
9. Yezdi Gundevia, who later rose to the position of foreign secretary.
10. My recollection is that the exodus of British members of the ICS had begun in late 1946. Accounts vary; according to Wikipedia, at the time of Partition there were 980 ICS officers of which 468 were Europeans. Most of these later left India, some for Pakistan

and the rest for Britain. Out of the 101 Muslim ICS officers, ninety-five opted for Pakistan.

CHAPTER TWO

1. Dutt, Subimal. *With Nehru In The Foreign Office*. Calcutta: Minerva Associates, 1955, p.37.

CHAPTER THREE

1. Indian National Army headed by Subhash Chandra Bose, a prominent leader of India's struggle for Independence.
2. Pandit, Vijaya Lakshmi. 'Chapter 34: Assignment in Washington'. In *The Scope of Happiness: A Personal Memoir*. Crown Publishers, 1979.
3. *National Herald* of 25 August 1949.
4. Gopal, Sarvepalli. *Radhakrishnan, a biography*. Oxford University Press, 1989.
5. For full account of the meeting see: Dayal, Rajeshwar. *A Life of Our Times*. Orient Blackswan, 1998, pp. 139–145. Dayal was Radhakrishnan's deputy in the embassy.
6. *Ibid*.
7. Annie Besant was a prominent British socialist, theosophist, women's rights activist, writer, orator and supporter of Irish and Indian self-rule. In pursuit of her theosophy-related work, she travelled to India and became involved in politics as a member of the Indian National Congress. In 1917, she was elected President of the Congress. She continued to campaign for Indian independence and for the causes of theosophy until her death in 1933.
8. Extracts from the memoranda of Present Eisenhower's White House conversations, kept in the Eisenhower Memorial Library; cited in the *International Herald Tribune* of 3–4 November 1979.
9. Panikkar, K.M. *In Two China's: Memories of a Diplomat*. London: Allen &Unwin, 1955, Chapter IX, p. 102.

10. Sarvepalli, Gopal. *Jawaharlal Nehru: A Biography*. India: Oxford University Press, 2003, Vol. 2, p. 102.
11. Dutt, Subimal. *With Nehru in The Foreign Office*. Calcutta: Minerva Associates, 1977, p. 43.

CHAPTER FOUR

1. *Sarvam dukham dukham; sarvam kshanikam, kshanikam.*
2. *Anityamasukhamlokam imam prapyabhajasva mam: IX:33.*

CHAPTER FIVE

1. A rendering in English would go something like this: Courtesy was the hallmark, once, of the mode of address in Delhi; now it is the curt 'Hey you'.

CHAPTER SIX

1. Acheson, Dean. *Present at the Creation: My Years in the State Department*. W.W. Norton and Company, 1987, p. 335.
2. *Ibid.*
3. Lippmann was the United States' most popular and respected columnist and political thinker.
4. Sarvepalli, Gopal. *Jawaharlal Nehru: A Biography*. India: Oxford University Press, 2003, Vol. 2, p. 182.
5. That this was indeed the considered US policy was confirmed by Dulles in his talks with Nehru in March 1956. He told Nehru that soon Pakistan's army would be as large as India's and it would have superior equipment.

CHAPTER EIGHT

1. The report of the British ambassador in Moscow, Sir Patrick Reilly on Moscow talks was released in 1990. A brief account of the talks based on Sir Patrick's report to the Foreign Office

appeared in the *Guardian* of London on 1 January 1990, when I was India's high commissioner in London.

2. Bachchan, as Hindi officer in the MEA did extremely useful work to coin Hindi equivalents of diplomatic words and phrases, and other official jargon. The irrepressible genius that he was, despite heavy pressures of official work he continued to enrich Hindi with his new writings in verse and prose.

3. J.N. Papers (M.O. Mathai). Subject file No. 29, Sheet 19.

CHAPTER TEN

1. Dutt, Subimal. *With Nehru In The Foreign Office*. Calcutta: Minerva Associates, 1955, p. 155.

CHAPTER ELEVEN

1. Secretary of State Rusk's Telegram 32 of 9 December 1961, cited in: Rakove, Robert B. *Kennedy Johnson, and the Non-aligned World*, p. 246.

CHAPTER TWELVE

1. Dutt, Subimal. *With Nehru In The Foreign Office*. Calcutta: Minerva Associates, 1955, p. 155.

2. *India Weekly*. London, Friday, 24 October 2003.

3. The late G. Parthasarathy (G.P.), a distinguished Indian diplomat, was a trusted adviser to prime ministers Nehru and Indira Gandhi. Ashok is the custodian of G.P.'s papers. Since I personally have seen no evidence of the Kennedy offer—I had heard rumours about it in Washington DC—I asked Ashok to let me see the letter. He said the letter was lost when the family shifted from one residence in Delhi to another after G.P.'s death, but he swore that he had seen and read the letter. Ashok, now living in retirement, had held responsible positions in government including that of science adviser to Prime Minister Indira Gandhi.

CHAPTER FOURTEEN

1. Maharaja Hari Singh was the last princely ruler of Jammu and Kashmir. He signed the document of accession leading to the state's integration with India following Pakistan's invasion of the state.

CHAPTER SIXTEEN

1. Kissinger, Henry. *White House Years*. Great Britain: George Weidenfeld and Nicolson, 1979, p. 855.
2. Kissinger, Henry. *White House Years*. Great Britain: George Weidenfeld and Nicolson: Great Britain, 1979.
3. He causes fear to none and none can frighten him; he is free from the agitation of the mood caused by euphoria, anger and excitement (XII.15).

CHAPTER SEVENTEEN

1. Westad, Odd Arne. *Restless Empire: China's America and the World since 1750*. New York: Basic Books, 2012, p. 369.

CHAPTER TWENTY

1. 'Inhale the soothing smoke of herb divine
   Draw it in deep and long
   Inhale it till your sorrows all
   Are drowned in song.
   Hare Krishna, Hare Ram.'

CHAPTER TWENTY-THREE

1. Nur Muhammad Taraki, President of Afghanistan, who was overthrown in a coup in 1979 by hardline communist Prime Minister Hafizullah Amin.

CHAPTER TWENTY-FIVE

1. In Samskrita: *Anudvega-karamvakyam, satyampriya-hitam cha yat.* (From: Radhakrishnan. The Bhagavad Gita. XVII.15).
2. In Samskrita: Apriyasya cha pathyasyavaktashrota hi durlabhah. (From: Shanti Parva. The Mahabharata. 63.17).

CHAPTER TWENTY-SIX

1. In his radio broadcast of 7 September 1956, Nehru had said: 'We propose as far as possible to keep away from the power politics of groups aligned against one another, which have lead in the past two world wars and which may again lead to disasters on an even vaster scale. We believe that peace and freedom are indivisible and the denial of freedom anywhere must endanger freedom elsewhere and lead to conflict and war . . .'
2. Eban, Abba. *The New Diplomacy: International Affairs in the Modern Age.* Random House, 1983, pp. 242–243.
3. In Samskrita, *Sainyadvinanaiva rajyamnadhanamnaparakramah, Balinovashagahasarvedurlabhasya cha shatravaha.*
4. Machiavelli, Niccolò. *The Prince.* London: Everyman's Library Dent & Sons Ltd: London, 1992, p. 13.
5. *Ibid.*, p. 93.
6. For an amusing incident connected with this situation see: Gundevia, Y.D. *Outside the Archives.* Sangam Books Ltd, 1983, pp. 271–272.

Appendix

MANDALA

~

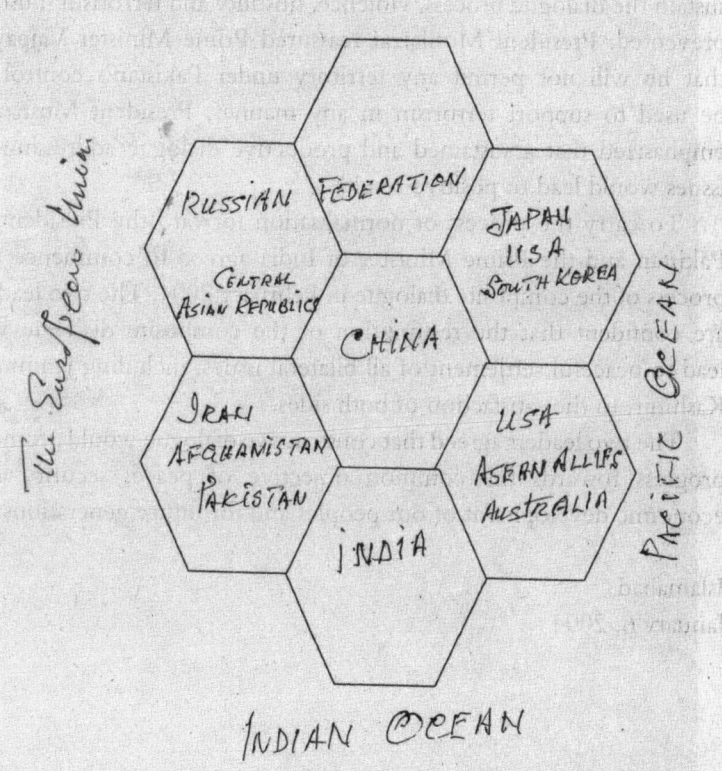

JOINT PRESS STATEMENT

~

The President of Pakistan and the Prime Minister of India met during the SAARC Summit in Islamabad.

The Indian Prime Minister while expressing satisfaction over the successful conclusion of the SAARC Summit appreciated the excellent arrangement made by the host country.

Both leaders welcomed the recent steps towards normalization of relations between the two countries and expressed the hope that the positive trends set by the CBMs would be consolidated.

Prime Minister Vajpayee said that in order to take forward and sustain the dialogue process, violence, hostility and terrorism must be prevented. President Musharraf reassured Prime Minister Vajpayee that he will not permit any territory under Pakistan's control to be used to support terrorism in any manner. President Musharraf emphasized that a sustained and productive dialogue addressing all issues would lead to positive results.

To carry the process of normalisation forward the President of Pakistan and the Prime Minister of India agreed to commence the process of the composite dialogue in February 2004. The two leaders are confident that the resumption of the composite dialogue will lead to peaceful settlement of all bilateral issues, including Jammu & Kashmir, to the satisfaction of both sides.

The two leaders agreed that constructive dialogue would promote progress towards the common objective of peace, security and economic development of our peoples and for future generations.

Islamabad
January 6, 2004

SARDAR PATEL'S LETTER TO PT NEHRU AFTER THE CHINESE INVASION OF TIBET

~

My dear Jawaharlal,

Ever since my return from Ahmedabad and after the cabinet meeting the same day which I had to attend at practically fifteen minutes' notice and for which I regret I was not able to read all the papers, I have been anxiously thinking over the problem of Tibet and I thought I should share with you what is passing through my mind.

I have carefully gone through the correspondence between the External Affairs Ministry and our Ambassador in Peking and through him the Chinese Government. I have tried to peruse this correspondence as favourably to our Ambassador and the Chinese Government as possible, but I regret to say that neither of them comes out well as a result of this study.

The Chinese Government has tried to delude us by professions of peaceful intention. My own feeling is that at a crucial period they managed to instill into our Ambassador a false sense of confidence in their so-called desire to settle the Tibetan problem by peaceful means. There can be no doubt that during the period covered by this correspondence the Chinese must have been concentrating for an onslaught on Tibet. The final action of the Chinese, in my judgement, is little short of perfidy. The tragedy of it is that the Tibetans put faith in us; they chose to be guided by us; and we have been unable to get them out of the meshes of Chinese diplomacy or Chinese malevolence. From the latest position, it appears that we shall not be able to rescue the Dalai Lama. Our Ambassador has been at great pains to find an explanation or justification for Chinese policy and actions. As the External Affairs Ministry remarked in one of their telegrams, there was a lack of firmness and unnecessary apology in one or two representations that he made to the Chinese Government on our behalf.

It is impossible to imagine any sensible person believing in the so-called threat to China from Anglo-American machinations in Tibet. Therefore, if the Chinese put faith in this, they must have distrusted us so completely as to have taken us as tools or stooges of Anglo-American diplomacy or strategy. This feeling, if genuinely entertained by the Chinese in spite of your direct approaches to them, indicates that even though we regard ourselves as the friends of China, the Chinese do not regard us as their friends. With the communist mentality of "whoever is not with them being against them", this is a significant pointer, of which we have to take due note. During the last several months, outside the Russian camp, we have practically been alone in championing the cause of Chinese entry into UN and in securing from the Americans assurances on the question of Formosa. We have done everything we could to assuage Chinese feelings, to allay its apprehensions and to defend its legitimate claims in our discussions and correspondence with America and Britain and in the UN.

Inspite of this, China is not convinced about our disinterestedness; it continues to regard us with suspicion and the whole psychology is one, at least outwardly, of scepticism perhaps mixed with a little hostility. I doubt if we can go any further than we have done already to convince China of our good intentions, friendliness and goodwill. In Peking we have an Ambassador who is eminently suitable for putting across the friendly point of view. Even he seems to have failed to convert the Chinese. Their last telegram to us is an act of gross discourtesy not only in the summary way it disposes of our protest against the entry of Chinese forces into Tibet but also in the wild insinuation that our attitude is determined by foreign influences. It looks as though it is not a friend speaking in that language but a potential enemy.

In the background of this, we have to consider what new situation now faces us as a result of the disappearance of Tibet, as we knew it, and the expansion of China almost up to our gates. Throughout history we have seldom been worried about our north-east frontier.

The Himalayas have been regarded as an impenetrable barrier against any threat from the north. We had a friendly Tibet which gave us no trouble. The Chinese were divided. They had their own domestic problems and never bothered us about frontiers. In 1914, we entered into a convention with Tibet which was not endorsed by the Chinese. We seem to have regarded Tibetan autonomy as extending to independent treaty relationship. Presumably, all that we required was Chinese counter-signature. The Chinese interpretation of suzerainty seems to be different.

We can, therefore, safely assume that very soon they will disown all the stipulations which Tibet has entered into with us in the past. That throws into the melting pot all frontier and commercial settlements with Tibet on which we have been functioning and acting during the last half a century. China is no longer divided. It is united and strong. All along the Himalayas in the north and north-east, we have on our side of the frontier a population ethnologically and culturally not different from Tibetans and Mongoloids. The undefined state of the frontier and the existence on our side of a population with its affinities to the Tibetans or Chinese have all the elements of the potential trouble between China and ourselves. Recent and bitter history also tells us that Communism is no shield against imperialism and that the communists are as good or as bad imperialists as any other. Chinese ambitions in this respect not only cover the Himalayan slopes on our side but also include the important part of Assam. They have their ambitions in Burma also. Burma has the added difficulty that it has no McMahon Line round which to build up even the semblance of an agreement. Chinese irredentism and communist imperialism are different from the expansionism or imperialism of the western powers. The former has a cloak of ideology which makes it ten times more dangerous. In the guise of ideological expansion lie concealed racial, national or historical claims. The danger from the north and north-east, therefore, becomes both communist and imperialist.

While our western and north-western threat to security is still as prominent as before, a new threat has developed from the north and north-east. Thus, for the first time, after centuries, India's defence has to concentrate itself on two fronts simultaneously. Our defence measures have so far been based on the calculations of superiority over Pakistan. In our calculations we shall now have to reckon with communist China in the north and in the north-east, a communist China which has definite ambitions and aims and which does not, in any way, seem friendly disposed towards us.

Let us also consider the political conditions on this potentially troublesome frontier. Our northern and north-eastern approaches consist of Nepal, Bhutan, Sikkim, Darjeeling and the tribal areas in Assam. From the point of view of communication, there are weak spots. Continuous defensive lines do not exist. There is almost an unlimited scope for infiltration. Police protection is limited to a very small number of passes. There, too, our outposts do not seem to be fully manned. The contact of these areas with us is by no means close and intimate. The people inhabiting these portions have no established loyalty or devotion to India. Even Darjeeling and Kalimpong areas are not free from pro-Mongoloid prejudices. During the last three years, we have not been able to make any appreciable approaches to the Nagas and other hill tribes in Assam.

European missionaries and other visitors had been in touch with them, but their influence was in no way friendly to India or Indians. In Sikkim, there was political ferment some time ago. It is quite possible that discontent is smouldering there. Bhutan is comparatively quiet, but its affinity with Tibetans would be a handicap. Nepal has a weak oligarchic regime based almost entirely on force: it is in conflict with a turbulent element of the population as well as with enlightened ideas of the modern age. In these circumstances, to make people alive to the new danger or to make them defensively strong is a very difficult task indeed and that difficulty can be got over only by enlightened firmness, strength and a clear line of policy. I am sure the Chinese and their source of inspiration, Soviet Union, would not miss any opportunity of exploiting these weak spots, partly in support of their ideology and partly in support of their ambitions.

In my judgement the situation is one which we cannot afford either to be complacent or to be vacillating. We must have a clear idea of what we wish to achieve and also of the methods by which we should achieve it. Any faltering or lack of decisiveness in formulating our objectives or in pursuing our policies to attain those objectives is bound to weaken us and increase the threats which are so evident.

Side by side with these external dangers, we shall now have to face serious internal problems as well. I have already asked Iyengar to send to the External Affairs Ministry a copy of the Intelligence Bureau's appreciation of these matters. Hitherto, the Communist Party of India has found some difficulty in contacting communists abroad, or in getting supplies of arms, literature, etc., from them. They had to contend with the difficult Burmese and Pakistan frontiers on the east or with the long seaboard. They shall now have a comparatively easy means of access to Chinese communists and through them to other foreign communists. Infiltration of spies, fifth columnists and communists would now be easier. Instead of having to deal with isolated communist pockets in Telengana and Warrangal we may have to deal with communist threats to our security along our northern and north-eastern frontiers, where, for supplies of arms and ammunition, they can safely depend on communist arsenals in China.

The whole situation thus raises a number of problems on which we must come to an early decision so that we can, as I said earlier, formulate the objectives of our policy and decide the method by which those objectives are to be attained. It is also clear that the action will have to be fairly comprehensive, involving not only our defence strategy and state of preparations but also problem of internal security to deal with which we have not a moment to lose. We shall also have to deal with administrative and political problems in the weak spots along the frontier to which I have already referred.

It is of course, impossible to be exhaustive in setting out all these problems. I am, however, giving below some of the problems which, in my opinion, require early solution and round which we have to build our administrative or military policies and measures to implement them.

a) A military and intelligence appreciation of the Chinese threat to India both on the frontier and to internal security.

b) An examination of military position and such redisposition of our forces as might be necessary, particularly with the idea of guarding important routes or areas which are likely to be the subject of dispute.

c) An appraisement of the strength of our forces and, if necessary, reconsideration of our retrenchment plans for the Army in the light of the new threat.

d) A long-term consideration of our defence needs. My own feeling is that, unless we assure our supplies of arms, ammunition and armour, we would be making our defence perpetually weak and we would not be able to stand up to the double threat of difficulties both from the west and north-west and north and north-east.

e) The question of China's entry into the UN. In view of the rebuff which China has given us and the method which it has followed in dealing with Tibet, I am doubtful whether we can advocate its claim any longer. There would probably be a threat in the UN virtually to outlaw China, in view of its active participation in the Korean war. We must determine our attitude on this question also.

f) The political and administrative steps which we should take to strengthen our northern and north-eastern frontier. This would include the whole of the border, ie. Nepal, Bhutan, Sikkim, Darjeeling and the tribal territory in Assam.

g) Measures of internal security in the border areas as well as the states flanking those areas such as Uttar Pradesh, Bihar, Bengal and Assam.

h) Improvement of our communication, road, rail, air and wireless, in these areas and with the frontier outposts.

i) The future of our mission at Lhasa and the trade posts at Gyangtse and Yatung and the forces which we have in operation in Tibet to guard the trade routes.

j) The policy in regard to the McMahon Line.

These are some of the questions which occur to my mind. It is possible that a consideration of these matters may lead us into wider question of our relationship with China, Russia, America, Britain and Burma. This, however, would be of a general nature, though some might be basically very important, e.g., we might have to consider whether we should not enter into closer association with Burma in order to strengthen the latter in its dealings with China. I do not rule out the possibility that, before applying pressure on us, China might apply pressure on Burma. With Burma, the frontier is entirely undefined and the Chinese territorial claims are more substantial. In its present position, Burma might offer an easier problem to China, and therefore, might claim its first attention.

I suggest that we meet early to have a general discussion on these problems and decide on such steps as we might think to be immediately necessary and direct, quick examination of other problems with a view to taking early measures to deal with them.

Vallabhbhai Patel,
7th November 1950

MEETING WITH GENERAL MUSHARRAF

~

ACCOUNT OF M. RASGOTRA'S MEETING WITH GENERAL PARVEZ MUSHARRAF

The Chief Executive (CE), General Parvez Musharraf received me at the PM's official residence in Islamabad at 2.00 P.M. on 7 August, 2000. The meeting lasted exactly one hour. *Mr. Salman Haider, my friend and former colleague in the Indian Foreign Service accompanied me to the meeting.*

C.E.'s Principal Staff Officer, General Ghulam Ahmed, and Pakistan's Foreign Secretary, Inam-ul-Haq were present throughout. The former intervened only once towards the end to raise the question of Iran-Pak-India Gas pipeline. Inam butted in two or three times briefly to highlight Indian's sins - stoppage of the SAARC process, lack of response to Pak initiatives for TALKS etc. On my side, Salman Haider gave me solid, silent support.

I. SUBSTANTIVE ISSUES DISCUSSED

After extending a warm and fulsome welcome, C.E. asked how our visit had gone and I said it had been a heart-warming experience: we had inter-acted with a wide cross-section of the people and my most outstanding impression was of a very wide-spread desire for peace and friendship with India.

1. KASHMIR

"I agree: that is so" C.E. said. "I also want peace: I am a man of peace. But the Kashmir problem has to be resolved: it cannot be forgotten and Pakistan cannot be sidelined. I don't want conflict. I have stopped shelling on the LoC. Your people were being killed and our people were being killed. It is pointless; I have stopped it. [U.S. Under Secretary Pickering had pressed Pakistan on this a couple of weeks earlier.)

"I read all your journals; they don't have a good word for us. They all say Pakistan has no role in Kashmir; that India should not talk to Pak. India does not want to talk to us on Kashmir: but Pakistan cannot be ignored; Kashmir has to be resolved; it cannot be put on the back burner" etc. etc.

I responded by saying that in India too there is great desire for peace and friendship with Pakistan. India is anxious for a peaceful solution of the Kashmir problem through dialogue. But for a dialogue to succeed proper conditions must be created. There are equally strong feelings on Kashmir in India, and there is a strong nationwide reaction to violence, sponsored and supported by Pakistan, which has made a complex problem even more intractable. Violence cannot lead to a solution: it has to be stopped.

C.E. Everyone is telling me to do something to end violence. I want peace; I have said so, so many times; made several offers but the response is always negative. India does not want to talk to us; India does not want to talk because there is a military government here.

I said that perception was not correct. India had dealt with military governments in Pakistan earlier. The real hindrance is Pakistan's material and other support for violence in Kashmir – training and equipping of militants, trans-border crossings etc.

(like Hizb-al-Mujahideen)

INAM chipped in: "Even India has said that the militants are indigenous Kashmiris".

"Indeed, but even those," I responded, "are trained and armed in and given financial support by Pak: the command centres of all jehadi groups are here in Pakistan".

"No one need expect India to be coerced into talks through pressure of violence. I cannot visualize Vajpayeeji, Advaniji or any other Indian leader being dictated to the table for talks with Pakistan under threat and pressure of violence".

C.E. "Kashmir is the central issue: it has to be resolved. It cannot be ignored; Pakistan cannot be sidelined and I cannot say that this issue will be set aside. It has to be **addressed**, (note the slight shift in his emphasis from 'resolved' to 'addressed'). India does not want to address this issue. It has to be addressed and resolved". I reminded him that at Lahore in February 1999, India had agreed to address the Kashmir problem along with other security related issues. Unfortunately, Kargil had torpedoed that process. *He felt abashed; I could see embarrassed flicker on his face: He was not angry, but was silent for a few moments.*

C.E. "They (Nawaz Sharief) were doing bad things: they were trying to put Kashmir on the back-burner; they were concealing things from the public. Nobody here would accept that. Shrief was trying to avoid the public about this: he did not want to meet the media.

"I am an upfront, direct, sincere and honest person. I cannot ignore this issue. It has to be addressed. I agree with you it is a very complex issue. It does not have to be resolved immediately, but it must be addressed. You mentioned other issues; they can all be addressed.

2. TRIPARTITE TALKS

I asked why Pakistan wanted tripartite talks on Kashmir. Where would tripartite talks lead ? I said: "Third party so-called has numerous representatives: A.P.H.C. represents only a small fraction of the Kashmiris: it is a divided group. Your Excellency, consider this scenario. On your side of the table will be the President of PoK, representatives from Gilgit and the other northern territories, Syed Salah-ud-Din and, possibly, chieftains of some other Jehadi groups and Syed Ali Shah Jilani and one or two others of the Hurriyat. Seated on the Indian side would be Farooq Abdullah, Mufti Mohd. Saeed, Soz, Gul Shah, three or four Hurriyat leaders, Shabir Shah; and representative leaders from Jammu and

Laddakh etc. etc". "What would your Excellency expect to get out of a multi-partite meeting of this kind ?" I asked.

C.E. was quiet and for the first time in this long interview looked a bit puzzled. He had not looked at it like this, *he said.*

3. PAK-SUPPORTED VIOLENCE

I added: "You sure have some problems in your part of Kashmir, we are not adding to your difficulties. (He did not cavil at or contest this). We have problems on our side, which Pakistan-sponsored violence has aggravated. Political wisdom demands that you handle your problems peacefully and leave us alone to handle ours peacefully. When the situation is calmed, India and Pakistan, as sovereign entities, should sit together and address the issue and amicably resolve it to mutual satisfaction or mutual dissatisfaction. The key lies in stopping violence and creating a proper environment for the dialogue.

C.E. "Rasgotra Sahib, as for violence I know what we are doing; and I also know what you are doing. I'll say no more". I tried to draw him out a bit, but he simply repeated the sentence and asked me not to press him, for elaboration.

This was the most enigmatic (and pregnant) sentence of this conversion. We should carefully consider its implications. Are we doing anything in Pakistan similar to what Pak is doing in the valley ?

4. HUM's CEASE-FIRE

I told C.E. that Hizb-ul-Majahideen's cease-fire had opened up a new opportunity and I expressed the hope that he would help expand its possibilities; Inam-ul-Haque intervened to say, that 'HUM' was only one group: India should talk to others also e.g. the All Parties Hurriyat Conference.

C.E. added briefly that there was a window of opportunity there and he wanted to "avail it". It was their impression from all Indian statements that India wished to exclude Pakistan from a Kashmir solution, he said.

I said I did not see how that would be possible considering that Pakistan holds a very large chunk of J&K territory. Lahore was about talks with Pakistan. But Kargil and the breach of trust had embarrassed and dismayed our leaders. The subsequent escalation of cross - border violence had given rise to strong feelings in India. The ending of violence would help restore confidence and trust. Furthermore, sorting out other issues – Siachen, Sir Creek, Wullar, Trade etc. – one by one would help generate the right kind of environment for addressing the more difficult problem.

C.E. agreed those issues could be addressed, but not to Kashmiri's exclusion. Kashmir should also be simultaneously addressed. "I am not saying issue can be quickly resolved, but we must talk about it". [He had come some way forward from his initial stance: namely, put Kashmir on the front burner; resolve it etc].

5. THE NUCLEAR ISSUE

I then mentioned the urgency and importance of the nuclear issue. I said India did not view Pakistan's nuclear deterrent in an adverse light. If it reassured Pakistan of its security vis-à-vis India, or gave Pakistan a sense of equality with India, well and good. But brandishing the threat of nuclear first-use made no sense. Deterrence did not require equality in the number of missiles and weapons: India's security concerns were much larger than Pakistan's. Pakistan and India should jointly manage mutual deterrence and jointly press the nuclear weapon powers to proceed with nuclear disarmament.

C.E. smiled and said he had never seen it in this light. He agreed that it should be discussed.

6. TRADE ISSUES AND SARRC

I mentioned the importance of economic relations and of trade in a globalising world environment; that cooperation in these areas in the W.T.O. framework would be good for both countries.

C.E. backed by Inam, spoke of India having blocked even the existing SAARC Channel. I said as one of SAARC's founders, I was deeply disappointed in its lack of progress over the last 16 years. What was really important was bilateral trade in the W.T.O. framework. INAM obviously felt strongly about the blockage of SAARC and asked whether meetings at the ministerial level could be allowed to take place, even if summit level meetings could not be considered for the present. I said I would convey this to the appropriate quarters in New Delhi.

7. IRAN-PAKISTAN-INDIA GAS PIPELINE

General Ghulam Ahmed brought up the question of the Iran-Pak-India Gas/Oil pipeline. He expatiated on the project's benefits to all three countries. C.E. said Turkmenistan-Afghanistan-Pak-India pipeline was also feasible as the related area of Afghanistan was stable and calm. However, he favoured the Iran-Pak-India line. He said the necessary security guarantees had already been given by Pak and added that the project being a multi-lateral one could be taken out of the total India-Pak agenda, _and dealt with expeditiously._ While offering to convey all this to our Government, I suggested that Pak and Iran might like to go ahead in any case with a pipeline of enhanced specifications leaving it to India to come in at a later stage. _I added that the issue being one of economic/trade significance, it would be easier to reach agreement on it in a more felicitous environment of cooperation in trade and economic projects._

8. NO WAR PACT

I asked C.E. whether his most recent offer, through the Pak Press, of a No War Pact, as in the case of past such offers, was conditional upon prior solution of Kashmir. [He seemed somewhat non-plussed and did not respond. Foreign Minister Sattar had told me on the 1st August that the matter had not been thought through], I mentioned for his information that as Foreign Secretary I had myself negotiated a NO WAR PACT/FRIENDSHIP TREATY with Pakistan between 1982 & 84, which Pakistan for some reason chose not to sign at the end. C.E. might, I said, have the matter looked into, and if he so felt fresh negotiations could be undertaken on the subject separately from other issues.

9. UN - BLOCKING DIPLOMATIC CHANNELS

I mentioned that the new Indian High Commissioner was due to arrive shortly and C.E. might consider using the occasion for triggering off something fresh e.g., a no-war pact proposal through the diplomatic channels. These latter were frozen since Kargil and needed to be de-blocked in any case. C.E's response was positive.

10. THE INDIAN POLITICAL SCENE

C.E. wanted to know how I viewed the Indian political scene. I said Indian democracy is going strong. Even though our government is a coalition of 20 odd parties, it is stable and would live its full term. It is led by experienced, strong and wise leaders. The economy is in good shape and the reform process is advancing well. The country under Shri Vajpayee's leadership had put Kargil behind it. In him Vajpayee Pakistan had a well-wisher, I added.

C.E. said; "I know Mr. Vajpayee is a strong and wise leader who can address difficult issues. Therefore, we have some expectations from him. Please convey my warm regards to him. I am a sincere, honest and open person and wish for peace and a happy future for both countries".

He presented me with a silver bowl as a "souvenir of your visit with me," and we took leave.

4P

II. My assessment of the MAN

General Parvez Musharraf is a calm, collected, pleasant - looking person of modest mien ~~and limited~~ *with occasional flashes of long vision.* vision. He is shrewd, and perhaps also not without cunning; but he is not wily like General Zia-ul-Haq. Nor does be possess the bluff exuberance of Gen. Mohd. Ayub Khan. He gives the impression of being forthright, efficient & quietly decisive.

He is a man of modern outlook; there is no aura of the religious zealot about him. Altogether, an unconvincing dictator.

He talks well and persuasively and is a good listener. In an hour-long conversation on ticklish issues, he did not show a whiff of impatience or irritation. He is open to argument and can, I think, be constructively engaged.

He needs advice on issues of larger international and domestic import. In matters pertaining to India his reliance on Foreign Minister Sattar and Foreign Secretary Inam-ul-Haq is not a helpful factor.

He enjoys the Army's solid support . The tasks confronting him are complex, ~~unenviable~~ and daunting. For the present, there are no contenders for his position. Would Aziz or another General want his job ? I doubt it.

The importance he attached to our meeting and the time (one hour) he gave it surprised me. I hope the argument might set him a thinking about the issue of violence. He seems to believe we are doing to his country what he is doing to us in J&K.

His feelings of respect for our leaders, especially P.M., seemed genuine.

III RECOMMENATIONS

1. The West is NOT in the least likely to declare PAKISTAN a terrorist state. General Musharraf is likely to be there for a couple of years/ *at the very least* We should not spurn him completely. It may not be time for summitry; but we should find ways of engaging him through official/non-official inter-locuteurs.

2. If at the U.N. a request or suggestion comes from the Pak side for a courtesy meeting, P.M. may receive him and impress upon him the wisdom and necessity of ending support for violence .

3. Normal contacts between the two High Commissions and the Foreign Offices to which they are accredited should be restored.

4. No harm can came from exploratory talks with Pakistan on the Iran Gas Pipeline. Even non-committal talks might lead to softening of Pakistan's stands on other issues.

5. Some guarded, inquisitive interest should be indicated (through MEA's spokesman) on Mussharaf's vague offers of No War Pact. Similarly our interest in nuclear related CBM's between the two countries should be indicated. In case of positive response, talks could be initiated at junior technical levels.

6. Show of some guarded, carefully calibrated flexibility on our part will bring us international appreciation without in any way detracting from our stand on the vital issue of violence. It might help generate even stronger international pressures on Pakistan.

7. My gut impression is that Pak will give up sponsorship of violence only when we can demonstrate, in actual deeds, that we can hurt them in PoK the same way as they are hurting us in the valley.

New Delhi
25.08.2000   M. Rasgotra

ARTICLE ON MRS RASGOTRA

~

Diplomatic entertaining with a hint of spice

A grand scale dinner party is planned at the Indian High Commissioner's Residence tonight. Eminent people in politics, the arts and diplomacy, will attend. The hostess, Kadambari Rasgotra, talks to Wendy Holden about the art of diplomatic entertaining. Photographs by John Parkes.

"I ALWAYS serve Indian food at my dinner parties," says Kadambari Rasgotra, wife of the High Commissioner for India. "People expect it, and really, it's very practical for me. I don't compete with the European food served by the Swiss and the French Embassies — they have their finest chefs and we brought ours with us from India. So I serve what we do best."

Tonight, the High Commissioner and his wife are giving a dinner in honour of Sir Patrick Wright, Permanent Under-Secretary of State at the Foreign Office. Among the 20 guests are other senior FCO officials (Sir John Fretwell, Deputy Permanent Under-Secretary at the Foreign Office and Mr John Boyd, Deputy Under-Secretary) a high court judge (The Hon. Justice Jean-Pierre Warner), the Deputy Director-General of the British Council (Mr John Hanson) and the Deputy Chairman of Rajya Sahab, Upper House of the Indian Parliament (Dr Najma Heptullah). "I like a mixed bag," Mrs Rasgotra says of guests. "Ideally, there should be people from the world of the arts and politics as well as other diplomats." Particularly well represented this evening is the literary world. Charles Wilson, editor of *The Times*, his wife Sally O'Sullivan, editor of *She* magazine and the poetess Kathleen Raine will all be there. Also due is the Rasgotras' recently-married banker son Dilip with his wife.

The table has been extended to full capacity, and is draped in soft primrose. "I wanted a golden, orangey feel to it," says Mrs Rasgotra. Setting out the gold-rimmed china and sparkling crystal began at 1pm "just," says the High Commissioner's wife, "as I went out to get my hair done." The table takes about four hours to set. Its freshly-laundered length is dotted with placecards, small silver ornaments, cruets, glasses containing cigarettes, a carnation centrepiece and two large candelabra circled with a warm display of tiger lilies and chrysanthemums. These are arranged by Barbara, the High Commissioner's Social Secretary. "I used to do the flowers myself," says Mrs Rasgotra, "until I discovered that Barbara had such a talent for it. She organises all the flowers in the house now."

At the moment, Barbara is busy organising the two extra waiting staff hired to supplement the three from the Residence. "Indian food is very complicated — quite different from serving roast beef and potatoes," says Mrs Rasgotra. "The waiters have to be very careful to get the dishes in the right order, and so, when I am invited out to dinner, I watch the waiters my friends use. If they are good and attentive, I hire them for my own parties." At a sit down dinner like tonight's, four waiters will serve the food and one the wine. Larger occasions would be buffet-style. The last one was held for 50 guests and involved two rooms, a variety of tables and great chafing dishes to keep all the food hot. "I prepared some fish European-style in case anyone didn't like Indian food," recalls Mrs Rasgotra, "and nobody touched it!"

Main picture: Kadambari Rasgotra awaits her guests. "Pink is a colour I love and feel happy in." Left: Elegant panelling in the main reception room.

*'The time is now quarter to eight.
The guests are due at 8.15. Home
from the office, the High Commissioner
casts his eye benignly around'*

Tonight's menu, wafting so tantalisingly through the Residence, includes pea palau rice, chicken curry, cauliflower Masala, cottage cheese with capsicum, dal, pickles and chutney and paratha bread. Dessert is Gajar halwa, a rich, creamy cake cooked in milk, fried in butter and served with cream. "It's delicious," says Mrs Rasgotra. "Thousands of calories!" She selects the menus herself and is, says Barbara, extremely efficient at organising the two cooks and the purchasing of the ingredients. All the ingredients are bought in London. "It's amazing," says Mrs Rasgotra. "You can get anything here. There are special things you can't buy in parts of India, but you can buy them all in London. And all good quality too." Mrs Rasgotra interferes as little as possible with the actual preparation. "Today I didn't go into the kitchens at all," she says. The wine cellar is the High Commissioner's domain, and he has selected a 1987 Sancerre, a Chateau de Pez 1983 and a 1979 Dom Ruinart to accompany tonight's dinner. French wine is usually served, "although," says Mrs Rasgotra, "I hear Indian champagne is very good."

The time is now a quarter to eight. The guests are due to arrive at 8.15, when white-gloved doormen will take their coats and usher them into the bar. Here they will be served aperitifs to take into the spacious gilt and wood-panelled reception room where sculptures and paintings brought by the Rasgotras from India give the European-style room an Eastern atmosphere. Dinner will be served at half past nine and last about an hour, after which guests will withdraw to the reception room for coffee. They will probably depart around 11pm. "They are all busy people," says Mrs Rasgotra, "and probably dine out most nights of the week."

The High Commissioner and his wife give about two such dinner parties a month, in addition to smaller, more informal gatherings for up to eight people. The Rasgotras themselves are invited to more dinner parties than they can possibly manage. "The size of the Indian community in Britain means we could be going out to dinner every night of the week," explains Mrs Rasgotra, "and my husband doesn't mind doing it, but it's not good for our health. We can't short-change ourselves on sleep like that!"

Everything is prepared. The High Commissioner, home from the office, casts his eye benignly around and goes to put on his black tie. The two house guests from New York disappear upstairs. Barbara, making last minute adjustments, fills glasses in the reception room with cigarettes.

Immaculate from top to toe, Mrs Rasgotra seats herself on one of the cream silk reception room sofas and smoothes the vivid pink folds of her sari. "Yes," she says in reply to my question, "I always wear a sari to dinner parties, and to lunches too. I bought this one in Delhi some years ago. Pink," she continues, "is a colour I love and feel happy in." □

*Main picture: The dinner table takes four hours to set. The flowers are chrysanthemums, carnations and tiger lilies. "I wanted an orangey-gold feel," says the hostess, Mrs Kadambari Rasgotra.
Left: A waiter in traditional dress.*

INDEX

~